VISUAL STATISTICS

2.0

VISUAL STATISTICS

2.0

David P. Doane
Kieran Mathieson
Ronald L. Tracy

Oakland University

Boston   Burr Ridge, IL   Dubuque, IA   Madison, WI   New York   San Francisco   St. Louis
Bangkok   Bogotá   Caracas   Lisbon   London   Madrid
Mexico City   Milan   New Delhi   Seoul   Singapore   Sydney   Taipei   Toronto

McGraw-Hill Higher Education

A Division of The McGraw·Hill Companies

VISUAL STATISTICS 2.0
Published by McGraw-Hill/Irwin, an imprint of The McGraw-Hill Companies, Inc. 1221 Avenue of the Americas, New York, NY, 10020. Copyright © 2001, by The McGraw-Hill Companies, Inc. All rights reserved. No part of this publication may be reproduced or distributed in any form or by any means, or stored in a data base or retrieval system, without the prior written consent of The McGraw-Hill Companies, Inc., including, but not limited to, in any network or other electronic storage or transmission, or broadcast for distance learning.
Some ancillaries, including electronic and print components, may not be available to customers outside the United States.

This book is printed on acid-free paper.

2 3 4 5 6 7 8 9 0 QPD/QPD 0 9 8 7 6 5 4 3 2 1 0

ISBN 0-07-240014-5 (book)
ISBN 0-07-240012-9 (CD)
ISBN 0-07-240094-3 (book with CD)

Vice president/Editor-in-chief: *Michael W. Junior*
Publisher: *Jeffrey J. Shelstad*
Executive editor: *Richard T. Hercher, Jr.*
Senior developmental editor: *Wanda J. Zeman*
Senior marketing manager: *Zina Craft*
Senior project manager: *Susan Trentacosti*
Lead production supervisor: *Heather D. Burbridge*
Senior designer: *Jennifer McQueen Hollingsworth*
Supplement coordinator: *Mark Sienicki*
Media technology producer: *Ed Przyzycki*
Cover design: *Anthony A. O'Neill*
Printer: *Quebecor Printing Book Group/Dubuque*

Library of Congress Card Number: 00-1-7930

www.mhhe.com

To

Blythe,
Cullyn and Teagan,
Kathy

Preface

What's New in the Revised Edition

In this new edition of *Visual Statistics* we have made several major enhancements and many minor improvements. Here are a few of the new features.

- Six new modules:
    - Random processes
    - Goodness-of-fit tests
    - Multiple regression analysis
    - Regression assumptions
    - Regression models
    - Binary predictors in regression

- Full integration of the worktext and software:
    - Adobe™ on-line worktext now has color and graphics
    - Jump to any desired part of the worktext chapter using bookmarks
    - Switch easily between worktext and software module
    - Worktext can be magnified, copied, or printed
    - View learning exercises and their solutions simultaneously

- Attractive one-screen main menu that lets you:
    - Select a chapter by clicking it
    - View the worktext for that chapter
    - Run the software module for that chapter
    - Run several modules simultaneously

- Hundreds of new and updated databases and examples
    - Revised examples
    - Updated databases
    - New multivariate databases

- Major changes in appearance and functionality in modules on:
    - Central Limit Theorem
    - Power and type I/II error
    - Trends and seasonality
    - Statistical process control

- Worktext enhancements
    - 2 levels of orientation (basic features, additional features)
    - 3 levels of exercises (basic, intermediate, advanced)

- Module enhancements:
    - Ability to copy/paste graphs as device-independent bitmaps
    - Improved use of color

Background

This textbook began near ten years ago when Tracy walked into Doane's office to see if he would be interested in writing a National Science Foundation (NSF) grant proposal to develop software to teach statistical concepts. The collaboration was natural. Each of us had taught statistics for many years, and had experience developing computer software. As our ideas began to take shape, we agreed that it was time to bring the computer into the *classroom* — not just have students do computer lab projects. We wanted to use computers to teach *concepts* rather than just analyze data. We wanted to stress visual displays rather than numbers, equations, and calculations. An equation is an explanation to some students, but it is a barrier to others. We felt that a series of pictures or a simple animation could illustrate fairly complex equations. Our proposal asked the National Science Foundation's support to develop software and learning tools that would bring the power of computers into the statistics classroom. After we were awarded the NSF grant, we asked Mathieson if he would serve as a Windows consultant to our project. Soon it was clear that Mathieson's skills were essential, and we became full partners.

Visual Learning

We assume that (1) for many students visualization is a key to learning; (2) most statistical packages are designed for data analysis, not visualizing concepts; (3) individual instructors lack the time and resources to design their own software. Accordingly, we set out to create learning modules to illustrate concepts that cannot easily be shown mathematically or with packages such as Minitab or Excel. We wanted to minimize duplication of software capabilities already available. We wanted to promote learning through active self-discovery (inductive learning) as well as to support the instructor in the traditional lecture/lab setting (deductive learning).

We came up with the idea of a worktext that is closely coupled with software devised to lead a learner through experiments that promote self-discovery. We designed learning projects for teams and individuals that pose less-structured problems to continue this process. Our software was designed to encourage experimentation, so a learner can use simulation to understand the "experimental" side of statistics. These same features can be used effectively by the instructor in the classroom or the computer laboratory to illustrate a concept (e.g., the relationship between a confidence interval and a test statistic) and reinforce it with a simulation experiment.

Overview of Features

Visual Statistics consists of 21 software modules and a worktext. Each chapter of the worktext begins with a list of the key concepts the chapter will cover and a short list of learning objectives. Each concept is reviewed and illustrated. A short (about 15–minute) orientation to each module is provided. *Past users have told us that this orientation is invaluable.* There is also an orientation to additional features that may be skipped if its topics are not required. Learning exercises (basic, intermediate, advanced) are provided for each module. These exercises guide self-discovery learning. There are open-ended learning exercises for individuals and teams. A self-evaluation quiz allows you to test your understanding of the material. Solutions and a guide to answering each question are provided. A glossary at the end of each chapter provides definitions of terms used in the chapter.

Visual Statistics is to be used with a textbook or other course materials. It complements these traditional sources—it does not replace them. However, you'll find topics in these sources easier to understand after you *see* them in *Visual Statistics*.

Every software module has its own Help system, similar to that in other Windows programs. It includes definitions, examples, equations, graphics, and hints. You can use the table of contents and hypertext capabilities to jump to topics you want to learn more about, or do keyword searches using the index. *You will get more out of the learning process if you use the Help system.*

Our software uses familiar Windows visual controls (command buttons, scroll bars, list boxes, option buttons, and so on). Input is mostly from a mouse rather than from the keyboard. This interface will seem quite natural to most people. If you have used other Windows programs, you already know how to use *Visual Statistics* controls.

Every *Visual Statistics* module opens with a virtual notebook (a familiar ring binder with pages you can turn) that organizes the options. Clickable tabs divide the notebook into different sections, including an introduction (general idea of what is in the module), list of concepts (main topics covered), and sources of more information (references to chapters or other textbooks). Other tabs that vary from module to module provide examples (illustrations using real data), scenarios (realistic context for simulations), databases (large number of related variables using real data), visual templates (icons that show a distribution or trend), do-it-yourself controls (control panels to manipulate parameters of an experiment), and a data editor (to enter data or paste data from a spreadsheet). You may return to the notebook while running the program (e.g., to change scenarios, pick a different example, or choose different options).

Level of Complexity
We have tried to write flexible software, so the instructor can omit topics or vary their order. No module requires knowledge of another module, except in a general way (e.g., simple regression precedes multiple regression). Because students learn in different ways and at different rates, each module is aimed at the average learner but with options for those who desire more analytical depth (or who are just adventuresome). For example, in some modules you can set parameters by manipulating do-it-yourself scroll bars (simple level), by typing parameter values (intermediate level), or by choosing a known distribution and its parameters (advanced level).

Acknowledgments
Although we take responsibility for all remaining errors, our project has benefited greatly from field testing, advice, and comments of faculty colleagues and their students at other universities. We thank these individuals for their dedication and interest in our project.

Revised Edition:
Sung K. Ahn—Washington State University
Nancy C. Aiello—Northern Virginia Community College
Priscilla Chaffe-Stengel—California State University- Fresno
Subha Chakraborti—University of Alabama
Patti Collings—Brigham Young University
Bradford R. Crain—Portland State University
William Duckworth II—Iowa State University
John C. Dutton—North Carolina State University
James Flynn—Cleveland State University
Robert Hannum—University of Denver
David C. Howell—University of Vermont
Glenn W. Milligan—Ohio State University
Pin Ng—University of Illinois
Roxy Peck—California Polytechnic State University- San Luis Obispo
Don R. Robinson—Illinois State University
Mark E. Rush—Washington & Lee University
Sue B. Schou—Idaho State University
Robert K. Smidt—California Polytechnic State University- San Luis Obispo
Michael P. Wegman—Keller Graduate School of Management

Previous Edition:
Richard Anderson-Sprecher—University of Wyoming
Mohamed Askalani—Mankato State University

David Booth—Kent State University
Tim Butler—Wayne State University
Patty Collings—Brigham Young University
Peyton Cook—University of Tulsa
Rick Edgeman—Colorado State University
Chris Franklin—University of Georgia
Bob Hordon—Rutgers University
William Jedlicka—William Rainey Harper
Anthony Keys—Wichita State University
Anne B. Koehler—Miami University of Ohio
Gerald Kohers—Sam Houston State University
Benny Lo—Northwest Polytechnic University
Gary Martin—DeVry University - Atlanta
Madhuri Mulekar—University of South Alabama
Sufi Nazem—University of Nebraska - Omaha
Ceyhun Osgur—Valparaiso University
Paul Paschke—Oregon State University
Andy Siegel—University of Washington
Boyd Swartz—Monmouth University
Mack Shelley—Iowa State University
Robert D. St Louis—Arizona State University
Bret Wagner—University of Delaware
Linda Young—University of Nebraska - Lincoln

 This project would have never begun without the initial support of the National Science Foundation, Department of Undergraduate Education (DUE # 9554967 and DUE # 9254182). For their sustained belief in our concept, we are grateful. Any opinions expressed are those of the authors and not necessarily those of the Foundation.

However, without the support of McGraw-Hill/Irwin, the project might never have reached the full audience of learners that we hope will benefit from our approach. Our executive editor, Richard Hercher has been an advocate of our project ever since he saw early versions of our first four modules, and has not wavered in his support. As we struggled to meet deadlines, he encouraged and cajoled us, offered advice, consulted us, and kept us informed of important strategic issues. We are grateful to Wanda Zeman for her patient advice and assistance in working with us on a day-to-day basis in developing this new edition, and in dealing with the many problems that naturally arise. We thank the entire staff of McGraw-Hill/Irwin for their able assistance in managing our project through the editorial and production process. We also acknowledge database development, field testing, and programming assistance by Steve Losey, Judith Gurney, Karen Helber, and Don Smith.

David P. Doane
Kieran Mathieson
Ronald L. Tracy

Contents

Introduction

Using *Visual Statistics*

OBJECTIVES

- Understand what *Visual Statistics* is all about

- Learn how to install *Visual Statistics*

- Learn how to use the Notebook, the starting point for every *Visual Statistics* module

- Learn about the worktext

What is *Visual Statistics*?

Statistics is a challenging subject for most people. Most of us have to work hard to understand probability distributions, statistical power, and confidence intervals. However, statistics is becoming more important. It's hard to design a product, create an advertising campaign, or play poker well without understanding statistics.

The main problem is that statistical ideas are abstract. When did you last speak with a probability distribution? Have you ever seen a correlation on the shelf at Sears? Or been almost run down by a wild confidence interval (except on an exam)? Formulas and numbers are fine for some people, but most of us learn best when we can see and interact with the thing we're learning about.

That's where *Visual Statistics* comes in. Computers have become more powerful and easier to use, so it's possible to explore statistical ideas in new ways. Graphics and animation can bring concepts to life in ways that formulas, tables, and static diagrams cannot. Rather than imagining what data for a particular situation looks like, *Visual Statistics* lets you create the situation and see it for yourself. You can change the circumstances and watch the result. *Visual Statistics* helps you build your statistical intuition, making it easier to understand the ideas behind data analysis.

It's important to understand that while you can analyze data with some *Visual Statistics* modules, that is not their main goal. Instead, *Visual Statistics* will help you *learn statistics*. Even the most powerful analysis tools, like Minitab, SAS, and SPSS, won't help you if you don't know what to do with them. On the other hand, if you are familiar with statistical ideas, you can do wonders with a simple calculator. The tools you use are less important than how you wield them. *Visual Statistics* will help you use statistical techniques more effectively because you will understand what they can be used for and what their limitations are.

Visual Statistics is not a tutorial, however. For example, the regression module won't explain why regression works or how to calculate regression statistics. Instead, it helps you explore regression, so you understand it better than you would without the visual tools. You'll get more value from your statistics text since you'll be able to experiment with the concepts. It'll be easier for you to *understand* statistics — and understanding brings more confidence and less worry.

The *Visual Statistics* suite consists of 21 modules. Each one helps you explore a specific set of statistical ideas. For example, the ANOVA module will help you understand one-way analysis of variance. It is designed for that purpose alone. It's different from the module that helps you understand statistical process control, since the two topics are different. However, every module shares some characteristics. First, they are all easy to use. Run through the 15-minute orientation for each module, and you should be able to use it effectively. If you have trouble, select Help for assistance. Second, they all use the Notebook. The Notebook introduces the module, and lets you choose how you want to explore the relevant statistical ideas. Different modules have different Notebook options. Some let you examine scenarios, while others allow you to analyze real data sets or enter your own data. The Notebook is described in more detail later in this introduction.

The best way to learn what *Visual Statistics* is all about is to try it. So go ahead. Install *Visual Statistics,* start the Univariate Data Analysis module and play around. You'll see how the same data can look very different, depending on how it is displayed.

Installing *Visual Statistics*

Visual Statistics runs under recent versions of Windows (95, 98, 2000, NT). You need at least a Pentium PC with 32 MB of memory. *Visual Statistics* takes about 7 MB of hard disk space for a Compact installation or about 37MB of hard disk space for a Complete installation. This includes the software (21 modules), the worktext (21 chapters plus the introduction), worktext solutions, help files, and databases containing over 1000 variables. The Compact installation runs off of the *Visual Statistics* CD while the Complete installation runs off your computer and only checks to see that you have a *Visual Statistics* CD.

Installing VS

This version of *Visual Statistics* is for a single user. Users needing a network version should contact their McGraw-Hill representative. To install *Visual Statistics*, first close down any other programs you are running. Place the *Visual Statistics* CD in your CD drive. The install program is setup.exe in the Setup folder in the Visual Statistics 2.0 folder. It can be executed in one of three ways:

- Use the Add/Remove Programs dialog box in the Windows Control Panel, *or*
- Double click the setup.exe file in Windows Explorer, *or*
- Press the Start button, select Run, and type d:\visual statistics 2.0\setup\setup.exe (where d: represents the drive letter for your CD reader).

You will be asked to select one of two setup types. *Both require that your Visual Statistics CD be in your computer.*

COMPACT installs the front-end of *Visual Statistics* on your computer and the necessary system files. It takes about 50 Mb LESS room on your hard drive.

COMPLETE installs the entire *Visual Statistics* system on your computer. It takes about 50 Mb MORE room on your hard drive, but runs faster on computers with slower CD readers.

Read the License Agreement during the install. After installing *Visual Statistics* it can be read by selecting the Visual Statistics 2.0 folder in the Programs folder. *Visual Statistics* can be started from this folder or by double clicking the VS icon that will be installed on your desktop. Once the system files have been installed on your computer, *Visual Statistics* can also be run directly from the CD by opening the *VisualStatistics*.exe file on the CD. This can be useful if your VS files have been corrupted and you want to run *Visual Statistics* without reinstalling the software.

Uninstalling VS

Visual Statistics can be uninstalled in two ways:

- Use the Add/Remove Programs dialog box in the Windows Control Panel, *or*
- Press the Start button and select Uninstall Visual Statistics 2.0 from the Visual Statistics 2.0 folder in the Programs folder.

Installing Adobe Reader 4.0

When you run the *Visual Statistics* install program, it will detect if you have already installed an Adobe Reader. If you do *not* have an Adobe Reader, VS will install the Adobe 4.0 Reader for you. If you *do* have an Adobe Reader, VS will *not* install the Adobe 4.0 Reader. In this case, you *should* determine which version of the Adobe Reader is on your computer. Although *Visual Statistics* will work with versions earlier than 4.0, the presentation of graphics improved considerably with version 4.0. If you have an earlier version, it is strongly recommended that you uninstall it and install the 4.0 version by executing the ar405en.exe file in the Reader folder on the *Visual Statistics* CD or by getting the latest version from Adobe at www.Adobe.com. Adobe warns that earlier versions should be uninstalled *before* installing version 4.0. If the earlier version is uninstalled *after* the 4.0 version is installed, problems will develop with the 4.0 Reader according to Adobe Corporation.

Starting *Visual Statistics*

Main Menu

To start *Visual Statistics*, click its icon on your desktop, or select *Visual Statistics* 2.0 in the Programs folder in the Start menu. After opening the cover, you will see the a menu like the one shown in Figure 1. From this menu, you can do three things: (1) view a chapter in the worktext (the Show Worktext button); (2) run a software module (the Run Module button); (3) exit *Visual Statistics* (the Exit button). Subject to your system's memory, you may simultaneously use as many chapters or modules as you wish (they will appear on the taskbar at the bottom of your screen). When a chapter is selected, its title will turn white and its icon will turn yellow. In Figure 1, for example, Chapter 1 (Visualizing Univariate Data Analysis) has been selected.

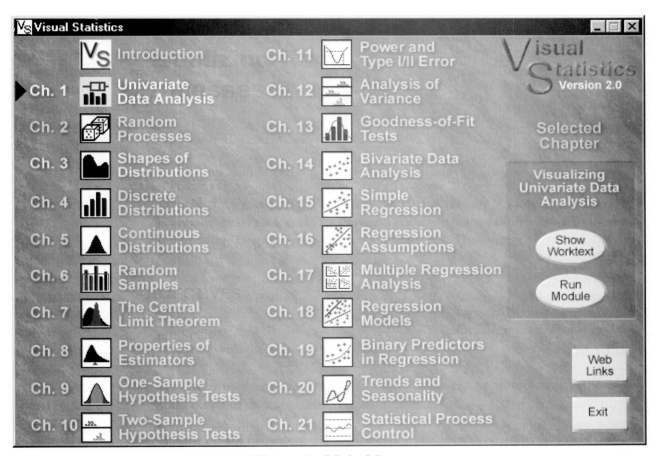

Figure 1: Main Menu

Selecting a Chapter

To select a chapter, click on its chapter number, its icon, or its title. If a chapter has not been installed, its title will be "grayed out" to indicate that it is inactive. When you click the chapter, a comet will streak across the screen to the Selected Chapter panel on the right, and the Show Worktext and Run Module buttons will appear in the panel. If either the module or worktext was not installed, the button will be "grayed out" and will be inactive. Each software module corresponds to a chapter in the worktext. The chapter's learning exercises will require that you run the corresponding software module. You can run several software modules at once, subject to your system's memory.

The *Visual Statistics* Worktext

The worktext has one chapter for each module. Each chapter in the worktext contains:

- A list of concepts and learning objectives
- An overview of concepts and illustrations of concepts
- An orientation to software features
- Structured learning exercises (basic, intermediate, and advanced)
- Suggested independent projects (team, individual)
- A bank of self-test questions
- A glossary of terms
- Answers to the self-test questions

Each chapter starts with a list of relevant concepts and learning objectives. Next, it offers an overview and illustration of each concept. Then there is a short section entitled Orientation to Basic Features. *Make sure you read this section.* It will quickly show you how to use the most important elements of the module. It only takes a few minutes and is well worth it. The Orientation to Additional Features illustrates other important capabilities of the software, which will be necessary to complete some of the exercises. These features are not necessarily more complex, but they intended to suggest priorities that may assist a busy learner or that might be recommended by an instructor if time permits.

The Learning Exercises ask questions you can answer using the module. They are to be completed in front of a PC. You will have a better understanding of the statistical ideas covered in the chapter once you run through the exercises. The Basic, Intermediate, and Advanced exercises are arranged in gradually increasing level of challenge. Your instructor might ask you to turn in some of the exercises. However, you can grade your own work using the Solutions.

The worktext also includes Learning Projects for individuals and teams. Where the Learning Exercises guide you through the module, the Learning Projects leave you to figure out how to use the module and do the analyses yourself or with your team. You may be asked to do a written report or make an oral presentation based on the Learning Projects. It is a good idea to do the Learning Exercises before you try the Learning Projects.

The Self-Evaluation Quiz lets you test your understanding of the ideas covered in the chapter. Try it after you have completed the Learning Exercises. The answers are at the back of each chapter, after the chapter's Glossary. You should do the entire quiz first, before you look at the answers. If you answer a question incorrectly, there are references to relevant sections of *Visual Statistics* that will help you understand the right answer. The exercises are arranged somewhat in increasing order of challenge. Some of the exercises can be answered by looking at the Overview, Illustration, and Glossary, while others may require using the software or working certain exercises.

The Glossary defines the terms used in the chapter. Much of the Glossary information (plus a lot more, such as formulas) will also be included in the module's Help file. Click Help on the menu bar to look at the Help file. It contains definitions, formulas, examples and explanations as well as usage instructions. The Help files are an oft-overlooked resource.

Using the *Visual Statistics* Worktext Reader

To view a worktext chapter, click the Show Worktext button (if the chapter has not been installed, the button will be "grayed out" to indicate that it is inactive) to bring up the Adobe reader, illustrated in Figure 2. Each chapter opens to its title page. You may jump to any section of the chapter by clicking the appropriate title in the Bookmarks window of the Adobe reader (on the left side of the screen) or you may use the scroll bar on the right. The Run Module button takes you to the chapter's software module. The Show Solutions button will display the answers to the learning exercises in a separate window at the bottom of the screen. The Return to VS button displays the *Visual Statistics* main menu.

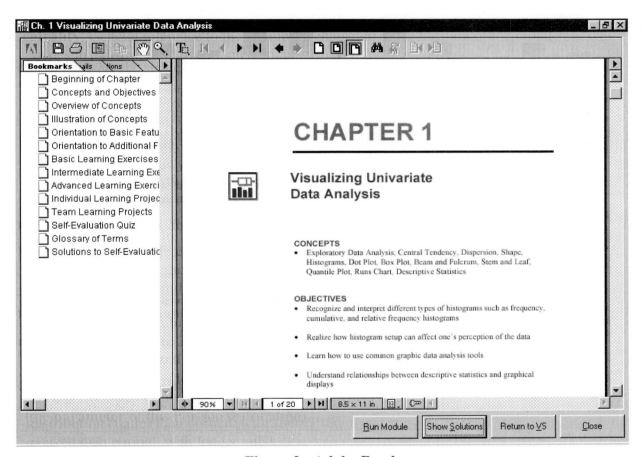

Figure 2: Adobe Reader

Adobe Buttons

The buttons across the top line of the Adobe reader offer many useful features. Each button has a tooltip that will appear when you allow the cursor to rest on the button.

The first group of buttons is:

- save file button (save a copy of the file)
- print file button (to print all or selected text)
- show/hide navigation panel (the "bookmark" area on the left of the screen)
- "hand" tool (to drag the document around in the window when it is too large to fit)
- magnify (to enlarge the document in the window; each click is one size larger)
- select text (so it can be copied using Ctrl-C)

The next group of buttons is:

- 4 page navigation buttons (first page, previous page, next page, last page)
- 2 view buttons (previous view, next view)
- 3 document size buttons (actual size, fit in window, fit width)

The last group of buttons is:

- rotate text (90° left or 90 ° right)
- find (a word or phrase of interest)
- jump to highlights (next, previous sections)

At the bottom of the Adobe screen are two other useful controls:

The first control permits you to set the size of the displayed document (or type in the desired size). The second control lets you page forward or backward in the document (or go to a given page by typing it).

Printing in Adobe

Each chapter of the worktext is in color, but it can be printed either in color or black-and-white. This depends on the printer you are using. The quality of printing of graphics depends on your printer, but also on the version of Adobe you are using (we strongly recommend version 4.0 or later).

Exercise Solutions

If you press the Show Solutions button you will see solutions to the learning exercises in a separate window at the bottom of your screen, as illustrated in Figure 3. This will allow you to check your answers to the learning exercises. If you are taking a class, the instructor may ask you to submit your original (uncorrected) answers along with your handwritten corrections and comments indicating the mistakes that you made or any explanations that you added after reading the exercise solutions.

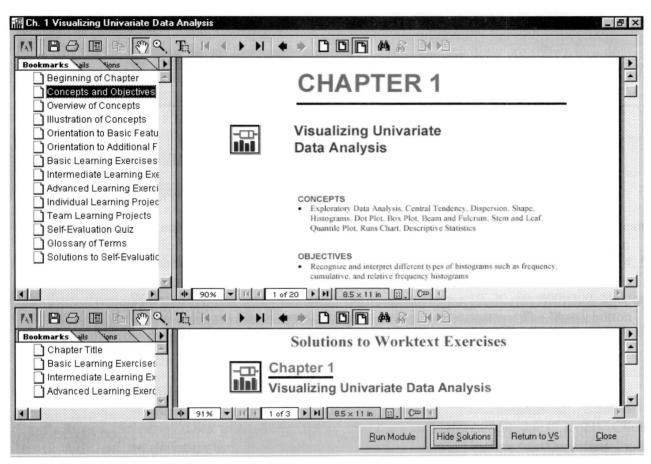

Figure 3: Adobe Reader with Solutions

The *Visual Statistics* Notebook

Every *Visual Statistics* module starts with the Notebook. There is a different Notebook for each module, but they all work in the same way. The main purpose of the Notebook is to let you choose the type of data you want to look at. Figure 4 shows the opening page of the Notebook for the Bivariate Data Analysis module.

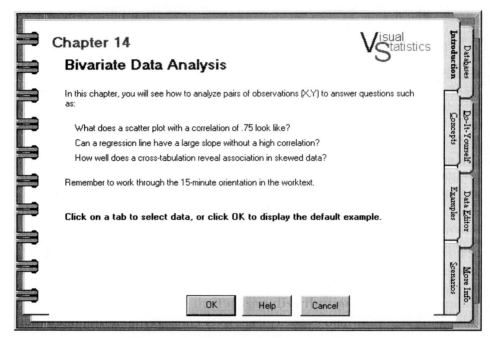

Figure 4: Notebook Opening Page

Navigating the Notebook
The Notebook is divided into sections, each with its own yellow tab. The Introduction section identifies the module and shows some questions the module will help you answer. The Concepts section lists some ideas the chapter covers. The More Information section identifies related modules, and lists relevant chapters in McGraw-Hill/Irwin textbooks.

The OK button closes the Notebook and returns to the module. It's only available when you have selected some data for the module to use. If you click the OK button on the Introduction page when the module first starts, default data will be chosen for you. The Help button gives you assistance in using the Notebook. The Cancel button closes the Notebook immediately.

Data Selection: Examples
Examples are real data sets that have been selected to illustrate the concepts of the module. For instance, to select an example in the Bivariate Data Analysis module, click on the Examples tab. You would see the display shown in Figure 5. Notice there are several different example categories (Sports, Consumer, etc.). You can jump directly to the category's page by clicking on its name. The names are in green and underlined, showing they are hyperlinks. Just as on the Web or in a Windows Help file, clicking on a hyperlink jumps to a different page. Alternatively, you can turn the page by clicking on Next page (lower right corner in Figure 5).

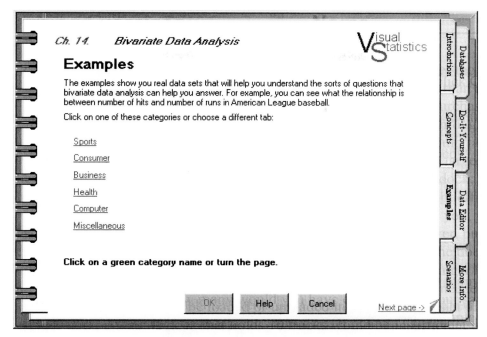

Figure 5: Categories of Examples

For instance, Figure 6 shows various sports-related examples. Click on an example's name to select it. You can read a description of the selected example in the yellow area to the right of the example list. Each page in the section gives examples from a different category. Turn the pages in a section by clicking on Previous page (upper right corner) or Next page. (lower right corner). You can also click on the "folded corners" of the page, as seen in the upper and lower right.

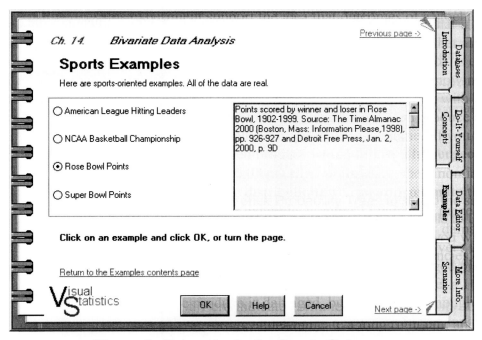

Figure 6: Examples in the Sports Category

Data Selection: Databases

A database contains many variables. You select the one(s) that you wish to analyze. The appearance of the database selection screen depends on the module. Figure 7 shows a database page from the Bivariate Data Analysis module. Note the categories Demographics, Economics, Crime, and so on. Click on the + and – signs to expand or collapse the category. The yellow area to the right describes the selected variable.

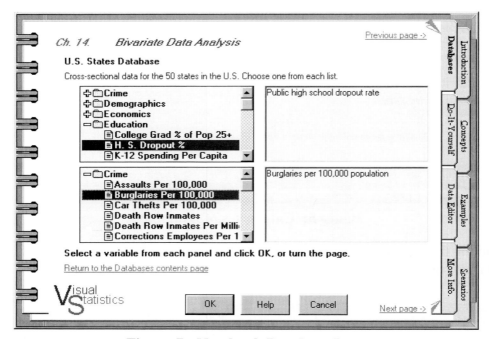

Figure 7: Notebook Database Page

Several modules use another type of variable selection screen. Figure 8 illustrates the one for Multiple Regression Analysis, which is similar to the others.

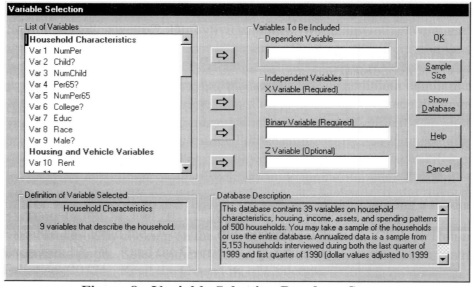

Figure 8: Variable Selection Database Screen

Data Selection: Using the Data Editor

The Data Editor lets you create your own data sets. Figure 9 shows an example from the Bivariate Data Analysis module. The spreadsheet is similar to Excel or 1-2-3. Each row is one observation (a person, a team, etc.). The first column is a label for the observation (a person's name, a team's name, etc.). The first column is optional; you don't have to label every point. The other columns contain the data that you want to analyze. Use the mouse or arrow keys to select a cell, then type data into it. You can rename a column by typing into the cell above the column (e.g., the cell with "Exam 2" in it).

The Data Editor has other useful options. Use the File menu to save your data to disk and retrieve it later. If you're running *Visual Statistics* on a network, make sure you save your data to a disk you can write to (e.g., a floppy). Use the Edit menu to modify the data or move data between applications (Copy, Paste, Insert Row, or Delete Rows). For example, you can copy data from the Data Editor and paste it into other Windows applications such as Excel, 1-2-3, Word, or WordPerfect. These operations are explained in Help in the Data Editor. You can also do the reverse—that is, paste data from another program into the Data Editor. Use the Options menu to sort the data, change its display format, and enter a title for the data set. Select Search under Help in the Data Editor for more information.

Different versions of the Data Editor are available in several programs (the number of columns and their headings will depend on the application). Figure 7 shows the data editor for the Bivariate Data Analysis Module. When you are finished editing your data, click Close Editor and Use Data (or click the "smiling face" icon). If you decide that you don't want to use the data, click Close Editor and Discard Data (or click the "sad face" icon).

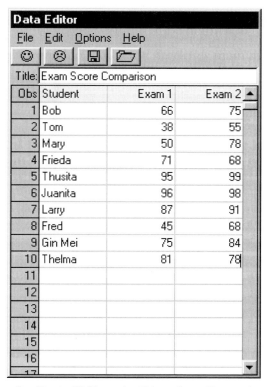

Figure 9: Data Editor in Bivariate Data Analysis

Data Selection: Scenarios

The Examples, Databases, and Data Editor sections are similar in one respect: they let you examine real data sets. The last three notebook sections are different. They let you experiment with the *process* that generates data sets. For example, suppose you rolled a normal six-sided die twice and got a 1 and a 3. The "1 and 3" is the data set. The "rolled a normal six-sided die twice" is the process that created the data set. If you run the same process again (that is, roll the die twice), you would probably get a different data set. Roll the die twice more, and you get yet another data set. You can ask many questions about this situation. Would the data be the same each time? How different would it be? Suppose you added the numbers together. What is the highest sum you can get? What is the smallest? Are you more likely to get the smallest sum or the largest sum? Are all sums equally likely, or are some values more common than others?

You can learn a lot about statistics by examining these questions. But you can learn even more by varying the process that creates the data. For example, what if you rolled a 10-sided die, as used in *Dungeons and Dragons*? What if you spun a roulette wheel twice? Would the answers be the same?

This is where the Scenarios, Templates, and Do-It-Yourself sections come in. The Scenarios let you choose from processes that have been set up for you. Each scenario generates data that you might see in a particular situation. For instance, one scenario looks at the relationship between the number of times at bat and home runs in major league baseball. It gives you a familiar context for statistical exploration. You can take repeated samples, and see how random chance leads to very different data from identical situations. Figure 10 shows one of the scenario pages from the Bivariate Data Analysis module. Most of the modules have a Scenarios section. Some modules have a version control (from 1 to 99) that lets you repeat the same scenario (selecting 0 will make a random scenario selection).

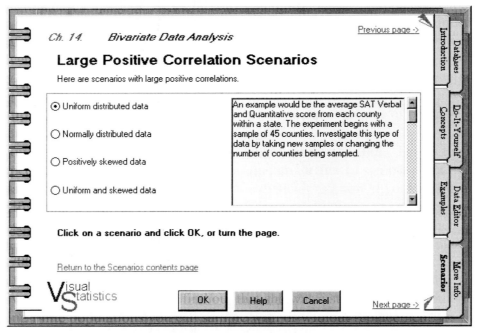

Figure 10: Scenarios

Data Selection: Templates

Templates let you generate data conforming to a particular shape. Several modules use templates. Figure 11 shows a template screen from the Properties of Estimators module. Each template represents a probability distribution (you'll learn what that is in your statistics class). To select a distribution to sample, click on its picture and click the OK button.

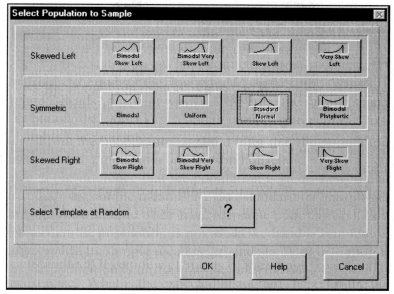

Figure 11: Templates

Data Selection: Do-It-Yourself

The Do-It-Yourself option gives you control over the process generating the data. Many of the modules have a do-it-yourself section. Figure 12 shows the do-it-yourself controls from the Simple Regression module. The appearance of the do-it-yourself screen depends on which module you are using. Figure 13 shows the do-it-yourself controls from the Visualizing Shapes of Distributions module.

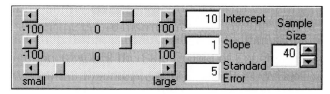

Figure 12: Do-It-Yourself Controls for Simple Regression

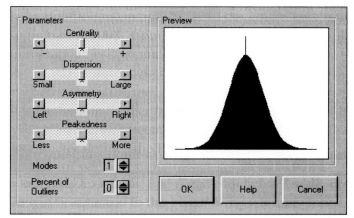

Figure 13: Do-It-Yourself Controls for Shapes of Distributions

Making Choices That Fit Your Needs

You can see that *Visual Statistics* is a powerful tool. There are quite a few modules, some of which have many options. There is something for everyone in *Visual Statistics,* from the novice to the expert. Beginners find it much easier to grasp basic statistical concepts when they use the package. The reason is simple: it's easier to understand something you can actually see than something you have to imagine. However, during our testing of *Visual Statistics,* we found that experts liked using the modules as well. The visualization and experimention capabilities gave them new insights into common statistical problems.

Don't let the suite overwhelm you. Although there's a lot of power available, you don't need to use every option in every module. In fact, you might find yourself using only a few of the features. That's fine if it gives you the level of understanding you want. This worktext will help you get what you need from *Visual Statistics*. In particular, make sure you run through each module's orientation. It only takes a few minutes, and then you'll have a good idea of how to use the module.

CHAPTER 1

Visualizing Univariate Data Analysis

CONCEPTS
- Exploratory Data Analysis, Central Tendency, Dispersion, Shape, Histograms, Dot Plot, Box Plot, Beam and Fulcrum, Stem and Leaf, Quantile Plot, Runs Chart, Descriptive Statistics

OBJECTIVES
- Recognize and interpret different types of histograms such as frequency, cumulative, and relative frequency histograms

- Realize how histogram setup can affect one's perception of the data

- Learn how to use common graphic data analysis tools

- Understand relationships between descriptive statistics and graphical displays

Overview of Concepts

At the beginning of a research project, statisticians feel that data should be examined and allowed to "tell its own story." The exploratory phase of the research can help us select appropriate methods of analysis. This is important because some statistical tests are sensitive to "ill-behaved" data (especially outliers or strange distributions) that are often encountered. John W. Tukey of Princeton University pioneered an approach known as **Exploratory Data Analysis** (EDA). He invented or popularized many useful visual tools (such as the box plot, stem and leaf display, and quantile plot) and argued for reliance on robust statistics (such as quartiles) whenever possible. Traditional tools of data analysis (such as parametric statistics) and visual displays (such as histograms) are also useful in EDA.

Statisticians rely on a variety of visual and numeric tools to do this analysis. One of the first goals of the analysis is to understand **central tendency** (middle or "typical" data values), **dispersion** ("spread" of data values), and the **shape** (degree of symmetry and peakedness) of the sample.

The first step is usually to sort the data from low to high to see if any anomaly stands out. **Descriptive statistics** are usually then calculated. From these statistics we can assess the data's central tendency, dispersion, and shape.

In order to visualize the data, statisticians use a variety of graphic displays. Visual alternatives to examining the entire sorted data array are the **dot plot** and the **stem and leaf** diagram. Visual displays of central tendency, dispersion, skewness, and peakedness are the **box plot** and the **beam and fulcrum**. The **quantile plot** provides a visual evaluation of the distribution of the sampled data (a 45-degree line for rectangular or uniformly distributed data, a lazy "S" for bell-shaped or normally distributed data, an upside-down "L" or a backwards "L" for skewed data, and an almost vertical line for very peaked data). The **runs chart** provides a visual check for randomness of the data in its original order (before sorting).

In creating a **histogram** the statistician must decide the number of intervals to display, the width of the histogram intervals, and whether the numbers on the horizontal axis are going to cover the range exactly or be aesthetically pleasing. A number of different histograms are available to the statistician. The most common is a *frequency histogram*. With this histogram we see the number of observations within each interval. A *relative frequency histogram* is used if we want to make inferences about the larger population since we see the proportion of the sample within each interval. The *cumulative histogram* is a histogram version of the quantile plot. A *frequency polygon* replaces the histogram bars with a line that connects the midpoints of the location of where the top of each histogram bar would be. It is generally used when there are a large number of intervals. The *standardized Z value histogram* is a frequency histogram which displays the standardized data (the difference between each data point and the sample mean divided by the standard deviation) that facilitates comparison between widely different data sets.

Only when we have explored the data thoroughly can we safely say that it is understood. We can draw conclusions or write a simple description of the data. If further analysis is required, the statistician is ready because he or she has allowed the data to "tell its own story."

Illustration of Concepts

The 1996 NCAA Division I national basketball tournament paired 64 teams, whose winners advanced to the second round. Consider a brief **Exploratory Data Analysis** of the number of points scored by the 32 opening-round winners.

Figure 1 shows a sorted data list. The list showed that the winning scores ranged from 43 (Princeton) to 110 (Kentucky). Figure 2 shows a table of **descriptive statistics**. Regarding **central tendency**, the mean was 77.03, the median was 75, and the midhinge was 78 (average of Q1 and Q3). These measures are almost equal, suggesting near-symmetry. Regarding **dispersion**, the range was 67 and the standard deviation was 13.70. Regarding **shape**, skewness was –0.04 (which confirms the notion of symmetry) and kurtosis was 3.07 (which is consistent with normality). Figure 3 shows the symmetric **dot plot** with two possible outliers (the **stem and leaf** would confirm these results).

Figure 1: Data List

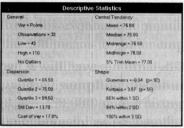

Figure 2: Descriptive Statistics

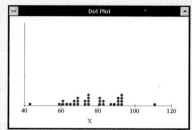

Figure 3: Dot Plot

Figure 4 shows a **box plot** and Figure 5 a **beam and fulcrum**. Both displays confirm that the data set is close to symmetric and about as peaked as a normal distribution. Similarity to a normal distribution is confirmed with the lazy "S" shape of the **quantile plot** in Figure 6. The **runs chart** in Figure 7 indicates that the data are random.

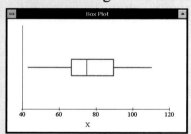

Figure 4: Box Plot

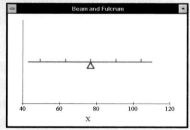

Figure 5: Beam and Fulcrum

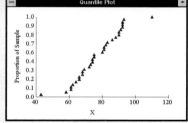

Figure 6: Quantile Plot

Two frequency **histograms** are shown. The histogram in Figure 8 uses six classes (based on Sturges' Rule) and uses nice labeling on the horizontal axis. The histogram in Figure 9 uses nine classes and covers the range exactly. It shows the two possible outliers. Which histogram is correct? Both of them! Full exploration of data requires trying many perspectives.

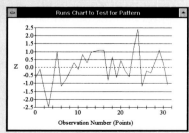

Figure 7: Runs Chart

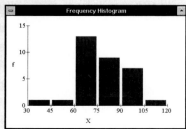

Figure 8: Nice Histogram

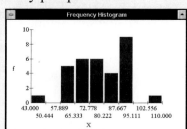

Figure 9: Exact Histogram

Orientation to Basic Features

This module familiarizes you with a variety of univariate data analysis tools. You can analyze a variety of different data sets by selecting them from the Notebook or create your own using the data editor.

1.   Opening Screen

Start the module by clicking on the module's icon, title, or chapter number in the *Visual Statistics* menu and pressing the Run Module button. When the module is loaded, you will be on the introduction page of the Notebook. The Introduction and Concepts sections describe what will be covered in this module. Click on the Examples tab, click on Financial, select an example, and press OK. A Hint appears in the middle of the display. Read it and press OK. The upper left of the screen shows a frequency histogram. The Histogram Control Panel appears on the right. On the bottom left is the Dot Plot. On the bottom right is a table of Descriptive Statistics. Other features are controlled from the menu bar at the top of the screen. A flashing Update Histograms button will indicate when you have changed one or more control settings.

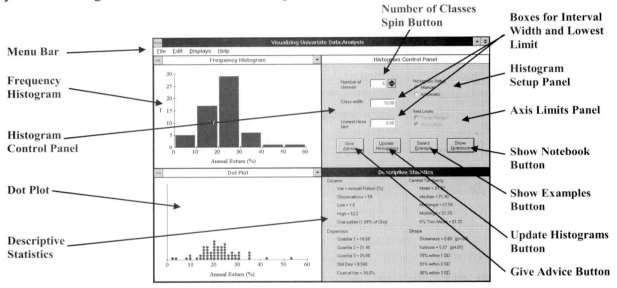

2.   Control Panel

a.   The Histogram Setup panel contains option buttons to select if the histograms are to be automatically or manually created. Click on Automatic.

b.   The Number of Classes spin button is used to control the number of histogram intervals. Click on the spin button and watch how the shape of the histogram changes.

c.   The Axis Limits panel contains option buttons that are active when Automatic is selected in Histogram Setup. Given the number of classes, Nice Limits usually creates the smallest possible interval width that is divisible by 10, 2, or 5 (to an appropriate power of 10). The starting value is the largest possible value (smaller than the minimum value in the data set) divisible by the class width. This option generally creates aesthetically pleasing labels on the horizontal axis. Cover Range calculates interval (class) width by dividing the sample range by the number of classes. The lower limit is the smallest sample value. Although the class limits may be unaesthetic, unlike the Nice Limits option, it does not create beginning or ending intervals that extend beyond the data's range. Try selecting each option.

d.   Clicking on the Give Advice button describes the data and suggests an optimal number of intervals, the starting value for the first interval (class), and the width of each class. Click either Cancel or Take Advice.

e.   Click on the Select Example button to select a new data set from the list of examples. This button changes to Select Databases or Edit Data depending upon the origin of the data you are analyzing. See (f) and (g) below. It is a shortcut to the Notebook tab previously used.

g.   Click on the Show Notebook button to bring up the Notebook. There are two large databases that you can access with this module: U.S. States and World Nations. Select the Databases tab. Click on either U.S. States or World Nations. Each database is organized by categories. Click on the + symbol of any category to expand the category and list its variables. A complete discussion of the databases is given in the Introduction to this text.

g.   Click on the Show Notebook button to bring up the Notebook. You can use your own data by selecting the Data Editor tab, and pressing OK. A simple two-column spreadsheet appears. You can copy data from any spreadsheet program and paste it into the data editor; directions are provided under Help. You can save the data in *Visual Statistics* format by using the Save button or selecting File and Save on the menu bar. When you are finished press the Exit and Use Data button or Exit and Discard Data button or select these options under File. A complete discussion of the Data Editor is given in the Introduction to this text.

3.   **Other Displays**

This module will make five different types of histograms, six different graphs, a table of descriptive statistics, and a list of the data. The Hint that was displayed as the module began said, "Click the right mouse button on a quadrant to select a different display." Displays can also be changed by selecting a quadrant and clicking on Displays in the menu bar. Only the Histogram Control Panel cannot be replaced. Under Histogram Types, a frequency histogram, cumulative histogram, relative frequency histogram, frequency polygon, and standardized Z histogram can be selected. All of these except the standardized Z histogram are controlled by the Histogram Control Panel. Under Graph Type, besides a dot plot there are options for a stem and leaf plot, a box plot, a beam and fulcrum, a quantile plot and a runs chart. Under Tables, in addition to a numeric summary, there is an option for a data list.

4.   **Copying Graphs**

Select Copy from the Edit menu (on the menu bar at the top of the screen), or the Copy option when you right click on a display, to copy the display. It can then be pasted into other applications, such as Word or WordPerfect, so it can be printed.

5.   **Help**

Click on Help on the menu bar at the top of the screen. Search for Help lets you search an index for this module, Contents shows a table of contents for this module, Using Help gives instructions on how to use Help, and About gives licensing and copyright information about *Visual Statistics*. Close Help by selecting Exit from the File menu on the Help screen.

6.   **Exit**

Close the module by selecting Exit in the File menu (or click ☒ in the upper right-hand corner of the window). You will be returned to the *Visual Statistics* main menu.

Orientation to Additional Features

Manual Histogram

Display a frequency histogram and the descriptive statistics by using the right click feature. To create your own histograms select Manual in the Histogram Setup panel in the Histogram Control Panel. The Class Width and Lowest Class Limit boxes are now active and can be used. When creating your own histogram two rules should be used:

1. All of the data should be included in the histogram.
2. Neither the first interval nor last interval should be empty. Both should contain observations.

The maximum and minimum values in your data are listed as High and Low in the Descriptive Statistics table. In the Lowest Class Limit box enter a number no larger than the minimum value in your data. The approximate class width will be:

$$\frac{(\text{Maximum} - \text{Minimum})}{\text{Number of Classes}}$$

Enter this number, or a number slightly larger, in the Class Width box. If you create a histogram that does not cover the sample range, an error message will appear but the histogram will be displayed. To fix the problem, adjust one or both of the numbers.

Example

Below is an example of a manually created histogram with 9 intervals using the New Home Prices data. It has 9 intervals of width 20,000. The first interval starts at 70,000. Note that 70,000 is less than the smallest observation (Low statistic = 74,189) and the last interval is larger than the largest observation (High statistic = 232,388). Therefore, all of the data points are included in the histogram. Also note that both the first and last intervals contain data (the first interval has a frequency of 12 and the last interval has a frequency of 1). Therefore, both rules are met.

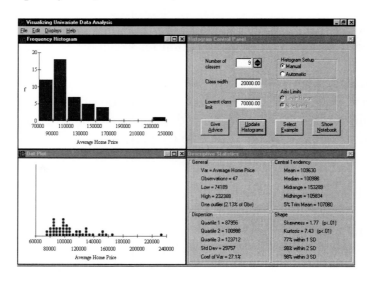

Basic Learning Exercises

Name _____

Press the Show Notebook button and select the Examples tab. Click on Consumer and select New Home Prices. Read the scenario.

1. a) Give the exact definition of the variable. b) What are its units of measurement? c) How do you think the *U.S. News* obtained the data? d) Are the data continuous or discrete?

Descriptive Statistics

2. Click on OK. Click the right mouse button to select your displays. Put the Numeric Summary in the lower right quadrant, the Data List in the lower left quadrant, and the Cumulative Frequency Histogram in the upper left quadrant. Using the sorted data list, which two cities had the lowest- and highest-priced homes? What were their standardized values?

3. What is the definition of an outlier? Get the definition from Help (click on Help on the menu bar and Search for Help. Type "outlier" and select the appropriate topic). Is either of these cities an outlier? Why or why not?

4. Give the value of each measure of centrality. If you are unfamiliar with a term, use Help. Are the measures different? What does this tell you about centrality and skewness?

    Mean _____   Median _____   Midrange _____   Midhinge _____
    5% Trimmed Mean _____

5. Give the value of each statistic. How does each relate to dispersion?

    Standard deviation _____   Range _____   First quartile _____
    Third quartile _____   Interquartile range _____

Graphs

6. Use the right click feature to view the dot plot, stem and leaf, and box plot in the three quadrants. The dot plot, and stem and leaf both illustrate the data. When would each be used?

7. How does the box plot illustrate centrality and dispersion? Use the Help feature for assistance.

Histograms

8. Use the right click feature to bring up the frequency histogram, frequency polygon, and relative frequency histogram in the three quadrants. All three of these displays have the same general appearance. Describe this appearance. Since each is similar, why would a statistician use one instead of another?

9. Use the right click feature to display the frequency, cumulative, and the standardized Z value histograms. Why would a statistician use either the cumulative or the standardized Z value histograms?

10. Click on Automatic in the Histogram Setup panel and Cover Range in the Axis Limit panel. Type the number "2" in the Number of Classes box and press Enter on your keyboard. Two histograms are redrawn. Use the spin button to increase the number of classes. a) Look at the frequency histogram; why does your impression of the shape of the data change as the number of classes changes? b) Look at the cumulative histogram; does its appearance change more or less and why? c) Why doesn't the standardized histogram change?

Intermediate Learning Exercises   Name _____

Press the Show Notebook button and select the Examples tab. Click on Consumer and select New Home Prices. Display the descriptive statistics, the box plot and the beam and fulcrum diagram.

Beam and Fulcrum
11. How does the beam and fulcrum illustrate centrality and dispersion? Use Help for assistance.

Shape Statistics
12. Record the value of each shape measure. What do these statistics tell us? If you do not know how to interpret these statistics, look up "Equations: Shape" in the Contents of Help.

Skewness _____   Kurtosis _____
% within 1 SD ____   % within 2 SD ____   % within 3 SD ____

13. The skewness measure tells us that this data is positively skewed. How can we see this skewness in the box plot, and beam and fulcrum diagram?

14. Kurtosis measures the peakedness of the distribution or the relative proportion of the distribution contained in its body versus its tails. How is kurtosis illustrated in the box plot and the beam and fulcrum? **Hint:** The new home price data are slightly peaked and positively skewed, the PC reliability data (press Show Examples and select PC Reliability) is almost normally distributed (mesokurtic or kurtosis near 3), and the lottery number data (press Show Examples and select Lottery Winners) is almost flat (very platykurtic or kurtosis << 3).

Runs Chart and Quantile Plot

15. Press the Show Examples button and select PC Reliability. Right click and show a quantile plot. How can we tell from the quantile plot that this data is almost bell-shaped (normal distribution)? Press Show Examples and select Lottery Winners. How can we tell from the quantile plot that this data is almost rectangular (uniform distribution)?

16. Return to the New Home Prices example. Right click and show a runs chart. How does the runs chart show that this data is random? Select the Technology section of the Examples tab of the Notebook and look at Importance of Job Abilities. Then select the Miscellaneous section of the same tab and look at Years Served by Popes. How does the runs chart show that these two data sets are not random?

Histograms

17. Return to the New Home Prices example. Right click on a diagram and show a frequency histogram. Set the Number of Classes spin button to 9. Click on Automatic in the Histogram Setup panel and Cover Range in the Axis Limit panel. Change the option button in the Axis Limit panel to Nice Limits. Did your impression of the data's shape change? Why or why not?

18. Change the number of intervals from 2 to 20 using both Cover Range and Nice Limits. With which setting does the appearance of the frequency histogram change less? Why?

19. Given these results when would a statistician use the Nice Limits option for histograms, and when would he or she use the Cover Range option?

Advanced Learning Exercises   Name _____

Histograms

20. Choose a variable from either the U.S. States or World Nations database. Click the Give Advice button, read its suggestions, and click Take Advice. Attach a copy of the histogram to this exercise. Describe the general appearance of the frequency histogram. List its noteworthy features (for example, does it have a single modal class?).

21. In the Histogram Setup panel select Manual. Construct a histogram of your own using nice labels, with the same number of classes used in exercise 20, but use a different class width and/or lower class limit. Copy the histogram and attach it to this exercise. Were you able to improve on the advice? What were the tradeoffs you had to consider? If you could vary the number of classes, could you have found nicer class limits?

22. Write down some principles for an algorithm to construct nice classes. Begin by looking in the Help file for Sturges' Rule. Discuss the logic of Sturges' Rule, which says that the correct number of classes is $1 + \log_2(n)$ where n is the sample size. **Hint:** Consider that $\log_2(2) = 1$, $\log_2(4) = 2$, $\log_2(8) = 3$, and so on.

Descriptive Statistics

23. Based on the descriptive statistics write a description of your data's shape. Explain what the skewness and kurtosis tell you. Next to the values of skewness and kurtosis is a p-value. What does this value tell you? If necessary, refer to the definitions and explanations in Help.

24. Two statistics reported in the descriptive statistics display and often not discussed in class or textbooks are the coefficient of variation and the 5% trimmed mean. Define each statistic and explain why each could be useful to a statistician.

Graphs

25. Reread exercise 16. What two types of data are most likely to suffer from non-randomness? What are their characteristics? Why is it likely to occur with these types of data?

25. Display either the beam and fulcrum or the box plot, and either the stem and leaf or the dot plot. List the advantages and disadvantages of each type of display. Are both needed?

Individual Learning Projects

Write a report on one of the three topics listed below. Use the cut-and-paste facilities of the module to place the appropriate graphs in your report.

1. Select a variable of interest and display its frequency histogram. Create five histograms with various numbers of classes, first using the Nice Limits option and then using the Cover Range option. In your paper give an exact definition of your variable, describe the shape of the distribution, explain in detail the effect the number of classes had on the appearance of your distribution, discuss the advantages and disadvantages of the Nice Limits and Cover Range options, and conclude with a decision (and reason) as to which histogram was most appropriate.

2. Select a variable of interest from one of the databases (U.S. States or World Nations) and do a complete Exploratory Data Analysis of the variable. Use the Learning Exercises and the Illustration of Concepts as a guide. Be sure to include a discussion of the units of measurement and possible inaccuracies or limitations in the data gathering process.

3. Select a variable of interest from one of the databases (U.S. States or World Nations) and explain how to construct the proper histogram manually to represent the data. You can use any other display (except automatic histogram creation) within the module to help in this task. Your paper should provide at least eight displays that illustrate the process you went through.

Team Learning Projects

Select one of the three projects listed below. In each case produce a team project that is suitable for an oral presentation. Use a large poster board(s) to display your results. Graphs should be large enough for your audience to see. Each team member should be responsible for producing some of the graphs. Ask your instructor if a written report is also expected.

1. Within one of the databases provided in this module or using another database of the team's choice, each team member should select a different variable and do an Exploratory Data Analysis of that variable. The objective of the project is to compare and contrast the central tendency, dispersion, shape, and general distribution of the variables selected. Include a discussion of the units of measurement and possible inaccuracies or limitations in the data gathering process for each variable.

2. A team of two or three should select a variable and do an in-depth analysis of constructing frequency histograms. Using Automatic classes with the Nice Limits option, create all possible histograms with 2 to 20 classes (make a display of each). Are the class limits always nice? For each that is not (but at least two), use the Manual feature to construct a histogram with nice limits that has the same number of classes (make a display of each). Of all the histograms, which histogram is most appropriate and why? Describe its overall shape. The objective of this project is to understand the importance of the number of classes in constructing histograms and the ease or difficulty in creating histograms with nice intervals.

3. A team of three should select three variables: one must be skewed with no outliers, one must be symmetric with no outliers, and one must contain outliers. For each variable the team is to construct 10 histograms varying the number of intervals and the type of labeling (five using the Nice Limits option and five using the Cover Range option). The objective of the project is to compare how different types of data have different issues involved in selecting the number of intervals and labeling. For each variable the team should select a "best" histogram.

Self-Evaluation Quiz

1.   Which statistics offer robust measures of central tendency when outliers are present?
      a.   Mean, midrange, and mode.
      b.   Median, midhinge, and trimmed mean.
      c.   Mean, midrange, and midhinge.
      d.   Mean, mode, and quartiles.
      e.   None of the above.

2.   The quartiles of a distribution are most clearly revealed in which display?
      a.   Box plot.
      b.   Dot plot.
      c.   Stem and leaf.
      d.   Frequency histogram.
      e.   Standardized Z histogram.

3.   The frequency of outliers can always be seen on which display?
      a.   Box plot.
      b.   Standardized Z histogram.
      c.   Dot plot.
      d.   Frequency histogram.
      e.   None of the above.

4.   The sorted stem and leaf display does *not* reveal
      a.   the modal groupings.
      b.   the mean.
      c.   all of the data values.
      d.   the mode(s).
      e.   the lowest and highest values.

5.   Which display(s) will show the position of each data item?
      a.   Box plot.
      b.   Standardized Z histogram.
      c.   Dot plot.
      d.   Frequency histogram.
      e.   None of the above.

6.   As we increase the number of classes in a histogram
      a.   central tendency becomes more obvious.
      b.   class interval width increases.
      c.   class intervals become rounder.
      d.   all of the above would be likely to happen.
      e.   none of the above would be likely to happen.

7. The mean and standard deviation are most easily seen in which display?
   a. Box plot.
   b. Beam and fulcrum.
   c. Stem and leaf.
   d. Dot plot.
   e. Histogram.

8. If nice classes are used in a histogram
   a. the scale range may not equal the true data range.
   b. the histogram classes may be easier to interpret.
   c. Sturges' Rule may be of secondary importance.
   d. all of the above are likely.
   e. none of the above is likely.

9. To ascertain the approximate range of a distribution we could use which display(s)?
   a. Box plot.
   b. Beam and fulcrum.
   c. Stem and leaf.
   d. Quantile plot.
   e. All of the above.

10. The quantile plot for a sample from a normal population would have what shape?
    a. L-shaped.
    b. Backward Z-shaped.
    c. Lazy S-shaped.
    d. Inverted U-shaped.
    e. Either a or b.

11. The runs chart is most useful to
    a. check for randomness.
    b. check for normality.
    c. check for skewness.
    d. check the interquartile range.
    e. check none of the above.

12. Sturges' Rule would be most helpful in constructing which display?
    a. Runs chart.
    b. Beam and fulcrum.
    c. Histogram.
    d. Stem and leaf.
    e. Dot plot.

Glossary of Terms

Beam and fulcrum A display that plots the position of the sample mean (the "fulcrum") and the standard deviation points (Mean ± 1 SD, Mean ± 2 SD, Mean ± 3 SD, etc.). This display reveals skewness (the longer tail will indicate the direction of skewness) and kurtosis (the more standard deviations displayed along the beam the more peaked the data).

Bimodal When a sample contains two modes, the data are bimodal.

Box plot Five-number graphical display plotting the positions of the minimum, quartiles (first, second, third), and maximum along a scale representing data values.

Central tendency General reference to the attempt to characterize the location of the middle or "typical" values in a distribution (mean, median, midrange, midhinge, trimmed mean, modal class).

Coefficient of variation The ratio of the standard deviation to the mean. It is often multiplied by 100 so that it can be expressed as a percentage. It shows dispersion in relative terms. The formula fails if the mean is zero. It is unit-free and thereby allows comparison of samples with different means.

Cumulative histogram Histogram showing accumulated frequencies of data values. It begins at zero and rises to the sample size as we move to the right.

Descriptive Statistics A variety of statistics that are use to summarize or describe a data set.

Dispersion General reference to the "spread" of data values around the center of a distribution (variance, standard deviation, range, interquartile range, and coefficient of variation).

Dot plot Display of each data point as a dot along a horizontal scale. It is a kind of histogram with many bins. Dots are stacked when they are very close to the same horizontal position.

EDA Acronym for Exploratory Data Analysis.

Exploratory Data Analysis A broad term encompassing a variety of methods of looking at data to understand its characteristics. Its common acronym is EDA.

Frequency histogram Histogram showing the frequency of individual data values on the vertical axis and the data value along the horizontal axis.

Frequency polygon Frequency histogram that connects the midpoints of its bar tops and then omits the bars, producing a line graph.

Histogram Bar chart showing on the horizontal axis the values of a variable grouped into discrete classes (intervals or bins) and on the vertical axis the frequency of occurrence within each class.

Interquartile range The difference between the third and first quartile. It is robust to outliers and extreme values.

Kurtosis Measure of relative peakedness. The Pearson coefficient of kurtosis is the ratio of the fourth sample moment about the mean to the square of the second sample moment about the mean. If a distribution is unimodal and symmetric, then $K = 3$ indicates a normal, bell-shaped distribution (mesokurtic); $K < 3$ indicates a platykurtic distribution (flatter than normal, with shorter tails); and $K > 3$ indicates a leptokurtic distribution (more peaked than normal, with longer tails).

Mean Average of the sample data. It may be interpreted as the fulcrum (balancing point) of the sample data if the n data points are plotted along the X-axis. It is the most common measure of central tendency. It is not robust to outliers and extreme values.

Median The point along the X-axis that defines the upper and lower 50 percent of the sample. If n is odd the median is a member of the data set, while if n is even the median is the average of two adjacent values. It is a robust measure of central tendency because it is insensitive to outliers and extreme values.

Midhinge The average of the first quartile and third quartile. It is a robust measure of central tendency when the data contain outliers or extreme values.

Midrange The average of the smallest and largest observation. It is a measure of central tendency that is easily affected by outliers or extreme values.

Modal class Bar on the histogram that is higher than the bars on either side. Histograms may have two modes (bimodal) or more than two modes (multimodal). Axis tick marks indicate the limits of the modal class. The modal class is a more useful indicator of central tendency than the mode when the data are continuous or have a large range.

Mode The data value that occurs most frequently in a sample. It is not necessarily unique. If there are two modes, the data are called bimodal. The mode is most useful for discrete data with a small range.

Moment See **Sample moment about the mean**.

Outlier Any sample observation that is more than 3 standard deviations from the mean. In general, it is an observation that may be from a different population because it differs markedly from the others in the sample. In a normal population, an observation more than 3 standard deviations from the mean is expected to occur only about 27 times in 10,000 observations.

Percent within k standard deviations In a normal population, we expect 68.26% of the observations within 1 standard deviation of the mean, 95.44% within 2 standard deviations of the mean, and 99.73% within 3 standard deviations of the mean.

P-value for shape A large-sample test for departure from normality may be used to yield a two-tailed p-value for normal skewness (if n > 8) and kurtosis (if n > 20). Small p-values (for instance, below 0.05) tend to indicate departure from normality.

Q_1, Q_2, Q_3 Abbreviation for the first, second and third quartiles.

Quantile plot Cumulative frequency plotted against original data values. Normally distributed data will resemble a lazy S-shaped curve; skewed data will more closely resemble an upside-down "L" or a backwards "L"; uniformly distributed data will resemble a 45-degree line; and peaked data will have a steeper line.

Quartiles The first quartile (Q_1) is the point along the X-axis which defines the lower 25 percent of the sample, located at observation (n + 1)/4. The second quartile (Q_2) is the median (see above). The third quartile (Q_3) is the point along the X-axis that defines the upper 25 percent of the sample, located at observation 3(n + 1)/4. If n + 1 is a multiple of 4, all quartiles are members of the data set; otherwise, we interpolate between adjacent observations.

Range The difference between the maximum and the minimum value in a sample. It is a measure of dispersion. It is not robust to outliers and extreme values.

Relative frequency histogram Frequency histogram that expresses frequencies as a fraction of sample size. Except for scaling of the frequency axis, it is identical in appearance to the frequency histogram.

Robust The quality of being unaffected by a particular factor. For example, the sample median is robust to the existence of an outlier (the sample median changes very little if an outlier is added to a data set).

Runs chart Plot of standardized data against the original order of entry in the sample, used to check for patterns that may occur when data are collected over time or in a systematic way.

Sample moment about the mean The kth sample moment about the mean is obtained by taking the average of all of the deviations about the mean raised to the kth power. The moments are used in the calculation of the Pearson coefficients of skewness and kurtosis.

Shape General reference to the degree of symmetry or asymmetry of a distribution, and to its degree of peakedness or flatness (see skewness and kurtosis).

Skewness Measure of relative symmetry. The Pearson coefficient of skewness is the ratio of the third sample moment about the mean to the square root of the second sample moment about the mean cubed. Zero indicates symmetry. Positive values show a long right tail. Negative values show a long left tail.

Standard deviation The square root of the sample variance. It is a measure of dispersion about the mean. It is measured in the same units as the mean (pounds, dollars, or whatever).

Standardized Z values Obtained from each observation when we subtract the mean and divide by the sample standard deviation. These transformed data are called Z values because they may be used to see how closely the sample resembles a standard normal distribution, to spot outliers, and to check symmetry about the mean. See **Percent within k standard deviations**.

Standardized Z histogram Histogram whose horizontal axis is scaled in terms of standard deviations instead of the original data units (usually from −4 to +4). It is useful for making comparisons with a standard normal distribution.

Stem and leaf Frequency tally in which each data point is tallied by displaying its "leaf" (its second significant digit) beside its "stem" (its first significant digit). The stem may be split into "high" and "low" stems if leaf frequencies become large. Data with more than two digits are expressed in appropriate units (10, 100, etc.). Leaf items are often sorted from low to high.

Sturges' Rule The number of histogram classes should be $1 + \log_2(n)$ where n is the sample size (e.g., 4 classes for 8 observations, 5 classes for 16 observations, 6 classes for 32 observations). It is only a suggestion to avoid having too many or too few classes. If the data are skewed, Sturges' Rule may not provide enough classes to reveal adequate detail.

Trimmed mean Mean calculated by omitting the highest 5% of the observations and the lowest 5% of the observations to mitigate the effect of extreme values. If 5% of the sample size is not an integer, we round the number of removed observations to the next smaller integer. It is generally robust to outliers and extreme values.

Univariate data Referring to any sample of observed values on a single variable (as opposed to bivariate or multivariate data).

Variance The sum of the squared deviations about the mean divided by the sample size minus one. The larger the variance the greater the dispersion or "spread" around the mean. It is not robust to outliers and extreme values.

Solutions to Self-Evaluation Quiz

1. b   Do Exercise 2–5. Read the Overview of Concepts.
2. a   Do Exercises 6–10. Consult the Glossary. Read the Overview of Concepts.
3. b   Do Exercises 6–10. Consult the Glossary. Read the Overview of Concepts.
4. b   Do Exercises 6. Consult the Glossary. Read the Overview of Concepts.
5. c   Do Exercises 6–10. Consult the Glossary. Read the Overview of Concepts.
6. e   Do Exercise 8–10. Do Exercise 10. Do Team Learning Project 2.
7. b   Do Exercises 6–11, 15, 16. Consult the Glossary.
8. d   Do Exercise 8–10, 17–19. Do Individual Learning Project 1 or Team Learning Project 2.
9. e   Do Exercises 11, 15, 16. Consult the Glossary. Read the Overview of Concepts.
10. c   Do Exercise 15. Consult the Glossary. Read the Overview of Concepts.
11. a   Do Exercise 16. Consult the Glossary. Read the Overview of Concepts.
12. c   Do Exercise 22. Consult the Glossary.

CHAPTER 2

Visualizing Random Processes

CONCEPTS
- Stochastic Process, Event, Sample Space, Random Variable, Variation, Probability of an Event, Empirical Probability, Probability Distribution, Centrality, Dispersion, Skewness, Parameter, Histogram

OBJECTIVES

- Recognize that the outcomes of a stochastic process may exhibit regularity even though the process is random

- Learn through experimentation how changing the parameters can affect the outcomes of an experiment

- Learn how a histogram can summarize the results of an experiment and suggest the shape of a probability distribution

- Visualize random data-generating processes that give rise to common probability distributions

- Understand how relative frequencies can be used to estimate the probability of an event if the sample is large

Overview of Concepts

A **stochastic process** is an experiment of chance whose outcomes cannot be predicted (e.g., flipping a coin). The **sample space** is the set of all possible outcomes (called elementary outcomes). For example, if you flip three coins the sample space {HHH, HHT, HTH, THH, HTT, THT, TTH, TTT} contains eight elementary outcomes. An **event** is a collection of elementary outcomes. For example, the set {HHT, HTH, THH} consists of all elementary outcomes containing two heads. A **random variable** is a number that is assigned to each event in the domain of X. For example, if X is the number of heads in the three-coin experiment, its possible values are {0, 1, 2, 3}.

A **probability distribution** assigns a probability P(X) to every value of X, such that $0 \leq P(X) \leq 1$. If the event cannot occur then P(X) = 0, and if the event is certain to occur then P(X) = 1. The **probability of an event** can sometimes be known *a priori* by thinking about the process. For example, in the three-coin experiment P(2) is 3/8 because three of the eight events in the sample space have two heads. An **empirical probability** is found by doing the experiment many times and finding the relative frequency of occurrence of each event. If we can flip three coins repeatedly, the relative frequency of 2's will be approximately 0.375 or 3/8. An empirical probability becomes better as the number of repetitions grows. Yet in a real-life stochastic experiment there is **variation** due to sampling, so unexpected things can happen in a given sample (e.g., you can get 0 heads in 3 flips).

We can describe a probability distribution in terms of its **centrality** ("middle" or "typical" value), its **dispersion** (the "spread" around the center), and its **skewness** (degree to which it lacks symmetry). The mode (most frequent value) is a simple measure of centrality. The range (from lowest to highest value) is a simple measure of dispersion. The visual length of the right and left tails are a simple measure of skewness. A **histogram** shows the sample frequencies.

Sometimes we can derive a mathematical equation for a probability if we assume certain conditions. For example, a binary experiment with independent trials and constant probability of "success" follows a known model called a *binomial distribution*. Its two **parameters** are the number of coins and the probability of "heads." In many binary processes the probability of "success" is not 0.50. For example, if motorists are stopped at random to check for expired licenses, the probability that a driver will have an expired license (the probability of "success") might be 0.03. An unknown parameter can be estimated empirically if a large sample is taken (e.g, using police records).

A second type of stochastic processe involves counting events over an interval of time or space. For example, how many phone calls will arrive at an L. L. Bean call center between 10:00 A.M. and 10:01 A.M. on the first Thursday in October? The lowest possible value is 0 but there is no obvious upper limit. If phone calls are independent and randomly distributed over time, such a probability distribution follows a known mathematical model called the *Poisson distribution* with one parameter (the mean arrival rate). This parameter is generally unknown *a priori* but can be estimated empirically (e.g., from L. L. Bean's database).

A third type of stochastic process is found in games of chance where all probabilities are the same (e.g., rolling a die), giving rise to a *uniform distribution*. Combining events gives rise to a more complex experiment. For example, if we roll two dice and add their outcomes we get a *triangular distribution*. These are examples of known distributions.

Illustration of Concepts

In a certain assembly facility, cars are produced with an average of 5 defects per car. The number of defects in a particular car is a **random variable**. Any particular **event** (such as finding 4 defects in a particular car) is the result of a **stochastic process**. The **histogram** in Figure 1 shows a count of the number of defects in each of 50 cars inspected at random. The range is from 1 to 10. It is symmetric and has two modes (4 and 6). Some events (such as 0 and 8) did not occur. There is **variation** around the presumed process mean of 5.

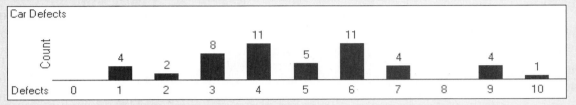

Figure 1: Histogram of Number of Defects in 1st Sample of 50 Cars

Figure 2 shows the results of inspecting 50 more cars. This sample histogram is quite different. Its range is from 2 to 10. It is unimodal (4) and has no "gaps" but is skewed (longer right tail). Logically the **sample space** {0, 1, 2, 3, ...} is best regarded as having no upper limit, but these two samples suggest that more than 10 defects is unlikely. Overall, these two samples reveal considerable **dispersion**, not very much **centrality**, and some skewness.

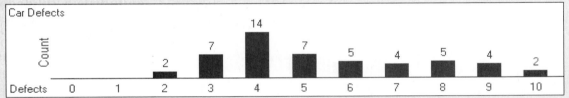

Figure 2: Histogram of Number of Defects in 2nd Sample of 50 Cars

To estimate the **probability of an event** empirically, we would prefer many repetitions of the experiment. Figure 3 shows the results of 1000 car inspections. The **empirical probability** of 4 defects is estimated to be 176/1000 or 0.176. For such a large sample, this histogram should provide a pretty good idea of the underlying **probability distribution**. Its range is from 0 to 14 and the mean number of defects is 4.942, which is very close to 5 (the true **parameter** of this Poisson distribution).

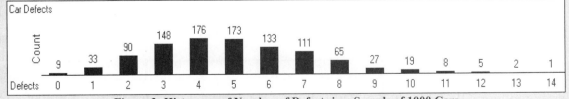

Figure 3: Histogram of Number of Defects in a Sample of 1000 Cars

As the number of repetitions in the experiment increases, we may also begin to see the shape of the unknown probability distribution. The histogram in Figure 3 (1000 cars) is somewhat more regular in its shape than the histograms in Figures 1 and 2 (50 cars). We would expect that another sample of 1000 would produce a histogram much like Figure 3. In smaller samples we would be reluctant to generalize about the distribution's shape.

Orientation to Features

This module is a simulation that illustrates random processes. You can choose four different scenarios from the Notebook.

1. **Opening Screen**

    Start the module by clicking on the module's icon number in the *Visual Statistics* menu and pressing the Run Module button. When the module is loaded, you will be on the introduction page of the Notebook. The Introduction and Concepts sections describe what will be covered in this module. Click on the Scenarios tab, select Probability Trees, and press OK. The upper part of the screen shows a tree with branch points, bins, a counter, and a Control Panel in the upper right. On the bottom is a histogram that tabulates the frequency of balls that are dropped.

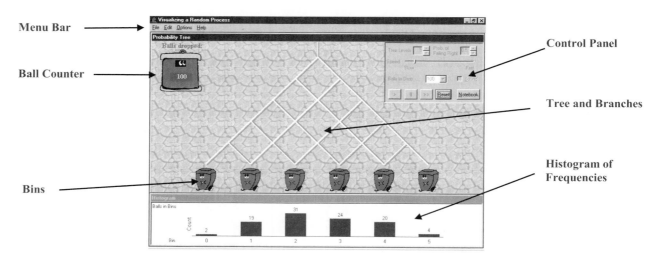

2. **Control Panel**

    a. In the Probability Trees scenario, at each branch point, a ball falls either left or right. The Tree Levels spin button sets the number of branch points (1 to 10). The Probability of Falling Right spin button goes from 0.1 to 0.9 (initially 0.5). The Speed slider controls the rate at which balls are dropped. The Balls to Drop combo box allows 10, 20, 50, 100, 200, 500, or 1000 balls. The Sound check box adds sound effects. The Reset Experiment button resets the counter to zero. The Run Experiment button initiates ball-dropping and the Pause Experiment button lets you pause to look at the histogram. If you get tired of watching each ball, the Skip to End of Experiment button finishes the simulation.

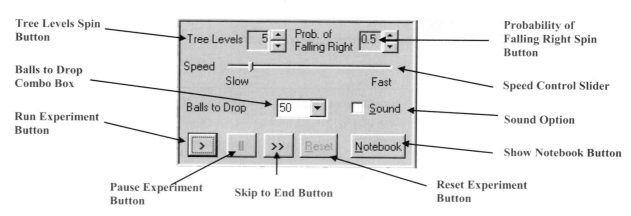

b.   Click the Notebook button. Select Tossing Coins, then click OK. In this scenario, several coins are flipped and the random variable is the total number of heads. Use the Number of Coins spin button to set the number of coins (1 to 8). These are fair coins, so the probabilities of heads and tails are the same at 0.5. The Speed slider is disabled. The Sound check box adds sound effects. With the Tosses to Make combo box you can choose 10, 20, 50, 100, 200, 500, or 1000 tosses. The Reset Experiment button resets the counter to zero. The Toss button flips the coins once. If you want to see the end result, click the Skip to End button to finish the random simulation.

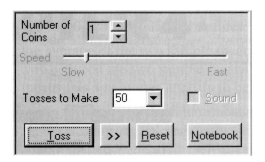

c.   Click the Notebook button. Select Throwing Dice, then click OK. In this scenario, you can toss several dice, then see the sum of the dots that you get. Use the Number of Dice spin button to set the number of dice (1 to 4). Each die is fair, so the probabilities of 1, 2, 3, 4, 5, 6 are identical at 1/6. The Speed slider is disabled. The Sound check box adds sound effects. With the Throws to Make combo box you can choose 10, 20, 50, 100, 200, 500, or 1000 throws. The Reset Experiment button resets the counter to zero. The Throw button throws the dice once. If you want to see the end result, click the Skip to End button to finish the random simulation.

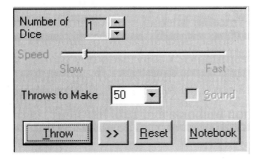

d.   Click the Notebook button. Click Scenarios, select Inspecting Cars, then click OK. In this scenario, you can set the Mean Defects Per Car (1 to 10). The Speed slider controls the rate at which cars move along the assembly line. Using the Cars to Test combo box you can choose 10, 20, 50, 100, 200, 500, or 1000 cars. The Sound check box adds sound effects. The Reset Experiment button resets the car counter to zero. The Run Experiment button initiates the process, and the Pause Experiment button lets you pause to look at the histogram. If you get tired of watching the cars go by, the Skip to End button finishes the random simulation.

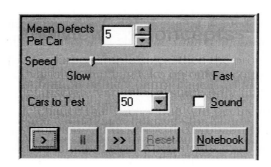

3. **Options**
    You can have each histogram frequency labeled as a relative frequency (the number of occurrences of each event divided by the number of times the experiment is repeated). This option makes it easier to estimate empirical probabilities.

4. **Copying Graphs**
    To copy the histogram, highlight the histogram, then select Copy from the Edit menu bar at the top of the screen (or type Ctrl-C).   It can then be pasted into another application, such as a spreadsheet or document.

5. **Help**
    Click on Help on the menu bar at the top of the screen. Search for Help lets you search an index for this module, Contents shows a table of contents for this module, Using Help gives instructions on how to use Help, and About gives licensing and copyright information about *Visual Statistics*.

6. **Exit**
    Close the module by selecting Exit in the File menu (or click ☒ in the upper right-hand corner of the window). You will be returned to the *Visual Statistics* main menu.

Basic Learning Exercises   Name _____

Tossing Coins
In the notebook, click Scenarios, click Tossing Coins to select the scenario, then click OK.

1. Set the Number of Coins spin button to 1 and the Tosses to Make spin button to 50. Click the Toss button ten times. How many times did you get tails (0)? Heads (1)? How many would you expect? Is your sample result much different from what you would expect?

2. Click the Skip to End of Experiment button. Now you have 50 tosses. How many times did you get tails (0) and heads (1)? How many would you have expected? Is your sample result very different from what you would expect? Would you expect the small sample (10 tosses) to differ more from its expected value than the large sample (50 tosses)? Explain.

3. Repeat Exercises 1 and 2. Did your results in this second set of experiments behave like the first series? How does this experiment support the idea that outcomes of a stochastic process exhibit regularity even though the underlying process is random?

Probability Trees
4. Click the Notebook button. Click Scenarios, click Probability Trees to select the scenario, then click OK. Set the Tree Levels to 1, Probability of Falling Right to 0.5, and Balls to Drop to 100. Click the Run Experiment Button. Drag the Speed slider to see its effect. If you wish, you can click the Skip to End of Experiment button. Are the sample histogram frequencies close to what you would expect? Is this experiment like the one-coin experiment? Explain.

5. Decrease the Prob of Falling Right to 0.3. How many times did you get "success"? Was this what you expected? Explain why this is like a baseball player whose batting average is 0.300 going to bat 100 times.

6. Set the Prob of Falling Right to 0.5. Increase the Tree Levels to 4. Conduct the experiment. What is the most frequent outcome? Explain why this is like flipping four coins.

7. If a professional basketball player is shooting free throws, what would be the probability of "success"? Set the Prob of Falling Right to that value. Set the number of Tree Levels to 10, to simulate shooting 10 free throws. Conduct the experiment. Was the most frequent outcome what you would expect? Why is this unlike flipping 10 coins?

8. Set the Prob of Falling Right to 0.20 and Tree Levels to 5. On the menu bar, select Options and click Display Relative Frequencies. Run the experiment and record the relative frequencies in the table below. Increase Balls to Drop to 500 and repeat. Repeat for 1000 balls. The theoretical (binomial) probabilities for 5 trials and a 0.2 probability of success are $P(0) = 0.3277$, $P(1) = 0.4096$, $P(2) = 0.2048$, $P(3) = 0.0512$, $P(4) = 0.0064$, and $P(X=5) = 0.0003$. Which of the three experiments (100, 500, 1000 balls) should give the best empirical estimate of the true probabilities? Explain your reasoning.

Balls	P(X=0)	P(X=1)	P(X=2)	P(X=3)	P(X=4)	P(X=5)
100						
500						
1000						

9. Why might it be advantageous to use relative frequencies in summarizing a random experiment? Why might it be disadvantageous?

Intermediate Learning Exercises   Name _____

Throwing Dice

In the notebook, click Scenarios, click Throwing Dice to select the scenario, then click OK. Select Options and deselect Display Relative Frequencies so that raw frequencies will be displayed.

10. Set the Number of Dice to 1 and the Number of Throws to 100. Click the Throw button 6 times. How many times did you get each outcome? How many would you expect? Then click the Throw button 6 more times (12 throws altogether). How many times did you get each outcome? How many would you expect? Would any of your sample results so far make you doubt that the die is fair?

11. Click the Skip to End of Experiment button. Describe the distribution. How many of each outcome would you expect? How different are the actual frequencies from your expectation? Do you think the die is fair? Are 100 throws enough to give you confidence in your answer?

12. Increase the Number of Throws to 1000. How many of each outcome would you expect? How different are the actual frequencies from your expectation? Does a large sample guarantee frequencies that are what we expect?

13. Set the Number of Dice to 2 and the Number of Throws to 100. Click the Skip to End of Experiment button. How many of each outcome would you expect? Describe the resulting sample histogram (e.g., its domain, mode, and general shape). Is this what you expected? Increase the Number of Throws to 1000 and repeat the experiment. Was 100 throws enough to give you confidence that you know the shape of the true distribution? Was 1000 enough?

Inspecting Cars
In the notebook, click Scenarios, click Inspecting Cars to select the scenario, then click OK. Select Options and select Display Relative Frequencies.

14. Set the Mean Defects per Car to 1 and the Number of Cars to 100. Click the Run Experiment button. Observe the process of data accumulation for a while and then click the Skip to End of Experiment button. Describe the resulting histogram (domain, mode, skewness, tails).

15. Increase the Number of Cars to 1000 and click the Skip to End of Experiment button. Record the relative frequencies below. Describe the resulting histogram (domain, mode, skewness, tails). Repeat this experiment two more times. The theoretical (Poisson) probabilities are P(0) = 0.3679, P(1) = 0.3679, P(2) = 0.1839, P(3) = 0.0613, P(4) = 0.0153, P(X=5) = 0.0031, P(X=6) = 0.0005, and P(X=7)= 0.0001. How close did you come?

Sample	P(X=0)	P(X=1)	P(X=2)	P(X=3)	P(X=4)	P(X=5)	P(X≥6)
1							
2							
3							

16. Keep the Number of Cars at 1000 but set the Mean Defects per Car to 5. What is the domain? Is there a clear mode? Is the distribution more or less skewed than in the previous exercise?

17. Keep the Number of Cars at 1000 but set the Mean Defects per Car to 20. Describe the domain, centrality, dispersion, and skewness of the distribution. Can you generalize about the effect of increasing the mean on the skewness of the distribution? On the mode?

Advanced Learning Exercises   **Name** _____

Distribution Shape

In the notebook, click Scenarios, click Tossing Coins to select the scenario, then click OK. Select Options and choose Show Relative Frequencies.

18. Set the Number of Coins to 2 and set the Tosses to Make to 1000. What is the expected relative frequency of 0, 1, and 2 heads? Explain why (i.e., describe the sample space). Click the Skip to End of Experiment button. Is 1000 a large enough number of repetitions to feel confident that the empirical probabilities are reliable?

19. Set the Number of Coins to 4. List a few elements of the sample space and tell how it differs from the previous exercise. What is the expected histogram shape for the number of heads? What mode would you expect? Click the Skip to End of Experiment button. Describe the resulting histogram. Were your *a priori* predictions correct? What is the empirical probability of P(1)? Do you have confidence in this empirical probability (repeat the sample a few times if you are not sure, to see how much variation there is)?

20. Set the Number of Coins to 8. What is the expected histogram shape for the number of heads? What mode would you expect? Click the Skip to End of Experiment button. Describe the resulting histogram. Were your *a priori* predictions correct? Would you say this histogram resembles a "normal" or "bell-shaped" curve?

Modes

In the notebook, click Scenarios, click Throwing Dice to select the scenario, then click OK. Select Options and choose Show Relative Frequencies.

21. Set the Number of Dice to 3 and the Number of Throws to 1000. Click the Skip to End of Experiment button. Describe the resulting sample histogram (e.g., its domain, mode, and general shape). Record the mode(s) for your sample. Repeat the sampling exercise four more times and record the mode(s) below. Is there a clear-cut mode?

	Sample 1	Sample 2	Sample 3	Sample 4	Sample 5
Mode(s)1					

22. Set the Number of Dice to 4 and the Number of Throws to 1000. Click the Skip to End of Experiment button. Describe the resulting sample histogram (e.g., its domain, mode, and general shape). What "ought" the mode to be? Would you consider this sample mode a reliable estimate of the theoretical mode? Generalize about what happens to centrality and dispersion as the number of dice increases.

Mean and Variation

In the notebook, click Scenarios, click Inspecting Cars to select the scenario, then click OK. Select Options and select Display Relative Frequencies.

23. Set the Number of Cars at 100 and set the Mean Defects per Car to 4. Click the Skip to End of Experiment button. Record the minimum, maximum, and calculate the range. Repeat for Mean Defects per Car of 8, 12, 16, and 20 defects. Describe what is happening to the range. Explain why the range changes as you increase the mean number of defects.

Sample	Mean = 4	Mean = 8	Mean = 12	Mean = 16	Mean = 20
Maximum					
Minimum					
Range					

Individual Learning Projects

Write a report on one of the three topics listed below. Use the cut-and-paste facilities of the module to place the appropriate graphs in your report.

1. Select either the coin tossing or dice scenario and the relative frequency option. Choose 1 coin and 10 tosses or 1 die and 10 throws. Do the sampling experiment 5 times, saving each sample histogram for your report. What was the maximum departure from the expected proportions? Discuss how the histograms illustrate the concept of sample variation. Repeat the experiment using 1000 throws. What was the maximum difference from the expected proportion? Discuss how these five histograms illustrate regularity. Using one histogram, deselect the relative frequency option. Explain how the count histogram contains the same information as the relative frequency histogram.

2. Select the probability tree scenario and deselect the relative frequency option (vertical axis on histogram should say Count). Choose 5 tree levels, 10 balls, and a 0.3 probability of falling right. Do the sampling experiment 5 times, saving each sample histogram for your report. Compare the histograms and explain how they illustrate the concept of sample variation. Repeat the experiment once using 1000 balls. Compare the histograms and explain how they illustrate the concept of regularity. Set the probability of falling right to 0.7 and conduct the experiment once with 1000 balls. For 1000 balls, describe the similarities and differences between the 0.3 and 0.7 probability of falling right.

3. Select the inspecting cars scenario and the relative frequency option. Choose 10 cars and set the mean number of defects to 1. Do the sampling experiment 5 times, saving each sample histogram for your report. In each experiment, what was the empirical probability of getting exactly the mean that you set? How does this illustrate sample variation? Repeat using 1000 cars. How does this demonstrate regularity? Are the 1000 car histograms symmetric? What is the mode in each case? Explain why the mean and mode are generally different in a non-symmetric histogram.

Team Learning Projects

Select one of the three projects listed below, and produce a team project that is suitable for an oral presentation. Use presentation software or a large poster board(s) to display your results. Graphs should be large enough for your audience to see. Each team member should be responsible for producing some of the graphs. Ask your instructor if a written report is also expected.

1. This project is for a team of 3. Select the probability tree scenario and the relative frequency option. Choose 1000 balls. One team member should choose 4 tree branches, another 6 branches, and the last 8 branches. Each team members should vary the probability of falling right from 0.1 to 0.9 in increments of 0.1, producing a histogram for each experiment. The objective is to demonstrate variation and regularity and to illustrate how the shape of a histogram varies as you change the parameters of the process. What type of distribution is this, and what are its parameters?

2. This is a project for a team of 2. Select the dice scenario and raw frequency option. Choose 100 throws. Each team member should choose a different number of dice (1 or 2). Calculate the *a priori* probability and expected frequency for each outcome. Do each sampling experiment 5 times, saving each sample histogram. Discuss how the histograms illustrate the concept of sample variation. Compare the actual and *a priori* frequencies by calculating their differences and their ratios. What was the maximum departure from the expected frequency? Repeat each experiment 5 times using 1000 throws. Compare the actual and *a priori* frequencies by calculating their differences and their ratios. Was the maximum departure from the expected frequency less than with 100 throws? The objective is to show if the empirical probabilities improve as you increase the number of repetitions.

3. This is a project for a team of 3 or 4. Select the inspecting cars scenario and the relative frequency option. Choose 10 cars. One team member should choose 4 as the mean number of defects, another 8, the third 12, and the fourth (if any) 16. Do the sampling experiment 5 times, producing a histogram for each experiment. In each experiment, what was the empirical probability of getting exactly the mean that you set? Repeat using 50 cars. Repeat using 200 cars. The objectives are to demonstrate variation and regularity, to see how the probability of getting exactly the process mean varies as the mean changes, and to see if the empirical probabilities stabilize as the number of repetitions increases.

Self-Evaluation Quiz

1.   What is a stochastic process?
     a.   One whose outcomes are known in advance.
     b.   One that produces the same outcome every time.
     c.   One whose outcomes are not known in advance.
     d.   One involving certainty.
     e.   Both c. and d. are correct.

2.   The sample space contains
     a.   elementary outcomes of an experiment.
     b.   random variables.
     c.   probabilities of events.
     d.   parameters of a process.
     e.   both b. and c.

3.   A random variable is
     a.   an elementary outcome.
     b.   an event in the sample space.
     c.   a number assigned to an event.
     d.   a probability of an event.
     e.   a parameter of a process.

4.   The histogram is used to assess
     a.   centrality.
     b.   variation.
     c.   dispersion.
     d.   symmetry.
     e.   all of the above.

5.   The probability $P(A)$ of an event A has which characteristics?
     a. $P(A)$ must not exceed 1.
     b. $P(A)$ must be non-negative.
     c. $P(A)$ may be determined empirically using relative frequencies.
     d. $P(A)$ may be known *a priori* in some cases.
     e. $P(A)$ has all of the above characteristics.

6.   The parameter(s) of a distribution
     a.   are needed to characterize the probability distribution.
     b.   are impossible to estimate from a large sample.
     c.   are usually known *a priori*.
     d.   have no effect on centrality or variation.
     e.   must be specified by design engineers.

7. As we increase the number of random trials we get
   a. a better idea of the probability of events.
   b. a smaller degree of dispersion.
   c. a narrower histogram scale.
   d. increasing parameter values.
   e. all of the above.

8. Which are the *parameters* of the distribution for the probability tree experiment?
   a. The number of balls dropped.
   b. The number of tree levels.
   c. The speed at which balls are dropped.
   d. The probability of falling right.
   e. Both b. and d. are correct.

9. If you roll 3 dice instead of 2, which will *not* occur?
   a. The center of the histogram will shift right.
   b. The mode of the histogram will increase.
   c. The range of the histogram will increase.
   d. The histogram will remain symmetric.
   e. The probability of rolling 7 will stay the same.

10. If you flip 4 coins 100 times
    a. you would see regularity in the relative frequencies of heads.
    b. you would expect a range from 0 to 4.
    c. you would expect to get 2 heads about 37.5 percent of the time.
    d. you would be observing a stochastic process.
    e. you would find all of these things.

11. The binomial model is used to describe a process
    a. with a constant probability of success for each trial.
    b. with a specified number of independent trials.
    c. that has only two outcomes.
    d. whose outcomes are discrete (e.g., 0, 1, 2, 3).
    e. with all of the above characteristics.

12. Which is *not* a characteristic of the Poisson model?
    a. It involves counting events over time or space.
    b. It has a definite upper limit on X.
    c. It describes a stochastic process with a known distribution.
    d. It has one parameter.
    e. It might be used to describe arrivals of telephone calls per hour.

Glossary of Terms

A priori probability A probability that is known prior to looking at actual sample results. The probability is calculated by reasoning alone, using the known sample space of the experiment. See **Empirical probability**.

Binomial distribution Two-parameter distribution describing discrete data generated by a binary (success/failure) experiment with n independent trials and constant probability of success.

Centrality General characterization of the location of the middle or "typical" values in a distribution (e.g., mean, median, mode).

Discrete random variable Random variable with a countable number of values.

Dispersion General characterization of the degree of variation about the center of a distribution (e.g., range).

Domain The values that can be assumed by a random variable (e.g., $X = 0, 1, 2, 3$).

Empirical probability A probability that is estimated by looking at relative frequencies of actual outcomes in a sampling experiment. It is based on evidence rather than reasoning. An empirical probability becomes closer to the *a priori* probability as the number of repetitions of the experiment increases. See **A priori probability**.

Event A collection of elementary outcomes of a stochastic experiment. For example, when you flip a coin once, "heads" or "tails" are the two events that could occur.

Frequency The number of occurrences of an event in a particular stochastic experiment.

Histogram Bar chart showing on the horizontal axis the values of a random variable and on the vertical axis the frequency of occurrence of each value.

Independent Reference to events that do not influence one another.

Mode The data value that occurs most frequently in a sample. It is not necessarily unique. If there are two modes, the data are called bimodal. The mode is most useful for discrete data with a small range. In a probability distribution, the mode is the X value that has the highest probability of occurrence.

Normal distribution The "bell-shaped" or Gaussian distribution. It is sometimes used as a point of reference with which to compare a sample histogram.

Parameter One or more numerical characteristics of a distribution that determine its probability distribution (centrality, dispersion, skewness, and other characteristics).

Probability distribution Value assigned to every value X of a random variable. These probabilities must sum to unity.

Probability of an event A number between 0 and 1 assigned to every value of a random variable.

Random variable An event of a stochastic experiment that is assigned a numerical value. For example, the number of heads in 15 flips of a fair coin is a random variable.

Regularity Tendency for stable patterns to emerge in relative frequencies when a random experiment is repeated many times.

Relative frequency The number of times an event occurs divided by the number of repetitions of the random experiment. For example, if you throw a pair of dice 216 times and get 7 exactly 35 times, the relative frequency of 7 is 35/216 or 0.162. See **Empirical probability**.

Sample space The set of all possible outcomes of an experiment of chance. Each element in the sample space is called an elementary outcome.

Skewness Degree of asymmetry of a probability distribution or a histogram. *Positive* skewness indicates a long right tail and *negative* skewness indicates a long left tail. See **Symmetry**.

Stochastic process Data-generating situation that produces an outcome which cannot be predicted in advance.

Symmetry Shape of a probability distribution or histogram whose tails are of equal length.

Triangular distribution Three-parameter distribution whose shape has a single sharp peak on either side of which the probabilities decline toward zero in a linear fashion.

Uniform distribution Two-parameter distribution which assigns the same probability to every value of X.

Variation Natural tendency for outcomes of a stochastic process to vary. See **Dispersion**.

Solutions to Self-Evaluation Quiz

1. c   Do Exercises 1–5. Consult the Glossary. Read the Overview of Concepts.
2. a   Do Exercises 1–7. Consult the Glossary. Read the Overview of Concepts.
3. c   Consult the Glossary. Read the Overview of Concepts.
4. e   Do Exercises 6–9. Consult the Glossary. Read the Overview of Concepts.
5. e   Do Exercises 7–8. Consult the Glossary. Read the Overview of Concepts.
6. a   Do Exercises 4–8. Read the Overview of Concepts. Do Team Projects 1 or 2.
7. a   Do Exercises 8–9. Consult the Glossary. Read the Overview of Concepts.
8. e   Do Exercises 6-9. Consult the Glossary.
9. e   Do Exercises 10–13. Do Individual Project 3 or Team Project 2.
10. e   Do Exercises 1–5 and 18–20. Do Individual Project 2.
11. e   Read the Overview of Concepts. Consult the Glossary.
12. b   Do Exercise 23. Read the Overview of Concepts. Consult the Glossary.

CHAPTER 3

Visualizing Shapes of Distributions

CONCEPTS
- Random Variable, Discrete Population, Continuous Population, Probability Distribution, Cumulative Distribution, Parameters, Shape Measures

OBJECTIVES
- Understand how a distribution is described by its parameters

- Be able to visualize common shape measures (mean, median, standard deviation, quartiles, skewness, kurtosis)

- Understand the relationship between a probability distribution and its cumulative

- Recognize discrete and continuous random variables and their probability distributions

Overview of Concepts

The value of a **random variable** is determined by chance. For example, your commuting time to work last Tuesday is a random variable. The universe of all possible values that the random variable can take is called the population. If a population consists only of countable values it is a **discrete population** (e.g., number of children in a family), whereas if it consists of a range of uncountable values it is a **continuous population** (e.g., the fraction of movie patrons who buy popcorn). Most discrete populations have a finite number of values (e.g., the numbers 2 to 12 representing the sum of two dice). However, as the number of values becomes very large the two types of populations become similar (e.g., all integers between 1 and 10,000).

The relative frequency with which the population values occur is given by its **probability distribution**. If the population is continuous, this distribution is an area graph. If the population is discrete, this distribution is a stick (or bar) graph. In a continuous population the area under the probability distribution between any two values gives the relative frequency, or probability, that the random variable will be between those values. In a discrete population the height of any bar (or stick) tells the relative frequency, or probability, that the random variable will equal a particular value in the population. A **cumulative distribution** gives the relative frequency that the random variable will be less than or equal to a specific value X_0. If X_0 is the maximum value in the population, the cumulative distribution will equal one.

Some probability distributions are so common they have been named. Three common distributions you may have heard of are the uniform distribution (a rectangle), the triangular distribution, and the normal distribution (the shape of a bell). Many named distributions are unbounded (i.e., they do not have an upper limit and/or lower limit). The distribution and range of values the random variable can take on depends on the distribution's **parameters**. For example, a three-digit lottery number or the number on a die that is rolled both follow a uniform distribution, which has two parameters: the minimum value and the maximum value. In choosing the lottery number, these parameter values are 000 and 999. In rolling a single die, the parameter values are 1 and 6. Although the uniform distribution has two parameters, other known distributions have as few as one parameter or as many as five parameters. In this module you will be able to manipulate a computer-created probability distribution using five parameters: centrality, dispersion (number of discrete points if the population is discrete), asymmetry, peakedness, and number of modes. This created distribution enables you to visualize over 1,200 different-shaped probability distributions. All of these distributions have an upper and lower bound.

You learned in Chapter 1 that the shape of data can be characterized by a variety of descriptive statistics, such as the sample mean, mode, standard deviation, and range. Similarly, the shape of probability distributions can also be characterized by a variety of **shape measures** (since these measures are not based on sample data but on the probability distribution itself, they are not called statistics). The shape measures presented in this module are the population mean, median, mode, midrange, standard deviation, interquartile range, range, skewness, and kurtosis. Each of these terms is defined in the glossary and is reviewed in the Learning Exercises.

Illustration of Concepts

Consider the distribution of the **random variable** "sum of numbers on two dice." This random variable is a **discrete population** since it consists of the set of numbers 2 through 12. The **probability distribution** is shown in Figure 1. It is a triangular distribution. Its **parameters** are 2 (minimum), 12 (maximum), and 7 (mode). Its **shape measures** are shown in Figure 2. It has a single mode at 7. This is also its mean, median, and midrange, as you would expect in a symmetric unimodal distribution. Skewness is 0. Its range is 10, interquartile range is 2, and standard deviation is 2.09. Kurtosis is 2.48, indicating that the distribution is platykurtic or less peaked than the bell-shaped distribution (whose kurtosis is 3.00). The ratio of the range to the standard deviation is 4.78 (for unimodal distributions, this ratio is typically less than 5 if the distribution is platykurtic). The single mode in the probability distribution is imperceptible on the **cumulative distribution** (Figure 3), as is often the case with discrete populations that have a small number of discrete points.

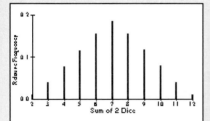

Figure 1: Discrete Population

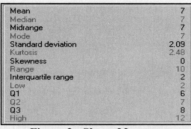

Mean	7
Median	7
Midrange	7
Mode	7
Standard deviation	2.09
Kurtosis	2.48
Skewness	0
Range	10
Interquartile range	2
Low	2
Q1	6
Q2	7
Q3	8
High	12

Figure 2: Shape Measures

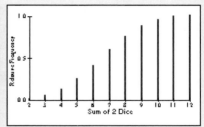

Figure 3: Cumulative Distribution

Now consider the distribution of annual incomes of females who work full time and are between the ages of 25 and 64. This is a **continuous population**, consisting of incomes from $500 to $95,500 (for illustrative purposes we are ignoring incomes above $95,500 though they do exist). It is a positively skewed distribution with two modes (Figure 4). One mode is at $14,350 and the other is at $35,140. Since the mode at $14,350 has the largest relative frequency, it is referred to as the global mode. It is the mode over the entire (global) population. The second mode is called a local mode since it is a mode within a portion (a localized range) of the population (about $25,000 and above in this case). The two modes are caused by differences in education. Females with a college degree earn substantially more than those without. The population's mean is $23,000, its median is $18,290, and its midrange is $48,000. The midrange is greater than the mean, which is greater than the median, as is typical of positively skewed distributions. Skewness is 1.12. The standard deviation is $13,910, the range is $95,000, and the interquartile range is $19,620. Kurtosis is 4.16. The ratio of range to standard deviation is almost 7, which is consistent with kurtosis being over 3. Figure 6 shows the cumulative distribution. Both modes on the probability distribution can be seen as slight inflection points on the cumulative distribution.

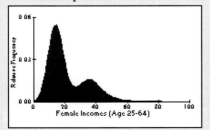

Figure 4: Continuous Population

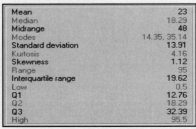

Mean	23
Median	18.29
Midrange	48
Modes	14.35, 35.14
Standard deviation	13.91
Kurtosis	4.16
Skewness	1.12
Range	95
Interquartile range	19.62
Low	0.5
Q1	12.76
Q2	18.29
Q3	32.39
High	95.5

Figure 5: Shape Measures

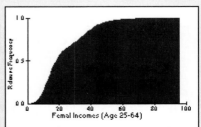

Figure 6: Cumulative Distribution

Orientation to Basic Features

This module allows you to change the shape parameters of a computer-created distribution and see the resulting probability distribution, cumulative distribution, and shape measures. Either continuous or discrete distributions can be created. The shape measures can be visually compared.

1. **Opening Screen**

   Start the module by clicking on the module's icon, title, or chapter number in the *Visual Statistics* menu and pressing the Run Module button. When the module is loaded, you will be on the introduction page of the Notebook. Read the questions and then click the Concepts tab to see the concepts that you will learn. Click on the Scenarios tab. Select One Mode from the list of choices. Select a scenario, read it, and press OK. The upper left of the screen shows the probability distribution. Controls to change the distribution's parameters and other module options appear on the right in the Control Panel. Below the probability distribution is its cumulative distribution. The shape measures are below the Control Panel. Other features are controlled from the menu bar at the top of the screen. A flashing Update button indicates that you have changed one or more control settings.

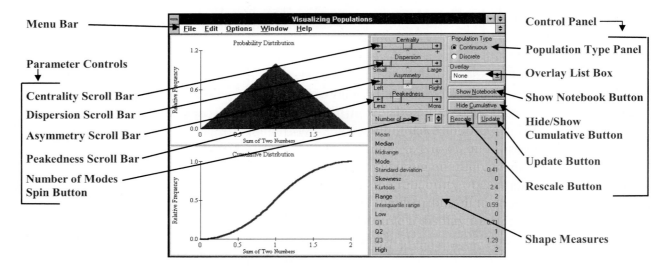

2. **Parameter Controls**

   The computer-created distribution's five parameters are set using either a scroll bar or a spin button located on the Control Panel. Move the Centrality scroll bar. Press the flashing Update button to redraw the displays. Try *large* changes (click on the scroll bar or drag the control button) and *small* changes (click on the arrows of the scroll bar). You can change the Dispersion, Asymmetry, and Peakedness parameters in the same way. The Number of Modes is changed using a spin button. Click on the up arrow on the spin button to increase the number of modes and the down arrow to decrease the number of modes in the probability distribution. Update the displays by pressing the Update button.

3. **Rescaling**

   If the probability or cumulative distribution is cut off or is too small, press the Rescale button. This will recenter the distributions and rescale both the vertical and horizontal axes.

4. **Overlays**
   There are five options listed in the Overlay list box:
   a.   No overlay (None) is the default.
   b.   Centrality gives a graphic display of the population mean, median, midrange, and mode(s) overlaid on the probability distribution.
   c.   Dispersion gives a graphic display of the population range, interquartile range, and standard deviation overlaid on the probability distribution.
   d.   Box Plot overlays a box plot of the population values on the probability distribution. The whiskers are drawn from the smallest to the largest value in the population.
   e.   Beam & Fulcrum overlays a beam and fulcrum of the population values on the probability distribution. The beam is drawn from the smallest to the largest value in the population.

5. **Notebook**
   Press the Show Notebook button to return to the Notebook. Click on other scenarios to read their descriptions. Any scenario can be selected by pressing OK. Click on the Previous page (upper right corner) or Next page (lower right corner) to page through the scenario section of the Notebook. You can return to the scenario's contents page by clicking on Return to Scenarios contents page. Selecting any other tab will take you to that section of the Notebook.

6. **Options**
   Three sets of options are available from the Options menu (two are discussed here, the last in the Orientation to Additional Features section) on the menu bar (top of the screen).
   a.   Select Change Title from the Options menu if you wish to retitle the current display.
   b.   Select Auto Update from the Options menu to automatically update each display after any change is made. Select Auto Rescale on Update from the Options menu to rescale automatically the distribution when any update occurs. Although useful at times, this option makes changes to the shape of the distribution difficult to see because the scale on the vertical and/or horizontal axis may have changed.

7. **Copying a Display**
   Click on the graph you wish to copy or click on the shape measures. Black handles appear indicating it has been selected. Select Copy from the Edit menu (on the menu bar at the top of the screen) or Ctrl-C to copy the display. It can then be pasted into other applications, such as Word or WordPerfect, so it can be printed. If you click on a graph and then decide not to copy it, the black handles can be removed by pressing the Esc key on your keyboard.

8. **Help**
   Click on Help on the menu bar at the top of the screen. Search for Help lets you search an index for this module, Contents shows a table of contents for this module, Using Help gives instructions on how to use Help, and About gives licensing and copyright information about *Visual Statistics*. Close Help by selecting Exit from the File menu on the Help screen.

9. **Exit**
   Close the module by selecting Exit in the File menu (or click ⊠ in the upper right-hand corner of the window). You will be returned to the *Visual Statistics* main menu.

Orientation to Additional Features

1. **Population Type**
   Change Population Type to Discrete by clicking its option button to see a discrete probability distribution. Notice that the Dispersion scroll bar has been renamed Number of Discrete Points. Clicking on the scroll bar will change the number of discrete points in the distribution (from 2 to 96). Reset Population Type to Continuous by clicking its option button.

2. **Showing/Hiding the Cumulative**
   The cumulative distribution that corresponds to the probability distribution in the top left quadrant is automatically displayed in the lower left quadrant. Click the Hide Cumulative button to remove the cumulative display and enlarge the probability distribution display.

3. **Creating Full Window Displays**
   Select Full Window Graph from the Options menu. This extends your distributions to the full width of your screen and hides the controls. To return to the normal display, de-select Full Window Graph from the Options menu. Use this option in conjunction with the Hide Cumulative button (see number 2 above) to have the probability distribution displayed on the entire screen.

Basic Learning Exercises

Name _____

Probability and Cumulative Distributions

1. Press the Show Notebook button, select the Scenarios tab, click on No Mode and select Roll of a Die. Read the scenario. Answer the exercises in the scenario.

2. Click OK. a) What does the probability distribution show? b) What does it mean in this scenario? c) What is the probability of rolling a 3?

3. a) What does a cumulative distribution show? b) What does it mean in this scenario? c) How was this cumulative distribution created? d) Calculate the cumulative probability for X = 5.

4. Press the Show Notebook button and click Next page (lower right hand corner of Notebook). Select Sum of Two Random Numbers, read the scenario, and answer the questions.

5. Press OK. How is the cumulative distribution created? What is the value at X = 2, why?

6. a) What value corresponds to the mode of the probability distribution? b) Why does the cumulative distribution equal 0.5 at this mode? c) In this scenario, what does the 0.5 mean?

Centrality Parameter

7. Many distributions have a centrality parameter. Use the Centrality scroll bar to change the value of the centrality parameter. Press the Update button and, if necessary, the Rescale button. Did changing centrality parameter change the shape of either the probability or cumulative distribution? Why or why not? This is generally true. Why?

8. Click on the Overlay list box and select Centrality. Lines representing four centrality statistics appear on the display. What is the value of the midrange, mean, median, and mode? Why are all four statistics the same? Click on the right portion of the Asymmetry scroll bar. Click the Update button. Rank these four statistics. In a unimodal, positively skewed probability distribution, this is *always* the relation between these four statistics. What is the relationship between these statistics for a negatively skewed unimodal distribution?

    Midrange _____   Mean _____   Median _____   Mode _____

Dispersion Parameter

9. Return the Asymmetry scroll bar to the middle (click on "^"). a) What is the height and range of your triangular distribution? b) Click *once* on the *right arrow* of the Dispersion scroll bar to change the scale of the probability distribution. This is equivalent to multiplying the random variable by a number (greater than 1 if you increase dispersion, less than 1 if you decrease dispersion). Press the Update button. What is the height and range of your new distribution? c) Press the Rescale button. How did changing dispersion affect the height, range, and shape of the probability and cumulative distributions? This is generally true.

10. Press the Show Notebook button and press OK to return to the original display. Click on the Overlay list box and select Dispersion. Lines representing the three dispersion statistics appear on the display. What is the value of the standard deviation, range and interquartile range? How many standard deviations and how many interquartile ranges cover the range?

    Standard Deviation _____   Interquartile Range _____   Range _____
    Range ÷ Standard Deviation _____   Range ÷ Interquartile Range _____

Intermediate Learning Exercises   Name _____

Continuous Distribution

11. Press the Show Notebook button, select the Scenarios tab, click on No Mode and select Random Numbers between 0 and 2. Answer the questions. Why is its height ½?

12. Press OK. Describe the cumulative distribution? Calculate its value for X = 0.5 and 1.2.

13. a) Using the probability distribution, what is the $P(1 \leq X \leq 2)$? b) $P(1 \leq X \leq 1.1)$?
     c) $P(1 \leq X \leq 1.01)$? d) Why does the $P(1 \leq X \leq 1) = P(X = 1) = 0$? e) Why is the probability that X equals a number, X_0, always equal to 0 in a continuous distribution?

Asymmetry Parameter

14. Press the Show Notebook button, select the Scenarios tab, click on One Mode, select Sum of Two Random Numbers, and press OK. Click on Options on the menu bar and select Auto Update. Create a positively skewed probability distribution by clicking on the right side of the Asymmetry scroll bar. Describe both distributions. Create negative skewness and describe both the probability and cumulative distribution. **Hint:** Watch the mode.

Peakedness Parameter

15. Click on "^" on the Peakedness scroll bar and on the Asymmetry scroll bar. This produces the bell-shaped curve. What is the value of the standard deviation, range, and interquartile range? How many standard deviations and interquartile ranges cover the range?

Standard Deviation _____   Interquartile Range _____   Range _____
Range ÷ Standard Deviation _____   Range ÷ Interquartile Range _____

16. Set the peakedness parameter to its maximum to produce a peaked or *leptokurtic* distribution. What is the value of the standard deviation, range, and interquartile range? How many standard deviations and interquartile ranges cover the range? Describe both distributions.

Standard Deviation _____   Interquartile Range _____   Range _____
Range ÷ Standard Deviation _____   Range ÷ Interquartile Range _____

17. Set the peakedness parameter to its minimum to produce a flat or *platykurtic* distribution. What is the value of the standard deviation, range, and interquartile range? How many standard deviations and interquartile ranges cover the range? Describe both distributions.

Standard Deviation _____   Interquartile Range _____   Range _____
Range ÷ Standard Deviation _____   Range ÷ Interquartile Range _____

18. Note that the number of standard deviations and interquartile ranges needed to cover the range increases and decreases as peakedness increases and decreases. This is generally true. Why?

Shape Measures or Shape Statistics
19. Click on "^" on all four scroll bars. Record the shape statistics. Change the Centrality scroll bar. Which statistic changes? Return the mean to 1. Change the Dispersion scroll bar. Which statistic changes? **Hint:** Recall from exercises 7 and 9 that changing centrality or dispersion does not change the shape of the distribution only its location and spread. The bell-shaped curve always has a skewness of 0 and a kurtosis of 3.0 (called *mesokurtic*).

Mean _____   Standard Deviation _____   Skewness_____   Kurtosis _____

20. Return all scroll bars to "^". Change the Asymmetry scroll bar. Why do all 4 statistics change when the symmetry changes? Return Asymmetry to "^". Change the Peakedness scroll bar. Why does the standard deviation change when the peakedness changes?

Advanced Learning Exercises   Name _____

Probability Distributions with Zero, Two and Three Modes

21. Press the Show Notebook button, select the Scenarios tab, click on No Mode, and select Random Numbers Between 0 and 2. Read the scenario. Answer the questions. Click OK. Note that the Asymmetry and Peakedness scroll bars are inoperative. Why is this? The Overlay feature can be turned off or set to whatever option you prefer.

22. Press the Show Notebook button. Click on Next page to turn a Notebook page. Turn another page to see examples of scenarios with two modes. Select the Traffic Flow scenario, read it, and answer the questions. Click OK. Describe the cumulative distribution. How can you tell by looking at the cumulative distribution that the probability distribution has two modes?

23. Change the skewness of the probability distribution by changing the Asymmetry scroll bar. Notice that the modes are no longer the same height. The taller one is the global mode (maximum over the entire distribution) and the shorter one the local mode (maximum within a region). How does the shape of the probability and cumulative distribution change as the probability distribution becomes more skewed?

24. Return skewness to 0 by changing the Asymmetry scroll bar. Increase the peakedness by clicking on the right end of its scroll bar. Watch both the probability and cumulative distribution and describe how both distributions change. Note the location of the two modes.

25. Decrease peakedness by clicking on the left end of the Peakedness scroll bar. Watch both the probability and cumulative distribution and describe how both distributions change. Note the location of the two modes.

26. Press the Show Notebook button, click on Next page to see scenarios with three modes and select Eating Habits. Read the scenario and answer the questions. Click OK.

27. Read the other scenarios under two and three modes. Describe your own scenario that has a probability distribution with two or three modes. What is the random variable? Is it a discrete or continuous population? Sketch what you think it would look like.

Exploring Chebyshev's Inequality
28. Chebyshev's Theorem says that, for any distribution, at least 8/9 of the area will lie between the mean ± 3 standard deviations and at least 3/4 of the area will lie between the mean ± 2 standard deviations. You will not be able to find a distribution that violates this theorem. What characteristics of a unimodal distribution will generate a probability distribution that comes closest to these limits. **Hint:** Use the Beam & Fulcrum in the Overlay list box.

29. Given your exploration in exercise 28, what are the characteristics of a unimodal distribution that has the entire distribution contained within the smallest number of standard deviations?

Individual Learning Projects

Write a report on one of the three topics listed below. Use the cut-and-paste facilities of the module to place the appropriate graphs in your report.

1. Changing the centrality or dispersion parameter does not alter the basic shape of a probability distribution (skewness and kurtosis do not change). However, changing the asymmetry or peakedness parameter can dramatically change the mean and standard deviation of the probability distribution. Explain and illustrate these concepts using graphs. Using the midrange and range measures, show why changing the centrality parameter is equivalent to adding or subtracting a number to the random variable. Similarly, using a continuous distribution, show why changing the dispersion parameter is equivalent to multiplying the random variable by a scale factor.

2. The box plot diagram and the beam and fulcrum diagram each give a representation of the probability distribution. Describe and illustrate how a trained statistician can tell the degree of skewness and peakedness in a unimodal probability distribution by looking at these diagrams. Use at least six different probability distributions (choose these distributions carefully so that they represent a wide variety of distributions) and *both* types of diagrams in your explanation. Which diagram do you find most informative and why?

3. Using a unimodal, continuous probability distribution, reduce the dispersion to its minimum. Notice that as the range is reduced, the ordinate (height of the distribution) is increased (actually exceeding 1). At first glance, untrained observers may think this is wrong. (a) Why might they think that a probability distribution can not have a height greater than one? (b) Illustrate (using graphs with different amounts of skewness, kurtosis, and dispersion) that this is possible and describe why it happens.

Team Learning Projects

Select one of the three projects listed below. In each case, produce a team project that is suitable for an oral presentation. Use a large poster board(s) to display your results. Graphs should be large enough for your audience to see. Each team member should be responsible for producing some of the graphs. Ask your instructor if a written report is also expected.

1. This project is for a team of three to five members. Investigate the relationship between the cumulative and the probability distribution. Each team member should select a specific setting on the Asymmetry scroll bar (the range of both positive and negative skewness values must be covered by the team). By changing the peakedness of the probability distribution (from minimum to maximum peakedness), each team member must generate at least five probability and cumulative distributions. Each team member should describe how peakedness affects both the probability and cumulative distributions for a specific asymmetry setting. The team should then describe how the symmetry of the probability distribution affects the cumulative distribution.

2. This project is for a team of three to five members. Investigate how discrete distributions become more like continuous ones as the number of discrete points increases. (Specify either Box Plot or Beam & Fulcrum in the Overlay list box to aid your investigation.) Each member should select three settings on the Asymmetry scroll bar (maximum right asymmetry, moderate right asymmetry, and symmetry) and one setting on the Peakedness scroll bar (the range of peakedness settings must be covered by the team). For each of the three pairs of settings (1) create at least three discrete probability distributions by changing the number of points in the probability distribution, and (2) create a continuous probability distribution to show the shape of the continuous version of the probability distribution and the value of its shape parameters. The team should describe what happens as the number of discrete points gets larger and how peakedness and asymmetry affect these results.

3. This project is for a team of two to three members. Investigate the Empirical Rule. The rule says that, if data is randomly selected from a probability distribution, almost all of the data will be within 3 standard deviations of the mean and approximately 95% of the data will lie within 2 standard deviations of the mean. (Use the beam and fulcrum diagram to determine where 2 and 3 standard deviations from the mean will be). Each member should select two settings on the Asymmetry scroll bar (the range of either right or left asymmetry settings must be covered by the team). For each asymmetry setting generate at least five probability distributions with different amounts or peakedness (the range of peakedness values from minimum to maximum must be covered by each team member). The team should describe how peakedness and asymmetry affect the accuracy of the Empirical Rule. Why doesn't changing the dispersion or centrality parameter affect the Empirical Rule?

Self-Evaluation Quiz

1. A cumulative distribution
   a. has a maximum of 1.
   b. has an indeterminate maximum.
   c. has the same maximum as the probability distribution.
   d. defines an area of 1 under the curve.
   e. has none of the above characteristics.

2. Which discrete variable would *most resemble* a continuous distribution?
   a. Number of strokes required by a seasoned pro golfer on the 18th hole.
   b. Number of daily charity solicitation calls received at a home phone.
   c. Number of points scored by SAT test takers (800 points possible).
   d. Number of red cards in five-card poker hands.
   e. Number of times per day the family dog is walked.

3. Centrality can be changed without changing dispersion.
   a. True.
   b. False.

4. If population A has a larger standard deviation than population B
   a. population A will have a greater range than population B.
   b. population A will have a smaller range than population B.
   c. skewness will be increased.
   d. skewness will be decreased.
   e. we cannot say which has the greater range or skewness.

5. Dispersion is often associated with which of the following?
   a. Mean, median, and mode.
   b. Standard deviation and interquartile range.
   c. Mode, quartiles, and peakedness.
   d. Skewness and kurtosis.
   e. None of the above.

6. If the standard deviation of a distribution is doubled, then generally we would expect that
   a. the kurtosis will increase.
   b. the skewness will increase.
   c. the range will increase.
   d. the mean will increase.
   e. all of the above will occur.

7. Which continuous variable is *least* likely to be skewed to the right by high values?
    a. Annual income of passengers on flights from New York to London.
    b. Weekend gambling winnings of customers at a major casino.
    c. Accident damage losses by renters of an auto rental company.
    d. Cost of a plain McDonald's hamburger in various U.S. cities.
    e. Size of itemized monthly charge account items by college students.

8. A positively skewed distribution will have a cumulative distribution that
    a. has a lazy "S" shape.
    b. is bowed outward.
    c. is bowed downward.
    d. is a straight line.
    e. is almost vertical.

9. If a probability distribution is right-skewed
    a. the distribution has a long left tail.
    b. the median will exceed the mean.
    c. the distribution has a long right tail.
    d. the standard deviation will be small.
    e. the mode will exceed the median.

10. If a probability distribution is platykurtic
    a. the distribution is usually skewed.
    b. the distribution has a "peaked" appearance.
    c. the distribution might also be skewed.
    d. the standard deviation usually is small.
    e. more than one of the above is correct.

11. Which of the following *must* be a symmetric probability distribution?
    a. Unimodal distribution.
    b. Bimodal distribution.
    c. Trimodal distribution.
    d. A distribution with no mode.
    e. None of the distributions *must* be symmetric.

12. Which is *not* true of quartiles?
    a. They define the upper and lower 25 percent of the probability distribution.
    b. They are shown in a beam and fulcrum display.
    c. They are shown in a box plot.
    d. They may be used to measure dispersion.
    e. They can be used with the minimum and maximum values to evaluate symmetry.

Glossary of Terms

Asymmetry   Generally, a reference to skewness. Within this module it is one of the parameters of the computer-created probability distribution.

Beam and fulcrum   Display that plots the position of the mean (the "fulcrum") and the standard deviation points ($\mu \pm 1\ \sigma$, $\mu \pm 2\ \sigma$, $\mu \pm 3\ \sigma$, etc.). Its appearance reveals skewness (the longer tail will indicate the direction of skewness) and peakedness (the larger the number of standard deviation ticks on the beam the more peaked the distribution).

Box plot   Five-number graphical display plotting the positions of the minimum, quartiles (first, second, third), and maximum along a scale representing the distribution's domain.

Centrality   General reference to the attempt to characterize the location of the middle or "typical" values in a distribution (mean, median, mode, etc.). Within this module it is one of the parameters of the computer-created probability distribution.

Continuous population   A distribution whose uncountable domain of values is defined over an interval on the X-axis (e.g., $3 \leq X \leq 9$).

Cumulative distribution   A function that maps each value of a random variable to the probability that the random variable is less than or equal to that value. The function begins at 0 and rises to 1 as you move to the right (or, less commonly from 1 to 0 as you move to the left). See **Probability distribution**.

Discrete population   A distribution whose domain is a countable set of points (e.g., $X = 0, 1, 2$).

Dispersion   General reference to the range and "spread" of values around the center of a distribution. Within this module it is one of the parameters of the computer-created probability distribution. See **Standard deviation**, **Range**, **Interquartile range**, and **Quartiles**

Distribution   See **Probability distribution**.

Interquartile range   The distance from the first quartile to the third quartile. It is a measure of dispersion. See **Quartile**.

Kurtosis   Measure of relative peakedness of the probability distribution. For unimodal distributions $K = 3$ is a mesokurtic distribution (normal or bell-shaped); $K < 3$ is a platykurtic distribution (flatter than normal, with shorter tails); and $K > 3$ is a leptokurtic distribution (more peaked than normal, with longer tails).

Mean   Sum (or integral) of the values of the random variable weighted by their probabilities, often denoted μ. It may be interpreted as the fulcrum (balancing point) of the distribution along the X-axis.

Median   The value, X_0, of the random variable such that $P(X < X_0) = 0.50$. If a random variable has a continuous, symmetric probability distribution, the median will equal the mean. If a random variable has a discrete, symmetric probability distribution, the median may not equal the mean because the median must be a value in the population whereas the mean is often not.

Midrange   Average of the lowest and highest values in the distribution.

Mode   In general, a peak on the probability distribution. If there is more than one mode (two modes is called bimodal, three modes is called trimodal), the one that is the highest is called the global mode (the most frequent population value). Other modes are called local modes (for each, the most frequent population value within a range of population values). Within this module it is one of the parameters of the computer-created probability distribution.

Parameters Values that define the probability distribution.

Peakedness Generally a reference to kurtosis. Within this module it is one of the parameters of the computer-created probability distribution.

Probability distribution For a discrete distribution, each value of the domain is mapped to a probability $P(X)$, such that $0 \leq P(X) \leq 1$. The sum of the probabilities is 1. For a continuous distribution, each value of the domain is mapped to a non-negative probability. The area under the probability distribution is 1. See **Cumulative distribution**.

Quartiles The first quartile (denoted Q_1) is the point along the X-axis which defines the lower 25 percent of the distribution. The second quartile (denoted Q_2) is the median. The third quartile (denoted Q_3) is the point that defines the upper 25 percent of the distribution.

Random variable A variable whose value is determined by chance. Possible values are determined by the population (either continuous or discrete) from which it is drawn.

Range The distance from the smallest to the largest value in the distribution's domain. It is a measure of dispersion.

Shape measures General reference to measures that describe the shape, location, and spread of a distribution. These measures include the population mean, median, midrange, mode(s), standard deviation, range, interquartile range, quartiles, skewness, and kurtosis.

Skewness Measure of relative skewness of the probability distribution. Zero indicates symmetry. Positive values show a long right tail. Negative values show a long left tail.

Standard deviation The square root of the variance, often denoted σ. The larger the standard deviation the greater the dispersion or "spread" around the mean.

Variance Measure of dispersion about the mean. Often denoted σ^2. It is the sum (or integral) of the squared difference between the values of the random variable and the mean, weighted by their probabilities.

Solutions to Self-Evaluation Quiz

1. a   Do Exercises 3–6. Read both the Overview and Illustration of Concepts.
2. c   Do Exercises 1–4. Read the Overview of Concepts.
3. a   Do Exercises 7, 8.
4. e   Do Exercises 9, 10.
5. b   Do Exercises 9, 10.
6. c   Do Exercises 9, 10.
7. d   Do Exercises 14, 20. Read the Illustration of Concepts.
8. b   Do Exercises 14, 20.
9. c   Do Exercises 14, 19–23
10. c   Do Exercises 15-17, 24, 25.
11. d   Do Exercises 1, 2, 14, 19–23.
12. b   Do Exercises 10, 19, 20, 28.

CHAPTER 4

Visualizing Discrete Distributions

CONCEPTS
- Discrete Variable, Binomial Distribution, Hypergeometric Distribution, Poisson Distribution, Uniform Distribution, Probability Distribution, Cumulative Distribution, Approximations

OBJECTIVES
- Recognize common discrete distributions and their cumulatives

- Identify the parameters of common discrete distributions and how they affect a distribution

- Interpret descriptive statistics for common discrete distributions

- Understand when to apply approximations and learn to assess their accuracy

Overview of Concepts

A **discrete variable** is a random variable that can take on only a countable number of alternative values. In this module, discrete variables assume only integer values. The **probability distribution** tells the chance that each value will occur. The binomial, Poisson, uniform, and hypergeometric distributions all describe the probability distribution of discrete variables under a variety of different situations or experiments.

A Bernoulli process refers to a two-valued or binary experiment (0, 1; no, yes; failure, success) whose probability of a success is fixed throughout and in which one trial has no effect on another trial. The **binomial distribution** tells the statistician the probability of obtaining r successes in an experiment of n trials (sample size n) when the binary variable is generated by a Bernoulli process. Generally, this means that the n observations are being selected from an infinite or very large population. It can, however, also mean that sampling is done with replacement from a smaller population. The binomial distribution can be used to find the probability of winning in many games of chance.

If the population size is finite and sampling is done without replacement, then the probability of a success changes as each sample is drawn. In this case the **hypergeometric distribution** tells the statistician the probability of obtaining r successes in an experiment of n trials (or sample size n) when sampling without replacement from a population of size N containing A successes. The hypergeometric distribution can be used to find the probability of an event in many card games.

When the statistician is interested in finding the probability of the number of occurrences (successes) over a fixed time or space, the **Poisson distribution** is used. It is named after the French mathematician Siméon Poisson (1781–1840). This distribution requires that the probability of the event (success) be proportional to the size of the interval being measured, that two events have zero probability of occurring at the same point in time or space, and that each event be independent of every other event.

The **uniform distribution** describes the situation where there are a finite number of events that each occur with equal probability. If there are k events in a uniform experiment, each event has a probability of 1/k of occurring.

Associated with every probability distribution is a **cumulative distribution**. This distribution tells the statistician the probability of selecting a value less than or equal to a specific value of the random variable. It sums the probability distribution from left to right or, in other words, accumulates the left tail of the probability distribution. Sometimes statisticians also like to accumulate the right tail of the distribution, which tells the probability of selecting a value greater than or equal to a specific value of the random variable.

The binomial, hypergeometric and Poisson distributions can each be **approximated** by other distributions. These approximations are useful because they often simplify the process of calculating probabilities. The accuracy of every approximation can be assessed using certain criteria. If the criteria are not met, the accuracy of the approximation must be questioned. The criteria are rough guidelines only. At times the criteria can suggest that an approximation is appropriate when it displays more error than the statistician deems appropriate.

Illustration of Concepts

Discrete distributions have useful applications in the everyday world. Consider the following example. Assume you operate a large produce distribution center in a major urban area. Every day numerous large trucks arrive with fresh fruits and vegetables, which are purchased from you by local retailers. Your trucks then deliver the fresh produce to retailers throughout the urban area for resale to consumers. Let us consider two problems that you would face.

First, in order to operate you need a loading dock to accommodate both the large trucks delivering the produce and your own delivery trucks. If you have too small a dock, trucks will have to wait to load or unload. If they are your own delivery trucks, you are not efficiently using your trucks or drivers. If they are growers' trucks delivering produce to you, you will alienate your suppliers who must pay their drivers to wait at the dock. However, building too large a dock is a waste of your own resources (both land and money to build the dock). In this scenario the number of trucks arriving in one hour is a **discrete variable** having a **Poisson distribution**. This can be used to help decide the size of loading dock that is needed. For example, if you know that a truck can be loaded or unloaded in one hour and that on average 6 trucks arrive every hour, a loading dock that holds 10 trucks would be insufficient 8.39% of the time (obtained from the **cumulative distribution**) while one that holds 11 trucks would be insufficient only 4.26% of the time (we have assumed that the trucks arrive independently and do not prefer certain hours of the day). Therefore, if you want less than a 5% risk of having a truck wait for docking space, an 11-berth dock would be appropriate for current needs.

Second, in order to operate a firm that delivers quality produce you must decide when to reject (or receive at a discount) a shipment from a grower as being of inferior quality. This means that you will need to sample produce from each delivery to determine if it meets your quality standard. For example, assume you have a contract with a grower that states if more than 5% of a shipment is damaged, you get a 10% reduction in price and if more than 10% of a shipment is damaged you get a 25% reduction in price. Experience tells you that it is equally likely that produce boxes throughout the truck contain damaged produce and that all produce within a box has an equal chance of being damaged. Because each produce box is equally likely to hold damaged produce, the boxes follow a **uniform distribution**. Knowing this **probability distribution** means that using random sampling will provide you with a representative sample of produce boxes. If 20 boxes are selected and each produce box holds 200 pieces of produce, you would have 4,000 pieces of produce to examine. If you sampled 200 pieces, the distribution of selecting damaged produce would follow a **hypergeometric distribution**. However, because $200/4,000 \leq 0.05$ (a criterion for using the binomial distribution to approximate the hypergeometric distribution) we can **approximate** this distribution with a **binomial distribution**. For example, assume 22 damaged pieces of produce were discovered out of the 200 samples. If only 5% of the produce is damaged, the probability of selecting 22 or more damaged pieces would be only be 0.0005 (very unlikely). If 10% of the produce is damaged, the probability of selecting 22 or more damaged pieces would be 0.3517 (a likely event). Therefore, in this example the distributor should get a 10% price reduction because more than 5% of the produce is damaged, but there is not enough evidence to suggest that more than 10% of the produce is damaged.

Orientation to Basic Features

This module illustrates the binomial, Poisson, hypergeometric and uniform discrete probability distributions and their cumulative distributions. Appropriate approximations can also be displayed.

1.   **Opening Screen**
     Start the module by clicking on the module's icon, title, or chapter number in the *Visual Statistics* menu and pressing the Run Module button. When the module is loaded, you will be on the introduction page of the Notebook. Read the introduction to see the types of questions this module will enable you to answer. Click on the Concepts tabs to see the concepts that this module covers. Click on the Scenarios tab. Select the Binomial Distribution from the table of choices. Select a scenario and press OK. The upper left of the screen depicts the binomial distribution. The module's Control Panel is on the right. On the bottom left is the table of the probabilities that are graphed. On the bottom right below the distribution are approximation options you may select. Other features are controlled from the menu bar at the top of the screen. A flashing Update button will indicate when you have changed one or more control settings.

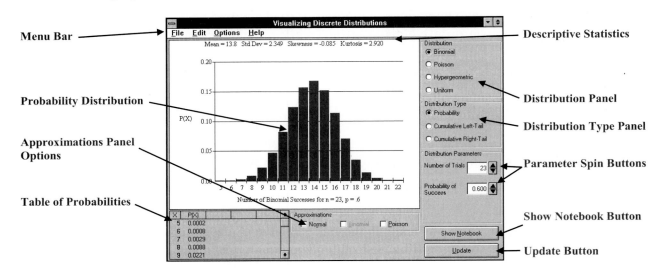

2.   **Changing Parameter Values**
     Use the spin buttons to change the parameters of the binomial distribution or to type in parameter values. Click on Update to view the new distribution.

3.   **Type of Display**
     Select either Cumulative Right-Tail or Cumulative Left-Tail on the Distribution Type panel. Click on Update. Notice that both the probability and cumulative probability values are displayed in the table below the graph.

4.   **Selecting a Distribution**
     Return to the Notebook by clicking on the Show Notebook button. Click on Return to the Scenarios contents page. Select either Poisson distribution, Hypergeometric distribution, or Uniform distribution. Select a scenario from the choices given. If you do not wish to deal with scenarios, you can simply select Poisson, Hypergeometric, or Uniform from the Distribution panel of the Control Panel and then click on Update.

5. **Options**
   Three options are available from the Options menu on the menu bar at the top of the screen.
   a.   You can choose to not display the descriptive statistics for the distribution. To remove the display, deselect Display Statistics on the Options menu.
   b.   You can also display your discrete distributions using either 2D or 3D histograms. Select 3D Graph on the Options menu in order to get 3D histograms. Select the kind of graph you prefer. Since 2D histograms more accurately display probabilities, they are the default.
   c.   Select Auto Update on the Options menu to automatically update the screen as the parameter values are changed.

6. **Copying Graph**
   Select Copy Graph or Copy Table from the Edit menu (on the menu bar at the top of the screen) to copy the graph or table onto the clipboard. It can then be pasted into other applications, such as Microsoft Word or WordPerfect.

7. **Help**
   Click on Help on the menu bar at the top of the screen. Search for Help lets you search an index for this module, Contents shows a table of contents for this module, Using Help gives instructions on how to use Help, and About gives licensing and copyright information about this module. Click on Contents. Click on any topic of interest (shown as green "hot text"). If there is green "hot text" on any screen, click on it to jump to a related help screen. Close Help by selecting Exit from the File menu on the Help screen.

8. **Exit**
   Close the module by selecting Exit in the File menu (or click ☒ in the upper right-hand corner of the window). You will be returned to the *Visual Statistics* main menu.

Orientation to Additional Features

1. **Approximations**

   Depending on the distribution you have selected either one or two standard approximations to the distribution may be superimposed on the display. For the binomial, both the normal and Poisson approximations are available; for the Poisson, the normal approximation is available; for the hypergeometric, both the normal and binomial approximations are available. No approximations are available for the uniform distribution. These options are shown in the Approximations panel below the distribution (if an option is not available, the approximation will be grayed out). The quality of the approximation is shown in the Approximation Indicator light at the bottom of the screen (red = poor, yellow = adequate, light blue = good, green = excellent). Notice that the table below the graph contains the probabilities using the approximations that have been selected. The figure below illustrates the display for a binomial distribution with n = 50 and p = 0.50.

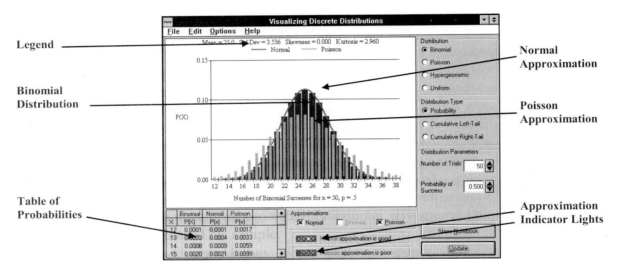

Basic Learning Exercises

Name _____

Binomial Distribution

1. Press the Show Notebook button. Select the Scenarios tab and click on Binomial Distribution. Select the Green Lights scenario and read it. Press the OK button. In this example, what are the values of its descriptive statistics? What parameters are associated with the binomial distribution and what are their values? How would you describe this distribution?

    Mean _____   Standard Deviation _____   Skewness _____   Kurtosis _____

2. Change the Probability of Success from 0.60 to 0.50. What are the new values of the descriptive statistics? How would you describe the new distribution? What would this tell you about how the traffic light is timed?

    Mean _____   Standard Deviation _____   Skewness _____   Kurtosis _____

3. Change the Probability of Success from 0.50 to 0.40. What are the new values of the descriptive statistics? How would you describe the new distribution? What would this mean about how the traffic light is timed?

    Mean _____   Standard Deviation _____   Skewness _____   Kurtosis _____

4. Change the Number of Trials to 70 from 23. a) What are the new values of the descriptive statistics? b) What happened to the shape of the distribution? b) Change the Probability of Success to 0.70. c) What are the new values of the descriptive statistics? d) What do you think the descriptive statistics would be if the Probability of Success were changed to 0.30? **Hint:** Reread exercises 1 and 3 together with your answers. Check your answer.

    Mean _____   Standard Deviation _____   Skewness _____   Kurtosis _____
    Mean _____   Standard Deviation _____   Skewness _____   Kurtosis _____
    Mean _____   Standard Deviation _____   Skewness _____   Kurtosis _____

Poisson Distribution

5. Press the Show Notebook button. Select the Scenarios tab and click on Poisson Distribution. Select and read the Billboards on I-75 scenario. Record the descriptive statistics for this distribution. What parameter defines the Poisson distribution?

    Mean _____   Standard Deviation _____   Skewness _____   Kurtosis _____

6.   a) How would you describe the distribution? b) What is the meaning of λ in this scenario?
     c) What is the relationship between Lambda (λ) and the distribution's mean and variance?

7.   If we changed the scenario to be the average number of billboards per 10 miles, what would
     the new λ be? What are the new descriptive statistics? What is the meaning of λ in this
     modified scenario? **Hint:** λ is proportional to the size of your interval.

     $\lambda = $ _____
     Mean _____   Standard Deviation _____   Skewness _____   Kurtosis _____

Uniform Distribution
8.   Press the Show Notebook button, select the Scenarios tab, click on Uniform Distribution, select
     the Gas Pump scenario and read it. What are the values of the descriptive statistics? What
     parameters are associated with the uniform distribution and what are their values? How
     would you describe the uniform distribution?

     Mean _____   Standard Deviation _____   Skewness _____   Kurtosis _____

Hypergeometric Distribution
9.   Deselect all approximations. Press the Show Notebook button. Select the Scenarios tab and
     click on Hypergeometric Distribution. Select and read the Refrigerator Configuration scenario.
     a) What are the values of its descriptive statistics? b) What parameters are associated with
     the hypergeometric distribution? c) How would you describe the distribution? d) What is the
     probability of a success (selecting a side-by-side) before the first refrigerator is selected?

     Mean _____   Standard Deviation _____   Skewness _____   Kurtosis _____

10. Increase Sample Size to 6. What are the new values of the descriptive statistics? Change
     Sample Size back to 4. Change Successes in Population to 6. What are the new values of the
     descriptive statistics? Notice that in both cases the distribution is symmetric. **Hint:** *A
     hypergeometric distribution is symmetric only if the sample size or the number of successes in
     the population are half the population size.*

     Mean _____   Standard Deviation _____   Skewness _____   Kurtosis _____
     Mean _____   Standard Deviation _____   Skewness _____   Kurtosis _____

Intermediate Learning Exercises   Name _____

Normal Approximation to the Binomial Distribution

11. Press the Show Notebook button, select the Scenarios tab, click on Binomial Distribution, select the Green Lights scenario and read it. Press the OK button. In the Approximations panel select Normal. Set the Probability of Success (p) to 0.5 and the Number of Trials (n) to 5 and press Update. a) What is the mean and variance of the approximating normal distribution? b) *In an "excellent" approximation, the normal curve goes through the middle of the top of each bar in the binomial distribution.* Does the normal curve go through the middle of each bar in this distribution? c) What does the Approximation Indicator light (at the bottom of the screen) say about the quality of the normal approximation? d) Increase n to 20 and answer questions (a)–(c).

12. Set n to 20 and p to 0.10. a) Does the normal curve intersect the center of each bar? b) Using the vertical distance between the middle of each bar and the normal distribution as a measure of the quality of the approximation, which bar has the largest absolute difference? c) From the table of probabilities in the lower left of the screen, record each binomial and normal probability, and find the absolute differences. Which absolute difference is largest? Does your answer agree with b)? d) What does the Approximation Indicator light say?

X	Binomial	Normal	Absolute Difference
0	_____	_____	_____
1	_____	_____	_____
2	_____	_____	_____
3	_____	_____	_____
4	_____	_____	_____
5	_____	_____	_____
6	_____	_____	_____
7	_____	_____	_____
8	_____	_____	_____
9	_____	_____	_____

13. Select Auto Update under Options on the Menu Bar. Keep p = 0.20. Increase the Number of Trials spin button, at what value of n does the Approximation Indicator light change to "adequate?" To "good?" To "excellent?" Does the graph reflect these assessments?

14. The Approximation Indicator light is based on the maximum absolute difference between the two distributions. Less than 0.005 is *excellent*, less than 0.01 is *good*, less than 0.02 is *adequate*, and all others are *poor*. However, most textbooks state that if $np \geq 5$ and $n(1-p) \geq 5$ the normal distribution adequately approximates the binomial distribution. This is true when p is between 0.20 and 0.80, but the approximation deteriorates when p gets either too large or too small. Here are several situations for which $np \geq 5$ and $n(1-p) \geq 5$. What does the Approximation Indicator light say about the accuracy of each normal approximation? If some are less than good, does the graph show the problem? Explain briefly.

n	p	np	Quality Indicator
10	0.50	5	_____
15	0.35	5.25	_____
50	0.10	5	_____
100	0.05	5	_____
125	0.04	5	_____
167	0.03	5.01	_____

Poisson Approximation to Binomial Distribution

15. Most textbooks state that if $n \geq 20$ and $p \leq 0.05$ the Poisson distribution adequately approximates the binomial distribution. To evaluate this statement in the Approximations panel, deselect Normal and select Poisson. *For an "excellent" approximation the green and blue bar should be the same height.* Set $p = 0.05$ and $n = 10$. a) What is the value of λ in the approximating Poisson distribution? b) At what value of n does the approximation become "good", based on the Approximation Indicator light? c) Become "excellent"? d) Set $p = 0.04$. At what value of n does the approximation become "adequate" or "poor"? e) What does this tell you about when to use the Poisson approximation to the binomial distribution?

Normal Approximation to Poisson Distribution

16. Most textbooks state that if $\lambda > 5$ the normal distribution adequately approximates the Poisson distribution. Press the Show Notebook button, select the Scenarios tab, click on Poisson Distribution, select and read the Billboards on I-75 scenario. Press OK. Change λ to 5.1. To see the normal distribution select Normal in the Approximations panel. a) What is the mean and standard deviation of the approximating normal distribution? b)Using the Approximation Indicator light, how good is this approximation? c) At what value of λ does the approximation become "adequate?" d) Given this result, why is $\lambda > 5$ used? e) At what value of λ does the approximation become "good?"

Advanced Learning Exercises   **Name** _____

Investigating the Hypergeometric Distribution

17. Press the Show Notebook button. Select the Scenarios tab and click on Hypergeometric Distribution. Select and read the Refrigerator Configuration scenario. Deselect all approximations. Set Population Size to 50 and Successes in Population to 35. Select Options on the menu bar and deselect Auto Update. a) Set Sample Size to 5 and click Update. Change Sample Size to 45 and click Update. How did the shape of the distribution change? b) Try other pairs of sample sizes equal to n and N-n. What general rule can you deduce if the number of successes in the population does not change? c) Set Population Size to 50 and Sample Size to 10. Change Successes in Population to 45 and click Update. Change Successes in Population to 5 and click Update. How did the shape of the distribution change? d) Try other pairs of successes equal to A and N-A. What general rule can you deduce if the sample size is unchanged?

18. Set Population Size to 50, Sample Size to 40, and Successes in Population to 25. a) Why is this distribution symmetric? b) How does the hypergeometric distribution change if Sample Size is changed to 10? Explain. c) How does the hypergeometric distribution change if Population Size is set to 30 and Successes in Population to 15? Explain.

19. Set Population Size to 50, Sample Size to 25, and Successes in Population to 40. a) Why is this distribution symmetric? b) How does the hypergeometric distribution change if Successes in Population is changed to 10? Explain. c) How does the hypergeometric distribution change if Population Size is set to 30 and Sample Size to 15? Explain.

20. Set Population Size to 50, Successes in Population to 25, and Sample Size to 10. Select Auto Update. Use the spin button to reduce Successes in Population to one. What happens to the number of intervals? Why does this happen?

21. a) What will happen to the distribution as you increase Successes in Population from 1 to 49? Try it. Was your supposition correct? If not describe what did happen. b) Explain why this occurs as the number of successes changes.

22. Many learners are surprised by the results of exercises 20 and 21. What is unique about the hypergeometric distribution that causes these unexpected results?

Binomial Approximation to the Hypergeometric Distribution
23. Select Binomial in the Approximations panel. Textbooks usually say the binomial approximation to the hypergeometric distribution is acceptable if $n/N < 0.05$. What is the value of n and p in the approximating binomial distribution? Evaluate the $n/N < 0.05$ criterion with different values of Population Size, Sample Size and Successes in Population.

Normal Approximation to the Hypergeometric Distribution
24. Select Normal in the Approximations panel. Set Population Size to 100, Successes in Population to 50, and Sample Size to 50. a) What is the value of the mean and variance in the approximating normal distribution? b) Decrease sample size, observing the approximation quality indicator. Why does the approximation deteriorate? c) Set Sample Size to 25. Decrease Successes in Population. Why does the approximation deteriorate?

Uniform Distribution
25. Press the Show Notebook Button. Select the Scenarios tab and click on Uniform Distribution. Select Gas Pump, read it, and click OK. Why is there no option to show an approximation?

Individual Learning Projects

Write a report on one of the three topics listed below. Use the cut-and-paste facilities of the module to place the appropriate graphs in your report.

1. Select two distributions to approximate. For both distributions investigate the accuracy of approximating the probability distribution function and the cumulative distribution function. First, you must select a criterion to evaluate the accuracy of each approximation. You can use a visual criterion (e.g., the vertical distance between the approximating distribution and the original distribution) or a criterion using a statistic (e.g., how much the skewness or peakedness statistics differ from one another). Second, for each distribution you are approximating, evaluate your approximation for a variety of parameter values. Third, decide whether the cumulative or probability distribution is easier to approximate and explain why.

2. Investigate the skewness of the binomial, Poisson, hypergeometric, and uniform distribution. For each distribution, explain when (or if) the distribution is symmetric, under what conditions the distribution is positively and negatively skewed, and how each of the distribution's parameters affects skewness. **Hint:** The hypergeometric distribution is complicated because there are three parameters, all of which can affect your result.

3. The binomial distribution can be used to approximate the hypergeometric distribution. The Poisson distribution can be used to approximate the binomial distribution. Using the Approximation Light indicator, investigate under what conditions the Poisson distribution can be used to approximate the hypergeometric distribution. Develop a rule for when the Poisson distribution can be used to approximate the hypergeometric distribution.

Team Learning Projects

Select one of the three projects listed below. Produce a team project that is suitable for an oral presentation. Use presentation software or large poster board(s) to display your results. Graphs and tables should be large enough for your audience to see. Each team member should be responsible for producing some of the exhibits. Ask your instructor if a written report is also expected.

1. This project is for a team of two. The team is to investigate the normal and Poisson approximation to the binomial distribution. One team member should investigate the normal approximation and the other the Poisson approximation. Start with a value of $p = 0.5$ and select n such that the *adequate* criterion is just met. Systematically decrease p and adjust n so that the criterion is just met. Each time evaluate the approximation. When is the approximation no longer *adequate* in your opinion? Repeat this process for the *good* and *excellent* criteria. Create a display that illustrates the accuracy of the approximation. Your displays should clearly illustrate how the approximation changes as the parameter values change.

2. This project is for a team of three or four. The team is to investigate the shape of the binomial distribution. Each team member should select a different value of n (make sure the values selected cover the range from 10 to 100). Investigate $p = 0.05, 0.10, 0.15, 0.20, 0.30, 0.40, 0.50$. Each team member should create the binomial distribution using each of the values of p. Create a display that shows how the parameter values affect the shape of the distribution. What happens to the distribution's shape as n increases with constant p? Does the value of p affect this answer? What happens to the distribution's shape as p increases with constant n? Does the value of n affect this answer? Why is it unnecessary to investigate values of p above 0.50?

3. This project is for a team of three. The team is to investigate the normal approximation to the hypergeometric distribution. The team should select a population size N (fairly large). Each team member should select one of the three approximation levels (*adequate*, *good*, *excellent*) to investigate by selecting A so that $A/N = 0.05, 0.10, 0.15, 0.20, 0.30, 0.40, 0.50$ (or as nearly as possible for the chosen N). Why is it unnecessary to investigate values of A/N above 0.50? Each team member should create a hypergeometric distribution (with the normal approximation superimposed) using each of the values of A/N. For each of these distributions, each team member should select a value of n that is consistent with the approximation level that he or she is investigating (or as closely as possible). Each team member should discuss when the approximation began to deteriorate. The team should arrive at a general conclusion.

Self-Evaluation Quiz

1. Which distribution is always asymmetric?
    a. Binomial.
    b. Poisson.
    c. Hypergeometric.
    d. Uniform.
    e. None of the distributions are always asymmetric.

2. Which distribution is most strongly right-skewed?
    a. Binomial with $n = 50$, $p = 0.25$
    b. Binomial with $n = 5$, $p = 0.9$
    c. Binomial with $n = 50$, $p = 0.5$
    d. Poisson with $\lambda = 1$
    e. Poisson with $\lambda = 15$

3. Which distribution is left-skewed?
    a. Binomial with $n = 10$, $p = 0.3$
    b. Poisson with $\lambda = 2.7$
    c. Hypergeometric with $N = 10$, $n = 5$, $A = 5$
    d. Uniform with $a = 10$, $b = 20$
    e. None of the above.

4. The Poisson distribution
    a. was named after French mathematician Siméon Poisson.
    b. was first applied in the French fishing industry.
    c. is always less peaked (flatter) than a normal distribution.
    d. is always less skewed than a normal distribution.
    e. has none of the above characteristics.

5. Which *most* resembles a Poisson random variable?
    a. the number of heads in 200 flips of a fair coin.
    b. the number of power failures in one year at a computer center.
    c. the number of face cards in a bridge hand.
    d. the number of bad floppy diskettes that are on a desk full of floppy diskettes.
    e. the number of dots showing when a pair of dice are rolled.

6. Which distribution has a mean of 5?
    a. Poisson with $\lambda = 25$.
    b. Binomial with $n = 200$, $p = .05$
    c. Uniform with endpoints 2 and 8
    d. Hypergeometric with $N = 100$, $n = 10$, $A = 5$
    e. More than one of the above.

7. Which binomial distribution would a normal distribution best approximate?
    a. n = 200, p = 0.05
    b. n = 100, p = 0.10
    c. n = 50, p = 0.20
    d. n = 25, p = 0.40
    e. All of the above.

8. Which Poisson distribution would a normal distribution best approximate?
    a. $\lambda = 25$
    b. $\lambda = 10$
    c. $\lambda = 3$
    d. $\lambda = 1.5$
    e. More than one of the above.

9. Which binomial distribution would a Poisson distribution best approximate?
    a. n = 35, p = 0.025
    b. n = 50, p = 0.03
    c. n = 20, p = 0.01
    d. n = 200, p = 0.05
    e. None of the above.

10. A binomial distribution with n = 75 and p = .02 is best approximated by which distribution?
    a. Poisson with $\lambda = 25$
    b. Poisson with $\lambda = 7.5$
    c. Poisson with $\lambda = 1.5$
    d. Poisson with $\lambda = 15$
    e. None of the above.

11. In a hypergeometric distribution with N = 20, n = 5, A = 4 the largest possible value of X (the number of successes) is
    a. 20
    b. 10
    c. 5
    d. 4
    e. none of the above.

12. Which hypergeometric distribution would a normal distribution best approximate?
    a. N = 100, n = 10, A = 5
    b. N = 150, n = 5, A = 75
    c. N = 20, n = 10, A = 5
    d. N = 200, n = 25, A = 100
    e. N = 50, n = 20, A = 10

Glossary of Terms

Approximations In this module, a reference to using one distribution to approximate another distribution.

Binomial distribution The discrete distribution that describes the number of "successes" in n independent trials with constant probability of success p.

Cumulative distribution A function that maps each value of a random variable to the probability of being less than or equal to that value. The function begins at 0 and rises to 1 as you move to the right (or, less commonly from 1 to 0 as you move to the left). See **Probability distribution**.

Descriptive statistics Statistics provided in this module are the distribution's mean, standard deviation, skewness, and kurtosis.

Discrete distribution A probability distribution whose random variable is defined over a discrete domain.

Discrete variable A random variable that takes on a countable number of different values.

Hypergeometric distribution The discrete distribution that describes the number of "successes" in a sample of size n from a finite population of size N containing a fixed number of "successes" A when sampling without replacement.

Kurtosis A measure of relative peakedness of a distribution. $K = 3$ indicates a normal bell-shaped distribution (mesokurtic). $K < 3$ indicates a platykurtic distribution (flatter than a normal distribution with shorter tails). $K > 3$ indicates a leptokurtic distribution (more peaked than a normal distribution with longer tails).

Mean The expected value of a random variable. It may be interpreted as the fulcrum (balancing point) of the distribution along the X-axis.

Median The point along the X-axis that defines the upper and lower 50 percent of the distribution. In a symmetric distribution, it is equal to the mean.

Mode The X value that defines the highest point of the probability function.

Normal distribution The standard bell-shaped or Gaussian distribution. It has two parameters called the mean and variance.

Parameter A numerical characteristic of a population. Each theoretical distribution is characterized by one or more parameters.

Poisson distribution The discrete distribution that describes the number of independent events occurring within an interval of time or space when the expected number of events within that interval is known.

Probability distribution A function that maps each value of a random variable to a probability. Each probability must be less than 1 and they must sum to 1. See **Cumulative distribution**.

Skewness A measure of relative symmetry. Zero indicates symmetry. The larger its absolute value, the more asymmetric the distribution. Positive values indicate a long right tail, and negative values indicate a long left tail.

Standard deviation The square root of the variance.

Uniform distribution The discrete distribution that assigns the same probability to each of n values of X in the domain. It is platykurtic (kurtosis = 1.8) and symmetric (skewness = 0).

Variance A measure of dispersion equal to the expected value of $(X - \mu)^2$. The larger the variance, the greater the dispersion or "spread" around the mean. See **Standard deviation**.

Solutions to Self-Evaluation Quiz

1. b   Do Exercises 1–10.
2. d   Do Exercises 1–7.
3. e   Do Exercises 1–10.
4. a   Read the Overview of Concepts.
5. b   Do Exercises 5–7. Read the Overview of Concepts.
6. c   Do Exercises 1–10.
7. d   Do Exercises 11–14.
8. a   Do Exercise 16.
9. c   Do Exercise 15.
10. c   Do Exercise 15.
11. d   Do Exercises 17–21.
12. d   Do Exercises 17, 24.

CHAPTER 5

Visualizing Continuous Distributions

CONCEPTS
- Continuous Distribution, Normal Distribution, Chi-Square Distribution, Student's t Distribution, F Distribution, Normal Approximations

OBJECTIVES
- Recognize common continuous distributions and their cumulatives

- Identify the parameters of common continuous distributions and how they affect the distribution

- Recognize shape measures for common continuous distributions

- Understand when common continuous distributions can be approximated by a normal distribution

- Understand the relation between a value of a distribution and the area in the distribution's tail

Overview of Concepts

Continuous distributions are used to describe variables that can take on an infinite number of values or at least a very large number of values. Unlike a discrete distribution, we cannot easily list the characteristics of a data-generating process (e.g., binomial) that will guarantee a particular continuous distribution. However, there are variables that we believe can be well approximated by a continuous distribution. For example, the height of seven-year old girls (in the U.S.) appears to be normally distributed with a mean of 120.5 cm and a standard deviation of 4.3 cm. We also know that process errors often are normally distributed. For example, if a door is supposed to be 32 inches wide, its actual width might be normally distributed with a mean of 32 inches and a standard deviation of 0.1 inches. But continuous distributions are primarily used to describe the distribution of sample statistics (e.g., the sample mean or the sample variance) or some transformation of these sample statistics.

The best-known distribution is the **normal distribution**. It describes the distribution of the sample mean if the statistic is based upon a large number of observations. This is proven by the Central Limit Theorem, which you will learn later in this book. This distribution has the classic symmetric bell-shape that you have probably seen elsewhere. It is defined by two parameters: its mean μ (mu) and its standard deviation σ (sigma).

If a normal distribution is sampled, the sample variance multiplied by its degrees of freedom is distributed as a **chi-square distribution**. This distribution is defined by one parameter called degrees of freedom. Unlike the normal distribution, the chi-square distribution is always positively skewed, with the degree of skewness decreasing with the degrees of freedom. For very large degrees of freedom, the chi-square distribution becomes normally distributed.

While the normal and chi-square distributions describe the behavior of the sample mean and variance, two other well-known distributions describe transformations of the sample mean and variance. The **Student's t distribution** describes the ratio of the sample mean divided by the square root of the sample variance divided by the sample size. This distribution has one parameter called the degrees of freedom. Like the normal distribution the t distribution is symmetric. For very large degrees of freedom increase, the t distribution becomes normally distributed.

The **F distribution** describes the ratio of two sample variances from independent samples. It is defined by two parameters, the degrees of freedom in the numerator and the degrees of freedom in the denominator. As both the numerator and denominator degrees of freedom get very large, the F distribution becomes normally distributed.

Under certain conditions, the chi-square, Student's t, and F distributions can be approximated by a normal distribution. The **normal approximation** improves in every case as the number of degrees of freedom increase.

Illustration of Concepts

Continuous distributions have been derived by mathematicians and statisticians in order to solve real-world problems. Abraham De Moivre (1667–1754) was investigating an approximation to the binomial distribution when he derived an expression that would later be known as the normal curve (i.e., the first occurrence of the **normal approximation**). His paper of 1738 is the first appearance in the English language of such an expression. Karl Gauss (1777–1855) was investigating the mathematics of planetary orbits when he derived what we now know as the **normal distribution** function (1809). His investigation was motivated by a need to explain why planetary orbits did not precisely correspond to the mathematical expressions that he derived. This need caused him to turn his attention to the distribution of errors. Independently, Pierre Laplace (1749–1827) was studying the anomalies in the orbits of Jupiter and Saturn when he derived an extension of De Moivre's limit theorem: "Any sum or mean will, if the number of terms is large, be approximately normally distributed." This is a simplified version of what we now call the Central Limit Theorem (1810).

The first derivation of a **chi-square distribution** was by Ernst Abbé in a paper written for his appointment as professor in the Faculty of Philosophy (1863). He derived the distribution while studying the distribution of the sum of squared errors. These were the same errors studied by Gauss, the difference being that Gauss studied their distribution while Abbé squared the errors and studied the distribution of their sum. Independently, Ludwig Boltzmann studied the distribution of kinetic energy of molecules (1878) when he derived the chi-square distribution for two and three degrees of freedom. However, it wasn't until Karl Pearson (1857–1936) provided numerous examples of how the chi-square statistic could be used (e.g., to study the heights of schoolgirls, barometric pressure, and pauperism) that the distribution became useful to most statisticians.

William Gosset (1876–1937) became a brewer for Messrs. Arthur Guinness Sons and Co., Ltd. in 1899. He was hired to study how the quality of hops and barley as well as the production process itself affected the quality of the beer produced. To study these relations he examined the ratio of $\overline{X}$ to s. However, because each experiment took a day to complete, very small samples were the norm. He noticed that comparing the ratio to the normal distribution seemed to produce incorrect results. Based upon this need, he developed a different approach that corrected these problems, which he published (1908) under the pseudonym "Student." Later, Harold Hotelling would derive the t distribution that "Student" first developed. It has become known as **Student's t distribution** in honor of William Gosset.

Sir Ronald Fisher (1890–1962) was one of the most important statisticians of all time. In one of his studies he examined differences in crop yields. However, to study these differences he had to develop a new distribution based upon the ratio of independent chi-square distributions. His variance ratio test later became known as an **F distribution,** in his honor.

Sources: M.G. Kendall and R.L. Plackett, *Studies in the History of Statistics and Probability, Volume II* (New York: Macmillan, 1977); E.S. Pearson and M.G. Kendall, *Studies in the History of Statistics and Probability, Volume I* (New York: Macmillan, 1970); and Stephen M. Stigler, *The History of Statistics: The Measurement of Uncertainty before 1900* (Cambridge, MA: Harvard University Press, 1986).

Orientation to Basic Features

This module illustrates the normal, chi-square, Student's t, and F probability distributions and their cumulatives. The distributions can also be compared visually to a normal distribution.

1. **Opening Screen**

    Start the module by clicking on the module's icon, title, or chapter number in the *Visual Statistics* menu and pressing the Run Module button. When the module is loaded, you will be on the introduction page of the Notebook. Read the questions this module covers and then click the Concepts tab to see the concepts that you will learn. Click on the Scenarios tab. Select Normal Distribution from the list of choices. Select a scenario and press OK. The upper left of the screen depicts the normal distribution. The module's Control Panel appears on the right. On the bottom left is the table of shape measures. On the bottom right are spin buttons that show the areas in each tail of the distribution. Other features are controlled from the menu bar at the top of the screen. A flashing Update button will indicate when you have changed one or more control settings.

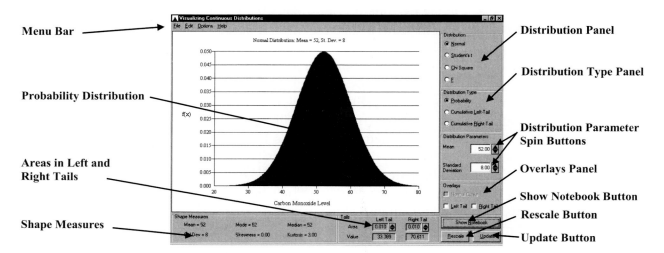

2. **Changing Parameter Values**

    Use the Parameter spin buttons to change the parameters of the normal distribution. Alternatively, you may type in parameter values. Click on Update to view the new distribution. Note how some of the shape measures change and some remain the same.

3. **Rescale**

    If the distribution is not fully visible, click the Rescale button.

4. **Viewing the Tails of the Distribution**

    In the Overlays panel on the Control Panel click on Right Tail. Note the shaded green area on the display. You can change the size of this area with the Right Tail spin button in the Tails panel below the distribution display. You can also view the left tail area.

5. **Type of Display**

    Select either Cumulative Right-Tail or Cumulative Left-Tail on the Distribution to Display panel. Click Update to see the graph selected.

6. **Selecting a Distribution**
   Return to the Notebook by clicking the Show Notebook button. Click on Return to the Scenario contents page. Select either Student's t distribution, chi-square distribution, or F distribution. Select a scenario from the choices given. Note that for each of these distributions the scenarios involve statistical tests. If you do not wish to deal with such scenarios you can alternatively select Student's t, Chi-Square, or F from the Distribution panel and click Update.

7. **Options**
   Two basic options are available from the Options menu on the menu bar on the top of the screen.
   a. Select Auto Update from the Options menu to update the distribution automatically as parameter values are changed.
   b. Select Auto Rescale on Update from the Options menu to rescale the distribution automatically when any parameter is changed. Although it guarantees plenty of graph detail, this option can make it difficult to see changes in the shape of the distribution because the scale on both axes changes each time you change a parameter.

8. **Copying a Display**
   Click on the display you wish to copy. Its window title will be highlighted. Select Copy from the Edit menu (on the menu bar at the top of the screen) or Ctrl-C to copy the display. It can then be pasted into other applications, such as Word or WordPerfect, so it can be printed.

9. **Help**
   Click on Help on the menu bar at the top of the screen. Search for Help lets you search a topic index, Contents shows a table of contents for this module, Using Help gives instructions on how to use Help, and About gives licensing and copyright information about this *Visual Statistics* module.

10. **Exit**
    Close the module by selecting Exit in the File menu (or click ☒ in the upper right-hand corner of the window). You will be returned to the *Visual Statistics* main menu.

Orientation to Additional Features

1. **Normal Curve**

   If you select any distribution but the normal you can select Normal Curve from the Overlays panel. This superimposes a normal curve on the distribution for a visual evaluation. For the Student's t distribution, the standard normal is shown (unless you have selected the option discussed below). For all other distributions, the normal is drawn using the mean and standard deviation that are indicated in the shape measures. In the figure below, the normal curve is shown superimposed on a chi-square distribution with 30 degrees of freedom.

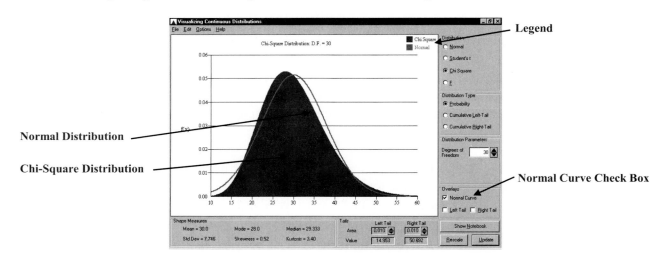

2. **Options**

   From the Options menu on the menu bar on the top of the screen you can select Standard Normal Overlay for t. This option is selected by default. It applies only if you display a Student's t distribution and select the Normal Curve overlay. The standard normal curve has mean 0 and standard deviation 1, as shown in most textbooks. However, if you look at the Shape Measures, you will notice that the standard deviation of the Student's t distribution is *not* exactly 1. In fact, the standard deviation varies with the degrees of freedom (d.f.) and approaches 1 only for large d.f. If you wish to see a normal distribution overlay with the true standard deviation, under Options you can deselect Standard Normal Overlay for t

Basic Learning Exercises   Name _____

Normal Distribution
Select a scenario under Normal Distribution in the Notebook. Make sure all of your overlays are turned off and select Auto Update, but do *not* select Auto Rescale under Options on the menu bar.

1.   Change the mean using the Mean spin button. What happens to the shape and location of the distribution? If it slides off the screen, click Rescale.

2.   Experiment with the Standard Deviation spin button. What happens to the shape of the distribution as the standard deviation increases? As it decreases? Click the Rescale button. Explain why the shape returns to the bell-shaped curve.

3.   The normal distribution has two parameters: μ and σ. Since the mean of the normal distribution is μ and its standard deviation is σ, we refer to them as the mean and standard deviation. Vary these two parameters and observe the three measures of central tendency (mean, median, and mode). How do they change? Do the shape measures (skewness and kurtosis) change as you vary μ and σ?

4.   Click the Show Notebook button. Select Carbon Monoxide Level. Answer the two questions in the scenario. On the Overlays panel select both Left Tail and Right Tail. Use the Left Tail and Right Tail spin buttons to find the approximate probabilities for the two questions.

5.   Type 0 for Mean and 1 for Standard Deviation (this is the standard normal distribution). In the Options, click Auto Rescale on Update. Use the Right Tail spin button to find the X axis values that correspond to areas of 0.01 and 0.025. What are these values if you set Standard Deviation = 2? If you set Standard Deviation = 3?

		$\sigma = 1$	$\sigma = 2$	$\sigma = 3$
Area = 0.01	Z Value = _____		Value = _____	Value = _____
Area = 0.025	Z Value = _____		Value = _____	Value = _____

6. What is the relationship between these X axis values and the standard deviation?

7. Set Mean = 4 and Standard Deviation = 3. Show algebraically that if the right-tail area is 0.05 the value of the normal distribution is 8.935. Can you write an equation that shows how to get the X value for a right-tail area of 0.05 for any values of μ and σ?

8. The standard normal variate is defined as $Z = (X - \mu)/\sigma$. In the Carbon Monoxide scenario, what would $Z = 0$ represent? What would $Z = 1$ represent?

9. Create a standard normal distribution ($\mu = 0$, $\sigma = 1$). a) From the graph, how likely is it that a standard normal random variable is within the range –2 to +2? b) Within the range –3 to +3? c) For any normal distribution, why is a value beyond the range $\mu \pm 3\sigma$ called an "outlier"?

10. In quality control, we sometimes hear that defects are controlled at the "6-sigma" level. This means that manufacturing capability is so refined that an extremely high proportion of the items produced will meet the desired specifications. How likely is it that a normal variate will fall outside the interval $\mu \pm 6\sigma$? Why might it be difficult to attain a "6-sigma" defect rate?

11. Keep the standard normal distribution (mean 0, standard deviation 1). In the Distribution Type control panel, select Cumulative Left-Tail. Click Update. a) From the graph, what is the probability that z will be below 0? b) Below 1? Below 2? Below 3? c) If you took a test and scored two standard deviations above the mean, how unusual would that be (assuming that exam scores are normally distributed)? d) If you scored three standard deviations above the mean, what would that tell you?

Intermediate Learning Exercises   Name _____

Student's t Distribution

Select Student's t Distribution and Probability Distribution. Set Degrees of Freedom = 1, display the Right Tail overlay (turn all others off). Deselect Auto Rescale under Options.

12. Set Right Tail area to 0.05. What t-value corresponds to this area? Find the t-value if DF = 6?
     DF = 11? DF = 16? DF = 21? What happens to the shape and location of the distribution?
     Click the Rescale button when necessary.

     DF = 1 _____   DF = 6 _____   DF = 11 _____   DF = 16 _____   DF = 21 _____

13. Change the DF and observe the shape measures. Find the mean, mode, median, and
     skewness. Do the standard deviation and kurtosis approach some value as the DF becomes
     very large?

14. Select Normal Curve on the Control Panel. Set the DF to 10. Compare the distributions.
     How are they different? Change the DF to 20, and then to 30. Has the difference increased or
     decreased? Why? **Hint:** The normal curve displayed has a mean of 0 and a variance of 1.

15. Select Cumulative Left-Tail. Change the DF to 10. Compare the two distributions. How are
     they different? Change the DF to 20. Has the difference increased or decreased? Why?

16.   Is the difference between the normal and t distribution more noticeable in the probability
      distribution or the cumulative distribution function? Why?

Chi-Square Distribution

Select Chi-Square and Probability Distribution. Set Degrees of Freedom = 10. Turn all the overlays off, and do *not* select Auto Rescale under Options on the menu bar.

17. What happens to the location and shape of the distribution as you increase and then decrease Degrees of Freedom (DF) using the spin button? If it slides off the screen, click Rescale.

18. Observe the shape measures as you vary the degrees of freedom. What relationship exists between the DF and the mean, mode, median, and standard deviation? What general observation can you make about skewness and kurtosis?

19. Change DF to 5 and select Normal Curve and Cumulative Left-Tail on the Control Panel. Click Rescale if necessary. Why are the cumulatives so different from one another? **Hint:** Look at their probability distributions.

F Distribution

Select F Distribution and Probability Distribution. Set Numerator DF = 3 and Denominator DF = 3. Select Auto Update and Auto Rescale on Update under Options on the menu bar.

20. Change Numerator DF to 10, then to 20, then to 200. What happens to the distribution's shape? Did the axis scale change?

21. Select the Normal Curve overlay. Keeping Numerator DF at 200, increase Denominator DF to 10, then to 20, then to 200. (a) What happens to the distribution's shape? Does it resemble the normal overlay? (b) What happens to the length of the right tail? (c) What happens to the mean, mode, skewness, and kurtosis as both degrees of freedom increase?

Advanced Learning Exercises   Name _____

Investigate the Chi-Square Distribution

Choose Normal Distribution and Cumulative Left-Tail. Set Mean = 0 and Standard Deviation = 1.
Select Auto Update and Auto Rescale under Options on the menu bar.

22. Using the standard normal cumulative left-tail distribution below, label the ordinate (vertical
     axis) when X equals -1.5, -1, -0.5, 0, 0.5, 1, and 1.5. As a guide, 1.5 has been done for you.

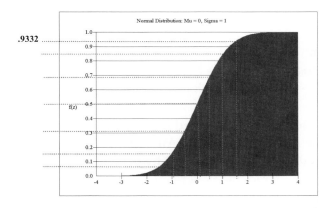

23. Click on Chi-Square Distribution and change Degrees of Freedom to 1. Using the chi-square
     cumulative left-tail distribution below, label the ordinate (vertical axis) when X equals 0, .25,
     1, and 2.25.

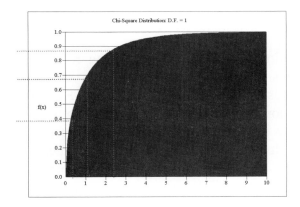

24. If a standard normal random variable is squared, the new random variable is distributed as a
     chi-square with 1 degree of freedom. Using the cumulatives above, show that the probability
     between −0.5 and 0.5 on the cumulative normal equals the probability that a chi-square
     variable will be less than 0.25. Also show that the probability between -1 and 1 on the normal
     cumulative is equal to the probability that a chi-square random variable will be less than 1.0.
     Finally, show that the probability between −1.5 and 1.5 on the normal cumulative equals the
     probability that a chi-square random variable will be less than 2.25.

25. Why are the answers in exercise 24 consistent with the fact that a standard normal random variable squared becomes a chi-square random variable?

Investigate the F Distribution

Choose F Distribution and Cumulative Left-Tail. Set Numerator DF = 1, Denominator DF = 10, and select Auto Update, and Auto Rescale under Options on the menu bar.

26. Student's t distribution is the ratio of a standard normal and the square root of an independent chi-square random variable divided by its DF. An F distribution is the ratio of two independent chi-square random variables divided by their DF. Therefore, if a variable that is distributed as t with k DF is squared, the new random variable is distributed as F with 1 and k DF. Design an experiment similar to the one in exercises 23–25 to illustrate this relationship.

27. An F distribution is the ratio of two independent chi-squares divided by their degrees of freedom. As a chi-square's DF increases, it approaches a normal distribution. Therefore, it is reasonable to assume that as Denominator DF increase, an F distribution approaches the ratio of the chi-square distribution (whose DF equals the F's Numerator DF) to its DF. Fill in the table below with the values along the horizontal axis that correspond to an area of 0.05 in the right tail of the F and the chi-square distributions. How do these results illustrate that an F with n and d DF approach a chi-square with n DF as d becomes large? Why does the F approach a chi-square divided by its DF rather than just a chi-square?

Values Along Horizontal Axis That Correspond to an Area of 0.05 in the Right Tail

	$F_{1,d}$	$F_{10,d}$	$F_{200,d}$
d=1	_____	_____	_____
d=50	_____	_____	_____
d=200	_____	_____	_____
	$\chi^2_1/1 =$ _____	$\chi^2_{10}/10 =$ _____	$\chi^2_{200}/200 =$ _____

Individual Learning Projects

Write a report on one of the three topics listed below. Use the cut-and-paste facilities of the module to place the appropriate graphs in your report.

1. Investigate the normal approximation to the Student's t, chi-square, and F distributions. Select a value of skewness and a value of kurtosis as criteria for when any of the three distributions can be approximated by a normal distribution. The criteria should provide a *Very Good* approximation. How did you select the values for skewness and kurtosis? Suggest a procedure to evaluate your criteria. Using this procedure, do the criteria work equally well for all three distributions? Repeat the process to establish and evaluate a *Fair* approximation criterion (not as stringent a criterion). **Hint:** A normal distribution has skewness of 0 and kurtosis of 3.

2. Investigate the shape of the chi-square distribution for a number of parameter values. Show clearly how degrees of freedom affect the appearance of this distribution and its shape measures. Over what range of degrees of freedom (if any) does it closely resemble a normal distribution, in your judgment? How would you determine the mean and variance of the normal distribution that approximates a chi-square distribution with k degrees of freedom? **Hint:** Use the Help files to obtain formulas for the various shape measures.

3. Investigate the Student's t distribution with 1 to 6 degrees of freedom. Compare the shape measures as well as the shape and size of the tails of the distribution. A Student's t distribution with 1 degree of freedom has an unusual appearance. How is it unusual? Why does the graph of its cumulative in this module not show the values of t whose probability appears to equal 0 or 1? **Hint:** Use the Tails spin buttons to find the t-value that corresponds to an area of 0.005 in each tail.

Team Learning Projects

Select one of the three projects listed below. In each case produce a team project that is suitable for an oral presentation. Use presentation software or large poster boards to display your results. Graphs should be large enough for your audience to see. Each team member should be responsible for producing some of the graphs. Ask your instructor if a written report is also expected.

1. This project is for a team of three. The team is to investigate the shape of the F distribution and how it depends on its two parameter values. The team should select five values for the numerator degrees of freedom (being sure that the range of values from 1 to 200 is covered). Each team member should select two values of the denominator degrees of freedom (the team should cover the range of degrees of freedom from 1 to 200). Each team member will produce ten distributions (one for each combination of the numerator and denominator degrees of freedom). The team should be able to show how increasing the numerator degrees of freedom with constant denominator degrees of freedom affects the shape of the F distribution. The team should also show how increasing the denominator degrees of freedom with constant numerator degrees of freedom affects the shape of the F distribution. Be sure to note the values of the shape measures and the height and width of each F distribution.

2. This project is for a team of two. The team is to investigate the normal approximation to the Student's t, χ^2, and F distributions. Many statisticians would say that a Student's t with 30 degrees of freedom can be approximated with a standard normal distribution. Compare the areas in the tails of the Student's t and standard normal distributions. Make this comparison at four different points. Many statisticians would say that a chi-square distribution with 200 degrees of freedom can be approximated with a normal distribution. Find its mean and standard deviation. Compare the areas in the upper and lower tails of the chi-square and normal distributions. Make these comparisons at four different points. Many statisticians would say that an F distribution with 200 and 200 degrees of freedom can be approximated with a normal distribution. Find its mean and standard deviation. Compare the areas in the upper and lower tails of the F and normal distributions. Make these comparisons at four different points. Based upon these three evaluations, characterize the quality of each approximation. **Hint:** Use the Help files to obtain relevant formulas.

3. Investigate the F distribution when both degrees of freedom are less than or equal to 9. Each team member should take a value for the denominator's degrees of freedom (the team should make sure the range from 1 through 9 is covered) and examine the F distribution for the case of 1 through 9 numerator degrees of freedom. Compare the distribution's shape, the values for both the skewness and kurtosis shape measures, and the area in the tails of the distribution.

Self-Evaluation Quiz

1. Which is *not* a characteristic of a continuous distribution?
    a. It always has an area of 1.
    b. It always has a height (probability) between 0 and 1.
    c. Its domain is defined as an interval rather than a series of points.
    d. It is characterized by one or more parameters.
    e. Its cumulative distribution approaches 1 as we move to the right.

2. In the normal distribution with $\mu = 100$, $\sigma = 20$, which X defines the smallest upper-tail area?
    a. 80
    b. 110
    c. 95
    d. 130
    e. Insufficient information is given.

3. A right-tail area of 0.10 in a normal distribution with $\mu = 80$, $\sigma = 15$ corresponds to an X value of
    a. 114.89
    b. 104.68.
    c. 99.23.
    d. 109.40.
    e. Insufficient information is given.

4. If the upper 1% point in a normal distribution with $\mu = 500$, $\sigma = 20$ is 546.52, then the upper 1% point in a normal distribution with $\mu = 500$, $\sigma = 40$ is
    a. 546.52
    b. 580
    c. 612.24
    d. 593.04
    e. Insufficient information is given.

5. Which X value defines the largest right-tail area in a standard normal distribution?
    a. 0.000
    b. 1.645
    c. 1.960
    d. 2.326
    e. 2.576

6. Which is *not* true of the Student's t distribution?
    a. It closely resembles a normal distribution for degrees of freedom above 10.
    b. It was discovered about a century ago.
    c. It is more symmetric for large degrees of freedom.
    d. It is always centered at 0.
    e. It was discovered by a beer brewer.

7. Which is *not* the name of a parameter of a common continuous distribution?
    a. Mean.
    b. Kurtosis.
    c. Variance.
    d. Numerator degrees of freedom.
    e. Denominator degrees of freedom.

8. The chi-square distribution
    a. is almost indistinguishable from a normal distribution for degrees of freedom above 30.
    b. is always skewed to the right.
    c. has two parameters (numerator and denominator degrees of freedom).
    d. has the same left-tail and right-tail 1% critical values except for the sign.
    e. fulfills more than one of the above.

9. The chi-square distribution
    a. has a mean equal to its degrees of freedom.
    b. has a mode equal to its degrees of freedom.
    c. is leptokurtic (more peaked than normal).
    d. has more than one of the above characteristics.
    e. has none of the above characteristics.

10. The F distribution looks quite like a normal distribution
    a. when $df_1 = 1$ and $df_2 = 10$.
    b. when $df_1 = 2$ and $df_2 = 30$.
    c. when $df_1 = 5$ and $df_2 = 100$.
    d. when $df_1 = 10$ and $df_2 = 200$.
    e. in none of the above cases.

11. Which is *not* true of the F distribution?
    a. It was discovered by Sir Ronald Fisher in the 20th century.
    b. It is nearly normal when $df_1 = 25$ and $df_2 = 25$.
    c. It is always unimodal.
    d. It is always a continuous distribution.
    e. Its mean decreases as we increase its denominator degrees of freedom.

12. The F distribution
    a. is symmetric if $df_1 = df_2$
    b. is always skewed left.
    c. is always platykurtic (flatter than normal).
    d. fulfills both b and c.
    e. fulfills none of the above.

Glossary of Terms

Chi-square distribution Right-skewed continuous distribution that describes the sum of squares of unit normal deviates. Its one parameter is called degrees of freedom.

Continuous distribution A distribution function where the random variable is defined over a continuous X domain.

Cumulative distribution A function that maps each value of a random variable to the probability of being less than or equal to that-value. The function begins at 0 and rises to 1 as you move to the right (or, less commonly from 1 to 0 as you move to the left). See **Probability distribution**.

Degrees of freedom Name given to parameters of certain distributions. Degrees of freedom will always be an integer. It is sometimes abbreviated DF or d.f. See **Chi-square distribution, F distribution, and Student's t distribution**.

F distribution Right-skewed continuous distribution used to describe the ratio of two independent sample variances. Its two parameters are called* the numerator and denominator degrees of freedom.

Kurtosis Measure of the relative peakedness of a distribution. $K = 3$ indicates a normal "bell-shaped" distribution (mesokurtic). $K < 3$ indicates a platykurtic distribution (flatter than a normal distribution with shorter tails). $K > 3$ indicates a leptokurtic distribution (more peaked than a normal distribution with longer tails).

Mean Expected value of a random variable. It may be interpreted as the fulcrum (balancing point) of the distribution along the X-axis. It is commonly denoted μ.

Median Point along the X-axis that defines the upper and lower 50 percent of the distribution. In a symmetric distribution, it is equal to the mean.

Mode X value that corresponds to the peak of the probability distribution function.

Normal approximation Using a normal distribution to approximate another distribution.

Normal distribution Standard "bell-shaped" or Gaussian distribution. It has two parameters called the mean and variance.

Parameter Numerical characteristic of a population that determines its distribution. Some distributions have several parameters.

Probability distribution Distribution that maps each value of a random variable to a probability. The area (integral) under the entire probability distribution must be 1. Also called a probability density function. See **Cumulative distribution**.

Shape measures Descriptive statistics such as the distribution's mean, median, mode, standard deviation, skewness, and kurtosis.

Skewness Measure of relative symmetry. Zero indicates symmetry. The larger its absolute value the more asymmetric the distribution. Positive values indicate a long right tail, and negative values indicate a long left tail.

Standard deviation The square root of the variance. It is commonly denoted σ.

Student's t distribution Symmetric continuous distribution used to describe the ratio of a normally distributed variable with zero mean divided by its standard deviation. Its one parameter is called degrees of freedom.

Variance A measure of dispersion equal to the expected value of $(X - \mu)^2$. The larger the variance, the greater the dispersion or "spread" around the mean. See **Standard Deviation**.

Solutions to Self-Evaluation Quiz

1. b   Read the Overview of Concepts.
2. d   Do Exercises 5–7.
3. c   Do Exercise 5.
4. d   Do Exercises 6 and 7.
5. a   Do Exercise 5.
6. c   Do Exercise 13. Read the Overview of Concepts.
7. b   Do Exercises 3, 12, 17, and 20–21. Read the Overview of Concepts.
8. b   Do Exercise 18. Read the Overview of Concepts.
9. d   Do Exercises 17–19. Read the Overview of Concepts.
10. e   Do Exercises 20–21. Read the Overview of Concepts.
11. b   Do Exercises 20–21. Read the Illustration of Concepts.
12. e   Do Exercises 20–21. Read the Overview of Concepts.

CHAPTER 6

Visualizing Random Samples

CONCEPTS
- Statistical Inference, Sample, Population, Infinite Population, Finite Population, Sample Size, Random Sample, Random Variation, Sample with Replacement, Sample without Replacement, Outliers

OBJECTIVES
- Understand the variability of samples in relation to their parent populations and the role sample size plays in that variability

- Recognize how the number of histogram intervals and the labeling of the horizontal axis affect the appearance of a sample

- Learn to infer a population's shape, mean, and standard deviation from a sample

- Understand the effects of sampling with or without replacement

- Recognize how outliers affect histograms and what they represent

Overview of Concepts

A **population** represents all possible outcomes of an experiment or a process. A **finite population** consists of N possible outcomes that can be enumerated or listed (e.g., the number on a roulette wheel). An **infinite population** has an inexhaustible and uncountable number of possible outcomes (e.g., waiting times for pizza deliveries). Some finite populations can be treated as if they are infinite because they are so large (e.g., prices of all new automobiles sold in California last year). Because many populations are very large, statisticians often make a judgment about a population based upon a small portion of the population called a **sample**. This judgment is called a **statistical inference**. For example, you are probably familiar with exit polls that make inferences about election results based upon a sample of voters.

If the sample represents the population, it can provide insight into the population at a fraction of the cost of analyzing the entire population. However, if a sample does not represent the population, it can lead to poor and even embarrassing decisions. Two related cases illustrate this point. The *Literary Digest* predicted that Alfred Landon would easily defeat the incumbent, Franklin D. Roosevelt, in the 1936 Presidential election. One week later, Roosevelt won by a record 11 million votes. What went wrong? The *Literary Digest* drew its sample from phone records, car registrations, and its own subscription list. This sample represented wealthier Americans who were more likely to vote Republican. The *Digest* incorrectly believed that because they had a very large **sample size** their results were very accurate. However, they had actually selected a biased sample, albeit a very large one.

In another case, George Gallup predicted that Thomas E. Dewey would defeat the incumbent Harry S. Truman in the 1948 Presidential election. Ten days later Truman won the election. That forecast was based upon the views of voters who preferred a candidate when the poll was taken — ten days before the election. However, there were a large number of undecided voters at the time of the poll, most of whom voted for Truman. By ignoring the undecided voters Gallup inadvertently biased his sample.

Ironically, in 1936, George Gallup, in his weekly newspaper column, had been critical of the *Literary Digest* poll because it over-represented wealthier Americans and hence was not a **random sample** (every outcome in the population has an equal chance of being selected). Yet 12 years later he inadvertently committed a similar error.

Even if you draw a random sample there will be **random variation**. This is the normal variation expected in a sample. However, if you find an **outlier** (a sample point that is more than three standard deviations from the mean) it is difficult to know if you are seeing random variation or if you have an observation from a different population. For example, you select 10 high school students at a football game and ask them the approximate size of their homes (in square feet). You collect the following data: 1500, 2000, 2200, 1800, 1600, 2300, 5000, 2800, 1900, and 2700. The 5000 is an outlier. Does it represent normal variation, or is it an observation from another population? You would not know unless you asked the subject where she lived. Only then might you find out that she was a student from another community.

In sampling finite populations you can sample with or without replacement. If you **sample with replacement**, after selecting an observation it is returned to the population, possibly to be drawn again. In contrast, if you **sample without replacement** the observation drawn is removed from the population, changing the probability of selecting the next observation. If the sample size is very small relative to the population size the methods are equivalent.

Illustration of Concepts

Consider the distribution of household size in the United States. Every three months the U.S. Bureau of Labor Statistics surveys consumers using the Consumer Expenditure Survey. This study used 5,153 households from the fourth quarter 1989 and the first quarter 1990. This is the **finite population** that will be sampled. A **random sample** of 25 consumers is drawn from this **population**. Since the population is large relative to our **sample size,** we can treat it as an **infinite population.** Therefore, it doesn't matter if we **sample with** or **without replacement**. A histogram of the **sample** is shown in Figure 1. What **statistical inferences** can be made about the population? From the histogram we would infer that the population is right skewed and is triangular in shape with a mode at a one-person household. For this sample size, we have more confidence in our inference that the population is right skewed than we do in its specific shape or its mode. Its sample mean is 2.2 and standard deviation is 1.27.

We draw a second and third sample of 25 from the same population (Figures 2 and 3). The second sample suggests that the population is not as skewed and is bimodal with modes at 2 and 4 persons per household. Its sample mean is 2.6 and standard deviation is 1.20. The third sample suggests that the population is uniform in the one- to four-person range with a slight tail to the right. Its sample mean is 2.60 and standard deviation is 1.26. The only similarity in the three histograms is that all suggest some positive skewness. None of the three samples has an **outlier** (an observation more than 3 standard deviations from the mean).

These histograms illustrate **random variation**. This differing picture of the population is not unusual, especially if the sample size is small. In contrast, note the similarity in the sample means and standard deviations. These statistics vary much less than the histograms.

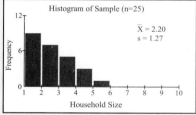

Figure 1: Histogram of First Sample

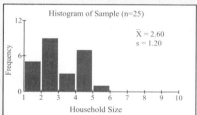

Figure 2: Histogram of Second Sample

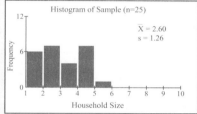

Figure 3: Histogram of Third Sample

For comparison, a histogram of the entire finite population is displayed in Figure 4. The second sample is most like the population, even though it incorrectly led us to suspect a bimodal distribution. Although it was not possible to infer the exact shape of the population from our samples of $n = 25$, our belief that the population was positively skewed was correct, and our estimates of the population mean and standard deviation were good. Figure 5 shows a histogram of a larger sample ($n = 100$). Compare its shape with the population histogram, and its sample statistics (sample mean is 2.66 and standard deviation is 1.50) to the population parameters ($\mu = 2.74$, $\sigma = 1.53$). Inferences from larger samples generally are more accurate.

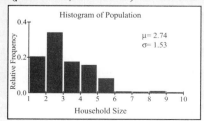

Figure 4: Histogram of Population

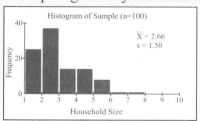

Figure 5: Histogram of Large Sample

Orientation to Basic Features

This module allows you to sample from a population distribution or a finite population that you select and create a histogram to display the sample. You can change the number of intervals in the histogram and superimpose the population for comparison.

1. **Opening Screen**

    Start the module by clicking on the module's icon, title, or chapter number in the *Visual Statistics* menu and pressing the Run Module button. When the module is loaded, you will be on the introduction page of the Notebook. Read the questions this module covers and then click the Concepts tab to see the concepts that you will learn. Click on the Scenarios tab. Select Normal Populations from the list of choices. Select the IQ Scores scenario, read it and press OK. The upper left of the screen depicts a histogram with eight intervals for a sample of size 25. The Control Panel appears on the right. The bottom left of the screen shows a box plot and a beam and fulcrum diagram of the sample. Descriptive statistics from the sample are shown to the right. Other features are controlled from the menu bar at the top of the screen.

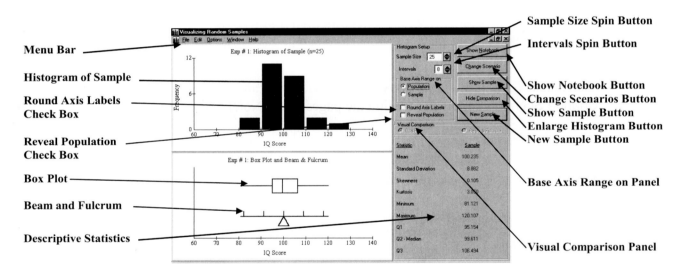

2. **Control Panel**

    a. Press the Intervals spin button. The histogram is automatically updated to reflect the number of intervals desired (2 to 20). Double clicking on the number in the spin box enables you to change it from your keyboard.

    b. Press the Sample Size spin button. A new sample size (2 to 1000) can be selected. The sample is drawn when the flashing New Sample button is pushed. Double-click the number in the spin box to change it from your keyboard.

    c. The Base Axis Range On panel contains two option buttons. Click Sample to base the histogram labels on the sample drawn. Click Population to base the axis scale on the population sampled. The Population option is useful if you are comparing the sample with the population from which it is drawn because it will not change with every sample.

    d. Click on the Round Axis Labels check box to improve horizontal axis labeling, making it more pleasing to the eye. When the histogram is based on the sample, this option usually improves the roundness of the numbers on the axis.

e. Click on the Reveal Population check box to see the population superimposed upon the sample histogram, a visual comparison of the sample and population, and the population statistics listed next to the sample statistics. The Visual Comparison panel is now active, allowing you to select a Box Plot or Beam & Fulcrum display.

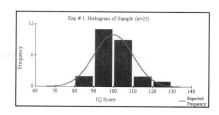

f. Press the Hide Comparison button to enlarge the histogram vertically. Press the Show Comparison button to return the histogram to normal size and show both displays.

g. Press the Show Sample button to see the sample in sorted order. Press the Show Frequencies button to see the observed frequency in each interval. If the population is being revealed, the expected frequency is also shown. Press the Copy to Clipboard button to copy a table to other applications.

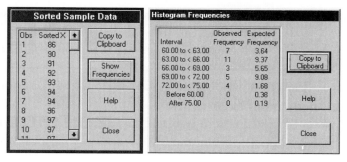

3. **Changing the Population**
    There are two easy ways to select the population being sampled.
    a. You can use a scenario. The purpose of a scenario is to provide a context showing how a statistician would use a sample. A different scenario can be selected by pressing the Change Scenario button and turning the pages of the Notebook.
    b. You can sample from 12 predefined populations. Press the Show Notebook button, select the Pop. Templates tab and click OK. A template like the one to the right appears. Click any population button or the random population button (?) and click OK. The Change Scenario button becomes the Change Templates button, providing a shortcut to the templates in the Notebook.

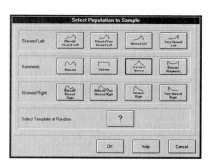

4. **Copying a Display**
    Click on the display you wish to copy. Its window title will be highlighted. Select Copy from the Edit menu (on the menu bar at the top of the screen) or Ctrl-C to copy the display. It can then be pasted into other applications, such as Word or WordPerfect, so it can be printed.

5. **Help**
    Click on Help on the menu bar at the top of the screen. Search for Help lets you search a topic index, Contents shows a table of contents, Using Help gives instructions on how to use Help, and About gives licensing and copyright information about this *Visual Statistics* module.

6. **Exit**
    Close the module by selecting Exit in the File menu (or click ☒ in the upper right-hand corner of the window). You will be returned to the *Visual Statistics* main menu.

Orientation to Additional Features

1. **Changing the Population**
    There are three advanced ways to change the population.

    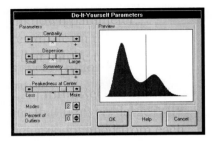

    a.   You can sample from a continuous population of your own creation. Press the Show Notebook button, select the Do-It-Yourself tab, click on User Created Distributions and click OK. Four scroll bars control the population's parameters. The Modes spin button sets the number of modes (0, 1, or 2) in the distribution being sampled. The Percentage of Outliers spin button sets the percent of outliers (1, 2, 3, 4, or 5). These are sampled from a second population with a mean 4 standard deviations away from the original mean. Click OK to sample from the population created. The Change Templates button becomes the Change Parameters button, providing a shortcut to this control in the Notebook.

    b.   You can sample from 9 known distributions. Press the Show Notebook button and click on Next page in the lower right corner. Click OK. Select a population from those listed. Change the parameter values using the text boxes. The range of values appears if the cursor is placed on a text box. The distribution is shown on the accompanying graph. Click on OK to sample from the population selected. The Change Parameters button becomes the Change Populations button, providing a shortcut to this control in the Notebook.

    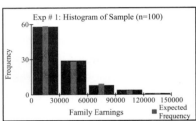

    c.   You can sample from either of two databases. Press the Show Notebook button and select the Databases tab. Read the descriptions and select a database. Each database is organized by categories. Click on the + symbol of any category that sounds interesting to expand the category and list its variables (the + symbol will become a − symbol). Click on the − symbol to shrink a category and hide its variables. Click on any variable and read its description in the text window at the right. Click on OK to sample from this finite population. You can sample with or without replacement. The Change Parameters button becomes Change Populations. Population frequencies can be superimposed on the sample histogram.

2. **Options**
    Two options are available from the Options menu:
    a.   Select Change Title from the Options menu to retitle the current display.
    b.   Select Full Window Graph from the Options menu to extend both graphs to the full screen width. Deselect Full Window Graph to bring back the Control Panel.

3. **Second Display**
    Under Window, click Copy Default Window or Copy Current Window from the Windows menu on the menu bar. This creates a second graph that can be tiled or cascaded. Using the Change Title option to retitle the displays, so you can keep track of them.

Basic Learning Exercises

Name _____

Sampling Variation

Select Sample in the Base Axis Range On panel. Press the Show Notebook button, select the Scenarios tab and click on Non-normal populations with one mode. Select The Sum of Two Random Numbers scenario. Read the scenario. Click OK. *Don't* select Population or Reveal Population yet.

1. Set Sample Size to 25. Use the Intervals spin box to create a histogram that best illustrates the sample (you may select Round Axis Labels if you wish). a) How many intervals did you select? Using only the sample histogram, sketch your impression of the shape of the population's distribution. Repeat this for three more samples. b) How do your sketches differ from one another? How are they similar? c) Why don't the sketches portray a consistent picture of the population's distribution?

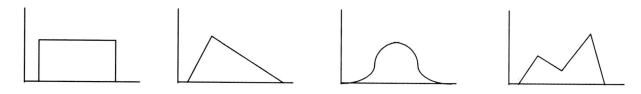

2. Take a new sample. Record the sample mean, standard deviation, skewness, kurtosis, and median. Repeat the process for three more samples. Subtract the smallest mean from the largest (this is the range of the sample means in this experiment). Calculate the ranges of the other sample statistics.

Sample	Mean	Std. Dev.	Skewness	Kurtosis	Median
1					
2					
3					
4					
Range					

3. Why is sample variation more evident in the histograms (exercise 1) than in the sample mean or sample median (exercise 2)?

Sample Size and Sample Variation

4.   Increase the sample size to 500 (use the spin button or enter 500 into the Sample Size box) and press the New Sample button. Using only the sample histogram, sketch your impression of the shape of the population's distribution. Repeat this for three more samples. Why are the sample histograms more consistent than in exercise 1?

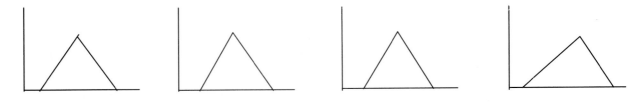

5.   Repeat exercise 2 using a sample size of 500.

Sample	Mean	Std. Dev.	Skewness	Kurtosis	Median
1					
2					
3					
4					
Range					

6.   a) Compare the range of each statistic in exercises 2 and 5. What do you observe? b) Compare your sketches in exercises 1 and 4. What do you observe? c) Give a general rule regarding the relationship between sample size, sample variation, variation in histograms, and variation in sample statistics. d) Why did increasing the sample size increase your confidence in your impressions about the population?

7.   Click the Reveal Population check box. Select Population in the Base Axis Range On panel. Were your impressions about the shape of the distribution and its statistics correct?

Intermediate Learning Exercises   Name _____

Making Inferences

One key to making inferences about unknown populations is seeing how the shape of the population's distribution affects the appearance of a sample histogram, while keeping the sample size and number of histogram intervals the same.

8. Push the Show Notebook button and select the IQ Test Scores scenario. Read the scenario and click OK. Change the sample size to 20, set the number of histogram intervals to 5, and take a sample. Sketch your impression of the shape of the population's distribution. Repeat this for four more samples. Then select Reveal Population. Were your sketches correct?

    IQ Test Scores: Population Distribution _____

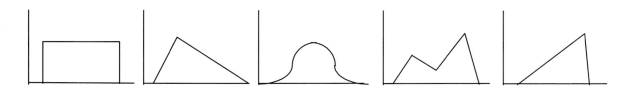

9. Repeat exercise 8 using The Accuracy of an Archer scenario from the Notebook.

    Accuracy of an Archer: Population Distribution _____

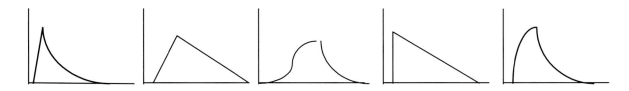

10. Repeat exercise 8 using the Choosing a Lottery Number scenario from the Notebook.

    Choosing a Lottery Number: Population Distribution _____

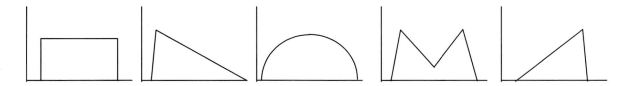

11. All of the following three histograms were generated by one of the three populations you analyzed in exercises 8–10. Which scenario is most likely to have generated these histograms? The least likely? Explain your reasoning.

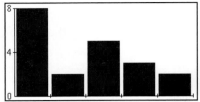 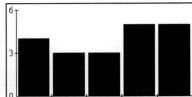 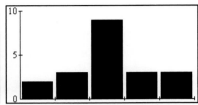

Sampling from a Finite Population

12. Press the Show Notebook button and select the Databases tab. Read about each database and select one that interests you. Read the descriptions of several variables and select one that interests you. Which variable did you select? Give its definition and population size (N).

13. Make sure that Sample with Replacement is checked. Click OK. Reveal Population should *not* be selected. Use a sample size of n = 40 for the grocery data or n = 100 for the expenditures data. Record the sample size and draw five samples, recording each mean. Calculate the range of the 5 sample means. Triple the sample size and repeat the process.

n	Sample 1	Sample 2	Sample 3	Sample 4	Sample 5	Range

14. Return the sample size to its original size (either 40 or 100). Press the Change Database button. Click on Sample with Replacement to deselect it. Press OK. Repeat exercise 13.

n	Sample 1	Sample 2	Sample 3	Sample 4	Sample 5	Range

15. a) For each sample size, calculate the ratio of the range of sample means when you sampled with and without replacement. b) What do you conclude from these comparisons? c) Why would the range of sample means be zero if you sampled without replacement and n = N?

Advanced Learning Exercises

Name _____

Sampling with Outliers

16. Click Reveal the Population to deselect this option. Press the Show Notebook button, select the Do-It-Yourself tab, click on User Created Distributions and click OK. A display will let you create your own distribution by changing the scroll bars and the Number of Modes spin button. Create any distribution you desire. Sketch and describe the shape of the distribution you created. What data might have this type of distribution? Defend your selection.

17. Use the Outliers spin button to set the percentage of outliers to 3%. Click OK to sample from the distribution selected. What is an outlier? (**Hint:** Use Help.) What could cause an outlier in a real sampling experiment? What warning does it give the statistician?

18. Not all samples will contain an outlier. Set your sample size to 100. Select the number of intervals that you believe is appropriate. Press the New Sample button. How can you tell if the data displayed contains an outlier? If it doesn't, draw new samples until it does (it would be very unusual to take more than two samples).

19. Click on Reveal the Population. From this display how can you tell that the outlier did not come from the population displayed?

20. Can a statistician assume that if a sample contains an outlier that the sample has an observation from another population?

Sampling from Known Distributions

21. Press the Show Notebook button. Select the Do-It-Yourself tab and click on Known Distributions. Press OK to bring up its Control Panel. Nine different continuous distributions can be sampled. The parameters of the selected distribution are listed in the Parameters panel. A sketch of the distribution is shown for reference. Select each and change its parameter values. The range of valid values is displayed in the tool tip (rest the cursor on a parameter value box). For each distribution, describe its shape and how its parameter(s) affect its shape.

Normal

Chi Square

F

Student's t

Gamma

Beta

Uniform

Exponential

Triangular

22. An exponential distribution is often used to model processes that have constant failure rates. Its single parameter is the failure rate, whose reciprocal is the mean of the distribution. For example, many 60W light bulbs have an advertised life of 1000 hours, which implies a failure rate of 0.001 or that 0.1% of the light bulbs fail every hour. Select an exponential distribution and enter 0.001 for its parameter value. Click OK. Take a sample of 100 light bulbs. Based on this sample, how many would fail in the first 250 hours? The first 500 hours? The first 1000 hours? How many hours before the last light bulb burns out?

Bimodal Populations

23. Bimodal distributions usually represent situations where two different populations are being sampled. Press the Show Notebook button, select the Scenarios tab and click on Populations with 0 or 2 modes. Read Heights of Students. Why is this distribution bimodal? Give your own example of a bimodal population. Press OK to study the sample. Can the two modes be identified in the sample? If a sample is bimodal does this mean that the population is also?

Individual Learning Projects

Write a report on one of the three topics listed below. Use the cut-and-paste facilities of the module to place the appropriate graphs and tables in your report.

1. Investigate the importance of sample size in reducing sample variability. Select a data set from one of the two databases to investigate. Describe the variable you selected. What do you think its upper and lower bound would be and why? Start your investigation with a sample size of 12. Draw three samples. For each sample provide a histogram (based upon the sample). Do the three samples provide a consistent impression of the shape of the distribution being sampled? If not, increase the sample size to 25 and reevaluate the histograms. Continue doubling the sample size until all three samples give a consistent impression of the distribution's shape. Include the histograms of these three samples (the histograms should all use the same sample size) in your report along with a histogram of the population. Repeat this process for a different data set that you believe will have a different distribution shape. Discuss the importance of sample size in overcoming random variation and how random variation was affected by the distribution's shape.

2. Investigate the effect sampling with or without replacement has on the variability of the sample mean. Select a data set to investigate. Conduct six experiments, sampling with and without replacement using three different sample sizes: less than 5% of the finite population size, 15 to 35% of the finite population size, and 60 to 85% of the finite population size. In each case take 10 samples and record the sample mean. For each experiment calculate the average and the variance of the 10 sample means. Your project should show that the variability of the sample means decreases as sample size increases and is further reduced if you sample without replacement, especially if the sample size is a large portion of the population size. Your report should include the histogram of the sample with the most variability and the histogram of the sample with the least variability from each of the six experiments.

3. Illustrate statistical inference. Select three different data sets (you must use both databases). Describe the variables you selected. Tell what you believe their upper and lower bounds would be and why. Use a sample size of 40 for the Grocery Expenditure Survey and 100 for the Consumer Expenditure Survey. Decide if you are going to sample with or without replacement and if you are going to use or not use Round Axis Labels. For each data set take one sample. Create a histogram (based upon the sample data) with the appropriate number of intervals. Analyze the box plot and beam and fulcrum diagrams. Evaluate the descriptive statistics. Make an inference about the population's shape and population statistics (mean, standard deviation, etc.) and your degree of confidence in the inferences. Reveal the population and evaluate your answer. Your answer will be judged on your explanation, not on whether you correctly identified the shape of the distribution. Your report should include evaluations of the usefulness of the box plot, the beam and fulcrum, histograms, and descriptive statistics in making inferences. Discuss the feasibility of creating a histogram based the population's upper and lower bound.

Team Learning Projects

Select one of the three projects listed below. In each case produce a team project that is suitable for an oral presentation. Use presentation software or large poster boards to display your results. Graphs should be large enough for your audience to see. Each team member should be responsible for producing some of the graphs. Ask your instructor if a written report is also expected.

1. A team of three to five individuals should investigate the importance of the number of intervals in producing a histogram. Each team member should choose a different shape distribution by using the Pop. Templates tab or the Do-It-Yourself tab in the Notebook (select distributions as diverse as possible). Give an example of data that would have such a distribution. Set Sample Size to 25, set Base Axis Range on to Sample, and, if you wish, click on Round Axis Labels. Draw four samples for each distribution. For each sample create two histograms, each with a different number of intervals. The project should illustrate how the number of intervals affects the impression of a distribution's shape and how variability is affected by the shape of the distribution that generates the sample.

2. A team of three to five should investigate the usefulness of the box plot and the beam and fulcrum diagrams in making inferences about a distribution's shape. Each team member should choose a different shape distribution by using the Pop. Templates tab or the Do-It-Yourself tab in the Notebook (select distributions as diverse as possible in skewness and peakedness). Give an example of data that would have such a distribution. Set Sample Size to 15, set Base Axis Range on to Sample, and, if you wish, click on Round Axis Labels. Using only the box plot, make an inference about the shape of the distribution that generated the data. Using only the beam and fulcrum, make an inference. Draw two more samples and repeat the process. Increase your sample size to 60 and repeat the process with 3 more samples. Which diagram is more useful in making an inference when n = 15? When n = 60? Consider the variability as well as the reliability of each diagram at each sample size. As a team, discuss how the shape of the distribution that generated the sample affected these results. Each team member should have a display illustrating six pairs of diagrams as well as a representation of the population.

3. A team of three to five should investigate how sample size, as well as the shape of the distribution that generates a sample, affects random variability. Each team member should choose a different shape distribution by using the Pop. Templates tab or the Do-It-Yourself tab in the Notebook (select distributions as diverse as possible in skewness and peakedness). Give an example of data that would have such a distribution. Set Sample Size to 10, set Base Axis Range on to Sample, and, if you wish, click on Round Axis Labels. Create a histogram that accurately displays the sample. Take two more samples using the same number of intervals. Increase your sample size to 30. Create three more histograms (adjust the number of intervals appropriately). Increase your sample size to 90 and create three more histograms. The project should illustrate how sample size reduces random variability and how variability is affected by the shape of the distribution that generates the sample.

Self-Evaluation Quiz

1. A sample has a histogram shaped like its population
   a. regardless of sample size.
   b. if the sample size is large enough.
   c. if the population is normal.
   d. if the sample is drawn randomly.
   e. More than one of the above are correct.

2. Sample means generally
   a. have the same variability as individual items in the population.
   b. have more variability than individual items in the population (due to sampling error).
   c. have less variability than individual items in the population.
   d. may be more or less variable than population items, depending on the population shape.
   e. may most easily be seen in the sample box plot.

3. Which is true of random variation?
   a. Variation is decreased as sample size is decreased.
   b. Variation is larger if a peaked distribution is sampled than a uniform distribution.
   c. As random variation is reduced, confidence in inferences is increased.
   d. Variation is smaller if a distribution has two modes rather than one.
   e. None of the above is correct.

4. If a normal population is sampled,
   a. the sample box plot should be roughly symmetric.
   b. the sample beam and fulcrum should be roughly symmetric.
   c. the sample median should roughly equal the sample mean.
   d. All of the above are correct.
   e. Only a and c are correct.

5. If we sample a given population, increasing the sample size will cause the
   a. sample means to vary more from sample to sample.
   b. sample standard deviations to vary more from sample to sample.
   c. histogram range for each sample to grow narrower.
   d. histogram of each sample to approach normality.
   e. histogram of each sample to approach the population shape.

6. As we increase the number of classes in a sample histogram, which would be expected?
   a. The population's mode (if any) becomes more apparent.
   b. The population's range becomes more apparent.
   c. The frequencies in each class interval become larger.
   d. Some empty intervals are likely to appear.
   e. All of the above would be expected.

7.   A right-skewed sample histogram is *least* likely to be from a
     a.   uniform population.
     b.   right-skewed population.
     c.   normal population.
     d.   left-skewed population.
     e.   bimodal population.

8.   When sampling a uniform population, a bimodal sample histogram
     a.   could be due to sampling variation.
     b.   could reflect the number of histogram intervals that were used.
     c.   could be due to the interval limits that were chosen.
     d.   could arise from using a small sample size.
     e.   could be due to any of the above.

9.   Which of the following statements is true?
     a.   Sampling with replacement decreases sample variability.
     b.   Sampling with or without replacement is not an issue in infinite populations.
     c.   Sampling without replacement decreases the accuracy of the sample mean.
     d.   Sampling without replacement is like sampling from an infinite population.
     e.   None of the above statements is true.

10. If a sample of 25 items is drawn without replacement from a uniform population of 50 items,
     a.   the sample mean will equal the sample median.
     b.   the sample beam and fulcrum will contain at least 6 standard deviations.
     c.   the sample box plot will have very long whiskers.
     d.   the sample histogram should be bell-shaped.
     e.   the sample mean is more accurate than if the sample was drawn with replacement.

11. Which of the following is *not* true of an outlier?
     a.   An outlier should be discarded since it is not part of the population being sampled.
     b.   An outlier is more than 3 standard deviations from the mean.
     c.   An outlier can be generated by a different population.
     d.   An outlier can be generated by the population being sampled.
     e.   All of the above are true of outliers.

12. Which of the following distributions can be either right-skewed or left-skewed?
     a.   Normal distribution.
     b.   Chi-square distribution.
     c.   Student's t distribution.
     d.   Triangular distribution.
     e.   Exponential distribution.

Glossary of Terms

Beam and fulcrum Display that plots the position of the sample mean (the "fulcrum") and the standard deviation points (Mean ± 1 SD, Mean ± 2 SD, Mean ± 3 SD, etc.). This display reveals skewness (the longer tail will indicate the direction of skewness) and kurtosis (the more standard deviations displayed along the beam, the more peaked the data).

Bimodal Population whose probability distribution has two peaks separated by a valley. In reference to a sample histogram, it would refer to two intervals that have higher frequencies than their adjacent intervals. See **Unimodal**.

Box plot Five-number graphical display plotting the positions of the minimum, quartiles (first, second, third), and maximum along a scale representing data values. The box encloses the quartiles and the span of the whiskers indicates the range.

Centrality General reference to measures of the middle of a distribution (for example: mean, median, mode, midrange).

Dispersion General reference to measures of "spread" of data values around the center of a distribution (for example: standard deviation, range).

Finite population Population with N elements.

Infinite population Population whose elements are uncountably large.

Kurtosis Measure of relative peakedness. If a distribution is unimodal and symmetric, then $K = 3$ indicates a normal bell-shaped distribution (mesokurtic); $K < 3$ indicates a platykurtic distribution (flatter than normal with shorter tails); and $K > 3$ indicates a leptokurtic distribution (more peaked than normal with longer tails).

Mean For a population, the mean is the expected value of X, denoted μ. It may be thought of as the probability-weighted average of the X values and may be interpreted as the fulcrum (balancing point) of the distribution along the X-axis. For a sample, the mean (denoted $\overline{X}$) is the sum of the sample items divided by the sample size.

Outlier Any sample observation that differs from the mean by 3 or more standard deviations.

Peakedness See **Kurtosis**.

Population Any collection of data values that are being sampled.

Population distribution The probability density function f(x) defined over the a range of values of a random variable. The ordinate shows the probability associated with each X value. The area under the entire distribution is 1.

Random sample A sample selected from a population by a method that ensures that every population element has the same chance of being chosen. Simple random sampling may be done using tables or computer-generated random numbers.

Random variation Sample items do not consistently lead to a perfect representation of a population. This variation is reduced if the sample size is increased. Such variation is expected, and can be quantified using the rules of statistics.

Replacement Sampling method used with a finite population in which an item is sampled and then returned to the population possibly to be sampled again. Sampling with replacement keeps the probability of drawing each item in the population unchanged. If sampling is done without replacement, the selected item is not returned to the population so the probability of selecting any of the remaining items from the population is changed.

Sample Set of observations taken from a population (usually, but not necessarily, by random sampling). See **Replacement**.

Sample size Number of items in a sample, usually denoted n.

Skewed population A population is skewed right and has a long right tail if its mean exceeds its median (and conversely if the population is skewed left).

Skewness Measure of relative symmetry. Zero indicates symmetry. Positive values show a long right tail. Negative values show a long left tail.

Standard deviation Denoted s (for a sample) or σ (for a population), it is the square root of the variance. It is a measure of dispersion about the mean. The larger the standard deviation, the greater the dispersion. See **Variance**.

Statistical inference Generalization about a population, based on a sample that has been drawn from the population. Often associated with a probability or confidence that the inference is correct.

Symmetry See **Skewness**.

Unimodal Population whose probability density function has one peak. In reference to a sample histogram, it would refer to an interval (bin) with higher frequencies than other intervals. See **Bimodal**.

Variance In a population, the variance is the expected value of $(X - \mu)^2$ and is denoted σ^2. In a sample, the variance is the sum of the squared deviations about the sample mean divided by $n - 1$ and is denoted s^2. It is a measure of dispersion about the mean.

Solutions to Self-Evaluation Quiz

1. b   Do Exercises 1–7, and 8–11. Read the Illustration of Concepts.
2. c   Do Exercises 2–6. Read the Illustration of Concepts.
3. c   Do Exercises 2–5. Read the Illustration of Concepts.
4. d   Do Exercise 8. Review Chapter 5.
5. e   Do Exercises 1–7. Review Chapter 2.
6. d   Do Exercise 1. Do Team Learning Project 1. Review Chapter 1.
7. d   Do Exercises 8–11. Review Chapter 2.
8. e   Do Exercises 10–11. Review Chapters 2 and 3.
9. b   Do Exercises 12–15. Read the Overview of Concepts.
10. e   Do Exercises 12–15. Read the Overview of Concepts.
11. a   Do Exercises 16–20. Read the Overview of Concepts. Review Chapter 1.
12. d   Do Exercise 21.

CHAPTER 7

Visualizing the
Central Limit Theorem

CONCEPTS
- Central Limit Theorem, Population Being Sampled, Sampling Distribution, Population Mean, Standard Error, Standard Deviation, Asymptotic

OBJECTIVES
- Recognize the difference between the population being sampled and the sampling distribution of the mean

- Comprehend the importance of the Central Limit Theorem

- Discern the difference between the standard error of the sampling distribution and the standard deviation of the population

- Understand the role of sample size in determining the standard error of the sampling distribution

Overview of Concepts

Pierre Simon Laplace's (1749–1827) major contribution to probability theory is now called the **Central Limit Theorem**, where the term *central* means fundamental rather than middle or center. His work was a generalization of the work of Abraham De Moivre. Whereas De Moivre (1667–1754) had shown that if the number of trials is very large, a symmetric binomial distribution becomes what we now call the normal distribution, Laplace showed that the sum or mean of independently drawn random variables will, if the sample size is large, be approximately normally distributed. Over the years this was further generalized and regularity conditions were added until the final form we use today was produced by Lindberg in 1922.

The Central Limit Theorem can be formally stated as follows: If $X_1, X_2, \ldots, X_n$ are identically distributed independent random variables from any population with finite mean μ and finite variance σ^2, then the sample mean $\overline{X} = (x_1 + x_2 + \ldots + x_n) / n$ will have a sampling distribution with mean μ and variance σ^2 / n. Further, the sampling distribution of $\overline{X}$ is asymptotically normally distributed.

This theorem has several important aspects. First, the **population being sampled** must have both a **population mean** (μ) and a **standard deviation** (σ). While the vast majority of distributions satisfy this requirement, there are distributions that lack a standard deviation, and some that have neither a standard deviation nor a mean. For example, a Student's t distribution with 2 degrees of freedom doesn't have a standard deviation (if you have not studied this distribution, you will later in the course), while a Student's t with 1 degree of freedom doesn't have a mean or a standard deviation. Second, all of the random variables $X_1, X_2, \ldots, X_n$ must be *independently* drawn from the same population. Therefore, drawing one random variable will not affect the chances of drawing any other random variable. This would be violated, for example, if you sampled from a hypergeometric distribution. Third, the sample mean has its own distribution called a **sampling distribution**. The mean of the sampling distribution is μ, the same as the mean of the population being sampled. The **standard error** (denoted $\sigma_{\overline{x}}$) of the sampling distribution is $\sigma / \sqrt{n}$ and is the square root of the variance of the sampling distribution. Note that the standard error will get smaller as your sample size n increases. Fourth, if the sample size is large enough, then the sampling distribution is approximately normally distributed, regardless of the population's shape. Since this will always be true only as $n \to \infty$, this is called an **asymptotic** result.

An intuitive explanation of the Central Limit Theorem is possible. Assume that you draw a sample of n observations from a population and calculate the sample mean. You then draw a new sample and calculate a new sample mean. If you redo this process many times, the average of these sample means will be near μ, and their standard error will be near $\sigma / \sqrt{n}$. Further, if n is large enough and you made a dot plot or histogram of all of the sample means, they would approximately form a normal distribution.

This is a very important theorem. It tells a statistician that even if the underlying population is skewed, or bimodal, the sample means will be approximately normally distributed if a large enough sample size is used. It also says that regardless of the size of the sample, the sample mean has the same mean as the original population and its standard error is much smaller than the standard deviation of the population sampled. This result will be invaluable when you learn to make inferences about a population.

Illustration of Concepts

A coal-fired electric power plant emits sulfur dioxide (SO_2). The power plant continuously measures these emissions and records its average emissions daily. To be in compliance with the EPA, a plant's daily emissions can exceed 140 parts per billion (ppb) only one day per year and must average below 30 ppb for the entire year. Twenty samples are taken. Is the power plant currently in compliance? Will the power plant be in compliance at the end of the year?

Below is a histogram of a sample of SO_2 emissions. The population being sampled has been superimposed as a line (this is drawn for your benefit but is not known to the company). It is clear from the histogram that the plant does not have any emissions over 140 ppb. However, it is not clear whether the plant will meet the yearly requirement of averaging under 30 ppb. Based on the 20 days sampled, the sample mean is 32 ppb. Although the **mean** of the **population being sampled** is unknown, the company's statistician knows, based on experience with the technology, that the population is positively skewed and has a **standard deviation** of 16. Therefore she poses the following question: "Is this sample mean consistent with the belief that the true mean is less than 30 ppb?"

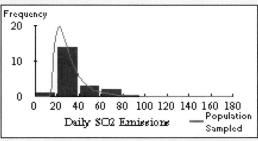

Figure 1: Histogram of Sulphur Dioxide Emissions

In order to answer this question she used the **Central Limit Theorem** to find out what the mean should be to make it very unlikely (since the EPA fine for noncompliance is very large) that the sample mean would be greater than 30 at the end of the year. The Central Limit Theorem provides the **asymptotic** result that if n $\to \infty$, then the **sampling distribution** is normally distributed. At the end of the year the company will have 365 samples. This is large enough to know that the sampling distribution is normally distributed. In addition, since the standard deviation is 16, the **standard error** of the sample mean at the end of the year is 0.8375 (16 divided by the square root of 365). Therefore, if the population mean is no more than 27.9 (= 30 − 2.5 × 0.8375), there is less than a 0.62% chance of being fined.

The question then becomes, "Is a sample mean of 32, after 20 observations, consistent with a population mean of 27.9?" To make this calculation, the statistician assumes that the sample of 20 is large enough so that the sampling distribution is approximately normally distributed (she knows, given the modest degree of skewness in the population being sampled, that this is not a bad assumption). The standard error of the sample mean with 20 observations is 3.578 (16 divided by the square root of 20). Therefore the probability that $\overline{X} \geq 32$ is

$Pr(\overline{X} \geq 32 \mid \mu = 27.9$ and $\sigma_{\overline{x}} = 3.578) = Pr (Z \geq (32\text{-}27.9)/3.578) = Pr (Z \geq 1.14) = 0.1271$. Hence, there is a 13% chance that the power plant's actual mean is 27.9 ppb or less. Given the size of the fine if the power plant does not meet the 30 ppb requirement, the company should use the 11 months still remaining to readjust their scrubbers and other pollution abatement equipment to increase their chances of meeting the EPA's yearly requirement.

Orientation to Basic Features

This module allows you to draw a sample from a normal, uniform, or skewed distribution, in order to demonstrate the similarity between the Central Limit Theorem's predictions and the sample results. You can also sample from two populations simultaneously to compare different population parameters or different sample sizes.

1.   **Opening Screen**
     Start the module by clicking on the module's icon, title, or chapter number in the *Visual Statistics* menu and pressing the Run Module button. When the module is loaded, you will be on the introduction page of the Notebook. Read the questions and then click the Concepts tab to see the concepts that you will learn. Click on the Scenarios tab. Select Normal Distribution from the table of choices. Select a scenario, read it, and press OK. The upper left of the screen shows the population being sampled. The Control Panel is to its right. On the lower left of the screen is the sampling distribution of the mean as stated in the Central Limit Theorem (assuming a large sample size). To the right of the sampling distribution is the statistics panel containing the population and sampling distribution statistics. The population mean is shown as a fulcrum below each distribution.

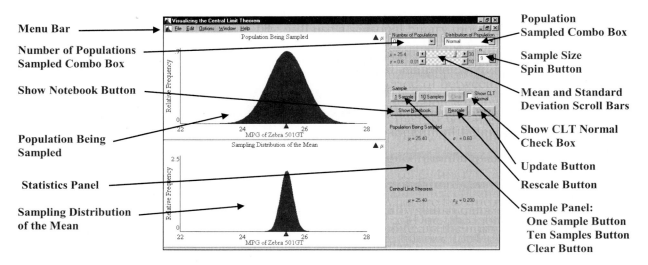

2.   **Control Panel**
     a.   Click the One Sample button in the Sample panel. A dot plot of the sample is superimposed on the population being sampled. A small fulcrum showing the sample mean appears below the dot plot (the large fulcrum is the population mean). That sample mean is placed on the

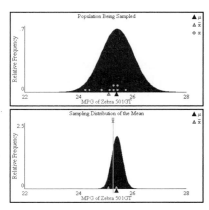

sampling distribution. Push the One Sample button again to generate a second sample and dot plot. The new sample mean is shown on the top display and is placed on the sampling distribution. The mean of these two sample means is shown as a vertical line on the sampling distribution. The fulcrum is the population mean.

Sample statistics appear in the statistics panel to the right. Push the Clear button in the Sample panel to clear the dot plot and sample statistics from the displays. Push the Ten Samples button to draw 10 samples and display them on the dot plot one after the other. Press the Stop Sampling button to quit after the last sample is displayed. Press the Skip to End button if you want to avoid redrawing the displays after each sample is drawn. The final result of taking the 10 samples is still displayed.

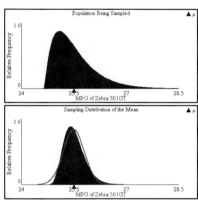

Population Being Sampled

$\mu = 25.40$ $\sigma = 0.60$

Current Sample $n = 9$

$\bar{x} = 25.58$ $s = 0.48$

Central Limit Theorem

$\mu = 25.40$ $\sigma_{\bar{x}} = 0.200$

Accumulation of 10 Samples

$\bar{\bar{x}} = 25.49$ $s_{\bar{x}} = 0.213$

b. Click the n spin button to change the sample size. Press the flashing Update button to redraw the display. Note that the sampling distribution changes.

c. Click the μ or σ scroll bars to change the mean or standard deviation. Press the flashing Update button to redraw the display with a new mean or standard deviation. Note how both distributions change. (Since you have changed the population parameters, the scenario may no longer have meaning.)

d. Push the Rescale button to rescale both distributions. A warning message appears if the distributions disappear from the screen.

e. Click on the population sampled combo box and select Skewed Population (since you have changed the population, the scenario may no longer have meaning). The population being sampled changes, as does the sampling distribution (illustrated on the right). The Central Limit Theorem says that sampling distribution of the mean will be normal *if* the sample size is large enough (its mean and standard error are shown on the Statistics panel). Click Show CLT Normal to superimpose the normal distribution predicted by the Central Limit Theorem on the sampling distribution in the lower diagram. In this illustration, the sampling distribution is not exactly normal.

3. **Copying a Display**

Click on the display you wish to copy. Its window title will be highlighted. Select Copy from the Edit menu (on the menu bar at the top of the screen) or Ctrl-C to copy the display. It can then be pasted into other applications, such as Word or WordPerfect, so it can be printed.

4. **Help**

Click on Help on the menu bar at the top of the screen. Search for Help lets you search a topic index, Contents shows a table of contents for this module, Using Help gives instructions on how to use Help, and About gives licensing and copyright information about this *Visual Statistics* module.

5. **Exit**

Close the module by selecting Exit in the File menu (or click ☒ in the upper right-hand corner of the window). You will be returned to the *Visual Statistics* main menu.

Orientation to Additional Features

1. **Two Populations**
   Click on the number of populations sampled combo box and select Two Populations. Two populations can now be sampled simultaneously. This can be useful to compare distributions with different means, standard deviations, or sample sizes. The area of overlap of the red and blue distributions is shown in magenta.

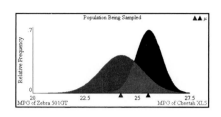

2. **Do-It-Yourself**
   Push the Show Notebook button and select the Do-It-Yourself tab. Press OK to return to the main screen with the illustrative scenario labels removed from the graphs. Use the μ and σ scroll bars to create your own examples.

3. **Options**
   Five sets of options are available from the Options menu on the menu bar.
   a. Select Change Title if you wish to retitle the current display.
   b. Select Auto Update if you wish to have the displays automatically updated when a Control Panel change is made.
   c. Select Auto Rescale if you wish to have the displays automatically rescaled when the displays are updated. With this option, graphs often look unchanged, but the scale on the axis has changed.
   d. Select Full Window Graph from the Options menu. This extends your graph to the full width of your computer screen. Deselect Hide Controls in the Options menu to make the controls reappear.

4. **Second Display**
   Select either Copy Default Window or Copy Current Window from the Windows menu on the menu bar. This creates a second graph that you can Tile or Cascade (from the Windows menu). Use the Change Title option (see 3a above) to retitle the display. This feature is useful to label different examples that are displayed simultaneously.

Basic Learning Exercises

Name _____

Sampling a Normal Population

Press the Show Notebook button, select the Scenarios tab, click on Normal Distribution, and select Fuel Economy. Read the scenario and click on OK.

1. What is the mean and standard deviation of the population being sampled? What is the mean and standard error of the sampling distribution? What is the relationship between the standard deviation of the population being sampled and the sampling distribution? If you aren't sure use the Help option on the menu bar.

    Population Being Sampled: Mean _____   Standard Deviation _____
    Sampling Distribution: Mean _____   Standard Error _____

2. Push the One Sample button on the Sample panel. Do all of the *individual* observations on mileage meet the company's expectation of at least 25 mpg? On *average*, do the cars meet the company's expectations? To which diagram (upper or lower) did you refer to answer these questions? If there is a difference in your answers to these questions, explain.

3. If the company were to advertise average mileage of 25 mpg, would this be misleading to its customers? Explain.

4. Increase the sample size to 25 by using the n spin button or by typing directly into the box and pressing the Enter key. Click Update. What is the standard deviation of the population? What is the standard error of the sampling distribution? Why did the latter change? How did the lower diagram's appearance change?

    Standard Deviation _____   Standard Error _____

5. If you wanted a standard error of 0.06 for the sampling distribution, what sample size would you need? Explain.

6. Give a formal statement of the Central Limit Theorem. In your own words, what does it mean? **Hint:** Use the Help feature if you do not remember the CLT.

7. How does exercise 5 use the Central Limit Theorem?

8. Reduce n to 2 using its spin button. Press the Ten Samples button five times. Is the sampling distribution formed by the dot plot normally distributed? Is so, why; if not, why not?

9. Press the Show Notebook button and select the Two Different Fruit Sorters scenario. Read the scenario and click OK. Describe the populations that you see.

10. Answer the two questions in the scenario (click the Show Notebook button if you need to re-read the scenario). How does the Central Limit Theorem help you answer the questions posed in the scenario?

Intermediate Learning Exercises   Name _____

Sampling a Nonnormal Population

Press the Show Notebook button, select the Scenario tab, and select Other Distributions. Select the Pizza Delivery scenario. Read the scenario and press the OK button.

11. Why would the time it takes to deliver a pizza have a skewed distribution like the one shown?

12. Select Show CLT Normal on the Control Panel. Press the Ten Samples button four times. This generates 40 sample means and displays them on the sampling distribution. Does the experimental sampling distribution you created look like the normal sampling distribution based on the CLT that is shown? Why or why not? Is this result consistent with the Central Limit Theorem?

13. If you increased your sample size to 20, would you expect the experimental sampling distribution to be similar to the normal sampling distribution? *Answer this exercise without using the computer.*

14. Increase your sample size to 20 by using the n spin button or entering the number directly into the spin button box and pressing Enter on your computer. Press the Ten Samples button four times. Did you answer exercise 13 correctly? If not, re-answer that same exercise below.

15. If you had a very skewed distribution, would a sample size of 20 always be large enough to generate a normal sampling distribution? **Hint**: Change the distribution to Very Skewed.

16. Push the Show Notebook button and select the Two Truck Drivers scenario. Read the scenario and push the OK button. Answer the scenario's questions. How does this scenario illustrate the Central Limit Theorem?

17. Push the Show Notebook button and select the Random Number scenario. Read the scenario and push the OK button. Answer the scenario's questions. How does this scenario illustrate the Central Limit Theorem?

18. Reduce n to 2 using its spin button. Press the Ten Samples button five times. Is the sampling distribution formed by the dot plot normally distributed? If so, why? If not, why not?

19. Increase n to 6. Press the Ten Samples button five times. Is the sampling distribution formed by the dot plot normally distributed? If so, why? If not, why not?

20. Is it easy or difficult to see the exact shape of the sampling distribution by looking at the dot plot of the sample means (the little triangles)? Explain.

Advanced Learning Exercises   Name _____

An Unbiased Estimator for μ

Push the Show Notebook button, select the Do-It-Yourself tab and press OK. Use the list boxes at the top of the Control Panel to show One Population and Skewed Population. Set σ to 20. Set μ to any value you wish. Push the flashing Update button.

21. Set sample size to 2 using the n spin button or entering the number in the spin button box. Press the One Sample button twice. The sample means from each draw are shown as a dot plot on top of the sampling distribution. Notice that a vertical line is drawn through the sampling distribution. This is the average of the two sample means. It is denoted as $\overline{\overline{X}}$. The average should be located halfway between the two sample means (because of the nature of the dot plot of the two sample means this sometimes appears to be incorrect, but it is not). Where is $\overline{\overline{X}}$ in relation to the population mean μ (the fulcrum below the sampling distribution)?

22. Press the One Sample button again. How did the position of $\overline{\overline{X}}$ change?

23. Press the One Sample button three more times watching what happens to the position of $\overline{\overline{X}}$ after each new sample is drawn. Do you notice a general pattern? If you do, explain what you have noticed. If you don't, continue to press the One Sample button until a pattern emerges, and then describe the pattern you observed. (Sometimes because of sampling variation a pattern was not evident. If this occurs after 10 samples are drawn, press the Clear button on the Sample panel and repeat exercises 21–22.)

24. Verify this pattern by pressing the Ten Samples button. Press the Ten Samples button a second time. Press the Ten Samples button a third time. What pattern did you observe?

25. If the average of many estimates equals the parameter's value, then the estimator provides an unbiased estimate for the parameter. *Therefore, the sample mean is an unbiased estimator for μ.* If this property is *only* true for large sample sizes, then the property is called asymptotically unbiased. Increase the sample size to 25. What do you observe; does the same pattern hold? Are there any modifications to your previous observation that you could make as a result of increasing the sample size?

A Consistent Estimator for μ

26. An estimator is called a consistent estimator for a parameter if the estimator is either an unbiased or an asymptotically unbiased estimator for the parameter *and* if as the sample size increases, the standard error of the sampling distribution gets smaller. What is the standard error if sample size is 4? 16? 64? 256? Is the sample mean a consistent estimator for μ? **Note:** Advanced students may recognize that this is not the correct formal definition of consistency. This type of consistency is sometimes called Mean Squared Error Consistency. However, for practical purposes, it is an appropriate substitute.

Standard error if n = 4 _____   Standard error if n = 16 _____
Standard error if n = 64 _____   Standard error if n = 256 _____

Individual Learning Projects

Write a report on one of the three topics listed below. Use the cut-and-paste facilities of the module to place the appropriate graphs in your report.

1. Investigate the normality of the sampling distribution. Set your sample size to 2 and draw 50 samples. Are your sample means normally distributed? If not, double your sample size and draw 50 more samples. Continue this process until your plot of sample means is normally distributed. What sample size was needed? Repeat the process for the other two populations. Write a report on what you have you learned describing in detail how this illustrates the Central Limit Theorem. Be sure to include a copy of *every* plot of sample means you evaluated.

2. Investigate how the sample means enable you to discriminate between two samples. Select Two Populations and select one of the three populations. Set both σ's to 5, sample sizes to 25, and μ's equal to one another. Draw 30 samples. Then increase one of the μ's by 1, update your graphs, and draw 30 more samples. Evaluate the overlap in the populations, the sampling distributions, and the dot plots of sample means. Repeat, continuing to separate the μ's until you can identify from which population *each* sample mean came. At that point, how far apart are the two means? Is this result consistent with the Central Limit Theorem? Write a report on what you have you learned. Do you think you could generalize this finding to other populations, σ's, or sample sizes? Include a copy of *every* population and sampling distribution you evaluated in your report.

3. Do project 2 with the following changes. Set both σ's to 8, set sample sizes to 25, and set one μ to be five units greater than the other μ. After evaluating the overlap, halve both σ's. Continue this process of halving the σ's until you can identify from which population *each* sample mean came. What is your value for σ? Is this result consistent with the Central Limit Theorem? Write a report on what you have learned. Do you think you could generalize this finding to other populations, sample sizes, or other differences in the μ's? Include a copy of *every* population and sampling distribution you evaluated.

Team Learning Projects

Select one of the three projects listed below. In each case, produce a team project that is suitable for an oral presentation. Use presentation software or large poster boards to display your results. Graphs should be large enough for your audience to see. Each team member should be responsible for producing some of the graphs. Ask your instructor if a written report is also expected.

1. A team of three can investigate the importance of sample size in discriminating between two samples. In the list box select Two Populations. Each team member should select a different population type (normal, uniform, skewed). Set both σ's to 2, sample sizes to 2, and set one μ to 1.0 greater than the other μ. Draw 20 samples. Each time evaluate the overlap in each of the following: populations, sampling distributions, and plot of sample means. Double both n's. Update your graphs, draw 20 more samples and again evaluate the overlaps. Continue this process until you can identify from which population *each* sample mean came. What is your value for n? Is this consistent with the Central Limit Theorem? Do you think you could generalize this finding if you sampled other populations, σ's, or differences in the μ's? Include illustrations of *every* population and sampling distribution you evaluated.

2. A team of three can investigate whether the sample mean is a consistent estimator for the population mean. Each team member should select a different population. Select any μ and σ. Set the sample size to 4. Draw 20 samples. Write down the average of the sample means and the standard error of the sample means. Repeat the process using sample sizes of 8, 16, 32, 64, and 128. How does this show that the sample mean is a consistent estimator for μ? Prepare an oral report on what you have you learned. Do you think you could generalize this finding if you sampled other populations? If you used other μ's? If you used other σ's? Be sure to include illustrations of the sampling distribution for *each* of the seven sample sizes for each population.

3. A team of three can investigate whether the sample mean is an unbiased estimator for the population mean. Each team member should select a different population. Select any μ and σ. Set the sample size to 2. Draw five samples. Write down the average of the sample means and the standard error of the sample means. Draw another five samples and write down the average of the sample means and their standard error. Continue drawing more samples and writing down the average of the sample means and their standard error for 20, 40, 60, 80, and 100 samples. How does this show that the sample mean is an unbiased estimator for μ? Prepare an oral report on what you have you learned. Do you think you could generalize this finding if you sampled other populations? If you used other μ's? If you used other σ's? If you used other sample sizes? Be sure to include illustrations of the sampling distribution showing *each* of your seven different numbers of samples (5, 10, 20, 40, 60, 80 and 100) for each population.

Self-Evaluation Quiz

1. The term "Central" in the Central Limit Theorem has which meaning?
    a. Middle.
    b. Fundamental.
    c. Central tendency.
    d. Sample mean.
    e. All of the above.

2. The Central Limit Theorem
    a. specifies certain asymptotic properties of the sample mean.
    b. is the basis for most statistical estimation.
    c. stems from work by many mathematicians, including De Moivre (1733), Laplace (1810), and Lindberg (1922).
    d. was discovered by Fra Luca Paciolo in 1494.
    e. all except d.

3. The Central Limit Theorem says
    a. that sample items will always form a normal, bell-shaped histogram.
    b. that the variance of the sample mean is the same as the population variance.
    c. that the variance of the sample mean exceeds the population variance.
    d. that the sample mean is a biased estimator of the mean if the population is not normal.
    e. none of the above.

4. If a normal population has parameters $\mu = 40$ and $\sigma = 8$, then for a sample of size $n = 4$
    a. the standard error of the sample mean is approximately 4.
    b. the standard error of the sample mean is approximately 2.
    c. the standard error of the sample mean is approximately 8.
    d. the standard error of the sample mean is approximately 10.
    e. the standard error depends on the population's shape.

5. If sample A with n items and sample B with 2n items are taken from a population, then
    a. the mean of sample A has a smaller expected variance than the mean of sample B.
    b. the mean of sample A has a greater expected variance than the mean of sample B.
    c. the ratio of the sample variances will be 2 to 1.
    d. the relative variance of the sample means will depend on the population shape.
    e. the variance of either sample will follow a normal distribution.

6. If the standard error of the mean is 12 when the sample size is 4, then if we increase the sample size to 16 the standard error will be
    a. 24
    b. 12
    c. 8
    d. 6
    e. None of the above.

7.   The standard error of the mean is
     a.   the standard deviation of the sample items.
     b.   a measure of bias in sampling.
     c.   the sample deviation of the standard normal distribution.
     d.   an unbiased estimator of the population variance.
     e.   none of the above.

8.   The Central Limit Theorem applies to
     a.   normally distributed populations.
     b.   right-skewed populations.
     c.   all populations with finite mean and variance.
     d.   platykurtic populations.
     e.   uniform populations.

9.   The distribution of the mean of a sample of n items is
     a.   normal if the population is normal and σ is known.
     b.   approximately normal if n exceeds 20 and the population is moderately skewed.
     c.   approximately normal if n exceeds 10 and the population is uniform.
     d.   not always approximately normal if n exceeds 20.
     e.   all of the above.

10. Which statement is correct?
     a.   The sample mean is always an unbiased estimator of the population mean.
     b.   The sample mean has a smaller variance than the population if n is at least 2.
     c.   The sample mean has approximately a normal distribution if n is large.
     d.   All of the above are correct.
     e.   None of the above is correct.

11. Which is *not* true of a sample mean based on n items from a skewed, bimodal population
     with mean μ and variance σ^2?
     a.   It will follow a bimodal distribution if n is very small.
     b.   It will follow a normal distribution if n is large.
     c.   It will be biased because of skewness.
     d.   It will follow a skewed distribution if n is small.
     e.   It has expected value μ.

12. A consistent estimator
     a.   collapses on the true parameter as the population variance increases.
     b.   collapses on the true parameter as the sample size increases.
     c.   consistently follows a normal distribution.
     d.   does not vary randomly from the true parameter.
     e.   is impossible to obtain from real sample data.

Glossary of Terms

Asymptotic Statistical properties that are evident in sufficiently large samples. Usually, this refers to a sample size that approaches infinity (denoted as $n \to \infty$).

Central Limit Theorem This well-known theorem says that if the sample size is large enough, sample means from any population (even a non-normal population) will follow a normal distribution with the same mean as the population but with a smaller variance. More formally, if $x_1, x_2, \ldots, x_n$ are identically distributed independent random variables from any population with finite mean μ and finite variance σ^2, then the sample mean $\overline{X} = (x_1 + x_2 + \ldots + x_n)\,/\,n$ will have a sampling distribution with mean μ and variance σ^2/n. Further, the sampling distribution of $\overline{X}$ is asymptotically normally distributed.

Consistent estimator One that is unbiased (or asymptotically unbiased) and whose standard error decreases as the sample size increases. For example, the Central Limit Theorem says that the sample mean is a consistent estimator of μ, because as the sample size increases the distribution of the sample mean is centered at μ and becomes narrower (as $n \to \infty$, the distribution collapses on μ). This definition of consistency is also known as mean squared error consistency.

Mean For a population or a sampling distribution, the mean is the expected value of X, denoted as μ. It may be thought of as the probability-weighted average of the X values and may be interpreted as the fulcrum (balancing point) of the distribution along the X-axis. For a sample, the mean is the sum of the sample items divided by the sample size. It is denoted $\overline{X}$.

Normal population Bell-shaped or Gaussian distribution. It has two parameters: the mean μ and the variance σ^2.

Population being sampled In the Central Limit Theorem, the population from which the sample is drawn. It can have any shape, but it must have a finite mean and standard deviation.

Population distribution Probability density function f(x) showing the probability associated with each x value. The area under the entire distribution is 1 (or the sum of the probabilities if x is a discrete variable).

Population mean See **Mean**.

Sampling distribution Theoretical distribution of an estimator derived from a sample, such as the sample mean. According to the Central Limit Theorem, regardless of the population being sampled, the sample mean's sampling distribution has a mean μ and standard deviation $\sigma/\sqrt{n}$. It is normally distributed if the sample size is large enough.

Skewed population A population is skewed right and has a long right tail if its mean exceeds its median (and conversely, if the population is skewed left).

Standard deviation Denoted σ, it is the square root of the population variance. It is a measure of dispersion about the mean. Larger σ values indicate greater dispersion.

Standard error Standard deviation of the sample mean, given by the Central Limit Theorem. The theoretical standard error of the sample mean is generally denoted $\sigma_{\bar{x}}$ and its formula is $\sigma/\sqrt{n}$ where σ is the population standard deviation and n is the sample size. If the standard error is estimated from a sample, it is generally denoted $s_{\bar{x}}$ and its formula is $s/\sqrt{n}$ where s is the sample standard deviation and n is the sample size.

Unbiased estimator An estimator is unbiased if its expected value equals the parameter it is estimating. The Central Limit Theorem says that the sample mean is an unbiased estimator of μ. That is, the average of a large number of sample means will equal μ.

Uniform population A distribution that assigns the same probability to each X value in the domain $a \leq X \leq b$. It is a rectangle with base $b - a$ (the range of X) and height $1/(b - a)$.

Variance In a population, the variance is the expected value of $(X - \mu)^2$ and is denoted σ^2. In a sample, the variance is the sum of the squared deviations about the sample mean divided by $n - 1$ and is denoted s^2.

Solutions to Self-Evaluation Quiz

1. b   Read the Overview of Concepts.
2. e   Read the Overview of Concepts.
3. e   Read the Overview of Concepts.
4. a   Do Exercise 1. Read the Overview and the Illustration of Concepts.
5. b   Do Exercises 1 and 4. Read the Overview of Concepts.
6. d   Do Exercises 1–4. Read the Overview of Concepts.
7. e   Do Exercise 1. Read the Overview of Concepts.
8. c   Do Exercises 11–15. Read the Overview of Concepts.
9. e   Do Exercises 8, 13–15, 18, and 19. Read the Illustration of Concepts.
10. d   Read the Overview of Concepts. Do Exercises 21–25.
11. c   Do Exercises 11–19 and 21–25.
12. b   Do Exercise 26.

CHAPTER 8

Visualizing Properties of Estimators

CONCEPTS
- Estimator, Properties, Parameter, Unbiased Estimator, Relatively Efficient Estimator, Consistent Estimator, Asymptotically Unbiased Estimator, Sufficient Estimator, Sampling Distribution, Empirical Sampling Distribution

OBJECTIVES
- Recognize how the distribution of an estimator is affected by sample size and the shape of the distribution being sampled

- Understand the properties of unbiasedness, asymptotic unbiasedness, relative efficiency, consistency, and sufficiency

- Realize that there are a variety of estimators for a parameter

- Recognize that not all estimators for a parameter are equally good in terms of their properties

Overview of Concepts

An **estimator** or sample statistic is a formula that enables the statistician to estimate an unknown **parameter** based upon a sample of data. The value obtained is called an estimate. This estimate provides the statistician with a possible value for the unknown parameter. However, because a variety of alternative estimators may be used to estimate an unknown parameter, statisticians have developed a list of desirable **properties** that can be used to evaluate the different estimators.

The most fundamental of these properties is called *unbiasedness*. An **unbiased estimator** is one whose expected value equals the unknown parameter. This means that if a very large number of samples are drawn and an estimate of the unknown parameter is obtained from each sample, the average value of those estimates will equal the parameter value. A related property is called *asymptotic unbiasedness*. An **asymptotically unbiased estimator** is a biased estimator whose bias goes to zero as the sample size approaches infinity.

Another important property is called *efficiency*. An efficient estimator is the estimator that has the smallest variance out of *all* unbiased estimators for the parameter. Because this is generally impossible to show (since there may be a very large number of unbiased estimators), statisticians have developed sophisticated methods to prove that an estimator is efficient. A less-encompassing but related property is called *relative efficiency*. Estimator A is a **relatively efficient estimator** compared with estimator B if A has a smaller variance than B *and* both A and B are unbiased estimators for the parameter.

Another asymptotic property is called *consistency*. A **consistent estimator** is an estimator whose probability of being close to the parameter increases as the sample size increases. The probability approaches 1 as the sample size approaches infinity. This property is often demonstrated by showing that an unbiased or asymptotically unbiased estimator has a standard error that decreases as the sample size increases. As a result, the estimator collapses on the parameter value as the sample size approaches infinity. This property is called mean squared error consistency. An estimator that is mean squared error consistent is a consistent estimator; however, it is possible for an estimator to be consistent even if it is not mean squared error consistent. This atypical situation will not be considered in this module.

The final statistical property considered here is *sufficiency*. A **sufficient estimator** is an estimator that uses all available information in a sample about the parameter it is estimating. Statisticians prefer sufficient estimators because they usually have a smaller variance.

In this module you can conduct experiments to construct the **empirical sampling distribution** for a variety of estimators for μ (population mean) and σ^2 (population variance). This empirical sampling distribution can be compared with the theoretical **sampling distribution** of either $\overline{X}$ or s^2. In addition, the mean of the empirical sampling distribution can be compared with the true population parameter, and the variance of the empirical sampling distribution can be examined to see if it decreases as the sample size is increased.

With the development of high speed computers, an entire class of new estimators has been developed. They are called resampling or bootstrap estimators (originally developed by Brad Efron and others since 1979). These estimators base the estimate on the average result after you resample your original sample K times. Using this technique, the bootstrap estimator for the variance was developed. This has turned out to be a relatively efficient estimator compared with the traditional sample variance estimator, s^2.

Illustration of Concepts

The **estimator** $\overline{X}$ (sample mean) is an **unbiased estimator** for the **parameter** μ (population mean). This can be verified by conducting a simulation experiment. Consider light bulb failures. Many light bulb packages state that a light bulb will last an average of 1,000 hours ($\mu = 1000$). This can be modeled using an exponential distribution with $\lambda = 0.001$ (reciprocal of the mean) as shown in Figure 1.

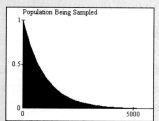

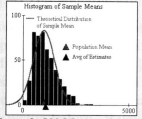

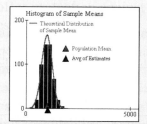

Figure 1: Exponential Distribution **Figure 2: 500 Means with n = 4** **Figure 3: 500 Means with n = 16**

We take 500 samples of size 4 from this exponential population, find the mean of each sample, and create a histogram of the 500 means to get an **empirical sampling distribution**.

The Central Limit Theorem says that $\overline{X}$ will have a normal distribution if the sample size is large enough. If we superimpose a normal **sampling distribution** (Figure 2) with a mean of 1000 and a variance of $\sigma^2/n = 1000^2/4 = 250,000$ on our histogram, we see that the histogram of means is somewhat skewed (although much less so than the exponential population). This suggests that n = 4 is not large enough for the sampling distribution to be normal when sampling an exponential distribution. For this experiment, the mean of the 500 sample means (980.4) was very close to the population mean ($\mu = 1000$), providing evidence that the sample mean is an unbiased estimator for μ (the difference is due to sample variation).

The sample mean is a **consistent estimator** of the population mean that will collapse on the true mean μ when n is large. For an unbiased or an **asymptotically unbiased estimator,** consistency can be demonstrated by showing that the estimator's standard error decreases as the sample size increases. To do this, we repeat the previous experiment using a larger sample size of n = 16, obtaining the histogram shown in Figure 3. Despite the skewed population, the histogram for n = 16 is nearly symmetric, is narrower than for n = 4, and is almost normally distributed, as suggested by the Central Limit Theorem. The 500 sample means have a mean of 1,005.1 and a variance of 61,504 (quite close to the theoretical values of $\mu = 1,000$ and $\sigma^2/n = 1000^2/16 = 62,500$). Because the variance of the sampling distribution decreased as the sample size increased, we see evidence that the sample mean is a consistent estimator for μ. that This is an *asymptotic* **property** because the sample mean slowly collapses on the population mean as the sample size approaches infinity.

The sample mean is a **sufficient estimator** because it uses *all* the information in the sample (i.e., all n sample points were used in its calculation). But to show that the sample mean is *efficient* requires showing that the sample mean has a smaller variance than *all* unbiased estimators for μ, which is impossible to do. However, we can show that it is a **relatively efficient estimator** compared with another unbiased estimator, the average of a subsample of size 2. Using this estimator, 500 estimates were calculated using a sample size of 16. The mean and variance of this sampling distribution were 998.1 and 495,630, respectively. Because the variance of the 500 sample means was only 61,504, we see that the sample mean is relatively efficient compared with the subsample of size 2 estimator for the population mean.

Orientation to Basic Features

This module conducts an experiment to create sampling distributions for six estimators for μ or five estimators for σ^2. The population being sampled may be selected from a scenario, chosen from a template of distributions, or specified by the user. The module illustrates the statistical properties of unbiasedness, relative efficiency, and consistency.

1.   **Opening Screen**

Start the module by clicking on the module's icon, title, or chapter number in the *Visual Statistics* menu and pressing the Run Module button. When the module is loaded, you will be on the introduction page of the Notebook. Read the questions and then click the Concepts tab to see the concepts that you will learn. Click on the Scenarios tab. Select Sample mean from the list of choices under Estimators for Mu. Select a scenario, read it, and press OK. The upper left quadrant of the display is empty, waiting to create a histogram of sample estimates. The upper right quadrant of the display contains the Control Panel. In the lower left quadrant is the distribution of the population being sampled, and to its right will appear an analysis of the experiment after it has been completed.

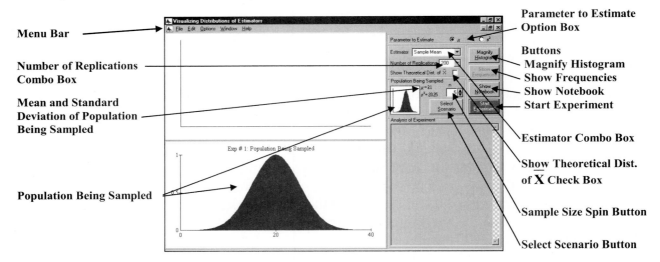

2.   **Start Experiment Button**

Click on the Start Experiment button. The experiment will sample from the population and estimate the sample mean 200 times. Click the Pause Experiment button. Superimposed on the population distribution is a dot plot of a sample and its sample mean (in red) as shown in the figure to the right. The

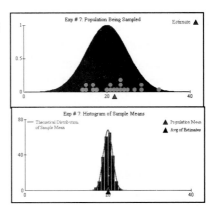

sample mean is also shown on the histogram in the upper left screen. Click the Continue Experiment button. At the end of the experiment a histogram of the sampling distribution has been created. It can be compared with the theoretical distribution of the sample mean (normal with mean of μ and a variance of σ^2/n) superimposed in red (see figure to the right).
During the experiment, if you do not want the graph updated one sample at a time, click the Finish Experiment button. Below the Control Panel appears an analysis of the experiment.

3. **Control Panel**

   a. The Number of Replications combo box sets the number of samples to be drawn. In general, 200 or more replications are needed to create a reliable representation of the true sampling distribution.

   b. Push the Show Frequencies button to see the number of estimates in each histogram class.

   c. Click the n spin button to change the sample size (or click inside its box and enter a number from your keyboard).

   d. Click on the Select Scenario button to change the scenario. This will return you to the Scenario section of the Notebook. You can browse through the scenarios by clicking on Next page or Previous page.

   e. Click the Show Theoretical Dist. of $\overline{X}$ check box. The theoretical sampling distribution of the sample mean appears (based on the Central Limit Theorem).

   f. Press the Magnify Histogram button to redraw the histogram using the entire left half of the screen and rescale the histogram so that its shape is more easily seen. Click the Reduce Histogram button to return to the original display.

   g. Click on the Estimator combo box. Six estimators for the mean are listed. Change the estimator to Sample Median. Start the experiment. The histogram displays the distribution of sample medians when you sample from the distribution in the lower left quadrant. Six estimators for the mean are listed.

   h. Select σ^2 using the Parameter to Estimate option buttons. The Estimator combo box lists five estimators of the variance. See Help for definitions of any estimator. The Show Theoretical Dist. of $\overline{X}$ check box is relabeled Show Theoretical Dist. of s^2.

4. **Copying a Display**

   Click on the graph you wish to copy or the Analysis panel. Black handles appear indicating it has been selected. Select Copy from the Edit menu (on the menu bar at the top of the screen) or press Ctrl-C to copy the display. It can then be pasted into other applications, such as Word or WordPerfect, so it can be printed or made part of a report.

5. **Help**

   Click on Help on the menu bar at the top of the screen. Search for Help lets you search a topic index, Contents shows a table of contents, Using Help gives instructions on how to use Help, and About gives licensing and copyright information about this *Visual Statistics* module.

6. **Exit**

   Close the module by selecting Exit in the File menu (or click ☒ in the upper right-hand corner of the window). You will be returned to the *Visual Statistics* main menu.

Orientation to Additional Features

1. **Population Templates**
    Press the Show Notebook button to return to the Notebook. Select the Pop. Templates tab and click OK. The display on the right will appear. Press the Very Skewed Left button (upper right corner) and click OK. The new distribution being sampled appears in the lower left quadrant and in the Population Being Sampled panel along with its mean and variance. The Select Scenario button has been replaced with a Select Templates button providing a short-cut to the templates display.

    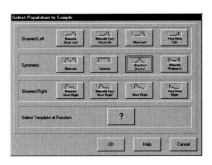

2. **Do-It-Yourself Distributions**
    Press the Show Notebook button and select the Do-It-Yourself tab. Select Known Distributions or User-Created Distributions. Pressing OK will bring up a display enabling you to create or select a distribution from which to sample. Accept the distribution by clicking OK. The Select Templates button will be replaced by a Select Distribution button if Known Distributions is selected or by a Show DIY Controls button if User-Created Distributions is selected.

    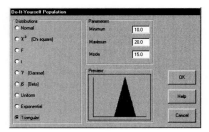

3. **Second Display**
    Select Copy Current Window from the Windows menu on the menu bar. You can now run two experiments and compare the results.

4. **Options**
    Click on Options on the menu bar and select Change Title to retitle the current display. This can be useful if you create a second display and need to keep track of them.

Basic Learning Exercises

Name _____

Replication Experiment

1. Press the Show Notebook button, select the Scenarios tab, click on Sample mean under Estimators for Mu, and select Golf Professional. Read the scenario and click on OK. What is the mean and variance of the population being sampled (look on the Population Being Sampled panel on the Control Panel)? What parameter is being estimated? What estimator is being used? What is the equation for this estimator? **Hint:** Select Help on the menu bar, click Search for Help, and type "sample mean" for its definition.

    Population being Sampled: Mean _____   Variance _____

2. Set the Number of Replications combo box to 50. Press the Start Experiment button. Press the Pause Experiment button after the experiment starts. a) Describe what is being displayed on the bottom graph. b) What does the triangle represent? c) What is being displayed on the top graph?

3. Press Continue Experiment to restart the experiment and watch the histogram build. Press Finish Experiment to suspend displaying each replication and complete the experiment. Read the Analysis of Experiment panel. What is the average of the sample means and the standard error of the sample means? What should each be according to the Central Limit Theorem (CLT)? Are the experiment results close to these predictions? What do the blue and red triangles on the top diagram represent? What do their relative positions tell you?

    Average of Sample Means _____   Standard Error of Sample Means _____
    CLT Predicted Mean _____   CLT Predicted Standard Error _____

Central Limit Theorem

4. Give a formal statement of the Central Limit Theorem. **Hint:** Use Help if you need it.

5. Increase the sample size to 100 by using the n spin button or typing the number directly into the box and pressing the Enter key on your computer. What is the standard deviation of the population being sampled? According to the CLT, what will be the standard error of the sampling distribution? What formula did you use to calculate the sampling distribution? What does the standard deviation measure? What does the standard error measure?

    Standard Deviation _____   CLT Predicted Standard Error _____

6. Select 500 from the Number of Replications combo box. Press the Start Experiment button and then the Finish Experiment button. What is the average of the sample means and the standard error of the sample means? Read the Analysis of Experiment. How do these results and those in exercise 3 illustrate the Central Limit Theorem?

    Average of Sample Means _____   Standard Error of Sample Means _____

7. Press the Select Scenarios button. Select the Smoke Stack Emissions scenario and read it. Press OK. Reduce the sample size from 30 to 10. Press the Start Experiment button. Read the Analysis of Experiment. Is the sampling distribution normally distributed? **Hint:** Press the Magnify Histogram button and make sure that Show Theoretical Dist. of $\overline{X}$ is checked in order to evaluate the histogram visually. When finished, press the Reduce Histogram button and uncheck Show Theoretical Dist. of $\overline{X}$ by clicking on it.

8. Increase the sample size to 30 and press Start Experiment. Is the sampling distribution normally distributed? How does exercise 7 illustrate the Central Limit Theorem?

Intermediate Learning Exercises   Name _____

Unbiased Estimators/Sufficient Estimators

9. What does it mean for an estimator to be unbiased? **Hint:** Click Search for Help in the Help menu and type "unbiased" if you are not sure.

10. How does the Central Limit Theorem prove that the sample mean is an unbiased estimator?

11. Press the Select Scenario button and click on Next page. Select Accuracy of Pistol Shooter and read the scenario. Click OK. What is the equation (estimator) for the sample median? Is the median a sufficient estimator? **Hint:** Use Help or the Glossary for definitions of terms.

12. Press the Start Experiment button. Does the median provide an unbiased estimator for μ in this case? Why or why not? **Hint:** Use the largest number of replications possible when you do an experiment. If the experiment took less than 15 seconds to finish, increase the number of replications from 500 to 1000 (or decrease the number of replications to 200 if it took longer than 30 seconds).

13. Press the Select Scenario button. Select the SAT Verbal Test Scores scenario and read it. Click OK. Press the Start Experiment button. Does the median provide an unbiased estimator for μ in this case? Explain.

14. Why does the median provide an unbiased estimator in exercise 13 but not in exercise 12?

Consistent Estimator

15. Push the Select Scenario button and click on Previous page. Select The Sum of Two Random Numbers scenario. Read the scenario and click OK. Press the Start Experiment button. Record the average of the sample means and their standard error. Increase n to 30 and repeat the experiment. Increase n to 90 and repeat the experiment.

n	Average of Sample Means	Standard Error of Sample Means
10	_____	_____
30	_____	_____
90	_____	_____

16. a) What is the definition of a consistent estimator? b) How can you show that an estimator is consistent? c) How do the results you recorded in exercise 15 demonstrate that the sample mean is a consistent estimator for μ? **Hint:** Use Help or the Glossary if you need guidance.

Relatively Efficient Estimator

17. Define a relatively efficient estimator. How would you show that an estimator is relatively efficient? **Hint:** Use Help or the Glossary if you need guidance.

18. Change the estimator to Sample Median using the Estimator combo box. Set the sample size to 10 and press the Start Experiment button. Record the average of the sample medians and their standard error. Increase n to 30 and repeat the experiment.

n	Average of Sample Medians	Standard Error of Sample Medians
10	_____	_____
30	_____	_____

19. Compare the results of exercises 17 and 18. How do these results show that the sample mean is relatively efficient compared with the sample median if a population with a symmetric distribution is being sampled?

Advanced Learning Exercises   Name _____

Unbiased Estimator for the Variance

Push the Show Notebook button, select the Do-It-Yourself tab, and click on Known Distributions. Read the description and press OK. Select the Exponential option button and enter 0.1 in the Scale parameter box. A sketch of the distribution appears in the window. Press OK. You are now sampling from the exponential distribution you specified. Click the σ^2 option button in the Parameter to Estimate panel. Make sure that the Sample Variance is appearing in the Estimator combo box. Use the Number of Replications combo box to specify the largest number of replications possible given the speed of your computer. The n spin button should be 9.

20. Press the Start Experiment button. a) Define the sample variance estimator. b) Read the Analysis of Experiment panel. What is the value of σ^2 in the population? c) What is the average of the sample variances? d) Is the sample variance an unbiased estimator for σ^2? e) How can you tell by looking at the Histogram of Sample Variances display?

21. Press the Select Distribution button. Select Normal distribution. Enter 5 for standard deviation and whatever mean you desire. Click OK. You are now sampling from the specified normal distribution. Press the Start Experiment button. What is the value of σ^2 in the population? What is the average of the sample variances? Given these results and those in exercise 20, does the distribution of the population being sampled cause the sample variance to become a biased estimator for σ^2?

Distribution of Sample Variance

22. Make sure the Show Theoretical Dist. of s^2 box is checked. The sample variance estimator has a χ^2 distribution that is scaled by $\sigma^2/(n-1)$. Notice how closely the histogram's shape corresponds to this theoretical distribution. Press the Select Distribution button. Select the t distribution and type 10 into the Degrees of freedom box. Although not normally distributed, the distribution has an approximate bell-shape. Press OK. Press the Start Experiment button. Read the Analysis of Experiment panel. Does the histogram have the scaled χ^2 distribution? Is the sample variance still an unbiased estimator?

23. Increase the sample size to 100 using the n spin button. Press the Start Experiment button. Read the Analysis of Experiment panel. Does the histogram have the scaled χ^2 distribution? The Central Limit Theorem says that the sample mean will have a normal distribution if the sample size is large enough. Given these results, do you think a similar theorem could be proven for the sample variance?

Asymptotically Unbiased Estimator

24. Press the Select Distribution button and select Normal. Set its standard deviation to 9 and its mean to 20. Press OK. Change the Estimator combo box to Sample MSD. Set the sample size to 4. Press the Start Experiment button. a) Define the sample MSD estimator. b) What is the variance of the population you are sampling? c) What is the average of the sample MSDs? d) Is the sample MSD an unbiased estimator for σ^2?

25. Increase the sample size to 100. Press the Start Experiment button. Read the Analysis of Experiment panel. What is the average of the sample MSDs? An estimator is asymptotically unbiased if the bias disappears as the sample size increases. Is sample MSD an asymptotically unbiased estimator for σ^2?

Bootstrap Estimator for σ^2

26. Change the Estimator combo box to Bootstrap-Variance and enter 50 in the dialog box. a) Define the bootstrap estimator for the variance. b) What does the 50 represent? c) Set the sample size to 20. Press the Start Experiment button. Why does this experiment take longer than the other experiments? d) Read the Analysis of Experiment panel. Why is the bootstrap estimator for σ^2 relatively efficient compared with the sample variance estimator?

Individual Learning Projects

Write a report on one of the three topics listed below. Use the cut-and-paste facilities of the module to place the appropriate graphs in your report. For each investigation use at least 200 replications (1000 is recommended).

1. Investigate three estimators for either μ or σ^2 and determine which are unbiased estimators. For each estimator investigate its bias by drawing a very small sample from three different distributions (symmetric, skewed, and very skewed). Define each estimator. To be unbiased, an estimator's experimental sampling distribution must be centered around the true parameter (μ or σ^2) for each investigation.

2. Investigate one estimator for the mean (not the sample mean) and one estimator for the variance (not the sample variance). Define each estimator and explain how it is calculated. Determine whether the estimator for the mean is unbiased (or asymptotically unbiased), whether it is consistent, and assess its relative efficiency compared with the sample mean. Determine whether the estimator for the variance is unbiased, whether it is consistent, and assess its relative efficiency compared with the sample variance. In your investigation, be sure to sample both from a symmetric and a very asymmetric distribution.

3. The Central Limit Theorem says that the sample mean is an unbiased estimator for the population mean and that its standard error is $\sigma/\sqrt{n}$ regardless of the distribution of the population being sampled. It goes on to say that the sampling distribution of the sample mean is normally distributed if the sample size is large enough. Illustrate the Central Limit Theorem. Select at least three different distributions to sample (they should be increasingly asymmetric). For each distribution, select three different sample sizes, ranging from very small (fewer than 8) to large (greater than 80). Discuss how these nine experiments illustrate the Central Limit Theorem.

Team Learning Projects

Select one of the three projects listed below. In each case, produce a team project that is suitable for an oral presentation. Use presentation software or large poster boards to display your results. Graphs should be large enough for your audience to see. Each team member should be responsible for producing some of the graphs. Ask your instructor if a written report is also expected. For each investigation use at least 200 replications (1000 is recommended).

1. A team of two to four should evaluate the relative efficiency of each estimator for either μ or σ^2. An estimator is relatively efficient compared with another estimator if both are unbiased and one has a smaller standard error than the other. For each estimator, investigate its relative efficiency by drawing a very small sample from four different distributions. Define each estimator. Tell which are unbiased and rank the relative efficiency of those that are unbiased. Support all findings with illustrations.

2. A team of three or four should evaluate the consistency of each estimator for either μ or σ^2. An estimator is consistent if it is unbiased or asymptotically unbiased (its bias disappears as n increases) and if the standard error of the sampling distribution decreases as n increases. For each estimator, investigate its consistency by drawing two samples, one very small and one moderate, from three different distributions (symmetric, skewed, and very skewed). Define each estimator and tell which are unbiased, asymptotically unbiased, and consistent. Support all findings with illustrations.

3. A team of two to four should evaluate the properties of estimators for the mean and variance. Each team member should select an estimator for μ and an estimator for σ^2 to evaluate. No one should select the sample mean or the sample variance. Define each estimator selected and explain how it is calculated. For each chosen estimator for μ, determine whether it is unbiased (or asymptotically unbiased), whether it is consistent, and assess its relative efficiency compared to the sample mean. For each chosen estimator for σ^2, determine whether it is unbiased, whether it is consistent, and assess its relative efficiency compared to the sample variance. For each estimator investigated, be sure to sample both from a symmetric and very asymmetric distribution. Support all findings with illustrations.

Self-Evaluation Quiz

1. Which of the following is an *unbiased* estimator of the population mean?
    a. The sample mean, regardless of the population sampled.
    b. The sample midrange, if the distribution of the population is symmetric.
    c. The sample median, if the distribution of the population is symmetric.
    d. The sample median, if the distribution of the population is skewed.
    e. All of the above are unbiased estimators.

2. The sample median
    a. is an unbiased estimator of μ if the population sampled is symmetric.
    b. is an asymptotically unbiased estimator of μ.
    c. is not efficient since it is not always an unbiased estimator of μ.
    d. has more than one of the above characteristics.
    e. has none of the above characteristics.

3. Relative efficiency requires an examination of
    a. the variability of a sample estimator.
    b. the bias of a sample estimator.
    c. both the bias and the variability of a sample estimator.
    d. neither the bias nor the variability of a sample estimator.
    e. none of the above.

4. If estimator A is relatively efficient compared with estimator B, then which is most likely?
    a. Estimator A is probably based on a smaller sample than is estimator B.
    b. Estimator A has a smaller bias than does estimator B.
    c. Estimator A is less sensitive to population shape than is estimator B.
    d. Estimator A has a smaller variance than does estimator B.
    e. Estimator A is based on a better sampling method than that of estimator B.

5. If you sample from a population with a symmetric distribution, which of the following is the relatively efficient estimator of the population mean?
    a. The average of a subsample of size K of the n sample observations (K < n).
    b. The sample midrange.
    c. The sample median.
    d. The sample mean.
    e. More than one of the above.

6. In a sample of size n, which is *not* a consistent estimator of the population mean?
    a. Subsample of size K of the n sample observations (K < n).
    b. Subsample of K% of the n sample observations (K < 100).
    c. The sample mean.
    d. All of the above are consistent estimator of the mean.
    e. None of the above is a consistent estimator of the mean.

7.   Which is a correct statement about the Empirical Rules?
   a.   The Empirical Rule of 4 is based on the $\mu \pm 2\sigma$ normal area (95.44 percent).
   b.   The Empirical Rule of 6 is based on the $\mu \pm 3\sigma$ normal area (99.74 percent).
   c.   The Empirical Rules are biased estimators even if the population is symmetric.
   d.   The Empirical Rules are inconsistent and inefficient estimators.
   e.   The Empirical Rules have all of the above characteristics.

8.   The bootstrap estimator
   a.   uses nonlinear variable transformations to improve accuracy.
   b.   was discovered long before powerful computers were available.
   c.   was initially developed by statistician Brad Efron (1979).
   d.   was first applied to quality sampling in the shoemaking industry.
   e.   provides biased but efficient estimates of a parameter.

9.   Which of the following is a biased estimator of the population variance?
   a.   The sample variance.
   b.   The sample MSD.
   c.   The sample Empirical Rule of 4.
   d.   The sample bootstrap estimator.
   e.   More than one of the above is a biased estimator.

10.   Which of the following is the most efficient estimator of the population variance?
   a.   The sample MSD.
   b.   The sample Empirical Rule of 4 estimator.
   c.   The sample Empirical Rule of 6 estimator.
   d.   The sample bootstrap estimator.
   e.   None of the above is an efficient estimator.

11.   Which of the following is an asymptotically unbiased estimator of the population variance?
   a.   The sample MSD.
   b.   The sample Empirical Rule of 4 estimator.
   c.   The sample Empirical Rule of 4 estimator.
   d.   The sample bootstrap estimator.
   e.   None of the above is asymptotically unbiased.

12.   Which is *not* true of the bootstrap estimator for the variance?
   a.   It often has a smaller variance than other estimators for the variance.
   b.   It is somewhat more difficult to calculate than other estimators.
   c.   It is widely used in the footwear industry to improve product quality.
   d.   It is growing in popularity partly because it requires few assumptions.
   e.   It may yield different results if the number of times the sample is resampled is not large.

Glossary of Terms

Asymmetric distribution Distribution that is skewed right or left. See **Symmetric**.

Asymptotic Refers to large sample sizes. Formally it refers to a limit as the sample size approaches infinity (denoted $n \rightarrow \infty$).

Asymptotic properties Properties of an estimator that can be evaluated only as the sample size approaches infinity. Essentially, this is a mathematical question, though it can be investigated using simulation of sampling as sample size is increased.

Asymptotically unbiased estimator Biased estimator whose bias decreases toward zero as the sample size increases (i.e., the probability of a given difference between the estimator and the parameter approaches zero as $n \rightarrow \infty$).

Average of K observations Same as the sample mean except that only K observations in the sample are used. It is unbiased but is not consistent (because K does not change as n increases) and has a larger variance than the sample mean. Because it is a mean, it is vulnerable to the presence of outliers in the sample.

Average of K% of the observations Same as the sample mean except that only K percent of the observations are included in the sample. It is unbiased and consistent, but is has a larger variance than the sample mean. Because it is a mean, it is sensitive to outliers in a sample.

Biased estimator An estimator whose expected value is not equal to the corresponding population parameter. See **Unbiased estimator**.

Bootstrap estimator Once the sample is taken, the sample is resampled K times, calculating the sample mean each time. The bootstrap estimator for the mean is the average of these sample means. It is unbiased and consistent. It has the same sampling distribution as the sample mean, and as a result is efficient. The bootstrap estimator of the variance is the square root of the variance of the K resampled means (an estimator of the sample standard error of the mean) multiplied by $\sqrt{n}$ and squared. It is unbiased and consistent. It has a smaller spread than the sample variance and is therefore relatively efficient compared with the sample variance.

Central Limit Theorem This famous theorem says that, if the sample size is large enough, sample means from any population will follow a normal distribution with the same mean as the population but with a smaller variance. More formally, if $x_1, x_2, \ldots, x_n$ are identically distributed, independent, random variables from any population with finite mean μ and finite variance σ^2, then the sample mean, $\overline{X} = (x_1 + x_2 + \ldots + x_n) / n$, will have a sampling distribution with mean μ and variance σ^2 / n. Further, the sampling distribution of the sample mean $\overline{X}$ is normally distributed as n approaches infinity.

Consistent estimator Estimator whose probability of being close to the parameter being estimated increases as the sample size increases. One can demonstrate that an estimator is consistent by showing that it is unbiased (or asymptotically unbiased) and that its standard error decreases as the sample size increases. This type of consistency is known as mean squared error consistency. The Central Limit Theorem implies that the sample mean is a consistent estimator of μ since, as the sample size increases, the distribution of the sample mean is centered at μ with a variance of σ^2/n. Therefore, as $n \to \infty$, the variance approaches zero and the sample mean collapses on μ.

Efficient estimator Estimator that has the smallest variance among *all* unbiased estimators for a parameter.

Empirical Rule of 4 $\left(\dfrac{X_{Max} - X_{Min}}{4}\right)^2$. This estimator of the variance is biased and is not consistent. Since it is biased it cannot be efficient. It is sensitive to outliers. It is based on the fact that 95.44 percent of the observations lie within 2 standard deviations of the mean in a normal distribution.

Empirical Rule of 6 $\left(\dfrac{X_{Max} - X_{Min}}{6}\right)^2$. This estimator of the variance is biased and is not consistent. Since it is biased it cannot be efficient. It is sensitive to outliers. It is based on the fact that 99.73 percent of the observations lie within 3 standard deviations of the mean in a normal distribution.

Empirical sampling distribution The empirical distribution created by applying the formula for an estimator to m different samples and producing a histogram of the m estimates.

Estimate Value of an estimator that results from applying its formula to sample data.

Estimator Any sample statistic that is used to estimate a population parameter of interest.

Known distributions A distribution that has been studied by statisticians and has been given a name. Known distributions that can be used in this module are the normal, Student's t, F, chi square, uniform, beta, gamma, exponential, and triangular.

Mean of sampling distribution The theoretical mean of a sampling distribution or the average of the estimates from an empirical sampling distribution.

Mean square deviation $\displaystyle\sum_{i=1}^{n}\dfrac{\left(x_i - \overline{X}\right)^2}{n}$. This estimator of the variance is biased but asymptotically unbiased (the bias decreases as n becomes large). It is consistent. It has slightly less spread than the sample variance, but since it is biased it is not efficient. It is sensitive to non-normal populations. See **Sample MSD**.

Normal distribution Standard bell-shaped or Gaussian distribution. It has two parameters called the mean μ and variance σ^2.

Parameter Population characteristic that determines the probability distribution of a particular population distribution.

Population distribution The probability density function f(x) that is defined over a set of values of X. The ordinate shows the probability associated with each X value. For a continuous random variable, the area under the entire distribution is 1.

Properties Desirable statistical attributes of an estimator that help a statistician evaluate a variety of estimators for an unknown parameter. See **Asymptotic properties**.

Relatively efficient estimator Unbiased estimator with the smallest variance. Suppose we have two unbiased estimators A and B. For a given sample size, if the variance of estimator A is smaller than the variance of estimator B, then estimator A is relatively more efficient than estimator B.

Sample mean $\overline{X} = \dfrac{1}{n}\sum\limits_{i=1}^{n} x_i$ (the average of n sample observations). It is unbiased, consistent, and efficient (no other estimator has a smaller variance). It is sensitive to outliers in a sample. Its theoretical distribution is normal if the population is normal or if n is large enough.

Sample median The middle sample observation (if n is odd) or the average of the two middle observations (if n is even). It is unbiased if a symmetric distribution is being sampled and is consistent but has a larger variance than the sample mean. It is relatively insensitive to outliers.

Sample midrange The average of the smallest and largest sample observations. It is unbiased if a symmetric distribution is being sampled, but it is not consistent and has a larger variance than the sample mean. It is very sensitive to outliers.

Sample MSD $\sum\limits_{i=1}^{n} \dfrac{\left(x_i - \overline{X}\right)^2}{n}$. This estimator of the variance is biased. However, the bias disappears as n approaches infinity and is therefore asymptotically unbiased. It is consistent. Its distribution is sensitive to non-normal populations. See **Mean squared deviation**.

Sample variance $\sum\limits_{i=1}^{n} \dfrac{\left(x_i - \overline{X}\right)^2}{n-1}$. This estimator of the variance is unbiased, consistent, and only the bootstrap estimator is more efficient. Its distribution is sensitive to non-normal populations. Its theoretical distribution is chi-square distribution with $n - 1$ degrees of freedom if the population sampled is normal.

Sampling distribution The theoretical distribution of an estimator derived from a sample, such as the sample mean. According to the Central Limit Theorem, regardless of the population being sampled, the sample mean's sampling distribution has a mean μ and standard deviation $\sigma/\sqrt{n}$. It is normally distributed if the sample size is large enough. See **Empirical sampling distribution**.

Standard deviation Denoted σ, it is the square root of the population variance. It is a measure of dispersion about the mean. Larger σ values indicate greater dispersion.

Standard error The square root of the variance of the sampling distribution. According to the Central Limit Theorem, the theoretical standard error of the sample mean is $\sigma/\sqrt{n}$, where σ is the population standard deviation and n is the sample size. It is generally written as $\sigma_{\overline{X}}$.

Sufficient estimator Estimator that uses all the information from a sample.

Symmetric distribution   A distribution whose mirror image looks the same on either side of its mean. The normal, uniform, and Student's t are symmetric distributions. Depending upon the parameter values used, the beta and triangular distributions may also be symmetric.

Unbiased estimator   Estimator whose expected value is equal to the parameter it is estimating. It is centered on the true population parameter (neither under- nor over-estimates the parameter). For example, the Central Limit Theorem says that the sample mean is an unbiased estimator of μ. Therefore, the average of a large number of sample means should equal μ.

Variance   In a population, the variance is the expected value of $(X - \mu)^2$ and is denoted σ^2. In a sample, the variance is the sum of the squared deviations about the sample mean divided by $n - 1$ and is denoted s^2.

Variance of Sampling Distribution   The theoretical variance of a sampling distribution or the variance of the estimates from an empirical sampling distribution.

Solutions to Self-Evaluation Quiz

1. e   Do Exercises 9–14. Do Individual Learning Project 1. Read the Overview of Concepts, Illustration of Concepts, and Glossary.
2. d   Do Exercises 9–14. Do Individual Learning Project 1. Read the Overview of Concepts, Illustration of Concepts, and Glossary.
3. c   Do Exercises 17–19. Do Individual Learning Project 2. Read the Overview of Concepts, Illustration of Concepts, and Glossary.
4. d   Read the Overview of Concepts.
5. d   Do Exercises 17–19. Do Individual Learning Project 2. Read the Overview of Concepts, Illustration of Concepts, and Glossary.
6. d   Do Exercises 15–16. Do Individual Learning Project 2. Read the Overview of Concepts, Illustration of Concepts, and Glossary.
7. e   Do Exercises 10–18 and 19–23.
8. c   Read the Glossary.
9. e   Do Exercises 20 and 21. Do Individual Learning Project 1. Read the Overview of Concepts, Illustration of Concepts, and Glossary.
10. d   Do Individual Learning Project 2. Read the Overview of Concepts, Illustration of Concepts, and Glossary.
11. a   Do Exercises 24 and 25. Read the Overview of Concepts, Illustration of Concepts, and Glossary.
12. c   Do Exercise 26. Read the Overview of Concepts and Glossary.

CHAPTER 9

Visualizing One-Sample Hypothesis Tests

CONCEPTS
- Null Hypothesis, Alternative Hypothesis, One-Tail Test, Two-Tail Test, Confidence Interval, Decision Rule, Level of Significance, Sampling Distribution, Critical Value, Test Statistic, P-Value, Type I Error, Type II Error, Power

OBJECTIVES
- Learn to distinguish between one-tail and two-tail null and alternative hypotheses

- Understand the roles of the critical value and test statistic in testing a hypothesis

- Be able to explain the meaning of level of significance and power

- Know the normality assumption and recognize the effects of violating it

Overview of Concepts

Hypothesis testing weighs theory against experimental evidence. Statistical techniques for hypothesis testing were pioneered by Karl Pearson (1857–1936) and R. A. Fisher (1890–1935). Its role in science was explained by Karl R. Popper in his *Logic of Scientific Discovery* (1934). The first step is to create two mutually exclusive hypotheses that exhaust all possibilities (i.e., if one is true, the other must be false). For example, the manufacturer of a CD ROM drive for a certain PC specifies the mean access time for a 2K block of data as 124 milliseconds (ms). If drives are repeatedly tested using randomly chosen 2K blocks of data, the hypotheses are

H_0: $\mu = 124$ ms   (access time conforms to the performance standard)
H_1: $\mu \neq 124$ ms   (access time fails to conform to the performance standard)

The **null hypothesis** (H_0) is a statement or belief that we try to reject. The **alternative hypothesis** (H_1) is the exact converse of the null hypothesis. Evidence to test the hypothesis is obtained from a sample. If the evidence contradicts H_0, then H_0 will be rejected in favor of H_1. This example depicts a **two-tail test** because a significant deviation in either direction indicates nonconformance to design. If someone (for example, a PC retailer) cares only whether access time is greater than claimed, a **one-tail test** (H_0: $\mu \leq 124$ and H_1: $\mu > 124$) might be useful.

One way to test a hypothesis is to construct a **confidence interval** around a sample estimate to see whether or not it includes the hypothesized parameter value ($\mu = 124$). Another way to test a hypothesis is to compare the sample statistic with the hypothesized parameter value, using our knowledge of the statistic's **sampling distribution**. For a hypothesis about a mean, the sampling distribution of the **test statistic** is normal (for known variance) or Student's t with $n - 1$ degrees of freedom (for unknown variance). The test statistic is compared with a **critical value** based upon the sampling distribution. A **decision rule** is established in advance, stating the criterion for rejecting H_0. If H_0 is not rejected, it is tentatively accepted. Some statisticians prefer to say simply that H_0 is "not rejected" because, although H_0 can be disproved, it *cannot* be proved once and for all.

If H_0 is true and we mistakenly reject it, we have committed **Type I error**, while if a false H_0 is mistakenly accepted we have committed **Type II error**. Otherwise, no error has been committed. The probability of Type I error is denoted α. The probability of Type II error is denoted β. The probability of correctly rejecting a false null hypothesis is called **power** and is equal to $1 - \beta$. The statistician prefers low values for α and β (and hence a high value for power). The value of α (called the **level of significance**) is chosen in advance (typically 0.10, 0.05, or 0.01) and is embodied in the decision rule. The value of β cannot be chosen because it depends on the true parameter value, which is usually unknown. However, power may be found for any possible true parameter value. This module lets you estimate Type I error or power empirically by sampling a known population many times.

Another way of thinking about a hypothesis test is to calculate its **p-value**, which is the probability that a given sample result (or one more extreme) would arise, assuming H_0 is true. The smaller the p-value, the stronger the evidence against H_0. Until recently, p-values were rarely used because they require calculating an exact area under the sampling distribution. Since modern computers can easily calculate such areas, the p-value approach now is widely used. An advantage of the p-value approach is that it avoids the need to specify α in advance (a choice the statistician must make with little basis except tradition).

Illustration of Concepts

To protect baby scallops, the U.S. Fisheries and Wildlife Service requires that in each "harvest" the average meat per scallop shall weigh at least 1/36 pound (12.6 grams). The population is normally distributed with a historic variance of 1.0 grams. A vessel arrives at a Massachusetts port with 11,000 bags of scallops. It is not feasible to weigh each bag, so the harbormaster chooses 18 bags at random. The **null hypothesis** (H_0) is that the average scallop weighs at least 12.6 grams, while the **alternative hypothesis** (H_1) is that this requirement is not met. This is a **one-tail test**, because only underweight scallops are of concern (whereas a **two-tail test** might be used by a biologist who is merely tracking mean scallop weight in general).

H_0: $\mu \geq 12.6$ (average scallop meets the minimum weight requirement)
H_1: $\mu < 12.6$ (average scallop falls short of the minimum weight requirement)

From each bag, a large scoop of scallops is taken and the average meat per scallop is weighed. For the 18 bags that are examined, the sample mean is 12.10 grams. The **sampling distribution** of the **test statistic** for the mean is normal because the population variance is known. Should the null hypothesis be rejected? In the dot plot (Figure 1) the sample mean is a bit below 12.6. The right end of the 95% **confidence interval** (Figure 2) does not include 12.6, which suggests that H_0 should be rejected. However, the decision is fairly close.

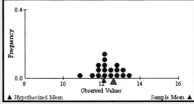

Figure 1: Dot Plot

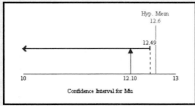

Figure 2: Confidence Interval

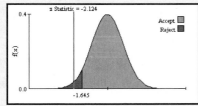

Figure 3: Decision Rule

Another approach is to create a **decision rule**, which will lead to the same conclusion as the confidence interval method. At the 5% **level of significance** we will reject H_0 if the test statistic is to the left of the **critical value** $z_{.05} = -1.645$ (for a normal distribution). Since the test statistic is $z = -2.124$, we reject H_0 (Figure 3). Thus, the captain may face fines for an underweight catch.

Could different samples lead to different results? Suppose this sampling experiment is repeated four more times, using 18 bags each time, with the results summarized below. Samples 1, 3, and 4 lead to rejection (and possible **Type I error**), while samples 2 and 5 lead to acceptance (and possible **Type II error**). The low **p-values** for samples 1, 3, and 4 suggest that these sample means are unlikely if H_0 is true, while samples 2 and 5 are more consistent with H_0. Which decision is correct? We don't know. The **power** of the test is unknown since the true mean is unknown.

Sample	Mean	Upper Limit	Test Statistic	P-Value	Decision
1	12.10	12.49	-2.124	0.016	Reject
2	12.48	12.87	-0.518	0.302	Accept
3	11.55	11.94	-4.450	0.000	Reject
4	11.93	12.32	-2.852	0.020	Reject
5	12.53	12.92	-0.299	0.383	Accept

*Based on A. Barnett, "Misapplications Reviews: Jail Terms," *Interfaces* 25, 2 (March–April 1995), pp. 18–24.

Orientation to Basic Features

This module helps you learn how to test hypotheses about a single mean (with known or unknown population variance) and about a single variance. It permits one-tail and two-tail tests and shows the relationship between confidence intervals and hypothesis tests using appropriate scenarios. You may also choose a population and specify its parameters. Using replication, you can study the meaning of power, Type I error, and Type II error.

1. **Select a Scenario**

    Start the module by clicking on the module's icon, title, or chapter number in the *Visual Statistics* menu and pressing the Run Module button. When the module is loaded, you will be on the introduction page of the Notebook. Read the questions and then click the Concepts tab to see the concepts that you will learn. Click the Scenarios tab. Click on Tests for Mu with Known Variance. Select a scenario, read it, and press OK.

2. **Main Display**

    The main display opens with a large Dot Plot and a Control Panel. Click Take New Sample and observe the changes in the sampled items (blue dots) and confidence interval (blue line segment labeled 95% CI). The hypothesized mean (red fulcrum) does not change, but the sample mean (blue fulcrum) will change to reflect each new sample. The Replicate button will remain inactive until you press Show 4 Displays (but do not do it yet).

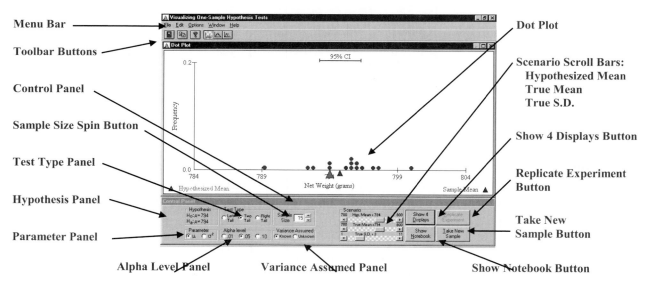

3. **Toolbar Buttons**

    Place the cursor over the fifth toolbar button located above the dot plot. A label will appear (Show True and Hypothesized Distribution). Click the button and see an overlay of the population to be sampled. This distribution does not change when you take samples, but will reflect any changes you make in the true or hypothesized parameters. Click the sixth toolbar button (Show True and Hypothesized Sampling Distribution) and observe the narrower sampling distribution. The sampling distribution will not change when you take samples, but will reflect any changes you make in the sample size or in the true and hypothesized parameters. Click the fourth toolbar button (Show Dot Plot Only) to restore the simple dot plot.

4. **Show 4 Displays**

Click Show 4 Displays. Read the Hint and press OK. The Control Panel will move to the upper right and its controls will be rearranged. The Dot Plot will become smaller and will be in the upper left. Two new quadrant displays will be on the bottom (Confidence Intervals for Mu, Normal Distribution). The Confidence Interval for Mu display shows more detail than the 95% CI on the Dot Plot. The Normal Distribution shows the decision rule. Right-click on the Confidence Intervals for Means 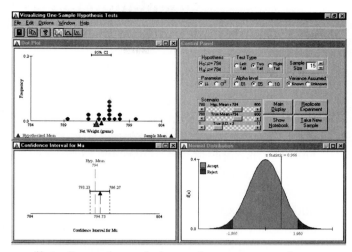 display and select Summary Statistics to see a list of sample statistics and parameter values. Right-click on the Summary Statistics display and select Analysis of Experiment to see a verbal description of the results of your experiment. Right-click the Analysis of Experiment display and select Confidence Interval to return to the original quadrant display. Any graph can be enlarged by maximizing its window.

5. **Using the Control Panel**

In the Test Type panel, click each option (Right-Tail, Left-Tail, Two-Tail). The normal distribution display will match the test type you have selected. Click each option (.10, .05, .01) in the Alpha Level panel and verify that the normal distribution tail area and the confidence intervals change to reflect your choices. Click Unknown in the Variance Assumed panel. The normal distribution is replaced by Student's t, and the confidence intervals will change. Click σ^2 in the Parameter panel. The Student's t distribution is replaced by a chi-square distribution and the confidence intervals now show variances instead of means. Click μ in the Parameter panel, and the displays again show a mean. Click Known in the Variance Assumed panel to return to the original scenario. Click the Sample Size spin button to alter the sample size (2 to 99). Click the fifth toolbar button to show an overlay of the population to be sampled. Change the position of any scroll bar in the Scenario panel (Hypothesized Mean, True Mean, True S.D.) and press Take New Sample to see its effect on the distributions.

6. **Copying a Display**

Click on the display you wish to copy. Its window title will be highlighted. Select Copy from the Edit menu (on the menu bar) or Ctrl-C. It can then be pasted into other applications.

7. **Help**

Click on Help on the menu bar at the top of the screen. Search for Help lets you search an index for this module, Contents shows a table of contents for this module, Using Help gives instructions on how to use Help, and About gives licensing and copyright information.

8. **Exit**

Close the module by selecting Exit in the File menu (or click ☒ in the upper right-hand corner of the window). You will be returned to the *Visual Statistics* main menu.

Orientation to Additional Features

1. **Replication**

   Click the Replicate Experiment button on the Control Panel. At the top are nine toolbar buttons. The new ones control the confidence level (99%, 95%, 90%) and the test type (Left-tail, Two-Tail, Right-Tail). On the left is the Confidence Intervals for Mu display. On the right is a Control Panel containing the Analysis of Experiment window and scroll bar controls (Hypothesized Mean, True Mean, True S.D.) and a Histogram/Distribution display. Click Number of Replications to vary the number of replications (20, 50, 100, 200, 500). If you click the Start Experiment button, it becomes Finish Experiment and Return to 4 Displays becomes Pause Experiment. If you click Pause Experiment, the displays are frozen in their current state and Pause Experiment becomes Continue Experiment. If you click Finish Experiment, the confidence interval and histogram displays go to their final state without showing any intermediate steps. Click Return to 4 Displays to exit replication.

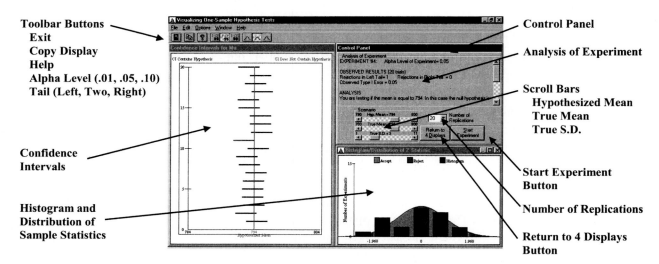

2. **Do-It-Yourself Controls**

   Click Show Notebook, choose the Do-It-Yourself tab, and click OK. Default values for the means and standard deviation are given on the Do-It-Yourself panel. You may change them using the edit boxes. Press Change Distribution and select any of six populations to sample (Normal, Uniform, Skewed Left, Skewed Right, Very Skewed Left, Very Skewed Right). The replication control panel will also show the Do-It-Yourself panel instead of scroll bars.

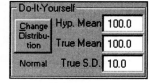

3. **Options**

   Click Options on the menu bar. You can change terminology from Accept Null Hypothesis to Do Not Reject Null Hypothesis. The latter option may be preferred by some, since we do not actually prove a null hypothesis.

Basic Learning Exercises   Name _____

Press the Show Notebook button, select the Scenarios tab, and click on Tests for Mu with Known Variance. Select the Filling Jars scenario, read it, and press OK.

Tests for a Mean with Known Variance
1. Record the hypothesized mean and true mean that are shown on the control panel. Based on this information, is the null hypothesis true or false?

    Hypothesized mean _____   True Mean   _____

2. Click Take New Sample 10 times. For each sample, estimate visually the lower and upper end of the range for individual sample items (blue dots) and the sample mean (blue fulcrum shown below the axis). Which shows less variation? Why?

    Smallest sample observation   _____   Largest sample observation   _____
    Smallest sample mean   _____   Largest sample mean   _____

3. Click the toolbar button for Show True and Hypothesized Distribution, and record its approximate end points (where it nearly reaches the X-axis). Then click the toolbar button for Show True and Hypothesized Sampling Distribution, and record its approximate end points. Do they agree with your answers in the previous exercise? Explain.

    Minimum of X distribution   _____   Maximum of X distribution   _____
    Minimum of sampling dist.   _____   Maximum of sampling dist.   _____

4. The decision rule is in the lower right. a) Why does the decision rule use a normal distribution? b) What are the critical values? c) Do the critical values change when you press Take New Sample? d) Does the test statistic change when you press Take New Sample?

5. Click Show 4 Displays. Click Take New Sample 20 times, and observe the confidence interval display in the lower left each time to see whether it includes the true mean. What percentage of the time did the confidence interval include the true mean? Does this agree with what you would expect, given the level of significance of this two-tailed hypothesis test?

6.   Click Take New Sample. Compare the decision about H_0 using the confidence interval (does the interval exclude the hypothesized mean?) and the normal decision rule (does the test statistic fall in the rejection region?). Repeat. Do the decisions always agree?

Tests for a Mean with Unknown Variance

7.   Click Return to 4 Displays and Press the Show Notebook button. Select the Scenarios tab and click on Tests for Mu with Unknown Variance. Select the GRE Test Scores scenario, read it, and click OK. Record the hypothesized mean, true mean, true standard deviation, and sample size. Based on these control panel settings, is the null hypothesis true or false?

Hypothesized mean   _____   True Std. Dev.   _____
True mean   _____   Sample size   _____

8.   a) Change Variance Assumed from Unknown to Known and watch what happens to the displays. Does changing this assumption of unknown population variances have a substantial impact on the decision rule and its critical values? b) Would your answer be the same if the sample size were larger? Explain.

9.   Be sure the Confidence Interval display is showing. Set Variance Assumed to Known. a) Press Take New Sample several times, each time assessing the width of the confidence interval for μ. Does the width vary from sample to sample? b) Set the variance assumption to Unknown and press Take New Sample several times. Does the width vary from sample to sample? Explain. c) Do statisticians have a choice about variances in actual sampling?

Intermediate Learning Exercises   Name _____

Press the Show Notebook button, select the Scenarios tab, and click on Tests for Mu with Known Variance. Select the Filling Jars scenario, read it, and press OK. Make sure all four displays are showing.

Type I/Type II Error and Power with Known Variance

10. Press Replicate. Set the number of replications to 100 and press Start Experiment. If the confidence interval fails to include the true value (shown in red), this indicates rejection of the null hypothesis ($\mu = 794$ grams). How many times did this occur? Repeat this experiment nine more times, entering the results below. What is the mean number of rejections? The range? Why does the number of rejections vary? Does it vary more than you expected?

Experiment: 1   2   3   4   5   6   7   8   9   10

Rejections: ____ ____ ____ ____ ____ ____ ____ ____ ____ ____

11. Explain what these findings say about Type I error in the context of the jar-filling scenario. If the level of significance were reduced, would that be helpful to the company? Explain.

12. Based purely on the samples, should the assembly line be shut down? **Hint:** Click Show Notebook and review the question posed in the scenario if necessary.

13. Press Replicate. Set the number of replications to 100 and press Start Experiment. Examine the Histogram/Distribution for your 100 replications. Describe its appearance. What does the Analysis of Experiment window tell you about empirical Type I error?

14. Move the True Mean scroll bar four clicks to the left (True Mean = 790 grams). Replicate the sampling experiment 100 times. Look at all three exhibits (Confidence Intervals, Analysis of Experiment, Histogram/Distribution) and describe how these results differ from the previous replication experiments. Would you say it is easy or difficult to detect a difference of 4 grams in this particular scenario? Is it safe to generalize your conclusion about the difficulty of detecting a difference of 0.1?

15. Click Return to 4 Displays and click the Show True and Hypothesized Sampling Distributions toolbar button. How do they help explain the results of exercise 11?

16. Set the True S.D. scroll bar to its largest value ($\sigma = 11$ grams) but leave Hypothesized Mean at 794 and True Mean at 790. Click the Take New Sample button. Describe the hypothesized and true sampling distribution. What is the implication for detecting a difference of 4 between the true and hypothesized means in this scenario?

17. Press Replicate. Set the number of replications to 100 and press Start Experiment. Look at all three displays (Confidence Intervals, Analysis of Experiment, Histogram/Distribution) and describe the results of your replication experiment. a) In this scenario (with $\sigma = 11$ grams) how often was the difference of 4 grams detected? b) What is the approximate power of the test? c) Why is Type I error not relevant in this case?

Type I/Type II Error and Power with Unknown Variance

18. Set Variance Assumed to Unknown (as in the original scenario) and press Replicate. Choose 500 replications. What is the empirical power? What is the empirical Type II error? What does the histogram of test statistics tell you? Interpret these results.

19. Click Return to 4 Displays, change the sample size to 25, and repeat exercise 18. Interpret your results. Does a larger sample size help?

20. Based purely on the sample evidence, would you conclude that the students' average GRE scores differ from the national average?

Tests for a Variance

21. Press the Show Notebook button, select the Scenarios tab, and click on Tests for Variance. Select the Vending Machine scenario, read it, and press OK. Record the hypothesized variance, true variance, sample size, and test type (left-tail, right-tail, two-tail) that are shown in the control panel. Based on the position of the scroll bars, is the null hypothesis true or false?

Hypothesized variance _____   True variance _____
Sample size   _____   Test type   _____

22. a) Why is the chi-square distribution the relevant distribution? How many degrees of freedom (DF) does it have, and why? What is the critical value? Why is this a right-tail test? Why is the mean of secondary importance in this scenario? **Hint:** Right-click to see the Statistics and Parameters or the Analysis of Experiment window if you need further information.

Degrees of freedom _____   Critical value _____

23. If it is not already displayed, bring up the Confidence Interval window. Why does this confidence interval extend all the way to the right? Is this true for a one-tailed test of a mean?

24. Press Take New Sample. Should H_0 be rejected? That is, did the confidence interval exclude the hypothesized value of the variance or did the test statistic fall in the rejection region of the chi-square distribution? Do these two approaches to hypothesis testing agree? Press Take New Sample several times. Did the two approaches always agree?

25. Press Replicate. Set Number of Replications to 200 and press Start Experiment. What is the empirical power for your experiment? Why is Type I error not relevant?

26. Press Replicate. Set Number of Replications to 500 and press Start Experiment. What is the empirical power for your experiment?

27. a) Does the number of replications affect the empirical power? b) Which experiment (200 replications or 500 replications) would give the best estimate of empirical power? c) Why do you suppose the maximum number of replications was limited to 500? **Hint:** Look at the display of confidence intervals.

Advanced Learning Exercises   **Name** _____

Press the Show Notebook button, select the Do-It-Yourself tab, and click OK. Accept the default parameters ($\mu_0 = 100$, $\mu = 100$, $\sigma = 10$) with a normal distribution. Use a right-tail test for one mean at $\alpha = 0.05$ for a normal distribution with known variance. Make sure all four displays are showing.

Tests of a Mean: Non-Normality and Type I Error

28. Set Sample Size to n = 4, press Replicate, choose 100 replications, press Start Experiment, and then Finish Experiment. Record the empirical Type I error (from the Analysis of Experiment window). Repeat twice and take the average. Compare the *shape* of the histogram of test statistics with its hypothesized normal sampling distribution. Use the Change Distribution button to do similar experiments for Uniform, Skewed Right, and Very Skewed Right populations. Briefly summarize your findings about the effects of population type on the shape of the histogram and on Type I error. How much do your results vary?

Distribution	Experiment 1	Experiment 2	Experiment 3	Avg Type I Error
Normal	_____	_____	_____	_____
Uniform	_____	_____	_____	_____
Skewed Right	_____	_____	_____	_____
Very Skewed R	_____	_____	_____	_____

29. Press Return to 4 Displays, set Sample Size to n = 25, and repeat exercise 28. What is the effect of a larger sample size on the *shape* of the histogram of test statistics and on the risk of Type I error when the population is non-normal? What do your results reveal about robustness of the sample mean as an estimator of the true mean? Do results vary less than in the previous experiment? Discuss. **Hint:** See the Glossary definition of robustness.

Distribution	Experiment 1	Experiment 2	Experiment 3	Avg Type I Error
Normal	_____	_____	_____	_____
Uniform	_____	_____	_____	_____
Skewed Right	_____	_____	_____	_____
Very Skewed R	_____	_____	_____	_____

Tests of a Mean: Non-Normality and Power

30. Press Return to 4 Displays. To create a false hypothesis, reduce the true mean to 96 and leave everything else the same ($\mu_0 = 100$, $\mu = 96$, $\sigma = 10$, two-tail test for one mean, $\alpha = 0.05$, known variance). Set Sample Size to n = 4 and click the Show True and Hypothesized Sampling Distributions toolbar button. From the appearance of these two distributions, do you expect the test of means to have high power? Explain.

31. Press Replicate and do three experiments of 100 replications for normal, uniform, skewed right, and very skewed right populations. Record the empirical power (from the Analysis of Experiment window) and take the average. Note the *position* of each histogram of test statistics in comparison with the hypothesized sampling distribution. Briefly summarize your findings about the effects of population shape on the histogram and empirical power.

Distribution	Experiment 1	Experiment 2	Experiment 3	Avg Power
Normal	_____	_____	_____	_____
Uniform	_____	_____	_____	_____
Skewed Right	_____	_____	_____	_____
Very Skewed R	_____	_____	_____	_____

32. Press Return to 4 Displays, set Sample Size to n = 25, and repeat exercise 31. What is the effect of increased sample size on power? Why? How much did the experiments vary?

Distribution	Experiment 1	Experiment 2	Experiment 3	Avg Power
Normal	_____	_____	_____	_____
Uniform	_____	_____	_____	_____
Skewed Right	_____	_____	_____	_____
Very Skewed R	_____	_____	_____	_____

Tests of a Variance: Skewness and Type I Error

33. Change Parameter to σ^2. Use the Do-It-Yourself controls to create a two-tailed test of a true null hypothesis with $\alpha = 0.05$, hypothesized variance of 100, true variance of 100, and sample size of 99 (the mean is irrelevant). Press Replicate Experiment and choose 100 replications. Start with a normal population. Do three replication experiments, record the Type I error, and take the average. Repeat the experiment for a skewed right population and a very skewed right population. Briefly summarize your findings about the effects of population skewness on Type I error in a test for a variance. Did the large sample size offer protection against the ill effects of population skewness? Would the direction of skewness matter?

Distribution	Experiment 1	Experiment 2	Experiment 3	Avg Type I Error
Normal	_____	_____	_____	_____
Skewed Right	_____	_____	_____	_____
Very Skewed R	_____	_____	_____	_____

34. Investigate the effect of population skewness on the distribution of the test statistic in a test of one variance with a true null hypothesis. Use the same setup as in exercise 33. Start with 100 replications using a normal population. Compare the *shape* of the histogram of test statistics with the hypothesized chi-square sampling distribution. Should they be the same? Are they? Use the Change Distribution button to do a replication experiment for a skewed right population and a very skewed right population. Briefly summarize your findings about the effects of population skewness on the shape of the histogram. How does this result relate to the previous exercise?

35. How does this conclusion differ from exercise 29 (a test for a mean)? Why do you suppose a test for a variance is so sensitive to the effects of skewness in the population? What implication, if any, is there for real-world tests of variances? **Hint:** Think about the dot plot as you take samples from various distributions.

Tests of a Variance: Sample Size and Power

36. Investigate the effects of sample size on power in a test of one variance. Create a false hypothesis by using the Do-It-Yourself controls to set up a right-tailed test at $\alpha = 0.05$ with hypothesized variance of 100, true variance of 150, and sample size of 6 (the mean is irrelevant). Be *sure* the population is normal. Use 200 replications, record the power of the test, and repeat the experiment. Average the power. Increase the sample size to 25 and repeat the process. Increase the sample size to 96 and repeat the process. What happens to power each time you quadruple the sample size? Should you generalize from these results concerning power? Would you say that H_0 is "very false" in this case?

Sample Size	Experiment 1	Experiment 2	Average
n = 6	_____	_____	_____
n = 24	_____	_____	_____
n = 96	_____	_____	_____

Individual Learning Projects

Write a report on one of the three topics listed below. Use the cut-and-paste facilities of the module to place the appropriate graphs in your report. Include in your report a copy of graphs and/or tables you feel are relevant for each different experimental setup.

1. Investigate the effects of sample size and the variance assumption on power in a test for the mean. Use a two-tailed test. Create a moderately false hypothesis using the Do-It-Yourself controls. Be sure the population is normal and Variance Assumed is set to Known. Start with a small sample size (n < 6). Choose the hypothesized mean, true mean, true standard deviation, and sample size in such a way that the difference in means is about one standard error so that the sampling distributions overlap substantially (use the Show True and Hypothesized Sampling Distribution toolbar button to display the sampling distributions). Use 500 replications to assess the power of the test (from the Analysis of Experiment window). Progressively double the sample size (n, 2n, 4n, 8n, 16n). Repeat, keeping every control the same, except set Variance Assumed to Unknown. Describe the effect sample size has on power, and discuss the effect of the assumption about variances (known or unknown).

2. Use the Do-It-Yourself controls to set up a two-tailed test of one mean at $\alpha = 0.05$ with a hypothesized mean of 100, a true mean of 97, and a *known* standard deviation of 10. Start with a small sample size (n < 5). Use 500 replications to assess the power of the test (from the Analysis of Experiment window). Through trial and error, find out approximately what sample size is required to achieve power of 0.10, 0.25, 0.50, 0.75, and 0.90. If you cannot achieve the desired power, speculate on the reason(s). Repeat the process with an *unknown* standard deviation. What generalizations can you draw?

3. Investigate the effects of level of significance (α) on power in a two-tailed test of one mean by creating a moderately false hypothesis using the Do-It-Yourself controls. Set Variance Assumed to Known. Choose a small sample size (n < 5). Choose the true mean, hypothesized mean, standard deviation, and sample size in such a way that the difference in means is about two standard errors. Use 500 replications to assess the power of the test (from the Analysis of Experiment window). Repeat two or three times and take the average. Try all available α values (0.01, 0.05, 0.10). Keeping everything else the same, change Variance Assumed to Unknown and repeat. Write a summary of your findings about the effect of level of significance on power and the effect of the unknown variance on power. What do you think would happen if sample size were increased (say to n = 30)?

Team Learning Projects

Select one of the three projects listed below. In each case, produce a team project that is suitable for an oral presentation. Use presentation software or large poster boards to display your results. Graphs should be large enough for your audience to see. Each team member should be responsible for producing some of the graphs. Include in your report a copy of all graphs and statistics that you evaluated. Ask your instructor if a written report is also expected.

1. This is a project for a team of five. Investigate the effects on power of population shape, sample size, and variance assumption in a two-tailed test of one mean at $\alpha = 0.05$. Start with *known* variance. Use the Do-It-Yourself controls to create a moderately false hypothesis about a mean by choosing the hypothesized mean, true mean, standard deviation, and sample size in such a way that the difference in means is about one standard error (use the Show True and Hypothesized Sampling Distribution toolbar button to display the sampling distributions). Each team member should choose a different population (normal, skewed right, very skewed right, skewed left, very skewed left) and should replicate the sampling experiment 500 times for sample sizes of 4, 10, and 30. Record the empirical power (from the Analysis of Experiment window). Compare each histogram of test statistics with the hypothesized sampling distribution. How does the population affect empirical power? Repeat for *unknown* variance. How does the assumption about the variance affect empirical power?

2. This is a project for a team of three. Investigate the effects of sample size and population skewness on power and Type I error in a test of the variance. First, create a true hypothesis by using the Do-It-Yourself controls to set up a two-tailed test at $\alpha = 0.05$ with hypothesized variance of 200 and true variance of 200 (the mean is irrelevant). Each team member should choose a different population shape (normal, skewed, very skewed) and should use sample sizes of 10, 25, and 50. Use 500 replications and record the Type I error of the test for each sample size. Repeat the experiment with the hypothesized variance set to 100 (so the null hypothesis is false) and this time record power. Discuss your findings.

3. This is a project for a team of three or four. Construct power curves for a right-tailed test of one mean with *unknown* variance with $\alpha = 0.05$. Using the Do-It-Yourself controls, choose a normal population. Each team member should choose a different sample size so that the range from 5 to 100 is covered. Create a true mean that exceeds the hypothesized mean by three standard errors (use the Show True and Hypothesized Sampling Distribution toolbar button to display the sampling distributions). Do 500 replications three times and find the average power. Record the true mean and average power. With other factors constant, repeat the replication for four other values of the true mean, moving the true mean progressively closer to the hypothesized mean until the sampling distributions are identical. Display the team results on a single graph. For each sample size, plot the power (on the Y-axis) against the true mean (on the X-axis) and connect the points. Discuss what the power curves tell you.

Self-Evaluation Quiz

1. In a right-tail test, the rejection region refers to
    a. the area to the left of the right-tail critical value.
    b. the area to the right of the left-tail critical value.
    c. the area between the left-tail and right-tail critical values.
    d. the area outside the left-tail and right-tail critical values.
    e. none of the above.

2. Which statement is *not* correct regarding the level of significance?
    a. It denotes the probability of Type I error.
    b. It is usually indicated by the symbol α.
    c. If it is reduced, it is harder to reject the null hypothesis.
    d. It is usually set at a high level (such as 90%, 95%, 99%).
    e. It indicates the percent of the time a true null hypothesis will be rejected.

3. Other things equal, in a left-tail test, if α is decreased from 0.05 to 0.01 the critical value
    a. will shift left.
    b. will shift right.
    c. could shift either left or right.
    d. will not shift.
    e. moves to the right tail.

4. In a normal population with known variance the distribution of the sample mean is
    a. normal.
    b. Student's t.
    c. chi-square.
    d. F.
    e. impossible to determine.

5. In a normal population with unknown variance the distribution of the sample mean is
    a. normal.
    b. Student's t.
    c. chi-square.
    d. F.
    e. impossible to determine.

6. Degrees of freedom for a sample mean with $n = 30$ from a normal population with a known variance will be
    a. 30
    b. 29
    c. 28
    d. 31
    e. irrelevant.

7.   Type I error is
     a.   the probability of correctly rejecting the null hypothesis.
     b.   the probability of correctly accepting the null hypothesis.
     c.   the probability of incorrectly rejecting the null hypothesis.
     d.   the probability of incorrectly accepting the null hypothesis.
     e.   none of the above.

8.   In a test of one mean, if the null hypothesis is true, the histogram of sample means in a replicated sampling experiment
     a.   will be shifted to the right of the hypothesized sampling distribution.
     b.   will be shifted to the left of the hypothesized sampling distribution.
     c.   could be shifted either left or right of the hypothesized sampling distribution.
     d.   will not be shifted relative to the hypothesized sampling distribution.
     e.   has none of the above behaviors.

9.   The distribution of the sample variance is
     a.   always symmetric.
     b.   always skewed right.
     c.   always skewed left.
     d.   more than one of the above.
     e.   none of the above.

10.   In a normal population the theoretical distribution of the sample variance is
     a.   normal.
     b.   Student's t.
     c.   chi-square.
     d.   F.
     e.   impossible to determine.

11.   Degrees of freedom for a sample variance with n = 10 from a normal population will be
     a.   10
     b.   9
     c.   8
     d.   irrelevant.
     e.   none of the above.

12.   In terms of Type I error (if H_0 is true) or power (if H_0 is false), a test of a hypothesis about a mean is fairly insensitive (robust) to non-normality of the population.
     a.   True.
     b.   False.

Glossary of Terms

Acceptance region Portion of the hypothesized distribution that is bounded by the critical value(s). Its area is $1 - \alpha$ where α is the chosen level of significance. Since a given sample can disprove (but cannot prove) the null hypothesis, it is more accurate to call it the *non-rejection region*. See **Type I error**.

Alternative hypothesis Denoted H_1, it is the converse of the null hypothesis (e.g., H_0: $\mu = 5$ and H_1: $\mu \neq 5$). If the sample evidence contradicts H_0, we would reject H_0 in favor of the alternative hypothesis H_1. Often, a test is motivated by the suspicion that the null hypothesis may be false.

Chi-square distribution When testing one sample variance against a hypothesized value of the population variance, the sampling distribution is chi-square with $n - 1$ degrees of freedom. More generally, the chi-square distribution describes the sum of squared independent identically distributed normal random variables (e.g., in the numerator of the sample variance).

Confidence interval Range of values that would enclose a true (generally unknown) population parameter (such as a population mean or variance) a given percentage of the time.

Confidence level Desired probability of enclosing an unknown population parameter when creating a confidence interval from sample data. The confidence level, denoted $1 - \alpha$, is chosen by the researcher and is usually expressed as a percent (typically 90%, 95%, or 99%). The higher the confidence level, the wider the confidence interval. See **Level of significance**.

Critical value Value on the X-axis that defines the rejection region for a hypothesis. In a one-tail test, the critical value defines a right-tail or left-tail area. In a two-tail test, there are critical values defining rejection regions in each tail. The critical value is determined by the level of significance. A test statistic beyond the critical value(s) is unlikely if the null hypothesis is true. Critical values may be found in a table or may be generated by a computer algorithm.

Decision rule Diagram that illustrates the criterion for rejection of the null hypothesis. It shows the hypothesized sampling distribution of the test statistic with its critical value(s) labeled and a shaded rejection region for the specified level of significance.

Degrees of freedom For a Student's t-test for one mean with unknown population variance, degrees of freedom will be $n - 1$. For a chi-square test of one variance, degrees of freedom will also be $n - 1$.

Level of significance The desired probability of Type I error. It is set by the researcher (typical values are 0.10, 0.05, and 0.01) and is denoted α. Other things equal, the power of a hypothesis test increases as the level of significance increases. See **Confidence level**.

Null hypothesis Denoted H_0, it is a statement that we try to reject (for example, H_0: $\sigma^2 = 5$). The null hypothesis is not necessarily chosen because we believe it to be true, but rather as an important reference point. If the sample evidence contradicts H_0, the null hypothesis is rejected. Otherwise, it awaits further testing and could be rejected at a later time.

One-tail test In a one-tail test, the alternative hypothesis always contains > (for a right-tail test) or < (for a left-tail test). For example, the hypotheses H_0: $\mu \geq 5$ and H_1: $\mu < 5$ imply a left-tail test.

P-value Probability that a result as extreme as (or more extreme than) the observed sample statistic would arise by chance if the null hypothesis were true.

Power If the null hypothesis is false, *theoretical* power is the probability of rejecting the null hypothesis H_0 when it is false (or $1 - \beta$ where β is the probability of Type II error). For example, in a test of $\mu = 5$, power will be low if the true mean is near 5, but will be higher if the true mean differs substantially from 5. The ideal power is near 1. *Empirical* power is the ratio of the number of rejections to the number of times the test is performed.

Rejection region Area under the hypothesized sampling distribution that lies beyond the critical value(s). It is determined by α, the probability of Type I error. If the test statistic falls within this region, we will reject the null hypothesis. See **Level of significance**.

Robustness Quality of being unaffected by a violation of an assumption. For example, the Student's t test is robust to non-normality in the population if the sample is moderately large.

Sample size Number of observations that are taken at random from the population. Other things equal, power increases as the sample size increases.

Sampling distribution Theoretical distribution of the estimator or the test statistic assuming the null hypothesis is true.

Test statistic Calculated value using the sample statistic and a hypothesized population parameter. Its distribution is known if the null hypothesis is true. The test statistic is compared with a critical value to see whether the null hypothesis should be rejected.

Two-tail test In a two-tail test, the alternative hypothesis always contains $\neq$. For example, the hypotheses H_0: $\mu = 5$ and H_1: $\mu \neq 5$ imply a two-tail test.

Type I error Error of rejecting a null hypothesis that is true. The probability of Type I error is denoted α. It is the area under the hypothesized sampling distribution that is beyond the critical value(s). See **Level of significance**.

Type II error Error of accepting a null hypothesis that is false. The probability of Type II error is denoted β. The probability of Type II error is the area under the true sampling distribution that is not in the rejection region. See **Power**.

Solutions to Self-Evaluation Quiz

1. e   Read the Overview of Concepts and Illustration of Concepts. Consult the Glossary.
2. d   Read the Overview of Concepts. Consult the Glossary.
3. a   Read the Overview of Concepts. Do Individual Learning Project 3.
4. a   Do Exercises 1–6. Read the Overview of Concepts.
5. b   Do Exercises 7–9. Read the Overview of Concepts.
6. e   Do Exercises 5 and 6. Consult the Glossary.
7. c   Do Exercises 10–13. Read the Overview of Concepts.
8. d   Do Exercises 13–16.
9. b   Do Exercises 21–25. Consult the Glossary. Read the Overview of Concepts.
10. c   Do Exercises 21–25. Consult the Glossary.
11. b   Do Exercises 21 and 22. Consult the Glossary.
12. a   Do Exercises 28–32. Read the Overview of Concepts.

CHAPTER 10

Visualizing Two-Sample Hypothesis Tests

CONCEPTS
- Null Hypothesis, Alternative Hypothesis, Two-Sample Tests, One-Tail Test, Two-Tail Test, Confidence Interval, Decision Rule, Level of Significance, Sampling Distribution, Critical Value, Test Statistic, Type I Error, Type II Error, Power

OBJECTIVES
- Become familiar with the sampling distributions used in two-sample parametric tests for means and variances

- Understand the relationship between a confidence interval and the corresponding two-sample hypothesis test

- Be able to explain the meaning of Type I error, Type II error, and power

- Know the assumptions underlying two-sample hypothesis tests and recognize the effects of violating each of them

Overview of Concepts

A one-sample test compares a sample statistic with an assumed parameter value (usually a historic benchmark). In contrast, a **two-sample test** compares two sample statistics with each other. Usually, the main issue is simply whether or not the two samples differ (e.g., in terms of means or variances). The first step is to create two mutually exclusive hypotheses that exhaust the possibilities. For example, in a laptop PC battery test, does brand A have a different mean rundown time than brand B? The hypotheses are

$H_0: \mu_A = \mu_B$ (mean battery rundown time is the same for both brands)
$H_1: \mu_A \neq \mu_B$ (mean battery rundown time differs for the two brands)

These hypotheses are a special case of a more general test for a specified difference of means:

$H_0: \mu_A - \mu_B = D$ (mean difference in battery rundown time is D)
$H_1: \mu_A - \mu_B \neq D$ (mean difference in battery rundown time is not D)

However, since $D = 0$ is the usual choice, only the first form will be discussed. The **null hypothesis** (H_0) is the statement or belief that we try to reject. The **alternative hypothesis** (H_1) is the exact converse of the null hypothesis. Evidence is gathered by testing randomly chosen batteries (n_A of brand A and n_B of brand B). Samples will be as large as possible, given the constraints of time and budget for the test. Equal sample sizes are logical, but are not necessary (and sometimes impossible). A **two-tail test** is commonly used when there is no prior belief about directionality. A **one-tail test** (e.g., $H_0: \mu_A \leq \mu_B$ and $H_1: \mu_A > \mu_B$) might be relevant if there are prior reasons (such as a manufacturer's claim) to believe that one brand lasts longer than the other.

If the **confidence interval** around the estimated difference of means includes zero ($D = 0$) we would reject H_0. But the usual way to test the hypothesis is to compute a **test statistic** and compare it with a **critical value** using our knowledge of the **sampling distribution** of the test statistic. The sampling distribution of the test statistic for the difference of two means is standard normal if the population variances are known or Student's t if the population variances are unknown. If the variances are unknown but are assumed equal, the t-test uses the sum of the sample degrees of freedom $(n_A - 1) + (n_B - 1)$. If the variances are unknown but are assumed unequal, a more complex approach is required (see Behrens-Fisher problem in the Glossary). The **decision rule** states the criterion for rejecting H_0. If H_0 is not rejected, it is tentatively accepted (many statisticians prefer to say that H_0 is "not rejected").

If H_0 is true and we mistakenly reject it, we have committed **Type I error**, while if a false H_0 is mistakenly accepted we have committed **Type II error**. Otherwise, no error has been committed. The probability of Type I error is denoted α. The probability of Type II error is denoted β. The probability of correctly rejecting a false null hypothesis is called **power** and is equal to $1 - \beta$. The value of α (called the **level of significance**) is chosen in advance (typically 0.10, 0.05, or 0.01) and is embodied in the decision rule. The value of β cannot be chosen because it depends on the true parameter value, which is usually unknown. However, power may be found for any possible true parameter value. This module allows you to estimate Type I error or power empirically by sampling a known population many times.

Illustration of Concepts

Do the weights of Bartlett pears have the same variance as the weights of D'Anjou pears? The **null hypothesis** (H_0) is that the variances are equal, while the **alternative hypothesis** (H_1) is that they are unequal. A **two-tail** test is appropriate when it does not matter which variance is greater (otherwise a **one-tail test** could be used).

H_0: $\sigma_1^2 = \sigma_2^2$ or $\sigma_1^2 / \sigma_2^2 = 1$ (population variances are the same)
H_1: $\sigma_1^2 \neq \sigma_2^2$ or $\sigma_1^2 / \sigma_2^2 \neq 1$ (population variances are different)

Early in the 20th century, the statistician R. A. Fisher (1890 – 1935) showed that these hypotheses may be tested using the F **sampling distribution** (named after its discoverer).

To test these hypotheses, two samples are taken. A sample of 18 Bartlett pears shows a mean weight of 242.4 grams with a standard deviation of 21.26 grams, while a sample of 13 D'Anjou pears shows a mean weight of 236.5 grams with a standard deviation of 9.563 grams. The dot plot (Figure 1) suggests that the D'Anjou pears (large dots) have less dispersion than the Bartlett pears (small dots). Also, the confidence intervals for each variance (top of Figure 2) do not overlap. More formally, the two-sided 95% **confidence interval** for the ratio of variances (bottom of Figure 2) does not include 1, suggesting that H_0 should be rejected. If H_0 is true (and if the population is normal) the ratio of the two sample variances will follow an F distribution with $df_1 = 18 - 1$ and $df_2 = 13 - 1$. The **test statistic** is $F = s_1^2 / s_2^2 = (21.26)^2 / (9.563)^2 = 4.940$. At the 0.05 **level of significance** the lower **critical value** is 0.354 and the upper critical value is 3.129, as illustrated in the **decision rule** (Figure 3). Since the test statistic lies in the right-tail rejection region, we reject H_0 and conclude that the population variances are unequal. The F-test must agree with the confidence interval approach.

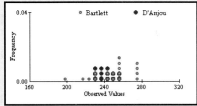

Figure 1: Dot Plot

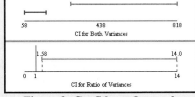

Figure 2: Confidence Intervals

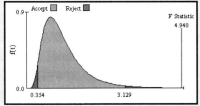

Figure 3: Decision Rule

Could different samples lead to different results? Yes. This sampling experiment was repeated four more times. The results of all five samples are shown in the table below. Samples 1, 2, 3, and 5 lead to rejection (and possible **Type I error**) while sample 4 leads to acceptance (and possible **Type II error**). Which decision is correct? We don't know. The **power** of the test is unknown since the true population variances are unknown. Uncertainty is inherent in all statistical decisions. Since only one sample usually is taken, we must accept the possibility of Type I or Type II error in any decision we make.

Sample	s_1^2	s_2^2	F Statistic	Decision
1	451.8	91.46	4.940	Reject
2	549.6	89.91	6.113	Reject
3	577.2	110.9	5.204	Reject
4	318.8	124.9	2.552	Accept
5	611.9	64.99	9.415	Reject

Orientation to Basic Features

This module helps you learn how to test hypotheses for two means (with known or unknown population variances) and for two variances. It permits one-tail and two-tail tests and shows the relationship between confidence intervals and hypothesis tests using appropriate scenarios. You may also specify two populations and set their means and standard deviations. Using replication, you can study the meaning of Type I error, Type II error, and power.

1. **Select a Scenario**

   Start the module by clicking on the module's icon, title, or chapter number in the *Visual Statistics* menu and pressing the Run Module button. When the module is loaded, you will be on the introduction page of the Notebook. Read the questions and then click the Concepts tab to see the concepts that you will learn. Click the Scenarios tab. Click on Unknown Variances Assumed Equal. Select a scenario, read it, and press OK.

2. **Main Display**

   The main display opens with a large display (Dot Plot and Estimates of the Mean) and a Control Panel. Click Take New Sample and observe the changes in the sampled items (red and blue dots) and confidence intervals (horizontal red and blue line segments). The sample means (red and blue fulcrums) will change to reflect each new sample. The Replicate button will remain inactive until you press Show 4 Displays (but do not do it yet).

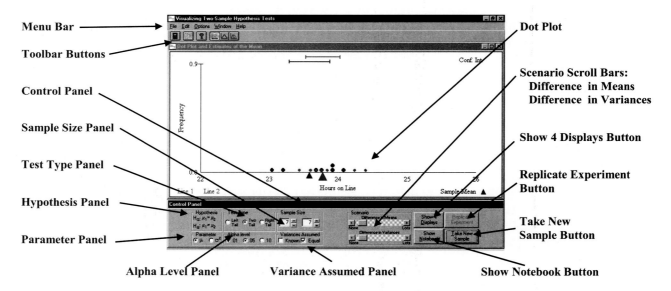

3. **Toolbar Buttons**

   Place the cursor over the fifth toolbar button located above the dot plot. A label will appear (Show Populations Sampled). Click the button and see an overlay of the population to be sampled. This distribution does not change when you take samples, but will reflect any changes you make in the true or hypothesized parameters. Click the sixth toolbar button (Show Sampling Distributions) and observe the narrower sampling distributions. The sampling distributions will not change when you take samples, but will reflect any changes you make in the sample sizes or in the true and hypothesized parameters. Click the fourth toolbar button (Show Dot Plot Only) to restore the simple dot plot.

4. **Show 4 Displays**
    Click Show 4 Displays. Read the Hint that appears and click OK. The Control Panel will move to the upper right and its controls will be rearranged. The dot plot will become smaller and will be in the upper left. Two new quadrant displays (Confidence Interval for Difference in Means and t Distribution) will be on the bottom. The dot plot and confidence interval will change as you take new samples, while the t Distribution display remains the same

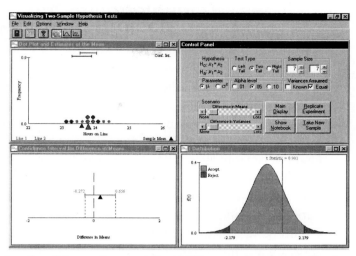

    except for the t-statistic. Right-click on the Confidence Interval for Difference in Means display and select Statistics and Parameters to see a list of sample statistics and parameter values. Right-click on the Statistics and Parameters display and select Analysis of Experiment to see a verbal description of the results of your experiment. Right-click the Analysis of Experiment display and select Confidence Interval to see the original displays.

5. **Using the Control Panel**
    In the Test Type panel, click each option (Right-Tail, Left-Tail, Two-Tail). The t distribution will match the test type you have selected. Click each option (.10, .05, .01) in the Alpha Level panel and verify that the t Distribution tail area and the confidence intervals change to reflect your choices. Check Known in the Variances Assumed panel and observe that the t distribution is replaced by a normal distribution. Uncheck Known to return to the t distribution. Uncheck Equal in the Variances Assumed panel. The t distribution and the confidence intervals will change. Click σ^2 in the Parameter panel. The t distribution is replaced by the F distribution and the confidence intervals now show variances instead of means. Click μ in the Parameter panel, and the displays again show a mean. Click the Sample Size spin button to alter the sample size (2 to 100). Click the fifth toolbar button to show an overlay of the population to be sampled. Change the position of any scroll bar in the Scenario panel (Difference in Means, Difference in Variances) and press Take New Sample. The population does not change as you take samples.

6. **Copying a Display**
    Click on the display you wish to copy. Its window title will be highlighted. Select Copy from the Edit menu (on the menu bar) or Ctrl-C. It can then be pasted into other applications.

7. **Help**
    Click on Help on the menu bar at the top of the screen. Search for Help lets you search an index for this module, Contents shows a table of contents for this module, Using Help gives instructions on how to use Help, and About gives licensing and copyright information.

8. **Exit**
    Close the module by selecting Exit in the File menu (or click ☒ in the upper right-hand corner of the window). You will be returned to the *Visual Statistics* main menu.

Orientation to Additional Features

1. **Replication**

   Click the Replicate Experiment button on the Control Panel. At the top are nine toolbar buttons. The new ones control the confidence level (99%, 95%, 90%) and the test type (Left-tail, Two-Tail, Right-Tail). On the left is the Confidence Intervals – Difference in Means display. On the right is a Control Panel containing the Analysis of Experiment window and scroll bar controls (Difference in Means, Difference in Variances) and a Histogram/Distribution display. Click the Number of Replications list box to vary the number of replications (20, 50, 100, 200, 500). If you click the Start Experiment button, it becomes Finish Experiment and Return to 4 Displays becomes Pause Experiment. If you click Pause Experiment, the displays are frozen in their current state and Pause Experiment becomes Continue Experiment. If you click Finish Experiment, the confidence interval and histogram displays go to their final state without showing any intermediate steps. Click Return to 4 Displays to exit replication.

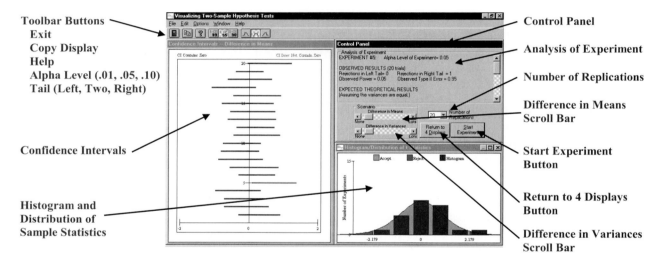

2. **Do-It-Yourself Controls**

   Click Show Notebook, choose the Do-It-Yourself tab, and click OK. The Parameters panel lets you change the means and standard deviations with scroll bars or by entering values into the edit boxes (not limited to the 1 to 10 scroll bar range). Choose any of six populations to sample (Normal, Uniform, Skewed Left, Skewed Right, Very Skewed Left, Very Skewed Right) by pressing its button. When you click OK, the Control Panel's scenario scroll bars are replaced by the Do-It-Yourself Summary panel shown at the right. Press Change DIY Parameters to use the Parameters panel again. The replication control panel also shows the Do-It-Yourself panel instead of scenario scroll bars.

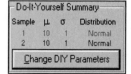

3. **Options**

   Click Options on the menu bar. You may change terminology from Accept Null Hypothesis to Do Not Reject Null Hypothesis. This option may be preferred by some, since we do not actually prove a null hypothesis.

Basic Learning Exercises

Name _____

Press the Show Notebook button, select the Scenarios tab, and click on Known Variances. Select the Day and Night Students scenario, read it, and press OK. Make sure all four displays are showing.

Tests for Two Means with Known Variances

1. Express the hypotheses in words. Do you believe a two-tail test is appropriate? Is the null hypothesis true or false? If there is a difference in means, do you expect it will be easy to detect using sampling? **Hint:** Look at the scenario scroll bars.

2. If you are using quadrant displays, click Main Screen. Click the Show Population Sampled toolbar button. Describe the distribution of the populations being sampled. Are the two population variances equal? How do you know?

3. Click Take New Sample a few times. Assess the overlap of sampled items and the relative positions of the sample means (red and blue fulcrums). Then click the Show Sampling Distribution toolbar button. Do these displays tend to confirm or disconfirm your answer to exercise 1 regarding the anticipated degree of difficulty of detecting the actual difference in means through random sampling? Why aren't the variances of the sampling distributions identical, given that the population variances are the same?

4. Click Show 4 Displays. a) Why does the decision rule show a normal distribution? b) Is this normal distribution justified on the basis of sample size? Explain. c) When you press Take New Sample, do its critical values change? d) Does the test statistic change? Explain.

5. Click Take New Sample 10 times, observing how often the null hypothesis is accepted (z statistic falls in the green acceptance region or the confidence interval for the difference of means includes zero). a) Did the z-test always agree with the confidence interval approach? b) Based on sampling results alone, what decision would probably be made about H_0? c) If you make this decision, would you commit Type I error? Type II error? d) What do you conclude about the power of the test in this example? Should this conclusion about power be generalized?

6. Right-click on the Dot Plot and Estimates of Means display (in the upper left quadrant) and select Statistics and Parameters from the menu. a) What are the true population means? b) How large is the true difference in population means? c) Does the table's CI for Difference always agree with the visual display called Confidence Interval for Difference in Means? Click Take New Sample several times, watching these two displays.

7. Right-click on the Statistics and Parameters display (in the upper left quadrant) and select Analysis of Experiment from the menu. What does the analysis tell you?

Intermediate Learning Exercises   Name _____

Test for Means with Known Variances
Press the Show Notebook button, select the Scenarios tab, and click on Known Variance. Select the Day and Night Students scenario, read it, and press OK. If the dot plot display is not visible, right-click the upper left display and select Dot Plot from the menu.

8. Press Replicate. Set the number of replications to 100. Press Start Experiment and then Finish Experiment (to avoid having to watch the graphs build). A confidence interval that fails to include zero (shown in red) indicates rejection of the null hypothesis (H_0: $\mu_1 = \mu_2$). Record the number of rejections from the Analysis of Experiment window. Repeat this experiment twice. Find the total number of rejections and compute the average power. What is the advantage of doing the experiment three times? Compare the histogram of test statistics with the hypothesized normal distribution and comment on its appearance.

Experiment:	1	2	3	Total	Avg. Power
Rejections:	____	____	____	____	____

9. Press Return to 4 Displays. Move the Difference in Means scroll bar to the middle (halfway between None and Lots). Examine the sampling distributions (by clicking the Show Sampling Distribution toolbar button) and make a general prediction about the power of the test. Press Replicate, do 100 replications three times, and record the results. Find the total number of rejections and compute the average power. Compare the histogram of test statistics to the normal distribution. Compare these results with exercise 8.

Experiment:	1	2	3	Total	Avg. Power
Rejections:	____	____	____	____	____

10. Press Return to 4 Displays. Double both sample sizes (to 44 and 52). Describe the sampling distributions. Press Replicate. Do 100 replications three times and record the results below. Find the total number of rejections and the average power. Did the larger sample sizes improve the power? What does the histogram of test statistics tell you? Explain.

Experiment:	1	2	3	Total	Avg. Power
Rejections:	____	____	____	____	____

Tests for Two Means with Unknown Variances

11. Press Return to 4 Displays. Press the Show Notebook button, select the Scenarios tab, and click on Unknown Variances Assumed Equal. Select the Making Cars scenario, read it, and click OK. Set the Difference in Means and Difference in Variances scroll bars to None and press Take New Sample. Why is the t distribution displayed instead of the normal distribution?

12. Right-click on the Confidence Interval for Difference in Means window and select Statistics and Parameters. Press Take New Sample several times. Do the degrees of freedom (df) and critical values change? Explain why or why not.

13. Set Variance Assumed to Unequal and press Take New Sample several times, watching what happens to degrees of freedom. Explain what you observe. **Hint:** Click Help or examine the formula for Welch's correction in the Glossary.

14. Set Variances Assumed to Equal and press Replicate. Choose 100 replications. What is the empirical Type I error? Repeat a few times. What does the histogram of test statistics tell you? Interpret these results.

15. Set the Difference in Variances scroll bar to Lots and again perform 100 replications. What is the empirical Type I error? Does it appear that Type I error is compromised if unknown, unequal variances are assumed equal? What does the histogram of test statistics look like?

16. Click Return to 4 Displays. Set Variances Assumed to Unequal and press Replicate. Choose 100 replications. What is the empirical Type I error? Repeat a few times. What does the histogram of test statistics tell you? Interpret these results.

17. Set the Difference in Means scroll bar to its midpoint. Write down the essential aspects of your sampling experiment, including sample size (use Return to 4 Displays if you need to refresh your memory). Then perform 100 replications. Estimate the empirical power. What does the histogram of test statistics look like?

18. Click Return to 4 Displays. Increase both sample sizes to 30, click Replicate Experiment, and perform 100 replications. Estimate the empirical power. Did the larger sample sizes have a strong effect on power? Compare these results with your answer in exercise 10.

Tests for Two Variances

19. Click Return to 4 Displays. Press the Show Notebook button, select the Do-It-Yourself tab, and press OK. Create unequal variances by setting $\sigma_1 = 1.5$ and $\sigma_2 = 1$ (the means are irrelevant). Make sure both populations are normal. Click OK. Choose *unknown* variances by unchecking Known in the Variances Assumed panel. Change Parameter from μ to σ^2. Set both sample sizes to 10. Be sure Test Type is Two-Tail and Alpha Level is 0.05. State the hypotheses in two different ways and explain their meaning. What is the true ratio of variances? Using sampling, how hard do you think it will be to detect the false null hypothesis you created?

20. Click Take New Sample. Why is the F distribution the relevant distribution? What are its degrees of freedom (df)? Explain. What are its critical values? **Hint:** Look at the Statistics and Parameters window or right-click on the lower left display to show the Analysis of Experiment window if you need further information.

    Numerator df   _____   Left-tail critical value   _____
    Denominator df   _____   Right-tail critical value   _____

21. Click Take New Sample 10 times, and count how many times the F test statistic falls in the red rejection region in either tail (refer to the F distribution that is displayed). Would you say the power of the test is high? Explain your reasoning.

22. Press Replicate. Set Number of Replications to 100 and press Start Experiment. Record the number of rejections. Repeat two more times. Find the total number of rejections and compute the average power. Why is Type I error not relevant?

Experiment:	1	2	3	Total	Power
Rejections:	_____	_____	_____	_____	_____

23. Describe the histogram of test statistics. Why doesn't it resemble the F distribution?

Advanced Learning Exercises

Name _____

Tests of Two Means: Skewness and Type I Error

Click Return to 4 Displays. Press the Show Notebook button, select the Do-It-Yourself tab, and click OK. Set $\mu_1 = 5$ and $\mu_2 = 5$ (equal means) and set $\sigma_1 = 1$ and $\sigma_2 = 1$ (equal variances). Make sure *both* populations are normal and click OK. Choose *unknown* variances by unchecking Known in the Variances Assumed panel. Set Parameter to μ. Set both sample sizes to 10. Set Test Type to Two-Tail and Alpha Level to 0.05. Check Equal in the Variances Assumed panel. Make sure the four displays are showing.

24. Press Replicate and do 100 replications. Record the empirical Type I error (from the Analysis of Experiment window). Repeat twice and take the average. Compare the histogram of test statistics with its hypothesized Student's t sampling distribution. Use the Change DIY Parameters button to do the same experiment with both populations Skewed Right. Does skewness affect the shape of the histogram and Type I error? How much do your results vary? In terms of Type I error, is the test for two means robust to skewness?

Distribution	Experiment 1	Experiment 2	Experiment 3	Avg Type I Error
Normal	_____	_____	_____	_____
Skewed Right	_____	_____	_____	_____

Tests of Two Variances: Skewness and Type I Error

25. Click Return to 4 Displays and change Parameter to σ^2. Increase both sample sizes to 50. Click Change DIY Parameters and set both populations to Normal. Do 100 replications and record the Type I error (from the Analysis of Experiment window). Repeat two times and take the average. Compare the histogram of test statistics with its hypothesized F sampling distribution. Use the Change Distribution button to do the same experiment with both populations Skewed Right. Describe the effects of skewness on the shape of the histogram and on Type I error. In terms of Type I error, is the test for two variances robust to skewness? Did the large sample size help? Are skewed populations encountered very often in reality?

Distribution	Experiment 1	Experiment 2	Experiment 3	Avg Type I Error
Normal	_____	_____	_____	_____
Skewed Right	_____	_____	_____	_____

Tests of Two Means: Skewness and Power

26. Press Return to 4 Displays and click Change DIY Parameters. To create a false null hypothesis about the means, set $\mu_1 = 6$ and $\mu_2 = 5$ (unequal means) but leave the variances unchanged at $\sigma_1 = 1.0$ and $\sigma_2 = 1.0$ (equal variances). Make both populations normal and click OK. Be sure the variances are still assumed unknown. Set both sample sizes to 10. Set Test Type to Two-Tail, Alpha Level to 0.05, and Variances Assumed to Equal. Click the Show Sampling Distributions toolbar button. From the appearance of these distributions, will this test of difference of means have high power? Is Type I error relevant here? Explain.

27. Press Replicate and do 100 replications. Record the empirical power (from the Analysis of Experiment window). Repeat twice and take the average. Compare the histogram of test statistics with the hypothesized Student's t sampling distribution. Use the Change DIY Parameters button to do the same experiment with both populations skewed right. How much do your results vary? Does skewness adversely affect power in a test for two means?

Distribution	Experiment 1	Experiment 2	Experiment 3	Avg Power
Normal	_____	_____	_____	_____
Skewed Right	_____	_____	_____	_____

Tests of Two Variances: Skewness and Power

28. Press Return to 4 Displays and click Change DIY Parameters. Create a false null hypothesis about variances with $\mu_1 = 5$ and $\mu_2 = 5$ (equal means) and $\sigma_1 = 1.5$ and $\sigma_2 = 1.0$ (unequal variances). Make sure both populations are *normal* and click OK. Change Parameter to σ^2. Do 100 replications three times, record the empirical power, and take the average. Compare the histogram of test statistics with its hypothesized F distribution. Do the same experiment when both populations are skewed right. Describe the effects of skewness on the histogram and on power. Compare this result with exercise 25. How does this illustrate the importance of the normality assumption in a test for variances?

Distribution	Experiment 1	Experiment 2	Experiment 3	Avg Power
Normal	_____	_____	_____	_____
Skewed Right	_____	_____	_____	_____

Individual Learning Projects

Write a report on one of the three topics listed below. Use the cut-and-paste facilities of the module to place the appropriate graphs in your report. Include in your report a copy of graphs and/or tables you feel are relevant for each different experimental setup.

1. Investigate the effects of the variance assumption and unbalanced sample size on Type I error in a test for two means. Using the Do-It-Yourself controls, set $\mu_1 = 5.0$ and $\mu_2 = 5.0$ (equal means), set $\sigma_1 = 3.0$ and $\sigma_2 = 1.5$ (unequal variances), make both populations normal, and let variances be assumed unknown. Specify a two-tailed test with $\alpha = 0.05$ and assume *equal* variances. Start with balanced samples $n_1 = 20$ and $n_2 = 20$ (combined sample size of 40). Do 100 replications several times, find the average Type I error of the test (check the Analysis of Experiment window), and compare the histogram of test statistics with the hypothesized t distribution. Repeat the replication for unbalanced samples $n_1 = 30$ and $n_2 = 10$ (combined sample size of 40) and again for unbalanced samples with $n_1 = 10$ and $n_2 = 30$ (combined sample size of 40). Then repeat the entire series of replication experiments with variances assumed *unequal*. Describe the effect on Type I error of the correctness of the assumption about variances with balanced or unbalanced sample sizes.

2. Construct two power curves for a two-tailed test of two means. With the Do-It-Yourself controls, set $\mu_1 = 5.0$ and $\mu_2 = 3.5$ (unequal means), $\sigma_1 = 1.6$ and $\sigma_2 = 1.6$ (equal variances), make both populations normal, and let variances be assumed *unknown* and equal. Choose $\alpha = 0.05$. Choose a small sample size (under 10) and make both samples the same size. Record the true difference of means, do 100 replications three times, and find the average power of the test. Repeat the experiment as you decrease μ_1 in steps of 0.5 until it equals μ_2 (true null hypothesis). Make a power curve by plotting the average power (on the Y-axis) against the true difference in means (on the X-axis). Then make a power curve for a sample size that is four times as large. Explain what the power curves tell you.

3. Investigate the effects of sample size on power in a test of two variances. Create a moderately false hypothesis using the Do-It-Yourself controls to set $\sigma_1 = 5.1$ and $\sigma_2 = 3.3$ (the means are irrelevant). Be sure the populations are normal. Choose $\alpha = 0.05$ and a two-tailed test. Start with small but equal sample sizes (under 6). Use 100 replications several times and average the power of the test (from the Analysis of Experiment window). Progressively double the sample sizes (n, $2n$, $4n$, $8n$, $16n$) and repeat the experiment. Describe the effect on power of progressively doubling the sample sizes. How large a sample is needed so the power of the test is at least 50%? At least 90%?

Team Learning Projects

Select one of the three projects listed below. In each case, produce a team project that is suitable for an oral presentation. Use presentation software or large poster boards to display your results. Graphs should be large enough for your audience to see. Each team member should be responsible for producing some of the graphs. Include in your report a copy of all graphs and statistics that you evaluated. Ask your instructor if a written report is also expected.

1. This is a project for a team of two. Investigate unbalanced samples on power in a test of two variances, and the possible mitigating effects of sample size. Create a moderately false hypothesis about variances using the Do-It-Yourself controls, setting $\sigma_1 = 6.0$ and $\sigma_2 = 4.0$ (the means are irrelevant). Be sure the populations are normal. Choose a two-tailed test for σ^2 with $\alpha = 0.05$. The first team member should do 100 replications several times and average the power of the test (from the Analysis of Experiment window) for sample sizes $n_1 = 6, 12, 24, 36, 42$ and $n_2 = 48 - n_1$ (so the combined sample size always remains at 48). The second team member will do a similar experiment for sample sizes $n_1 = 12, 24, 48, 72, 84$ and $n_2 = 96 - n_1$ (so the combined sample size always remains at 96). Are unbalanced sample sizes injurious to power? To what extent do larger sample sizes enhance power and/or mitigate any adverse effects that may exist?

2. This is a project for a team of three. Investigate the effects of population non-normality and sample size on Type I error. With the Do-It-Yourself controls set $\mu_1 = 6.0$ and $\mu_2 = 6.0$ (equal means) and $\sigma_1 = 2.0$ and $\sigma_2 = 2.0$ (equal variances). Be sure the variances are assumed *unknown*. Each team member should choose a different population shape (normal, uniform, skewed) and should use sample sizes of 6, 24, and 96, first in a test for equal means (a true hypothesis) assuming equal variances, and then in a test for equal variances (also a true hypothesis). Use 100 replications three times, find the average Type I error of the test for each sample size, and examine the histogram of test statistics. Summarize your findings about Type I error. Does larger sample size mitigate potential adverse effects of non-normality for means and variances?

3. This is a project for a team of three or more. Construct power curves for a two-tailed test of two means. With the Do-It-Yourself controls, set $\mu_1 = 6.0$ and $\mu_2 = 5.0$ (unequal means), set $\sigma_1 = 1.5$ and $\sigma_2 = 1.5$ (equal variances), make both populations normal, and let variances be assumed *unknown*. Assume equal variances and choose $\alpha = 0.05$. Each team member should choose a different sample size so that the range from 5 to 100 is covered (keep both samples the same size). Record the true difference of means, do 100 replications three times, and find the average power of the test. Repeat the experiment as you increase μ_2 in steps of 0.2 until μ_2 equals μ_1 (true null hypothesis). Present the combined team results on one graph with a power curve for each sample size. For each power curve, plot the average power (on the Y-axis) against the true mean (on the X-axis). Discuss what the power curves tell you.

Self-Evaluation Quiz

1. Type II error is
    a. the probability of correctly rejecting the null hypothesis.
    b. the probability of correctly accepting the null hypothesis.
    c. the probability of incorrectly rejecting the null hypothesis.
    d. the probability of incorrectly accepting the null hypothesis.
    e. none of the above.

2. To compare two sample means with known variances, the statistician would use the
    a. Student's t distribution.
    b. chi-square distribution.
    c. normal distribution.
    d. F distribution.
    e. binomial distribution.

3. Which procedure might be used to compare two sample means?
    a. Draw dot plots for the samples and compare them visually.
    b. Calculate a test statistic and compare it with a critical value.
    c. Calculate a confidence interval and see if it contains zero.
    d. Calculate a p-value for a test statistic and compare it with an α level.
    e. All of the above are useful procedures.

4. To compare two sample means with unknown variances, the statistician would use the
    a. Student's t distribution.
    b. chi-square distribution.
    c. normal distribution.
    d. F distribution.
    e. binomial distribution.

5. The one-sided confidence interval for a difference of means
    a. always extends to infinity on one side.
    b. is similar to a one-sided hypothesis test.
    c. would signal rejection of the hypothesis of equal means if it does not include zero.
    d. puts the entire α risk in one tail.
    e. has all of the above characteristics.

6. In a test of two means with samples of size n_1 and n_2, if the population variances are unknown and assumed unequal, which statement is *incorrect*?
    a. We face a problem known as the Behrens-Fisher problem.
    b. The sample variances are biased estimators.
    c. Degrees of freedom will generally be less than $n_1 + n_2 - 2$
    d. Degrees of freedom will generally be greater than the minimum of $n_1 - 1$ or $n_2 - 1$
    e. It is appropriate to use Welch's correction for degrees of freedom.

7. In a two-sample test from unknown populations with sample sizes $n_A = 10$ and $n_B = 15$, which statement is correct?
    a. To compare variances we would use F with $df_1 = 10$ and $df_2 = 15$.
    b. To compare means we would use Student's t with $df = 23$, assuming unequal variances.
    c. To compare means we would use Student's t with $df = 23$, assuming equal variances.
    d. To deal with unequal variances, we might rely on Chebychev's inequality.
    e. To find the confidence interval for the difference of means, we would use $F_{9,14}$.

8. With unknown but equal variances, the test statistic for equality of two means
    a. will increase when the level of significance increases.
    b. will decrease when the level of significance increases.
    c. could either increase or decrease when the level of significance increases.
    d. is unchanged when the level of significance increases.
    e. is affected both by sample size *and* the level of significance.

9. To compare two sample variances, the statistician would use which distribution?
    a. Normal.
    b. Student's t.
    c. Chi-square.
    d. F.
    e. None of the above.

10. The $1 - \alpha$ confidence interval for the ratio of two unknown variances
    a. will enclose unity if the true population variances are equal.
    b. will enclose unity with probability $1 - \alpha$ if the true population variances are equal.
    c. will enclose unity if the hypothesis of equal variances is rejected at α.
    d. will be reliable even if the populations are skewed (i.e., non-normal).
    e. is based on the Student's t distribution if the populations are normal.

11. If either sample size is increased, the critical value for a right-tail test for equality of two variances would be likely to
    a. increase.
    b. decrease.
    c. stay the same.
    d. either increase or decrease.
    e. depend on the test statistic.

12. Type I error in a two-sample test for variances is quite sensitive to population skewness, while the Type I error in a two-sample test for means is fairly robust to population skewness.
    a. True.
    b. False.

Glossary of Terms

Acceptance region Portion of the hypothesized distribution that is bounded by the critical value(s). Its area is $1 - \alpha$ where α is the chosen level of significance. Since a given sample can disprove (but cannot prove) the null hypothesis, it is more accurate to call it the *non-rejection region*. See **Type I error**.

Alternative hypothesis Denoted H_1, it is the converse of the null hypothesis (e.g., H_0: $\mu_1 = \mu_2$ and H_1: $\mu_1 \neq \mu_2$). If the sample evidence contradicts H_0, we reject H_0 in favor of the alternative hypothesis H_1. A hypothesis test may be motivated by suspicion that H_0 is false.

Behrens-Fisher problem When population variances are unknown and assumed unequal, the distribution of the test statistic for a difference of two means is uncertain. Various approaches to this problem are used, but the simplest is to adjust the degrees of freedom. See **Welch's correction**.

Chi-square distribution If the population is normal, the sample variance has a chi-square distribution with $n - 1$ degrees of freedom.

Confidence interval Range of values that would enclose a true (generally unknown) population parameter (such as a difference of means or a ratio of variances) a given percentage of the time.

Difference of means with known variances:

$$\overline{X}_1 - \overline{X}_2 - z\, \sigma_{\overline{X}_1 - \overline{X}_2} < \mu_1 - \mu_2 < \overline{X}_1 - \overline{X}_2 + z\, \sigma_{\overline{X}_1 - \overline{X}_2}$$

Difference of means with unknown variances:

$$\overline{X}_1 - \overline{X}_2 - t\, s_{\overline{X}_1 - \overline{X}_2} < \mu_1 - \mu_2 < \overline{X}_1 - \overline{X}_2 + t\, s_{\overline{X}_1 - \overline{X}_2}$$

Ratio of two population variances:

$$F_{\text{Lower}}\left(\frac{s_1^2}{s_2^2}\right) < \frac{\sigma_1^2}{\sigma_2^2} < F_{\text{Upper}}\left(\frac{s_1^2}{s_2^2}\right)$$

Confidence level Desired probability of enclosing an unknown population parameter when creating a confidence interval from sample data. The confidence level, denoted $1 - \alpha$, is chosen by the researcher and is usually expressed as a percent (typically 90%, 95%, or 99%). The higher the confidence level, the wider the confidence interval. See **Level of significance**.

Critical value Value on the X-axis that defines the rejection region for a hypothesis. In a one-tail test, the critical value defines a right-tail or left-tail area. In a two-tail test, there are critical values defining rejection regions in each tail. The critical value is determined by the level of significance. A test statistic beyond the critical value(s) is unlikely if the H_0 is true.

Decision rule Diagram that illustrates the criterion for rejection of the null hypothesis. It shows the hypothesized sampling distribution with its critical value(s) labeled and a shaded rejection region for the specified level of significance.

Degrees of freedom For a Student's t-test for the difference of two means with unknown population variances that are assumed equal, degrees of freedom will be $n_1 + n_2 - 2$. If the unknown variances are assumed unequal, degrees of freedom may be modified using Welch's correction. For an F test of the ratio of two variances, the numerator and denominator degrees of freedom will be $df_1 = n_1 - 1$ and $df_2 = n_2 - 1$.

Equal variances   When the population variances are unknown, the formula for the standard error of the difference of two means depends on whether the variances are assumed equal or unequal. The hypothesis of equal variances may be tested using an F test based on the sample variances.

F distribution   If the null hypothesis of equal variances is true and the populations being sampled are normal, the sampling distribution of the ratio of two sample variances s_1^2 / s_2^2 is F. See **Degrees of freedom.**

Known variances   If the variances in a test for two sample means are known, the normal distribution may be used for the sampling distribution of the test statistic. If the variances are unknown, the test statistic follows the Student's t distribution. If the sample sizes are large, the difference between the normal and Student's t distributions is slight.

Level of significance   The desired probability of Type I error. It is set by the researcher (typical values are 0.10, 0.05, and 0.01) and is denoted α. Other things equal, the power of a hypothesis test increases as the level of significance increases. See **Confidence level.**

Normality assumption   In tests of two means or two variances, the theoretical sampling distributions are predicated upon the assumption that the populations being sampled are normal. If the populations are not normal, the Type I error and power of the test for two variances may be compromised. However, because of the Central Limit Theorem, the test for two means is fairly insensitive to violations of the normality assumption. See **Robustness.**

Null hypothesis   Denoted H_0, it is a statement that we try to reject (for example, H_0: $\sigma_1^2 = \sigma_2^2$). The null hypothesis is not necessarily chosen because we believe it to be true, but rather as a reference point. If the sample evidence contradicts H_0, the null hypothesis is rejected. Otherwise, it awaits further testing and could be rejected at a later time.

One-tail test   In a one-tail test, the alternative hypothesis always contains > (for a right-tail test) or < (for a left-tail test). For example, the hypotheses H_0: $\mu_1 \geq \mu_2$ and H_1: $\mu_1 < \mu_2$ would require a left-tail test.

Power   If the null hypothesis is false, *theoretical* power is the probability of rejecting the null hypothesis H_0 when it is false (or $1 - \beta$ where β is the probability of Type II error). For example, in a test comparing two means, power will be lower if the true means are nearly equal, but will be higher if the true means differ substantially. The ideal power is near 1. *Empirical* power is the ratio of the number of rejections to the number of times the test is performed.

P-value   Probability that a result as extreme as (or more extreme than) the observed sample statistic would arise by chance if the null hypothesis were true.

Rejection region   Area under the hypothesized sampling distribution that lies beyond the critical value(s). It is determined by α, the probability of Type I error. If the test statistic falls within this region, we will reject the null hypothesis. See **Level of significance.**

Robustness   Quality of being unaffected by a violation of an assumption. For example, the Student's t test for two means is robust to non-normality in the population if the sample sizes are moderately large.

Sampling distribution   Theoretical distribution of the test statistic assuming the null hypothesis is true. For example, if H0: $\sigma_1^2 = \sigma_2^2$ is true, the sampling distribution of s_1^2/s_2^2 is F.

Standard error Another name for the standard deviation of a sampling distribution. The formula for standard error is derived from statistical theory, but the standard error is usually estimated from samples.

Difference of two means with known variance:

$$\sigma_{\overline{X}_1 - \overline{X}_2} = \sqrt{\frac{\sigma_1^2}{n_1} + \frac{\sigma_2^2}{n_2}}$$

Difference of two means with unknown variances assumed equal:

$$s_{\overline{X}_1 - \overline{X}_2} = \sqrt{\frac{(n_1 - 1)s_1^2 + (n_1 - 1)s_1^2}{n_1 + n_2 - 2}} \sqrt{\frac{1}{n_1} + \frac{1}{n_2}}$$

Difference of two means with unknown variances assumed unequal:

$$s_{\overline{X}_1 - \overline{X}_2} = \sqrt{\frac{s_1^2}{n_1} + \frac{s_2^2}{n_2}}$$

Student's t distribution If the populations being sampled are normal but with unknown variances, the test statistic for the difference of means follows the Student's t distribution. This distribution is also used to construct confidence intervals for one mean or for the difference of two means. See **Welch's correction**.

Test statistic Calculated value resulting from the comparison of a sample statistic and a hypothesized population parameter. Its distribution depends on the null hypothesis. The test statistic is compared with a critical value to see whether the null hypothesis should be rejected.

Difference of two means:

$$z = \frac{\overline{X}_1 - \overline{X}_2}{\sigma_{\overline{X}_1 - \overline{X}_2}} \text{ (known variances)} \qquad \text{or} \qquad t = \frac{\overline{X}_1 - \overline{X}_2}{s_{\overline{X}_1 - \overline{X}_2}} \text{ (unknown variances)}$$

Ratio of two variances:

$$F = \frac{s_1^2}{s_2^2}$$

Two-sample test Any statistical test that utilizes two samples to test a hypothesis about two populations. For example, two sample means may be used to test whether the population means are equal. In contrast, a one-sample test compares a sample with a fixed point of reference, such as a hypothesized value of a true population parameter, to test a hypothesis about the population.

Two-tail test In a two-tail test, the alternative hypothesis always contains $\neq$. For example, the hypotheses H_0: $\mu_1 = \mu_2$ and H_1: $\mu_1 \neq \mu_2$ imply a two-tail test.

Type I error The error of rejecting a true null hypothesis that is true. The probability of Type I error is denoted α. It is the area under the hypothesized sampling distribution that is beyond the critical value(s). See **Level of significance**.

Type II error The error of accepting a null hypothesis that is false. The probability of Type II error (denoted β) is the area under the true sampling distribution that is not in the rejection region. See **Power**.

Welch's correction When population variances are unknown and assumed unequal, the t test for a difference of two means may be used with modified degrees of freedom. The degrees of freedom will be between Min (n_1, n_2) and $n_1 + n_2 - 2$. See **Behrens-Fisher problem**.

Welch's correction:
$$\text{d.f.} = \frac{\left(\dfrac{s_1^2}{n_1} + \dfrac{s_2^2}{n_2}\right)^2}{\dfrac{\left(s_1^2/n_1\right)^2}{n_1 - 1} + \dfrac{\left(s_2^2/n_2\right)^2}{n_2 - 1}}$$

Solutions to Self-Evaluation Quiz

1. d   Read the Overview of Concepts. Consult the Glossary.
2. c   Do Exercises 1–7. Read the Overview of Concepts. Consult the Glossary.
3. e   Do Exercises 1–5. Read the Illustration of Concepts.
4   a   Do Exercises 11-18. Read the Overview of Concepts. Consult the Glossary.
5. e   Consult the Glossary. Read Overview of Concepts.
6. b   Do Exercises 12 and 13. Consult the Glossary.
7. c   Do Exercises 12, 13, and 20. Consult the Glossary.
8. d   Read the Overview of Concepts. Consult the Glossary.
9. d   Do Exercises 19–23. Read the Illustration of Concepts. Consult the Glossary.
10. b   Do Exercises 19–23. Read the Illustration of Concepts.
11. b   Consult the Glossary. Do Team Learning Project 1.
12. a   Do Exercises 25–28. Do Team Learning Project 2.

CHAPTER 11

Visualizing Power and Type I / Type II Error

CONCEPTS
- Power, Type I Error, Type II Error, β Level, Power Curve, α Level, Null Hypothesis, Alternative Hypothesis, True Parameter Value

OBJECTIVES
- Understand relationships between Type I error, Type II error, and power

- Recognize the shape of a power curve and how to compare points along the parameter axis

- Understand how a point on the power curve is obtained

- Understand how power is affected by alpha level, sample size, and true parameter values

Overview of Concepts

In hypothesis testing, we compare the **null hypothesis** and the **alternative hypothesis**. These statements often concern a mean (μ) or a proportion (π). For example:

Application	Hypotheses
Manufacturing quality assurance	H_0 : wire tensile strength meets or exceeds specification : H_1 : wire tensile strength is below specification
Medical clinic client relations	H_0 : patient complaints are at or below the historical level : H_1 : patient complaint rate has risen above historical level

Testable hypotheses must be mutually exclusive and collectively exhaustive. They may be right-tail, left-tail, or two tail tests. When we make a decision, we seek to avoid both **Type I error** (rejecting a true null hypothesis) and **Type II error** (accepting a false alternative hypothesis). The probability of Type I error is the α **level**. The probability of Type II error is the β **level**. If neither error is committed, we have reached a correct decision.

Even if the null hypothesis is accepted, there is only a probability of $1 - \alpha$ that a correct decision was made. If the null hypothesis is true, the sum of the probabilities of its acceptance or rejection ($1 - \alpha$ plus α) must be 1. Similarly, if the null hypothesis is false, the sum of the probabilities of its acceptance or rejection (β plus $1 - \beta$) must be 1. Just as there are two types of *incorrect* decisions, there are two ways a *correct* decision can be made: a true null hypothesis can be correctly accepted, or a false null hypothesis can be rejected. The probability of correctly rejecting the null hypothesis is called **power**.

		True State	
		Null Hypothesis is True	*Null Hypothesis is False*
Decision	*Accept H_0*	Correct Decision $1 - \alpha$	Type II Error β
	Reject H_0	Type I Error α	Correct Decision (Power) $1 - \beta$

A statistical test that has a high probability of correctly rejecting a false H_0 (high power) is a desirable test. When the power is calculated for all possible true values of the true parameter and plotted on a graph, a **power curve** is generated. Since the **true parameter value** is unknown (otherwise why would we be testing a hypothesis?) there is no way of knowing which error, if any, we have committed when we make our decision. But we can define the relationships among α, β, and power. Power is lowest (near α) when the true parameter differs only slightly from the value hypothesized in H_0, and rises toward unity as H_0 becomes more obviously false. If we increase α, the power curve shifts up at all parameter values. Increasing the sample size increases power at every level of the true parameter (though only slightly near H_0). In testing a mean, a smaller standard deviation σ will improve power.

Illustration of Concepts

The diameter of a piston is designed to be 100.12 mm. The assembly line should be stopped if the piston is either too large or too small. In this case the **null hypothesis** and **alternative hypothesis** would be

$$H_0 : \mu = 100.12 \text{ mm}$$
$$H_1 : \mu \neq 100.12 \text{ mm}$$

Unless there is enough evidence to refute the null hypothesis, it is assumed to be true. If the diameter is not 100.12 mm and the hypothesis is accepted (i.e., not rejected) then an error has been made. This is **Type II error** and its probability is the β **level**. (the probability of incorrectly accepting the null hypothesis). In the example Type II error would mean that the piston is either too small (insufficient compression) or too large (excessive friction) leading to poor engine performance or premature piston failure. If detected during manufacture, rework may be possible, but often the result is scrappage. If the problem is not detected in manufacture, the company will experience extra repair claims (if failure occurs during the warranty period) or loss of consumer goodwill (if failure occurs after the warranty period or goes unreported). Type II error is costly to any company. Because the **true parameter value** is *unknown,* Type II error is generally unknown.

Costs arise if we continue operating an assembly line that is making inferior parts, but **Type I error** is also costly, because it means shutting down the line when adjustment is unnecessary (downtime, lost wages, disrupted schedules). Because the parameter's value under H_0 is *known, the* α **level** can be specified. It is generally set to 0.10, 0.05, or 0.01. In this example, if $\alpha = 0.01$, it would mean that there is 1 chance in 100 that the assembly line would be stopped to realign the equipment when the line is actually producing proper-sized pistons.

Since the statistician can specify any α that is desired it is natural to suppose that α should always be kept low. But choosing lower α will, *ceteris paribus,* increase β and hence reduce **power** (the converse of β). Saying that low β is preferable is the same as saying that high power is preferable. In testing a mean, there are two ways to reduce both α and β simultaneously: (1) to increase the sample size (but in quality control, the sample size is often kept small), or (2) to decrease the variance of the piston-making process. Manufacturers are well-aware of this latter strategy, and variance reduction is one of their major goals. Low σ will make the product perform more consistently in its intended use, and will lend power to quality tests. Thus, reducing σ is a good way to raise the **power curve** (near the mean specified in H_0 the difference may be small, but slight departures from the specification are intrinsically less damaging).

In many applications, the tradeoff between α and β is elusive. For example, has excessive F.D.A. concern over adverse side effects caused the U.S. to approve potentially useful new drugs too slowly, or has their policy saved consumers from disasters such as Thalidomide, which caused horrifying birth defects in some Western European nations (but not the U.S., which withheld approval)? Responding to criticism of its caution, the FDA has changed some of its testing requirements to allow drug companies to offer apparently effective drugs to the public with warnings that the long-term side effects are still being tested. This policy change has probably been a good one that allows some individuals access to potentially life-saving drugs, even if in the long run it exposes them to unknown risks. At least the individuals may live long enough to see what the long run has to offer.

Orientation to Basic Features

This module enables the user to visualize how Power and Type II error are affected by the alpha level (Type I error), sample size, type of test (two-tailed, left-tailed, or right-tailed), standard deviation, and the value of the true parameter. It also illustrates what a power curve is and how it is generated. These concepts can be shown using either a test for the mean or a test for the proportion.

1. **Opening Screen**

   Start the module by clicking on the module's icon, title, or chapter number in the *Visual Statistics* menu and pressing the Run Module button. When the module is loaded, you will be on the introduction page of the Notebook. Read the questions and then click the Concepts tab to see the concepts that you will learn. Click on the Scenarios tab. Select Mean from the list of choices. Select a scenario, read it, and press OK. A screen similar to the one below will appear. The top left of the screen shows a power curve. The bottom left of the screen shows two distributions. The true distribution is shown in blue and the hypothesized distribution in gray. The module's control panel is on the right. Other module features are controlled on the menu bar at the top of the screen. The amount of power illustrated in the bottom display is shown on the top graph.

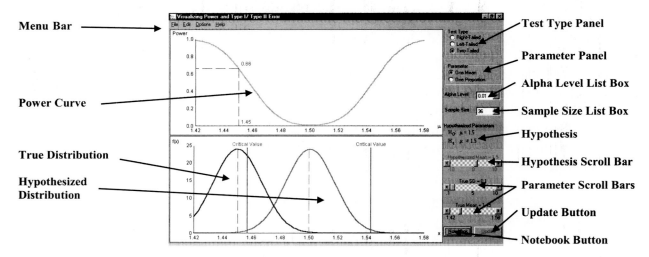

2. **Hint**

   A hint message appears on the upper diagram. It says, "Hold down the Alt key and click the left mouse button on the top graph to show power values." After reading the message, press the OK button. Try it. There are several ways you can remove these lines: (1) click on Options on the menu bar at the top of the screen and select Clear Power Values, or (2) press Esc, or (3) press Ctrl-P, or (4) change an aspect of the problem and press the flashing Update button. If you forget what the hint said while you are in the module, select Help and select Show Hint.

3. **True Mean**

   Try changing the scroll bar for the True Mean. Note how the true distribution moves right or left. Each power illustration on the lower diagram represents a single point on the upper diagram. If you hold down the mouse button on the scroll bar (the arrow for small steps, or the bar for large steps), the true distribution will shift continuously until you release it.

4. **Change the Experiment**
    a. Try changing the scroll bars for the Hypothesized Mean or True SD (standard deviation). Changing either of these controls represents a new experiment, and the power curve is redrawn after pressing the flashing Update button. Similarly, if you change the Sample Size list box or the Alpha Level list box, a new power curve will be redrawn once you press the Update button.
    b. You can also press the Notebook button to return to the Notebook to select a new scenario, read a section of the Notebook, or select the Do-It-Yourself tab. Pressing OK on the Do-It-Yourself section returns you to the module without descriptive labels on the horizontal axis.

5. **Test Types**
    The Test Type panel contains three option buttons: Right-Tailed, Left-Tailed, or Two-Tailed. These options change the null and alternative hypotheses. The power curve and the critical values in the lower diagram are redrawn after you press the Update button.

6. **Options: Graph Labels**
    In addition to clearing power values, several basic graph labeling options are available from the Options menu on the menu bar at the top of the screen.
    a. Click on Show Numeric Critical Value(s) to provide the numeric value for the critical value(s).
    b. Click on Options and select Label Reject/Accept Region to label these regions on the lower graph.
    c. Click on Options and select either Show Type I and Type II Error, or Show Power and Type II Error to reveal these regions as shaded areas on the lower graph.

7. **Copying a Graph**
    When you click on a graph, black handles will appear indicating it has been selected (they can be removed by pressing "Esc"). Select Copy under Edit on the menu bar at the top of the screen (or press Ctrl-C) to copy the display. It can then be pasted into other applications, such as Word or WordPerfect, so it can be printed. Graphs are copied as bitmaps

8. **Help**
    Click on Help on the menu bar at the top of the screen. Search for Help lets you search an index for this module, Contents shows a table of contents for this module, Using Help gives instructions on how to use Help, and About gives licensing and copyright information about *Visual Statistics*.

9. **Exit**
    Close the module by selecting Exit in the File menu (or click ☒ in the upper right-hand corner of the window). You will be returned to the *Visual Statistics* main menu.

Orientation to Additional Features

1. **Options: Families of Curves**
   Click on Options and select Families of Power Curves to compare the positions of power curves for different sample sizes, alpha levels, or standard deviations. For example, here are power curves representing 2n (light green), n (cyan), and n/2 (dark green).

   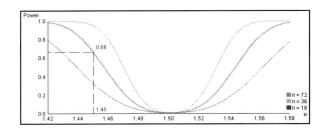

2. **Proportions**
   Click on the Notebook button, select the Scenario tab, and click on Proportion. Select a scenario. A screen similar to the one on the right appears. The display illustrates the power of a test for the proportion (π). The Control Panel has changed to reflect a test for a proportion. There

   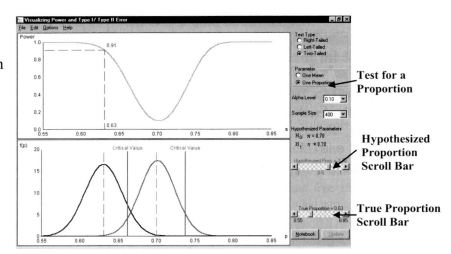

   no longer is a True SD scroll bar, and the True Mean and Hypothesized Mean scroll bars have been replaced with the True Proportion and Hypothesized Proportion scroll bars. As an alternative to using the Notebook to switch between a test for a proportion and a test for a mean, you can click on the One Mean or One Proportion option buttons in the Parameter panel.

Basic Learning Exercises   Name _____

Reject/Accept Regions

1. Press the Notebook button, select the Scenarios tab, and click on Mean. Select the Quiz
    Scores scenario, read the scenario, and click OK. What are the null and alternative
    hypotheses in this scenario if you want a left-tailed test?

2. Select Show Numeric Critical Values from Options on the menu bar. What is the value of the
    critical value? Explain how it is calculated. **Hint:** Select Contents from Help on the menu
    bar and click on Power for a Sample Mean under Equations. Read Step 1.

3. On which side of the critical value is the rejection region? **Hint:** Select Options on the menu
    bar and select Label Rejection Reject/Accept Region.

4. Change the test type from left-tailed to right-tailed by clicking on the Right-Tailed option
    button and clicking on Update. State the null and alternative hypotheses for this test. On
    which side of the critical value is the rejection region now?

5. What is the relationship between the rejection region and the direction of the alternate
    hypothesis?

6. Change the test type from left-tailed to two-tailed by clicking on the Two-Tailed option button
    and clicking on Update. Why are there now two critical values? Where are the rejection
    regions in the two-tailed test?

Power and the Power Curve

7. Power is the probability of *correctly* rejecting a null hypothesis that is *false*. Press the Notebook button, select Quiz Scores, read the scenario. Answer the first question after you have pressed the OK button (this resets all of the controls to their original settings). Interpret this answer in the context of this scenario. How is power illustrated on the bottom diagram? Is power in the rejection or acceptance region? **Hint:** Select Options on the menu bar and select Show Power and Type II Error.

8. Answer the second question in the scenario. What is the power if the true mean is 6.6? 6.4? 6.2? 7.0? **Hint:** Click the True Mean scroll bar to change the value of the true mean (or Alt-Click the desired μ values along the X axis of the upper diagram).

9. If you connect these points you have created a power curve. The number on the horizontal axis is the value of the true mean μ. The value on the vertical axis is the power. This graph tells us that if the true value of μ is 6.6, the test will reject the null hypothesis 57% of the time. In this scenario, explain why power *decreases* as the value of the true mean increases from 6.0 to 7.0. Why is the power 0.05 at $\mu = 7.0$? Why is Type II error 0.95 at $\mu = 7.0$?

10. What do you think the power would be when the true mean equals the critical value? Why?

11. Change the test type to Two-Tailed and the True Mean (μ) to 6.6. What is the power? Why is it different from the answer using a one-tailed test (exercise 8)? **Hint:** Select Show Numeric Critical Values from Option on the menu bar and look at your answer to exercise 2.

Intermediate Learning Exercises   **Name** _____

Alpha Level

12. What is the alpha level of the current test? Alpha level is shown on the lower graph by the area under the null hypothesis (gray distribution) in the rejection region (left of the left critical value and right of the right critical value). Change Alpha Level to 0.01. Notice how this area becomes much smaller. Change True Mean to 6.6. What is the power? **Hint:** Click on Options on the menu bar and select Label Accept/Reject Region.

13. Change Alpha Level to 0.10. What is the power when the true mean μ equals 6.6? Why has the power increased from exercises 11 and 12?

14. *At any value of μ the power increases with an increase in alpha.* This relationship is illustrated by clicking Options on the menu bar, selecting Families of Power Curves, selecting Alpha and clicking OK. This will display three power curves (for $\alpha = 0.01$, 0.05, and 0.10). Use the scroll bar to change the true mean μ to 6.5. Reading from the graph, approximately what is the power if alpha equals 0.01, 0.05, and 0.10?

    $\alpha = 0.01$ _____ $\alpha = 0.05$ _____ $\alpha = 0.10$ _____

15. What rule would you suggest regarding the relationship between power and alpha?

16. Click Families of Power Curves and select None to remove the three power curves. What happens to Type II error when Type I error increases from 0.01 to 0.05 to 0.10? **Hint:** Select Show Type I and Type II Error from Options on the menu bar.

17. What rule would you suggest regarding the relationship between Type I and Type II error?

Sample Size

18. Press the Notebook button, select Battery Voltage, and read the scenario. Answer the first question after you press the OK button. Interpret this answer in the context of the scenario. What does 1.45 represent on the bottom graph? How is power illustrated on the bottom diagram? **Hint:** From the Options menu select Show Power and Type II Error.

19. Click the Notebook button, reread the scenario and press OK. Answer the last question in the scenario by setting Sample Size to 100 (press Update). Use the scroll bar to set the true mean to 1.45 and determine the power.

20. *At any value of μ, power increases with an increase in sample size.* Click Options on the menu bar, select Families of Power Curves, select Sample Size and click OK. This will display three power curves (for a sample size n/2 = 50, n = 100, and 2n = 200). Use the scroll bar to set the true mean to 1.48. Reading from the graph, approximately what is the power when the sample size is 50, 100, and 200?

    n/2 = 50 _____   n = 100 _____   2n = 200 _____

21. What rule would you suggest regarding the relationship between power and sample size?

22. Click Families of Power Curves and select None to remove the three power curves. What happens to Type II error when sample size is increased from 100 to 200 to 400? **Hint:** Select Show Type I and Type II Error from Options on the menu bar.

23. What rule would you suggest regarding Type II error and sample size?

24. Total error is Type I error plus Type II error. What rule would you suggest regarding the relationship between total error and sample size?

Standard Deviation

25. Press the Notebook button, select Beer Mug Diameter and read the scenario. Answer the first question after you press the OK button. Interpret this answer in the context of the scenario. What does 3.60 represent on the bottom graph? How is power illustrated on the bottom diagram? **Hint:** From the Options menu select Show Power and Type II Error.

26. Click the Notebook button, reread the scenario and press OK. Answer the last question in the scenario by changing the True SD (Standard Deviation) scroll bar to 0.4 and pressing Update. What is the power if $\mu = 3.60$?

27. *At any value of μ, power decreases with an increase in the standard deviation.* This relationship is illustrated by selecting Families of Power Curves and Standard Deviation. This will display three power curves (for a standard deviation equal to $\sigma/2$, σ, or 2σ). Use the scroll bar to set the true mean μ to 3.65. Reading from the graph, approximately what is the power when the standard deviation is 0.2, 0.4, and 0.8?

    $\sigma/2 = 0.2$ _____ $\sigma = 0.4$ _____ $2\sigma = 0.8$ _____

28. What rule would you suggest regarding the relationship between power and standard deviation?

29. Click Families of Power Curves and select None to remove the three power curves. What happens to Type II error when standard deviation is increased from 0.2 to 0.4 to 0.8? **Hint:** Select Show Type I and Type II Error from Options on the menu bar.

    Type II error increases.

30. What rule would you suggest regarding the relationship between Type II error and power? Do you believe that this rule would work with a two-tailed hypothesis about μ? Try it.

Hypothesized Mean

31. Press the Notebook button, select the Do-It-Yourself tab and click OK. The null hypothesis is that $\mu = 2$ against the alternative that $\mu > 2$. Give an example of a situation where a statistician would want to test this null and alternative hypothesis. What is the standard error in this situation? State the critical value and the true mean of the distribution. **Hint:** Click on Options and select Show Numerical Critical Values.

    Example:
    Standard Error = $\sigma_{\bar{x}} = \sigma/\sqrt{n}$ =_____   Critical Value = _____   True Mean = _____

32. Power in this situation is calculated by finding $Pr(Z > (CV - \mu_1)/ \sigma_{\bar{x}})$, where CV is the critical value, μ_1 is the true mean, and $\sigma_{\bar{x}}$ is the standard error. Use the numbers from exercise 40 to calculate the Z value. What is the power of the test? **Hint:** A complete derivation of power is given in Help.

33. Since in this case $CV = \mu_0 + Z_{0.05} \times \sigma_{\bar{x}}$, substituting into the probability statement in exercise 41 gives $Pr(Z > \mu_0 + Z_{0.05} \times \sigma_{\bar{x}} - \mu_1)/ \sigma_{\bar{x}} = Pr (Z > (\mu_0 - \mu_1))/ \sigma_{\bar{x}} + Z_{0.05})$. Use this formula to find the Z value and report the power if the true mean is 2.2 and the hypothesized mean is 1.8? 1.6? 1.4? 2.2? **Hint:** $Z_{0.05} = 1.645$.

    Hypothesized Mean = 1.8   CV = _____   Z value = _____   Power = _____
    Hypothesized Mean = 1.6   CV = _____   Z value = _____   Power = _____
    Hypothesized Mean = 1.4   CV = _____   Z value = _____   Power = _____
    Hypothesized Mean = 2.2   CV = _____   Z value = _____   Power = _____

34. a) What rule would you suggest regarding the relationship between power and the difference of the hypothesized mean and the true mean? b) These calculations have been done with a right-tailed test. Does this relation change if it is a left-tailed test? A two-tailed test?

35. Why in exercise 42 is power equal to 0.05 (the alpha level) when the Hypothesized Mean scroll bar is set to 2.2? Instead of power, can you suggest a better label? Explain.

Advanced Learning Exercises   **Name** _____

Test for Proportion

36. Press the Notebook button, select the Scenarios tab, and click on Proportion. Select the Certification Exam scenario, read the scenario, and click OK. a) State the null and alternative hypotheses in this scenario. b) Answer the three questions in the scenario. c) Set $\alpha = 0.05$ and note the power. What happens to power if you decrease the Sample Size to 200? **Hint:** Press the Notebook button to read the scenario, and then press Cancel to return to the diagram.

Exploring the Dispersion in a Test for a Proportion

37. The rules regarding sample size, alpha level, and the difference between the true and hypothesized proportion are the same when examining the power of a proportion instead of a mean. However, there is no standard deviation scroll bar because the standard deviation of a binomial is always $\sqrt{\frac{\pi\,(1-\pi)}{n}}$. Set the experiment values to the following: Left-Tailed, Alpha Level = 0.05, Sample Size = 100, and Hypothesized Proportion = 0.13. Press Update. Select Show Power and Type II Error from Options on the menu bar. What is the power when the true proportion is 0.12? Briefly describe the true and hypothesized distribution.

38. Click on the left arrow of True Proportion and hold it down. Notice what happens to the true distribution relative to the hypothesized distribution. Stop at 0.04; what is the power? Briefly describe the true and hypothesized distribution.

39. The hypothesized distribution has not changed in exercises 37 and 38, yet the true distribution has changed dramatically. The mean of the true distribution is 0.12 in exercise 32 and 0.04 in exercise 33, while the mean of the hypothesized distribution is 0.13 in both cases (the values specified on the respective scroll bars). Calculate the standard error for both the true and hypothesized distribution for both cases. **Hint:** To find the formula for standard error, click Help, select Contents, click on Equation: Power of a Sample Proportion, and read Step 1.

True Distribution	$\pi = 0.12$ _____	$\pi = 0.04$ _____
Hypothesized Distribution	$\pi = 0.13$ _____	$\pi = 0.13$ _____

Exploring the Normality Assumption in a test for a Proportion

40. Press the Notebook button, select the Scenarios tab, and click on Proportion. Select the Certification Exam scenario, read the scenario, and click OK. Examine the power curve. Then change Hypothesized Proportion to 0.04 by clicking on its scroll bar. Why did the message come up that the proportion estimate may not be normally distributed?

41. Look at the area under the hypothesized distribution to the left of the critical value. Why does the distribution stop at zero and not meet the horizontal axis?

42. Change Hypothesized Proportion to 0.03. Has the hypothesized distribution become less normally distributed? Why do you believe this? Change the hypothesized mean to 0.02; note the placement of the critical value under the normality assumption. Where should the critical value be? What does this mean about the Type I error and power (look at the power curve)?

43. If you changed to a right-tailed test and did the same experiment using hypothesized proportions of 0.96, 0.97, and 0.98, would the same problem occur? Why?

44. Why is it important that $n \pi_0 \geq 5$ and $n(1-\pi_0) \geq 5$?

Individual Learning Projects

Write a report on one of the three topics listed below. Use the cut-and-paste facilities of the module to place the appropriate graphs in your report.

1. Investigate the relationship between a one-tailed and a two-tailed power curve. Using either a test for a mean or a proportion, explain and illustrate how the power curve for a two-tailed hypothesis test conducted at a 0.10 alpha level is related to the power curves for a right-tailed and left-tailed hypothesis test conducted at a 0.05 alpha level. The comparison should be made at seven points spread along the horizontal axis and common to the two-tailed power curve and one of the one-tailed power curves (be sure that you examine a point slightly greater and slightly less than the hypothesized value). For each comparison, the probability distributions that generated the power curve should be used in your explanation.

2. Investigate how a power curve for a proportion is created. Using a test for a proportion and at least five different values of the true proportion, explain and illustrate how power is calculated. Also calculate the range of the true proportion over which the power curve has a non-zero slope (power less than one). How is this range affected by the sample size and hypothesized value of the proportion? How is it affected by a two-tailed test, left-tailed test, or right-tailed test?

3. Investigate how power is affected by the standard error in a test for μ. Using a test for the mean, explain and illustrate how the standard deviation and the sample size interact in determining the power curve. Use at least six illustrations in your project. The project should culminate in a precise rule involving the relationship between power, sample size, and standard deviation.

Team Learning Projects

Select one of the three projects listed below. In each case, produce a team project that is suitable for an oral presentation. Use presentation software or large poster boards to display your results. Graphs should be large enough for your audience to see. Each team member should be responsible for producing some of the graphs. Ask your instructor if a written report is also expected.

1. A team of two should investigate how a power curve is created. Create your own two-tailed scenario that can be illustrated with the module. On a large poster board, draw the power curve. For each value of the true parameter along this power curve (using the True Mean or True Proportion scroll bar) make a copy of the probability distributions. Use these illustrations to show how power is calculated at each point along your power curve. Explain what a power curve illustrates.

2. A team of two should investigate the peculiarities of a power curve for a proportion. Select a sample size of 100 for a two-tailed test when $\pi = 0.40$. Try all the different true values of π. Notice what happens to the hypothesized and true distributions. Draw the power curve on a poster board using at least seven points (each point should have an illustration of the probability distributions associated with it). Redo the experiment using the same sample size but $\pi = 0.05$. Try all the different true values of π. Notice what happens to the hypothesized and true distributions. Draw the power curve on another poster board using at least 11 points (each point should have an illustration of the probability distributions associated with it). Explain why the hypothesized and true distributions behave so differently in the two examples. Why would this not be true in a test for μ?

3. A team of three should investigate the range of values over which a power curve exists. Using a one-tailed test for the mean, illustrate four different power curves (use two different hypothesized means and, for each hypothesized mean, two different true standard deviations). Each power curve should consist of at least six points (each point should have an illustration of the probability distributions associated with it). Derive a rule for the range of values over which the power curve has a non-zero slope (power is less than one).

Self-Evaluation Quiz

1. Type II error is
   a. the probability of correctly rejecting the null hypothesis.
   b. the probability of correctly accepting the null hypothesis.
   c. the probability of incorrectly rejecting the null hypothesis.
   d. the probability of incorrectly accepting the null hypothesis.
   e. none of the above.

2. Power is
   a. the probability of correctly rejecting the null hypothesis.
   b. the probability of correctly accepting the null hypothesis.
   c. the probability of incorrectly rejecting the null hypothesis.
   d. the probability of incorrectly accepting the null hypothesis.
   e. none of the above.

3. Which of these relationships is correct?
   a. Alpha + Power = 1
   b. Power + Beta = 1
   c. Alpha + Beta = 1
   d. All of the above are true.
   e. None of the above is true.

4. In a hypothesis test for the mean μ, which represents movement along the power curve as opposed to a shift of the power curve?
   a. Using a different α level.
   b. Using a different value for true μ to calculate the power.
   c. Using a different value for the true variance.
   d. Using a different sample size.
   e. Using a different hypothesized value for μ.

5. The power of a statistical test for the mean (with known variance) is affected by
   a. alpha level.
   b. variance of the variable.
   c. sample size.
   d. true value of the mean.
   e. all of the above.

6. Which statement is most nearly correct concerning the level of significance α?
   a. If α is increased from 0.05 to 0.10, the power curve will shift up.
   b. If α is increased from 0.05 to 0.10, the power curve will shift down.
   c. If α is increased from 0.05 to 0.10, the power curve will not shift.
   d. Changing α is a movement along the power curve, not a shift.
   e. None of the above is correct.

7. Which statement is most nearly correct concerning the sample size?
    a.   If the sample size is increased, the power curve will shift up.
    b.   If the sample size is increased, the power curve will shift down.
    c.   If the sample size is increased, the power curve will not shift.
    d.   Changing the sample size is a movement along the power curve, not a shift.
    e.   None of the above is correct.

8. In conducting a hypothesis test for the mean, doubling the standard deviation
    a.   doubles the power.
    b.   increases the power.
    c.   leaves the power unchanged.
    d.   reduces the power.
    e.   halves the power.

9. In conducting a hypothesis test for the mean μ, which statement is correct?
    a.   If the variance increases, power decreases.
    b.   If the true value of μ increases, the test's power changes.
    c.   Increasing the sample size increases a test's power.
    d.   Increasing the α level will increase the test's power, all other things held constant.
    e.   All of the statements are true.

10. A firm wants to know whether at least half of its 617 hourly employees are satisfied with the company's health care plan. A sample of 25 employees shows that 16 are satisfied with the company's health care plan. If the true proportion of satisfied employees is 0.51, the right-tailed test for $\pi > 0.5$ would have
    a.   relatively low power.
    b.   relatively high power.
    c.   relatively low β level.
    d.   relatively low α level.
    e.   both a and c are correct.

11. In the preceding problem, if the sample size were increased to 100 employees and the alpha level stayed the same,
    a.   the β risk would decrease.
    b.   the Type I would decrease.
    c.   both power and β risk would decrease.
    d.   neither Type I error nor β risk would decrease.
    e.   we cannot say without knowing the true proportion.

12. Other things equal, in the preceding problem, if the α level is decreased from 0.05 to 0.01,
    a.   the β error is decreased.
    b.   the power is increased.
    c.   the power is decreased.
    d.   the β error does not change.
    e.   a and b only.

Glossary of Terms

Acceptance region Portion of the hypothesized distribution that is bounded by the critical value(s). A given sample can disprove (but cannot prove) the null hypothesis, so it is more accurate (but awkward) to call it the "non-rejection region." See **Type I error**.

Alpha level Desired probability of Type I error. It is set by the researcher and is denoted α. Typical values are 0.10, 0.05, and 0.01. Other things equal, power increases as α increases.

Alternative hypothesis Denoted H_1, it is the converse of the null hypothesis. For example, H_0: $\mu = 5$ might suggest H_1: $\mu \neq 5$. If the sample evidence contradicts H_0, we would reject H_0 in favor of the alternative hypothesis, H_1. Often, a hypothesis test is motivated by the suspicion that the alternative hypothesis may be correct.

Beta level Denoted β, it is the probability of accepting a false null hypothesis. See **Type II error**.

Critical value Value on the X-axis that defines the rejection region for a decision rule. In a right-tailed test, the critical value defines a right-tail area, and conversely for a left-tailed test. A two-tailed test requires two critical values to define a rejection region in each tail. The critical value is determined by the α level. If H_0 is true, it is unlikely that the test statistic will lie beyond the critical value(s). When this does occur, it is unlikely that the null hypothesis is true.

Hypothesized mean Denoted μ_0, it is the assumed value of the population mean that is specified in the null hypothesis (e.g., H_0: $\mu_0 = 5$).

Hypothesized proportion Denoted π_0 (or p_0), it is the assumed value of the population proportion that is specified in the null hypothesis (e.g., H_0: $\pi_0 = 5$). See **Proportion**.

Mean Population parameter characterizing central tendency. It is the expected value of X and is denoted μ.

Null hypothesis Denoted H_0, it is a maintained statement that we try to reject (for example, H_0: $\mu_0 = 5$). The null hypothesis is not necessarily chosen because we believe it to be true, but rather to serve as a reference point (e.g., do at least half the voters support campaign reform?). If the sample evidence contradicts H_0, the null hypothesis is rejected. Otherwise, it awaits further testing that could disprove it at a later time.

Power Probability of correctly rejecting a null hypothesis that is false. Ideal power would be near 1. Power is $1 - \beta$ (the complement of Type II error). Power is the area under the true distribution that is also in the rejection region.

Power curve Result of calculating power for all possible values of the true parameter and plotting the results on a graph. Its minimum value is α. For a two-tailed test, it resembles a valley between two plateaus. For a left-tailed test it increases from 0 toward 1, going from right to left (and conversely for a right-tailed test).

Proportion Population parameter representing the probability that a randomly chosen population item will have a particular characteristic (e.g., proportion of computer chips that are defective). Some textbooks call it π (following the convention that Greek letters denote population parameters) while others call it p to avoid confusion with the trigonometric constant π (the ratio of a circle's circumference to its diameter).

Rejection region Area under the hypothesized distribution that lies beyond the critical value(s). It is determined by α, the probability of Type I error. The rejection region usually is small, since we usually choose a low value for α. If the test statistic falls within this region, we will reject the null hypothesis. See **Alpha level**.

Sample size Number of observations taken at random from the population. Other things equal, power increases as the sample size increases.

Standard deviation Population parameter characterizing dispersion. It is denoted σ. In a test involving a sample mean, power increases as the standard deviation decreases, other things being equal.

True mean Power is low when the true mean μ is close to the hypothesized mean μ_0, but increases the farther μ is from μ_0 as we move along the power curve. See **Mean**.

True parameter value Specific value of the true mean in a test for μ or the true proportion in a test for π.

True proportion Power is low when the true proportion π is close to the hypothesized proportion π_0, but increases the farther π is from π_0 as we move along the power curve. See **Proportion**.

Type I error Error of rejecting a null hypothesis that is true. The probability of Type I error is denoted α. It is the area under the hypothesized distribution that is beyond the critical value(s). When it is set by the researcher it is called the alpha level.

Type II error Error of accepting a null hypothesis that is false. The probability of Type II error is denoted β (beta). The probability of Type II error is the area under the true distribution that is not in the rejection region. It is also called β risk.

Solutions to Self-Evaluation Quiz

1. d Do Exercises 7–9. Read the Overview of Concepts.
2. a Do Exercise 7. Read the Overview of Concepts.
3. b Do Exercise 9. Read the Overview of Concepts.
4. b Do Exercises 7–9.
5. e Do Exercises 8, 12, 18, 19, 26, and 33.
6. a Do Exercises 12–17.
7. a Do Exercises 17–24.
8. d Do Exercises 25–30.
9. e Do Exercises 12–30.
10. a Do Exercises 9 and 36–37.
11. a Do Exercises 18–24 and 36–37.
12. c Do Exercises 12–16 and 36–37.

CHAPTER 12

Visualizing Analysis of Variance

CONCEPTS
- Analysis of Variance (ANOVA), Variation within Groups, Variation between Groups, F Ratio (F Statistic), ANOVA Table, Critical Value, Type I Error, Type II Error, Power, Equal Variances Assumption, Normality Assumption

OBJECTIVES
- Be familiar with situations in which one-factor ANOVA is applicable

- Understand how much difference must exist between group means to be detected using an F test

- Appreciate the role of sample size in determining power

- Know the ANOVA assumptions and recognize the effects of violating each of them

Overview of Concepts

When several sample means are compared, the question arises whether the group means are truly different or whether we are merely seeing sample variation. To compare c sample means, we rely on **analysis of variance** (or **ANOVA** for short) to test the hypotheses:

H_0: $\mu_1 = \mu_2 = \ldots = \mu_c$ (The true group means are the same.)
H_1: Not all μ_i are equal   (The true group means are not all the same.)

Suppose we have c groups with sample sizes n_1, n_2, . . . , n_c. Comparison of dot plots for each group may reveal differences in means and/or variances. We can do the ANOVA calculations in a spreadsheet or use specialized software to produce the **ANOVA table**. This table shows us the **variation between groups**, the **variation within groups**, and the **F ratio**. The sample F ratio (also called the **F statistic**) is the ratio of the mean variation between groups to the mean variation within groups. The F ratio is a measure of how strongly the sample contradicts the null hypothesis H_0. A large F ratio suggests that H_0 may be false, while an F ratio near 0 says that the sample evidence is not inconsistent with H_0. We would reject H_0 if the sample F ratio exceeds the F **critical value**.

Critical values of F may be found in a table (or calculated by a computer) for any α level (level of significance). Commonly used α levels are 0.10, 0.05, or 0.01. If the null hypothesis is true and if you do an ANOVA test repeatedly on different samples drawn from the same populations, then you can calculate the empirical **Type I error** as the ratio of the number of rejections to the number of times the test is performed. This should be approximately equal to α. If the null hypothesis is false, the empirical **power** of the test is the ratio of the number of rejections to the number of times the test is performed. Empirical **Type II error** is one minus the empirical power. If the test is able to reject a false null hypothesis every time, then the power of the test is 1. Power is higher when the means are more unequal, when the variances are smaller, when the sample sizes are larger, or when α is larger.

In order to investigate Type I error or power empirically, we must repeat the sampling experiment many times *and* must know whether the null hypothesis is true or false. Under normal situations this is impossible (even if we could conduct the experiment 100, 200, or even 1,000 times, we would not know if the null hypothesis is true or false). However, this type of experiment is possible with computer simulation. Suppose we design an experiment and replicate it 1,000 times with a true H_0. The laws of chance say that we would expect 1000α rejections (that is, if $\alpha = 0.05$, we would expect about 50 rejections, while if $\alpha = 0.01$, we would expect about 10 rejections). For a true H_0, the histogram of replicated sample F statistics should closely resemble the F distribution. But if we replicate the experiments with a false H_0, the histogram will be more symmetrical and will be shifted right. The number of rejections would exceed 1000α. Empirical power would be the number of rejections divided by 1,000. If the means differ by a great deal, power will be near 1, while if they differ very little, the power will be near α. The test's empirical Type II error would equal 1 minus its empirical power.

The ANOVA procedure rests on two assumptions. The **equal variance assumption** says that the variances are the same for all groups. The **normality assumption** says that samples from all groups are drawn from normal populations. Real data often violate one or both of these assumptions. It is therefore useful to study how violations of these assumptions affect Type I error, Type II error, and the power of the F test.

Illustration of Concepts

We would like to know if there are differences in the sizes of California navel oranges sold by three fresh produce retailers. We purchase oranges at each store, taking care to choose them at random from the stack of fresh oranges at each market. Our sample sizes are similar but not identical. We weigh each orange and calculate the sample means and standard deviations.

Retailer	Sample Size	Weights of Sampled Oranges (grams)	Mean	S.D.
Mercado Uno	10 oranges	263 290 284 298 250 308 317 277 357 280	292.51	30.29
Papa Jose	8 oranges	309 317 271 367 242 387 290 268	306.33	49.79
Green Grow	9 oranges	299 288 195 208 231 327 305 226 278	261.79	47.40

The standard deviation of each group is a measure of the **variation within groups**. The difference between the means (relative to their standard errors) suggests that there is also **variation between groups**. In order to test this observation we use **analysis of variance** (or **ANOVA**). Our hypothesis is:

H_0:   Mean weight of oranges is the same in all three markets.
H_1:   Mean weight of oranges is not the same in all three markets.

Only if the sample information is inconsistent with the null hypothesis will it be rejected. Using a spreadsheet or a statistical analysis program we create an **ANOVA table**:

Source of Variation	Sum of Squares	DF	Mean Square	F Ratio	P-Value
Between groups	8959.1	2	4479.57	2.463	0.106
Within groups	43651.2	24	1818.80		
Total	52610.3	26			

The sample **F ratio** (or **F statistic**) is 2.463. Since the **critical value** is 2.54 using $\alpha = 0.10$ (**Type I error**), we accept (do not reject) the null hypothesis. That is, in this particular sample, there is not enough evidence to refute the null hypothesis. However, the p-value tells us that it was a close decision. The p-value says that, if H_0 were true, an F ratio of 2.463 would arise by chance about 10.6% of the time. By accepting the null hypothesis we know that there is some chance (it could range from 0% to $1-\alpha$, or 90% in this case) that we have made a **Type II error** (the probability that we incorrectly accepted H_0). In this case, since the true means are unknown, we have no insight into the **power** of the test.

Is the **equal variances assumption** valid? To find out, we use Hartley's F_{max} test statistic. It is the ratio of the largest to the smallest sample variance, or $F_{max} = (49.79)^2/(30.29)^2 = 2.70$. From a table of F_{max} critical values with c = 3 groups we find that $F_{c,n/c-1} = F_{3,26/2} = 4.16$ using a 0.05 level of significance. Since F_{max} is < 4.16 we conclude that this sample does *not* provide enough evidence to reject the equal variances assumption.

A number of questions remain unanswered. Since the decision was close (p-value was 0.106) would we again accept the null hypothesis if the test were redone using a new sample? Would we have obained different results if we had used larger sample sizes? Is the **normality assumption** valid? The only way to answer these questions is to collect additional data, perform new ANOVA tests, and do tests for normality (e.g., probability plots or at least a histogram of each sample).

Orientation to Basic Features

This module allows you to conduct an ANOVA experiment to determine if you would accept or reject the null hypothesis that the means of several groups are equal. In addition, you can replicate the experiment up to 1,000 times to examine Type I error, Type II error, and power.

1. **Opening Screen**

   Start the module by clicking on the module's icon, title, or chapter number in the *Visual Statistics* menu and pressing the Run Module button. When the module is loaded, you will be on the introduction page of the Notebook. Read the questions and then click the Concepts tab to see the concepts that you will learn. Click on the Scenarios tab. Select Agriculture from the table of choices. Select a scenario, read it, and press OK. The upper left of the screen shows dot plots from each sample. The vertical black line represents the overall sample mean. The short blue vertical lines represent the sample mean from a particular group, while the red line connecting the black and blue line is the difference between the group sample mean and the overall sample mean. Below these dot plots are two tables. The ANOVA table is on the left, and a table of Summary Statistics is on the right. To the right is the Control Panel.

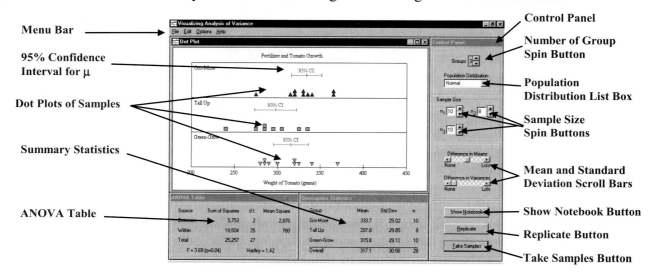

2. **Control Panel**

   a. Push the Take Samples button in the lower right of the Control Panel. Note that the dot plot, ANOVA Table and table of Summary Statistics change to reflect the new sample.

   b. Use the Sample Size spin buttons to change the sample size. Push the flashing Take Samples button. The dot plot and both tables reflect the new sample size.

   c. Click on the Difference in Means scroll bar to change the difference between the largest and smallest population means. When set to None there will be no difference in the means, and when set to Lots there will be a large difference in the means. Push the Take Samples button to draw a sample from the new populations. The Difference in Variances scroll bar works in the same way. Remember that an assumption of ANOVA is that the variance of each group is the same.

   d. Click the Groups spin button to change the number of groups in your experiment. You can select two, three, or four groups. Press the flashing Take Samples button so that the displays correspond to your new experiment.

e.   Click on the Population Distribution list box. You can select either Normal, Uniform, or Skewed. If you select a skewed distribution, the program will randomly choose either left or right skewness (it will not change the choice unless you make a change in the Number of Groups spin button or Population Distribution list box). Push the Take Samples button to update your displays.

f.   Push the Show Notebook button to select a new scenario or change to the Do-It-Yourself controls.

3. **Copying a Display**

Click on the display you wish to copy. Its window title will be highlighted. Select Copy from the Edit menu (on the menu bar at the top of the screen) or Ctrl-C to copy the display. It can then be pasted into other applications, such as Word or WordPerfect, so it can be printed.

4. **Help**

Click on Help on the menu bar at the top of the screen. Search for Help lets you search an index for this module, Contents shows a table of contents for this module, Using Help gives instructions on how to use Help, and About gives licensing and copyright information about *Visual Statistics*.

5. **Exit**

Close the module by selecting Exit in the File menu (or click ☒ in the upper right-hand corner of the window). You will be returned to the *Visual Statistics* main menu.

Orientation to Additional Features

1. **Replication**
   Push the Replicate button to initiate a replication experiment.
   a. The Number of Replications list box permits 50, 100, 200, 500, or 1,000 replications.
   b. Push the flashing Start Experiment button to start the experiment. Histograms of the sample means from each group appear to the left, a histogram of the F statistics appears at the top right, and a panel showing the Results of Replication Experiment is below the histogram of F statistics.
   c. Finish Experiment and Pause Experiment buttons now appear. Push the Pause Experiment button to pause the experiment. The Pause Experiment button changes to a Continue Experiment button. Press this to resume the experiment. Pressing the Finish Experiment button suspends the building process and updates the display at the end of the experiment.
   d. When the experiment is finished, a display similar to the one on the right appears. The histogram of F statistics has an F distribution superimposed upon it. The critical values corresponding to α = 0.05 and 0.01 are drawn in blue and green, respectively. The Results of Replication table shows the number and percentage appearing to the right and left of each critical value.

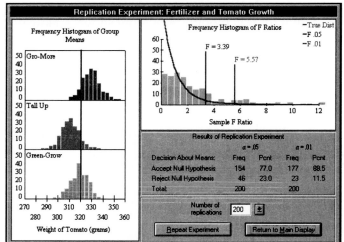

   e. Push the Repeat Experiment button to redo the experiment or the Return to Main Display button to leave replication mode.

2. **Do-It-Yourself**
   Press the Show Notebook button. Select the Do-It-Yourself tab and click OK. This will replace the Difference in Means and Difference in Variances scroll bars with a panel containing μ and σ boxes in which you can type your own values. An example with default values is to the right. Change any of these parameter values using your keyboard. Press the Take Samples button to draw a sample from the populations you have defined.

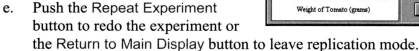

Basic Learning Exercises

Name _____

Understanding ANOVA

Press the Show Notebook button, select the Scenarios tab, and click on Agriculture. Select the Fertilizer and Tomato Growth scenario. Read the scenario. Click OK.

1. State the null and alternative hypotheses. Are the means equal, based on the Difference in Means scroll bar setting? Does this indicate that the null hypothesis is true or false?

    H_0:
    H_a:

2. What two assumptions are required to do ANOVA? Are they met in this scenario? How do you know? **Hint:** Look at the Population Distribution combo box and the Difference in Variances scroll bar.

3. Based only on the dot plots, would you conclude that the groups differ in central tendency or dispersion? Does any of the three samples have outliers or unusual data points? If so, what might be their effects?

4. Based on the 95% confidence intervals, would you conclude that the means are equal? What decision does this suggest about H_0?

5. Do you see anything in your samples that seems inconsistent with the belief that the population is normal? If you did not know whether or not the population was normal (see exercise 2) what would you conclude about normality?

6. Look at the Summary Statistics. Do the sample means and standard deviations confirm your comparisons of central tendency and dispersion among the groups?

7. To check your understanding of the ANOVA table, verify each of the following calculations. **Hint:** c is the number of groups and n is the total number of observations. If you need to review the formulas, click Help.

DF Between: $c-1 =$

DF Within: $n-c =$

Total DF: $n-1 =$

Mean Square Between: $MSB = SSB \, / \, (c-1) =$

Mean Square Within: $MSW = SSW \, / \, (n-c) =$

F ratio: $F = MSB \, / \, MSW =$

8. Move the Difference in Means scroll bar to None and press Take Samples. Refer to the dot plots to explain what is measured by Mean Square Between (MSB) and Mean Square Within (MSW). Why are they nearly equal if H_0 is true?

9. At $\alpha = 0.05$, does the F statistic (and its p-value) indicate that you should reject the null hypothesis of equal means? Would you expect to reject H_0?

10. Move the Difference in Means scroll bar to Lots and press Take Samples. Use the dot plots to explain why, if H_0 is false (unequal means), MSB is usually greater than MSW.

11. At $\alpha = 0.05$, does the F statistic (and its p-value) indicate that you should reject the null hypothesis of equal means? Would you expect to reject H_0?

Intermediate Learning Exercises   Name _____

Type I Error, Type II Error, and Power
Press the Show Notebook button, select the Scenarios tab, and click on Agriculture. Select the Fertilizer and Tomato Grow scenario. Read the scenario and Click OK.

12. Move the Difference in Means scroll bar all the way to the *left* (so it is set to None). You have made the null hypothesis true (no difference in means). Push the Take Samples button 10 times. Out of the 10 samples, how many times did you reject the null hypothesis? Since the null hypothesis is true in this case, based on these 10 trials what is the empirical Type I error of the ANOVA test? Do you think 10 samples are enough to estimate empirical Type I error? **Hint:** Empirical Type I error is the relative frequency of rejecting a false null hypothesis.

13. Push the Replicate button. Set the number of replications to 1,000 using the Number of Replications list box, and then press Start Experiment. When the experiment is finished, examine the table of results. How many rejections did you get using $\alpha = 0.05$? Using $\alpha = 0.01$? What is the empirical Type I error for $\alpha = 0.05$? For $\alpha = 0.01$? Do you feel that 1,000 samples is enough to yield a reasonable estimate of empirical Type I error?

14. Why is the empirical Type I error generally not exactly equal to the α-level?

15. Describe the histogram of F statistics. Does it closely resemble the theoretical F distribution that is superimposed on the histogram? Should it? Explain.

16. Describe the shapes of histograms of sample means (on the left). Do the means appear to be equal? Do the variances appear equal? Is this what you would expect? Explain.

17. Press the Return to Main Display button. Create a *slightly* false null hypothesis (i.e., slightly unequal means) by moving the Difference in Means scroll bar two clicks to the right of None. Push the Take Samples button 10 times. At $\alpha = 0.05$, how many times did you reject the null hypothesis (based on the p-value)? Since the null hypothesis is false in this case, based on these 10 trials what is the empirical power of the ANOVA test? **Hint:** Empirical power is the relative frequency of rejecting a false null hypothesis.

18. Press the Replication button. Press the Start Experiment button. Watch the table of results. After about 100 replications, press the Pause Experiment button. Look at the histograms of sample means (on the left). What do you notice about them? Press the Finish Experiment button. Describe the final histograms of means.

19. At the conclusion of the experiment, compare the distribution of the sample F statistics to the superimposed F distribution that is based on the assumption of equal means. How does this histogram indicate that the null hypothesis is false? Explain.

20. Refer to the table of results. Using $\alpha = 0.05$, how many rejections did you get? What was the empirical power? What was the empirical Type II error? Why is the empirical power relatively low in this exercise? **Hint:** Empirical Type II error is the relative frequency of accepting a false null hypothesis.

Effects of Sample Size

21. Press the Return to Main Display button. Use the Sample Size spin buttons to double each sample size. Push the Take Samples button to reset all of the displays. Choose 1,000 replications and push the Replicate button. Using an α-level of 0.05, what is the empirical power and empirical Type II error of the test? How does this answer compare with your answer to exercise 20? What generalization can you make about the effect of sample size on power and Type II error in the F test?

Advanced Learning Exercises   Name _____

Investigate Equal Variances Assumption

22. Press the Show Notebook button, select the Do-It-Yourself tab and click OK. At the top of the Control Panel set the number of groups to three and the population to Normal. The Difference in Means and Variances scroll bars have been replaced with boxes to enter the mean and standard deviation of each group. Set all three means to 3,000 and all three standard deviations to 500. Set all three sample sizes to 10 using their spin buttons. Press the Take Samples button. Record the value for the Mean Square Within (MSW), Hartley's statistic, and the p-value of the F statistic. Is its p-value below 0.05? Why is this important? Define Hartley's statistic and tell what it is used for. What is its critical value in this situation? **Hint:** Type Hartley after selecting the Search for Help feature under Help on the menu bar.

    MSW _____   Hartley's Statistic _____   p-value of F _____

23. Press the Takes Samples button 10 times. Each time record the value of MSW, Hartley's statistic, and the p-value of the F statistic. Could you tell that the variances were equal by looking at the dot plots? What is the median of the 10 MSWs? Circle each value of Hartley's statistic that is greater than the critical value. How many rejections are there? Circle each p-value below 0.05. How many are there? Is the average MSW what you would expect; why or why not? Is the number of circled Hartley's statistics what you would expect? Why or why not? Is the number of circled p-values what you would expect? Explain.

    MSW 1 _____   2 _____   3 _____   4 _____   5 _____   6 _____
        7 _____   8 _____   9 _____   10 _____   Median _____

    Hartley's   1 _____   2 _____   3 _____   4 _____   5 _____
            6 _____   7 _____   8 _____   9 _____   10 _____

    p-value   1 _____   2 _____   3 _____   4 _____   5 _____
          6 _____   7 _____   8 _____   9 _____   10 _____

24. Press the Replications button. Set the Number of Replications list box to 1,000. Press the Start Experiment button (if you wish you can press the Finish Experiment button). What percentage of the time was the null hypothesis rejected at the 5% and 1% α-level? What percentages would you have expected? Are your results plausible given sampling variation?

25. Change two of the standard deviations to 400 and 580 to create *slightly* unequal variances. Verify that the MSW is still about 250,000. Press the Takes Samples button 10 times. Can you tell that the variances are unequal by looking at the dot plots? Each time, record Hartley's statistic and the p-value of the F ratio. Circle each value of Hartley's statistic that is greater than the critical value. How many are there? What does this say about the power of Hartley's statistic to detect *slightly* unequal variances? Circle each p-value below 0.05. How many are there? Is the number of circled p-values what you would expect? Explain.

Hartley's	1 _____	2 _____	3 _____	4 _____	5 _____
	6 _____	7 _____	8 _____	9 _____	10 _____
p-value	1 _____	2 _____	3 _____	4 _____	5 _____
	6 _____	7 _____	8 _____	9 _____	10 _____

26. Press the Replications button. Press the Start Experiment button. What percentage of the time was the null hypothesis rejected at the 5% and 1% α-level (empirical Type I error)? What does this mean about the robustness of one-way ANOVA to slightly unequal variances? Can you tell that the variances are unequal by looking at the histograms of sample means?

27. Change the standard deviations to 300, 500, and 640 to create *moderately* unequal variances. Verify that the MSW is still about 250,000. Press the Takes Samples button 10 times. Can you tell that the variances are unequal by looking at the dot plots? Each time record Hartley's statistic and the p-value of the F ratio. Circle each value of Hartley's statistic that is greater than the critical value; how many are there? What does this say about the power of Hartley's statistic to detect *moderately* unequal variances? Circle each p-value below 0.05; how many are there? Is the number of circled p-values what you would expect? Why or why not? Since comparing dot plots is not a reliable test for equal variances, why look at the dot plots?

Hartley's	1 _____	2 _____	3 _____	4 _____	5 _____
	6 _____	7 _____	8 _____	9 _____	10 _____
p-value	1 _____	2 _____	3 _____	4 _____	5 _____
	6 _____	7 _____	8 _____	9 _____	10 _____

28. Press the Replications button. Press the Start Experiment button. What percentage of the time was the null hypothesis rejected at an α-level of 5% and 1% (empirical Type I error)? Is one-way ANOVA robust to moderately unequal variances? Can you tell that the variances are unequal by looking at the histograms of sample means?

29. Change the standard deviations to 100, 500, and 706 to create *very* unequal variances. Verify that the MSW is still about 250,000. Press the Takes Samples button 10 times. Can you tell that the variances are unequal by looking at the dot plots? Each time, record Hartley's statistic and the p-value of the F ratio. Circle each value of Hartley's statistic that is greater than the critical value; how many are there? Circle each p-value below 0.05. How many are below 0.05? What does this say about the power of Hartley's statistic to detect *very* unequal variances? Is the number of circled p-values what you would expect? Why or why not?

Hartley's   1 _____   2 _____   3 _____   4 _____   5 _____

            6 _____   7 _____   8 _____   9 _____   10 _____

p-value   1 _____   2 _____   3 _____   4 _____   5 _____

            6 _____   7 _____   8 _____   9 _____   10 _____

30. Press the Replications button. Press the Start Experiment button. What percentage of the time was the null hypothesis rejected at the 5% and 1% α-level (empirical Type I error)? What does this mean about the robustness of one-way ANOVA to very unequal variances?

31. Change the standard deviations to 10, 10, and 865 to create *extremely* unequal variances. Verify that the MSW is still about 250,000. Press the Takes Samples button five times. Can you tell that the variances were unequal by looking at the dot plots? Note the size of the Hartley's statistic. Press the Replications button and the Start Experiment button. What percentage of the time was the null hypothesis rejected at the 5% and 1% α-level? What does this mean about the robustness of one-way ANOVA to *extremely* unequal variances?

32. How big is Hartley's statistic in the case of extremely unequal variances? From these experiments, what can you conclude overall about the robustness of one-way ANOVA to the equal variance assumption? *Note this result is only true for one-way ANOVA!*

33. Set all three σ's to 500 and the three μ's to 100, 300, and 500 (so the null hypothesis of equal means is false). Conduct a replication experiment. What is the power of one-way ANOVA in this case? Change the σ's to 300, 500, and 640. What is the empirical power of one-way ANOVA in this case? Why is the power reduced? Do you think this is a general result?

Investigate the Normality Assumption

34. Set all three standard deviations equal to 500 and all three means equal to 100. Set the Population Distribution to Uniform. The normality assumption is now being violated. Conduct a replication experiment. What percentage of the time is the null hypothesis rejected at the 5% and 1% α-level? This is empirical Type I error. What does it say about the robustness of one-way ANOVA to sampling from a uniform distribution?

35. Set the Population Distribution to Skewed. Conduct a replication experiment. What percentage of the time is the null hypothesis rejected at the 5% and 1% α-level? What does this say about the robustness of one-way ANOVA to sampling from a skewed distribution? What is the shape of the histograms of sample means? What do the results in exercise 33 and this exercise tell you about the robustness of one-way ANOVA to *some* violations of the normality assumption? *This result is only true for one-way ANOVA.*

36. Set all three standard deviations to 500 and the three means to 100, 300, and 500. Conduct a replication experiment. What is the power of one-way ANOVA in this case? Compare your results with those in exercise 33. Is this a general result, or is it only true for some violations of the normality assumption?

Individual Learning Projects

Write a report on one of the three topics listed below. Use the cut-and-paste facilities of the module to place the appropriate graphs in your report.

1. Derive a power curve using any scenario or make up your own scenario using the Do-It-Yourself controls (use at least three groups). Set the Difference in Means scroll bar to None (the null hypothesis is true) and the Difference in Variances scroll bar to None (equal population variances). Set the Population Distribution to Normal. Use replicate (with 1,000 replications) to find the empirical Type I error. Copy the F distribution and the histogram of sample means (click on a display and press Ctrl–C on your keyboard to copy the display to the clipboard). Return to the main display. Move the Differences in Means scroll bar two clicks to the right. Repeat the replication experiment finding the power of the test. Continue moving the scroll bar two clicks to the right and repeating the experiment (a total of six experiments will be done). How should you measure the difference in the means ? (**Hint:** The histogram of sample means will give you a good indication of each group's mean.) Place this measure on the horizontal axis and sketch a power curve. Write a report on the power of one-way ANOVA. Describe the scenario, state the null and alternative hypotheses, and discuss how you measured the difference in means. Each point on your power curve should be validated with a display of the F distribution and the histogram of the means. How much difference must there be before there is a 50% chance that the ANOVA test will reject the null hypothesis? Are these results generalizable?

2. Select any scenario or make up your own scenario using the Do-It-Yourself controls (you must use at least three groups). Examine the dot plot of samples, the Summary Statistics and the ANOVA Table. Is the null hypothesis accepted (not rejected) or rejected? How is this reflected in all three displays? Take a second sample. Redo the previous analysis. Do this analysis a total of 10 times. Each time make a copy of your dot plot, the Summary Statistics and ANOVA Table. Write a report on the results of your 10 samples. Describe the scenario, state the null and alternative hypotheses, and discuss how you analyzed all three displays (what you looked for in each display). Based on these 10 samples, are the means equal? If you had used only your first sample, would you have gotten the same result? Why would a statistician always like to replicate an experiment a number of times? Why is it usually infeasible?

3. Sketch two power curves using any scenario or make up your own scenario using the Do-It-Yourself controls (you must use at least three groups). Set the Difference in Means scroll bar to None (the null hypothesis is true) and the Difference in Variances scroll bar to None (equal population variances). Set the Population Distribution to Normal. Follow the process described in project 1, using *three* clicks instead of two (four experiments will be created). Set the population being sampled to skewed and repeat the four experiments. How should you measure the difference in the means? (**Hint:** The histogram of sample means will give you a good measure of each group's mean.) Place this measure on the horizontal axis and sketch both power curves (you have only three points). Write a report discussing how sampling from a skewed distribution affected one-way ANOVA (both Type I error and power). Describe the scenario, state the null and alternative hypotheses, and discuss how you measured the difference in means. Are these results generalizable?

Team Learning Projects

Select one of the three projects listed below. In each case produce a team project that is suitable for an oral presentation. Use presentation software or large poster boards to display your results. Graphs should be large enough for your audience to see. Each team member should be responsible for producing some of the graphs. Ask your instructor if a written report is also expected.

1. Derive a family of power curves to illustrate the effect of sample size. Use any scenario or make up your own scenario using the Do-It-Yourself controls (you must use at least three groups). Set the Difference in Means scroll bar to None (the null hypothesis is true) and the Difference in Variances scroll bar to None (equal population variances). Set the Population Distribution to Normal. Each team member will generate a power curve using different sample sizes. One member will set each group sample size to 5, one member will set each to 50, and all other members will use sample sizes in between (as equally spaced as possible). Each team member will complete the six experiments described in Individual Learning Project 1. After all team members have completed their experiments, one graph showing each team member's power curve should be produced. Discuss the effect sample size has on power. Each team member should have graphs that validate his or her own power curve. Are these results generalizable?

2. Derive a family of power curves to illustrate the effect violating the equal variances assumption has on the power of one-way ANOVA. Use any scenario or make up your own scenario using the Do-It-Yourself controls (use at least three groups). Set the Difference in Means scroll bar to None (the null hypothesis is true). Set the Population Distribution to Normal. Each team member will generate a power curve using a different setting of the Differences in Variances scroll bar. One member will set the scroll bar to None, one member will set the bar to Lots, and all other members will use settings in between (as equally spaced as possible). Each team member will complete the six experiments described in Individual Learning Project 1. After all team members have completed their experiments, one graph showing each team member's power curve should be produced. Discuss the effect on power of the degree of inequality in variances. Each team member should have graphs to validate his or her own power curve. Are these results generalizable?

3. Derive a family of power curves to illustrate how the distribution of sample size among the groups affects the power of one-way ANOVA. Use any scenario or make up your own using the Do-It-Yourself controls. Set the Population Distribution to Normal and select three groups. Use a total sample size of 45. Each team member will generate a power curve using a different distribution of this total sample size. One member will set each group sample size to 15. Another member will set one group sample size to 39, and the other two to 3. Other members will use any sample sizes that sum to 45 (select an interesting distribution of sample sizes). Each team member will complete the six experiments described in Individual Learning Project 1. After the experiments are completed, produce a single graph showing each team member's power curve. Discuss how the distribution of sample size among the groups affects power and explain why. Each team member should have graphs that validate his or her own power curves. Are these results generalizable?

Self-Evaluation Quiz

1. The F statistic for analysis of variance is
    a. used to identify significant differences in means.
    b. either a left-tail or a right-tail test.
    c. based on the assumption of normal populations.
    d. all of the above.
    e. either a or c.

2. A dot plot in connection with ANOVA often
    a. reveals differences in means.
    b. reveals differences in variances.
    c. reveals differences both in means and variances.
    d. reveals nothing about means or variances.
    e. requires a normal population to be effective.

3. The sample F statistic
    a. is always positive.
    b. must be less than or equal to 1.
    c. is based on the ratio of sample means.
    d. goes to zero unless the population is normal.
    e. has more than one of the above characteristics.

4. The effect of increased group sample sizes in ANOVA would be
    a. to improve the utility of the dot plots in assessing the data.
    b. to improve the power of the F test for equality of means.
    c. to improve the power of Hartley's test of homogeneity of variance.
    d. to improve the estimates of the sample means and standard deviations.
    e. all of the above.

5. The F test in analysis of variance
    a. lacks validity unless each group has at least 30 items.
    b. requires equal group sizes in order to be accurate.
    c. suffers a sharp loss of power with slight departures from normality.
    d. is used because computations are easy.
    e. has none of the above characteristics.

6. The p-value for the sample F statistic shows
    a. the probability that the null hypothesis is false.
    b. the probability of obtaining the statistic by chance if H_0 is true.
    c. the probability of committing Type I error if H_0 is rejected.
    d. more than one of the above.
    e. none of the above.

7.   If the null hypothesis of equal group means is true, the population is normal, and the group variances are equal, then
     a.   the distribution of replicated sample F statistics should be normal.
     b.   the distribution of replicated sample F statistics should be chi-square.
     c.   the distribution of replicated sample F statistics should be Student's t.
     d.   the distribution of replicated sample F statistics should be F.
     e.   the distribution of replicated sample F statistics is uncertain.

8.   If the null hypothesis of equal group means is false, the population is normal, and the group variances are equal, then
     a.   the distribution of replicated sample F statistics should be shifted right.
     b.   the distribution of replicated sample F statistics should be shifted left.
     c.   the distribution of replicated sample F statistics should be centered on zero.
     d.   the distribution of replicated sample F statistics should be the same as the true F.
     e.   the distribution of replicated sample F statistics is uncertain.

9.   In an ANOVA experiment with four groups of five observations and a true null hypothesis,
     a.   the mode of the theoretical F distribution is positive.
     b.   the mode of the theoretical F distribution is zero.
     c.   the mode of the theoretical F distribution is negative.
     d.   the mode of the theoretical F distribution is indeterminate.
     e.   the mode of the theoretical F distribution is undefined.

10.   If an ANOVA sampling experiment is replicated many times, the histograms of sample means for the groups will
     a.   be approximately normal if the sample size is large.
     b.   resemble a chi-square distribution with $n - 1$ degrees of freedom.
     c.   reflect differences in group variances, if they exist.
     d.   have the same scale from the histogram of F statistics.
     e.   have more than one of the above characteristics.

11.   In the ANOVA comparison of k groups, which is *not* true of Hartley's F_{max} test statistic?
     a.   It is used to assess whether or not the population variances are homogeneous.
     b.   It is the ratio of the smallest to the largest sample variance.
     c.   It is generally larger when there is inequality of variance.
     d.   It requires special tables because it is not the same as Fisher's F.
     e.   It tends to be near 1 when the variances are homogeneous.

12.   Which is *not* true of heterogeneity of group variances?
     a.   One-way ANOVA is robust to a great deal of heterogeneity.
     b.   It may lead to non-parametric alternatives (e.g., Kruskal-Wallis test).
     c.   It refers to the skewness of each group's distribution.
     d.   In general, it reduces the power of the F test.
     e.   It is detected through Hartley's F_{max} test statistic.

Glossary of Terms

Analysis of variance Abbreviated ANOVA, this is the partitioning of variation about the overall mean into several additive categories. Part of the variation is attributed to the proposed ANOVA model, and the rest is attributed to error. In one-factor ANOVA there are two categories: *between-group variation* (model) and *within-group variation* (error). This partitioning of variance may be written SSE = SSB + SSW.

ANOVA table Worksheet summarizing the calculations for analysis of variance. In one-factor ANOVA there are three columns: sum of squares, degrees of freedom, and mean square. The first two columns also include a column sum.

Between treatments Refers to variation between groups. See **Analysis of variance**.

Critical value Separates the rejection and acceptance (non-rejection) region in the distribution of the test statistic assuming that the null hypothesis is true. It is a function of α, the level of significance used in a test.

Degrees of freedom For a one-factor ANOVA the variation *between* c treatment groups has c − 1 degrees of freedom, and the variation within the groups has n − c degrees of freedom.

Empirical power See **Power of a test**.

Empirical Type I error See **Type I error**.

Empirical Type II error See **Type II error**.

Equal variance assumption To derive the test statistic in one-factor ANOVA we assume that the population of each group being sampled has the same variance. If this assumption is violated, the distribution of the test statistic under the null hypothesis is open to question. If a test is relatively unaffected by a violation of an assumption, the test is said to be robust.

F ratio Ratio of the mean square between groups to the mean square within groups for a sample. If group means are equal, this ratio will tend to be near 0. A large ratio suggests that the group means may be unequal.

F statistic See **F ratio**. These terms are used interchangeably.

Mean square The sum of squares divided by its degrees of freedom.

Normality assumption To derive the test statistic in one-factor ANOVA we assume that the population of each group being sampled is normally distributed. If this assumption is violated the distribution of the test statistic under the null hypothesis is open to question. If a test is relatively unaffected by a violation of an assumption, the test is said to be robust.

Power of a test If the null hypothesis is false, *theoretical* power is the probability of correctly rejecting the null hypothesis $(1 - \beta)$. If the null hypothesis is known to be false, the *empirical* power is the ratio of the number of rejections to the number of times the test is performed. Ideally, the power of the test would be near 1. See **Type II error**.

Robust The quality of being relatively unaffected by a particular problem (e.g., non-normality or unequal variances). For example, one-way ANOVA is moderately robust to non-normality.

Source of Variation See **Analysis of Variance**.

Sum of Squares The sum of squared deviations about the mean.

Theoretical power See **Power of a test.**

Treatment In the context of one-factor ANOVA the "treatment" simply refers to a group (e.g., Freshman, Sophomore, Junior, Senior). The test is looking for possible differences among the treatments (e.g., does GPA vary among the four class "treatments").

Type I error If the null hypothesis is true, the *theoretical* Type I error is the probability of incorrectly rejecting the null hypothesis. Its probability is denoted α. When the null hypothesis is known to be true, the *empirical* Type I error is the ratio of the number of rejections to the number of times the test is performed.

Type II error If the null hypothesis is false, the *theoretical* Type II error is the probability of incorrectly accepting (not rejecting) the null hypothesis. Its probability is denoted β. When the null hypothesis is known to be false, the *Empirical* Type II error is the ratio of the number of acceptances to the number of times the test is performed.

Within treatments Refers to variation within groups. See **Analysis of variance.**

Solutions to Self-Evaluation Quiz

1. e Do Exercises 1, 2, and 7. Read the Overview of Concepts.
2. c Do Exercise 3.
3. a Do Exercises 1–9.
4. e Do Exercises 18–21.
5. e Do Exercises 7, 12–19.
6. d Do Exercises 13–17. Read the Illustration of Concepts.
7. d Do Exercises 13–15. Read the Overview of Concepts.
8. a Do Exercises 17–20.
9. a Do Exercises 12–15.
10. e Do Exercises 2 and 13–16.
11. b Do Exercises 22–23. Read the Illustration of Concepts.
12. c Do Exercises 22–23.

CHAPTER 13

Visualizing
Goodness-of-Fit Tests

CONCEPTS
- Theoretical Distribution, Parameter, Fitted Distribution, Goodness-of-Fit Test, Chi-square Test, ECDF plot, Kolmogorov-Smirnov test, Probability Plot

OBJECTIVES
- Recognize the characteristics of data-generating situations that will suggest an appropriate theoretical distribution to be fitted

- Interpret common data displays that may reveal whether a specified theoretical distribution is compatible with a given data set

- Learn how the chi-square goodness-of-fit test works and how the number of histogram classes affects the results of the test

- Recognize limitations of the chi-square goodness-of-fit test and the alternatives that are available

- Use visual and analytical ECDF-based tests for goodness-of-fit and compare their results with chi-square tests

Overview of Concepts

Goodness-of-fit tests (or **GOF** tests) have many important applications. For example, a quality control analyst may need to test whether defects are Poisson-distributed, or whether a finished product dimension is normally distributed. In exploratory data analysis (EDA) statisticians feel that sample data should "tell its own story." But in a GOF test *a priori* logic plays a strong role. First, we consider the data generating situation and choose a **theoretical distribution** (perhaps more than one) that is consistent with the data type (continuous or discrete), the sampling method, and the data's magnitude and range. Second, we examine sample statistics and visual displays (such as a histogram) to assess central tendency, dispersion, shape (skewness and kurtosis), and unusual features (e.g., outliers). Third, we may proceed to formal tests to see whether the chosen theoretical distribution provides an acceptable fit to the data.

In this module, you may specify the **parameters** of the proposed distribution *a priori*, or you may use the sample data to create a **fitted distribution**. Setting the parameters from the sample data will give a "better fit" but may violate the logic of the data generating situation. Purists oppose fitting the parameters from the data, arguing that a GOF test is inappropriate when there is no *a priori* basis for specifying the parameters. Yet sometimes logic dictates a distribution but not its parameter values.

This module superimposes your proposed distribution on the histogram, so you can see how it looks. This visual test may rule out the proposed distribution. The next step usually is a **chi-square test** based on the number of histogram classes (bins) you have chosen. In this module, the histogram covers the data range exactly, to avoid introducing unnecessary imprecision in the end classes. Bin width is the data range divided by the number of classes, so class limits will not be "nice." To maintain a "nice" axis scale, the histogram is allowed to "float" on top of the horizontal axis (the actual class limits are shown in the chi-square test).

The **empirical cumulative distribution function** (or **ECDF plot**) graphs the cumulative proportion of observations against the data values. The proposed theoretical distribution may be superimposed on the ECDF to check its fit. More formally, the **Kolmogorov-Smirnov test** (or **K-S test**) is based on the largest vertical difference between the ECDF and the proposed theoretical distribution. The K-S calculations may also be shown in tabular format. Critical values for the K-S test are found in published tables. The **probability plot** is a visual test that compares actual and expected data values under the proposed distribution. It will resemble a straight $45°$ line if the proposed distribution gives a good fit to the data.

Some words of caution are in order. In the chi-square test, expected frequencies should not be small (Cochran's Rule says at least 5, but other rules exist). To enlarge the frequencies, classes can be collapsed from the ends (this module tries to get frequencies of at least 2) but with discrete data this may not suffice. You can let the computer choose classes to maximize the expected frequencies (though this leads to unequal class sizes that no longer correspond to the histogram). You can also treat discrete data as if they are continuous.

Some distributions have logical approximations. For example, a binomial will resemble a normal if its mean is large (e.g., if $np \geq 5$ and $nq \geq 5$) and similarly for a Poisson (e.g., if $\lambda \geq 5$). A Poisson approximation can be used for a binomial (e.g., if $n \geq 20$ and $p < 0.05$). An exponential can approximate a geometric with a large mean. You can explore these possibilities in this module.

Illustration of Concepts

From a grocer's shelf, 22 D'Anjou pears are chosen at random and weighed. We expect the weights to be normally distributed, but since we have no *a priori* idea of the mean (μ) or standard deviation (σ) we must estimate the **parameters** from the sample. Figures 1, 2, and 3 show histograms using 4, 5, and 10 classes, along with a normal **fitted distribution** ($\mu = 248.1$ grams and $\sigma = 9.471$ grams). The 10-class histogram is rather sparse (its **chi-square test** would have small expected frequencies) so we will consider only the first two cases.

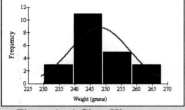

Figure 1: 4-Class Histogram

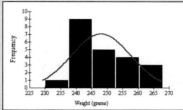

Figure 2: 5-Class Histogram

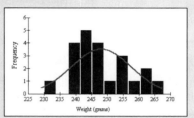

Figure 3: 10-Class Histogram

If the fit is good, the chi-square statistic will be near zero, using k–1–m degrees of freedom where m is the number of parameters estimated from the sample (m = 2 in this case) and k is the number of classes. In Figure 4 (for k = 4) the chi-square test statistic is 2.191 (p = 0.139), while Figure 5 (for k = 5) shows a chi-square test statistic of 4.605 (p = 0.100). The p-values indicate that we are unable to reject the hypothesis of normality at $\alpha = 0.05$. In this example, the number of classes affects the test statistic and degrees of freedom, but has little impact on the p-value. Figure 6 shows that the second class contributes heavily to the chi-square statistic.

Chi Square Calculations

Weight (grams)	Obs	Exp	Obs-Exp	Chi-Square
Under 239.5	3	4.01	-1.01	0.254
239.5 < 249.0	11	7.83	3.17	1.281
249.0 < 258.5	5	7.17	-2.17	0.656
258.5 or more	3	2.99	0.01	0.000
Total	22	22.00	0.00	2.191

d.f.=1   p < .139

Small expected frequency.   Big impact on test statistic.

Figure 4: Chi-Square Test (k=4)

Chi Square Calculations

Weight (grams)	Obs	Exp	Obs-Exp	Chi-Square
Under 237.6	1	2.95	-1.95	1.287
237.6 < 245.2	9	5.41	3.59	2.375
245.2 < 252.8	5	6.83	-1.83	0.490
252.8 < 260.4	4	4.68	-0.68	0.098
260.4 or more	3	2.13	0.87	0.354
Total	22	22.00	0.00	4.605

d.f.=2   p < .100

Small expected frequency.   Big impact on test statistic.

Figure 5: Chi-Square Test (k=5)

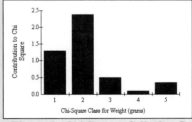

Figure 6: Chi-Square Cells (k = 5)

The descriptive statistics in Figure 7 show that the sample minimum and maximum (230 and 268) are almost exactly what we would expect in a sample of this size (229.1 and 267.0), calculated as the 0.5/n and 1-0.5/n fractiles of the **theoretical distribution**. The data are slightly right skewed (skewness 0.34) and platykurtic (kurtosis 2.45). The **ECDF plot** in Figure 8 resembles the fitted normal distribution, and the **K-S test** statistic of 0.14 shows no significant departure from normality. The **probability plot** In Figure 9 is close to a straight line. Overall, the normal distribution gives a reasonable fit in our **GOF** tests.

Statistical Summary

Statistic	Weight (grams)	If Normal
Minimum	230	229.1
Maximum	268	267.0
Mean	248.1	248.1
St. Dev.	9.471	9.471
Quartile 1	241.5	241.7
Quartile 2	247.0	248.1
Quartile 3	256.0	254.5
Skewness	0.34	0.00
Kurtosis	2.45	3.00
Cases	22	---

Figure 7: Statistical Comparison

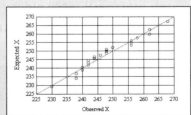

Figure 8: ECDF and K-S Test

Figure 9: Probability Plot

Orientation to Basic Features

This module does goodness-of-fit tests. You can analyze a variety of different data sets by selecting them from the Notebook or create your own using the data editor.

1. **Opening Screen**

   Start the module by clicking on the module's icon, title, or chapter number in the *Visual Statistics* menu and pressing the Run Module button. When the module is loaded, you will be on the introduction page of the Notebook. Click on the Introduction and Concepts tabs to see what will be covered in this module. Click on the Examples tab, select Class Projects, select Weight of D'Anjou Pears, and press OK. Read the Hint that appears in the middle of the display and press OK. The upper left shows a frequency histogram with a normal distribution (the default). The Control Panel appears on the right. On the bottom left is a statistical summary that compares the sample with the specified theoretical distribution. On the lower right is a table of calculations for the chi-square test. Other displays may be chosen from the menu bar at the top of the screen or by right-clicking a display and using the menu. The flashing Update Displays button will indicate when you have changed one or more control settings.

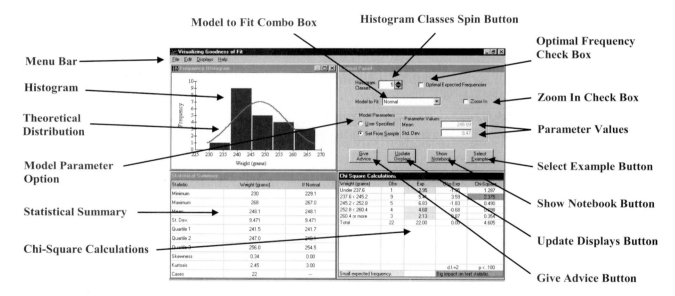

2. **Control Panel**
   a. The Histogram Classes spin button affects the number of histogram intervals and also the number of classes for the chi-square test. The number of classes is set initially using Sturges' Rule ($k = 1 + \log_2 n$). When too many classes are used, the chi-square test may generate a warning because the expected frequency in each class will become small.
   b. When the Zoom In check box is chosen, the axis on the histogram is chosen to reflect the actual data range. By default, the histogram axis scale is based on the theoretical maximum and minimum (usually wider than the actual data range), though in some data sets the results will be the same. Watch the histogram scale as you select this option.
   c. The Optimal Expected Frequencies check box forces the classes in the chi-square test to be chosen so that expected frequencies are maximized. For continuous data, this helps avoid small expected frequencies and may improve the power of the test. However, the unequal class sizes that arise may be less attractive. Note that this option is inactive for a discrete

distribution since the "classes" are integers that cannot easily be converted to class limits. However, you can use this option for a discrete model if you also select the option to treat the data as continuous.

d. The Model Parameters default is to use Set From Sample to ensure a properly centered distribution. Choose the User Specified option if you want to specify the parameter values. If you make strange choices (e.g., specifying a distribution that is off the scale) you will receive a warning or, in extreme cases, be asked to choose different values.

e. The Model To Fit combo box lets you select another distribution. Select a Uniform distribution. If you specify an inappropriate distribution, you will be warned (or prevented if your choice would make computation impossible) and an explanation will be given.

f. Click the Give Advice button to see a commentary on your data. If you are selecting a model or setting its parameters, this button may also suggest options of interest.

g. Click the Select Example button to pick a new data set from the list of examples. This button changes to Select Databases or Edit Data depending upon the origin of the data you are analyzing. It acts as a shortcut to the Notebook tab previously selected.

h. Click the Show Notebook button to bring up the Notebook. There are two large databases that you can access with this module: U.S. States and World Nations. Select the Databases tab. Click on either U.S. States or World Nations. Each database is organized by categories. Click on the + symbol of any category to expand the category and list its variables. The + symbol will become a − symbol. Click on the − symbol to shrink a category and hide its variables. Within any category of interest, click on several variables and read their descriptions in the text window at the right. A complete discussion of the databases is given in the Introduction.

i. Click on the Show Notebook button to bring up the Notebook. You can use your own data by using the Data Editor. Select the Data Editor tab, and press OK. A simple two-column spreadsheet appears. You can enter data and corresponding labels directly into this spreadsheet. You can title each column by entering its label in the top row. You can copy data from another spreadsheet and paste it into the data editor. From File on the menu bar you can save the data in *Visual Statistics* format. When you are finished, click on File and choose Exit Editor and Use Data or Exit Editor and Discard Changes. A complete discussion of the Data Editor is given in the Introduction to this book.

3. **Copying Graphs**
To copy a display, select Copy from the Edit menu on the menu bar or the Copy option when you right click on a display. It can then be pasted into other applications, such as Word or WordPerfect. Graphs are copied as bitmaps, and tables as tab-delimited text.

4. **Help**
Click on Help on the menu bar at the top of the screen. Search for Help lets you search an index for this module, Contents shows a table of contents for this module, Using Help gives instructions on how to use Help, and About gives licensing and copyright information.

5. **Exit**
Close the module by selecting Exit in the File menu (or click ☒ in the upper right-hand corner of the window). You will be returned to the *Visual Statistics* main menu.

Orientation to Additional Features

This module offers seven different types of graphs, four types of tables, and a verbal interpretation. The Hint that was displayed as the module began said, "Click the right mouse button on a quadrant to select a different display." This can also be done by selecting a quadrant and clicking on Displays in the menu bar. Only the Control Panel cannot be replaced.

1.   **Additional Graphs**
     Click on the upper left quadrant and choose Graphs and Kolmogorov-Smirnov Test. Click on the lower left quadrant and choose Graphs and Probability Plot. Click the lower left quadrant and choose Graphs and Dot Plot. The screen will look like the following:

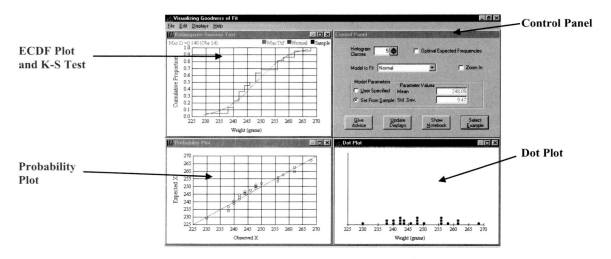

2.   **Additional Tables**
     Click on the upper left quadrant and choose Tables and K-S Calculations. Click on the lower left quadrant and choose Tables and Data List. Click the lower left quadrant and choose Interpretation. The screen will look like the following:

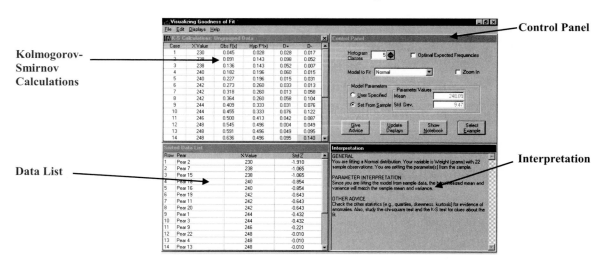

Basic Learning Exercises

Name _____

Descriptive Statistics

Press the Show Notebook button and select the Examples tab. Click on Sports and select Kentucky Derby Winners. Read the description of the data set and click OK.

1. Give the exact definition of the variable. What are its units of measurement? Are the data continuous or discrete? Do you think the sample size is large enough to give insight into the shape of the distribution?

2. Click on OK. Click the right mouse button to select your displays. Right-click the display in the lower right quadrant and select Tables and Data List. From the sorted data list, which horse had the best winning time? The worst? What are their standardized z-values? Is either an outlier?

3. What is the value of each statistic shown below? Based on these measures, what can you say about centrality and skewness? If you are unfamiliar with any term, use Help.

    Mean _____   Median _____   1st Quartile _____ 3rd Quartile _____

4. Record the value of each measure of shape. Click "Give Advice" to obtain the percent of observations within 1, 2, and 3 standard deviations. What do these statistics tell you?

	Skewness	Kurtosis	% within 1 SD	% within 2 SD	% within 2 SD
Sample					
If normal					

Histograms

5. Visually assess the histogram in comparison to the fitted normal distribution. Vary the number of classes (k) from 4 to 9. Does your impression of "fit" change as k changes?

Chi-Square Tests

6. Right-click the lower left display, select Tables, and choose Chi-Square Calculation. Consider the hypotheses

H_0: Derby winning time follows a normal distribution
H_1: Derby winning time does not follow a normal distribution

Record the chi-square test statistic, degrees of freedom, and p-value as you vary the number of classes (k) from 4 to 9. For each test at $\alpha = 0.05$ state the conclusion about H_0 (accept, reject). What conclusion you would reach about H_0 overall?

	k = 4	k = 5	k = 6	k = 7	k = 8	k = 9
Chi-square						
D.F.						
P-value						
Decision						

7. Repeat the previous exercise, but this time click Optimal Expected Frequencies. What is meant by "optimal expected frequencies"? **Hint**: Use Help. What conclusion you would reach overall? What was the effect of using equal expected frequencies on the apparent power of the test? **Hint**: Compare the p-values with those in Exercise 6.

	k = 4	k = 5	k = 6	k = 7	k = 8	k = 9
Chi-square						
D.F.						
P-value						
Decision						

Intermediate Learning Exercises   Name _____

Chi-Square Tests

8. Press the Show Notebook button, select the Examples tab, click on Sports and select Kentucky Derby Winners. Read the description of the data set and click OK. Vary the number of classes from 4 to 9, noting the number of degrees of freedom in the chi-square test. Why did D.F. not always increase? **Hint**: How many end classes were combined?

9. Click the Optimal Expected Frequencies option. Why do you consistently get one extra D.F. each time you add a class?   Contrast this with Exercise 8. **Hint**: Observe the expected frequencies and explain how they arise.

10. Does adding more classes lead to a better chi-square test (i.e., more powerful test)? Explain. **Hint**: Using optimal expected frequencies, keep adding classes (beyond 9) and see what happens to the expected frequencies.

11. Choose 7 classes and select Optimal Expected Frequencies. Right-click the display in the lower left and select Graphs and Chi-Square Test. Right-click the display in the upper left and select Graphs and Difference in Frequencies. What does the green highlighting in the chi-square table of calculations tell you? Relate it to the graphs.

12. Does the Chi-Square Test graph always agree with the Difference in Frequencies graph? **Hint**: Try varying k with and without Optimal Expected Frequencies.

Probability Plot

13. Right-click the display in the lower left and select Graphs and Probability Plot. What does this probability plot indicate? **Hint**: Use Help. Right-click the display in the lower right and select Tables and Data List. On the probability plot, locate the lowest data point in the data list (Secretariat in 1973). Estimate its coordinates on the graph and tell what the coordinates indicate. Repeat for the highest data point in the data list (Tiny Tam in 1958).

14. Right-click the display in the upper left and select Graphs and Frequency Histogram. Right-click the display in the lower right and select Tables and Chi-Square Calculation. Select Uniform Continuous on the control panel's Model to Fit. Use 7 classes. What does the chi-square test tell you? What does the probability plot tell you? Compare the two tests.

15. Again select Normal on the control panel's Model to Fit. Use 7 classes. Set Model Parameters to User Specified. Set the mean to 123.0 and the standard deviation to 1.0, and click Update Displays. What does the frequency histogram with overlaid normal distribution tell you? What does the chi-square test tell you? What does the probability plot tell you? Explain the problem that you have introduced.

Empirical Cumulative Distribution Function

16. Set Model Parameters to Set From Sample and click Update Displays. Right-click the display in the lower right and select Tables and Descriptive Statistics. Right-click the display in the upper left and select Graphs and Empirical Distribution Function. What does the ECDF tell you? Estimate the median from this graph, and check it against the descriptive statistics.

Advanced Learning Exercises   Name _____

Kolmogorov-Smirnov Test
Press the Show Notebook button and select the Examples tab. Click on Sports and select Kentucky Derby Winners. Read the description of the data set and click OK.

17. Right-click the display in the lower right and select Tables and Kolmogorov-Smirnov Calculation. Right-click the display in the lower left and select Graphs and Kolmogorov Smirnov Test. How does the K-S graph differ from the ECDF graph? Explain the meaning of the magenta line segment on the K-S graph, and relate it to the table of K-S calculations. Does this test support or disconfirm the hypothesis that the true distribution is normal?

18. Click Help and choose Search for Help On and Kolmogorov Smirnov and Equations. Using this information, try to calculate the critical value for $\alpha = 0.20$ and verify the conclusions of the K-S test. Was the decision close?

19. What does the help file say about the power of the Kolomogorov-Smirnov test? What does this mean?

20. Select Uniform Continuous on the control panel's Model to Fit. Use 7 classes. What does the K-S test tell you? Describe what the K-S graph shows.

Discrete Distributions

Press the Show Notebook button and select the Scenarios tab. Click on Binomial distribution and select True-false exam Scores. Read the scenario and click OK.

21. Right-click the display in the upper left and select Graphs and Frequency Histogram. Right-click the display in the lower left and select Graphs and Kolmogorov Smirnov Test. Right-click the display in the lower right and select Tables and Chi-Square Calculation. Do these tests support the hypothesis that the true distribution is binomial with $p = 0.50$ (i.e., the students were guessing)? Explain in your own words what the histogram suggests. How does the histogram appearance differ from the previous examples?

22. Leave the sample size at 50 but enter a probability of success somewhat greater than 0.50, and click Update Displays. Look at the histogram, K-S graph, and chi-square test. Use trial-and-error to vary the probability of success until you find a value that gives a good fit to the data, based on these visual displays. Explain in your own words what this experiment suggests.

23. Select Normal on the control panel's Model to Fit. Use 7 classes. Set Model Parameters to Set from Sample. Click Update Displays. Describe the results of this test. How does the appearance of the K-S graph and chi-square calculation differ from the previous discrete case?

Exponential Distribution

Press the Show Notebook button and select the Scenarios tab. Click on Exponential distribution and select Light bulb life. Read the scenario and click OK.

24. Is light bulb life exponentially distributed with a mean of 1,000 hours?

Individual Learning Projects

Write a report on one of the three topics listed below. Use the cut-and-paste facilities of the module to place the appropriate graphs and tables in your report.

1. Select a continuous variable from one of the normal scenarios. Create five histograms with various numbers of classes, and record the chi-square test statistic and its p-value for each. What effect does the number of classes have on the p-value? What do you consider the "best" number of classes? Do all the histograms appear normal? Discuss any anomalies that you notice. Repeat this exercise with one of the uniform scenarios. Discuss the similarities and differences in doing the chi-square test for the two variables.

2. Select a continuous variable of interest from one of the databases (U.S. States or World Nations) and test it for normality using the chi-square test, the K-S test, and the probability plot using the Set From Sample option for the parameters. Try more than one chi-square test. Do the tests agree? Examine the descriptive statistics (minimum, maximum, quartiles) and tell whether the sample and hypothesized normal values are similar. Repeat this exercise using another variable of interest. Tell which variable is closer to "normal." Discuss the similarities and differences in doing the K-S test for the two variables.

3. Select a Poisson scenario and carry out a hypothesis test using the chi-square test, the K-S test, and the probability plot. Click User Specified Values and try several parameter values to see whether the fit can be improved. How sensitive is the test to changes in the parameter? Finally, try the Set From Sample option. Was the fit improved? Choose a continuous distribution to fit to this data set (try more than one if appropriate). Do you get a reasonable fit? Compare and contrast the fit with the original Poisson distribution.

Team Learning Projects

Select one of the three projects listed below, and produce a team project that is suitable for an oral presentation. Use presentation software or a large poster board(s) to display your results. Graphs and tables should be large enough for your audience to see. Each team member should be responsible for producing some of the exhibits. Ask your instructor if a written report is also expected.

1. A team of two should select a continuous variable from any source and test the data for normality, using the chi-square test with various frequency histograms. Use 2 to 20 classes (make a display of each). Record each chi-square test statistic and its p-value. Describe whether the tests agree, and discuss any problems that arise. If the tests disagree, suggest reasons. Would you say that the chi-square test is robust to the number of bins (classes)? What does Sturges' Rule say about the number of classes? Which chi-square classification(s) would you recommend, and why? The objective of this project is to understand the effect of the number of classes on the results of a chi-square test.

2. Each member of a team of three should select a different variable from the normal-lognormal scenarios. Using the chi-square test, do a goodness-of-fit test first for a normal distribution, then for a lognormal distribution, and finally for a uniform continuous distribution. For each test, try at least three different classifications using different numbers of bins (classes). Which of the three proposed distributions is most compatible with your data? Would you say that more than one is acceptable? Explain any disagreements or difficulties that arise. The objective of the project is to explore the sensitivity of the chi-square test under various competing hypotheses about the population distribution.

3. This project is for a team of three to five. The team should agree on one of the discrete scenarios (binomial, Poisson, geometric, uniform) in the Notebook. Each team member should select a different variable and do various goodness-of-fit tests (chi-square, K-S, probability plot) to see whether the data are compatible with the hypothesized distribution and its parameters. Click User Specified Values and try several parameter values to see whether the fit can be improved. Finally, try the Set From Sample option. Compare the fit from the various tests for each set of parameter values. The objective of the project is to see whether the *a priori* distribution is reasonable, to see whether the hypothesized parameters were correct, and to see whether the tests agree. Discuss any problems that arise. If a different distribution might be better than the hypothesized one, explain why.

Self-Evaluation Quiz

1. Ideally, the choice of a theoretical distribution to be fitted to a sample is *not* based on
    a. the nature of the data-generating situation.
    b. the data type (continuous, discrete).
    c. the magnitude and range of the data.
    d. the sample statistics that give the best fit.
    e. the assumptions upon which the distribution is based.

2. The histogram is *least* likely to reveal
    a. the modal class(es).
    b. the mean and standard deviation.
    c. the general degree of skewness.
    d. the general shape of the distribution.
    e. the approximate range.

3. The chi-square GOF test on frequencies
    a. yields an inflated test statistic if the expected cell frequencies are small.
    b. usually requires that the parameters be estimated from the sample.
    c. requires a reasonably large sample size.
    d. is not essentially a visual test.
    e. has all of these characteristics.

4. Increasing the number of histogram classes with the exact range covered generally leads to
    a. more degrees of freedom in the chi-square test.
    b. decreasing class interval width.
    c. smaller expected frequencies in each class.
    d. a more powerful chi-square test.
    e. all of the above.

5. The probability plot is *primarily* used to
    a. check for randomness.
    b. check for normality.
    c. check for skewness.
    d. check the interquartile range.
    e. check more than one of the above.

6. To ascertain the approximate range of a sample we could *not* use which display(s)?
    a. Dot plot.
    b. Table of descriptive statistics.
    c. ECDF plot.
    d. Probability plot.
    e. Chi-square test with open-end classes.

7. The probability plot does *not* have which characteristic?
   a. It reveals outliers.
   b. It is easy to generate without a computer.
   c. It is approximately linear along the diagonal if the null hypothesis is true.
   d. It presents the data in sorted order.
   e. It is difficult to interpret if the data values are clustered.

8. The ECDF plot
   a. is a step function.
   b. works better for discrete data.
   c. presents the sample data in unsorted order.
   d. is generally U-shaped.
   e. has all of the above characteristics.

9. The Kolmogorov-Smirnov test
   a. requires the data to have a normal distribution.
   b. compares the ECDF and hypothesized distribution.
   c. is based on a minimum difference.
   d. has all of the preceding characteristics.
   e. has none of the above characteristics.

10. Which statement is *not* correct?
    a. The lognormal model is suitable when $\ln(x)$ is believed to be normal.
    b. The uniform distribution may be either discrete or continuous.
    c. The geometric distribution is skewed and has a very long right tail..
    d. The uniform distribution may be skewed either right or left.
    e. The geometric may be approximated by an exponential if the range is large.

11. Which is *not* a characteristic of the Poisson model?
    a. It is suitable only for discrete data.
    b. It can be approximated by a normal if the range is large.
    c. It is a versatile candidate for many kinds of samples.
    d. It is appropriate only for certain specific data-generating situations.
    e. It is useful in quality control.

12. The exponential distribution
    a. is right-skewed.
    b. is used as a model of waiting time for event arrivals.
    c. is appropriate only for non-negative data.
    d. is a continuous distribution.
    e. has all of the above characteristics.

Glossary of Terms

Binomial distribution Two-parameter distribution describing discrete data generated by a binary (success/failure) experiment with n independent trials and constant probability of success.

Chi-square test Non-parametric test for goodness-of-fit that groups the data into k classes and calculates the class frequency that would be expected under the hypothesized distribution. The parameters may be specified *a priori*, but often are estimated from sample data.

Degrees of freedom The number of independent pieces of information remaining after a statistical calculation. In a chi-square test with k classes, if m parameters are estimated the degrees of freedom will be k − 1 − m.

ECDF plot Acronym for *Empirical Cumulative Distribution Function*, a step function that plots the cumulative proportion of the sample against the corresponding sample X value. It is customary to superimpose the hypothesized distribution on the ECDF for comparison.

Expected frequency In a chi-square test, the number of observations that would be expected to fall within a defined interval if the data came from the hypothesized distribution.

Exponential distribution Continuous distribution used to characterize waiting time until a Poisson arrival (e.g., failure of a component). X must be non-negative. It has one parameter, the mean arrival rate.

Fitted distribution Distribution whose parameters have been estimated from sample data.

Geometric distribution Discrete distribution that describes the number of trials until the first "success" in a binomial experiment. It has one parameter (the probability of "success").

Goodness-of-fit test Any test that compares a hypothesized distribution with data from a sample. It may be visual (see **Probability plot**) but usually is a formal mathematical test.

Histogram Bar chart showing on the horizontal axis the values of X grouped into classes (intervals or bins) and on the vertical axis the frequency of occurrence within each class.

Kolmogorov-Smirnov test The K-S test statistic is the largest difference between the ECDF and the hypothesized distribution, measured in a vertical direction. It is a non-parametric test.

Kurtosis Measure of relative peakedness. For a unimodal, symmetric distribution K = 3 indicates a *mesokurtic* (normal, bell-shaped) distribution; K < 3 indicates a *platykurtic* distribution (flatter than normal, with short tails); and K > 3 indicates a *leptokurtic* distribution (more sharply peaked than normal, with long tails).

Lognormal distribution Continuous two-parameter distribution appropriate if ln(x) may be supposed to be normal. It is useful for certain kinds of positive, right-skewed data.

Nonparametric test Method of hypothesis testing that does not rely on an assumption about the population distribution from which the sample was drawn (e.g., normality).

Normal distribution "Bell-shaped" or Gaussian distribution with two parameters, the mean and variance. In a normal population, we expect 68.26% of the observations within 1 standard deviation, 95.44% within 2 standard deviations, and 99.73% within 3 standard deviations.

Observed frequency In a chi-square test, the actual frequency of sample data in a class interval.

Outlier Sample observation that is more than 3 standard deviations from the mean (suspected to come from a different population because it differs markedly from other sample data).

Parameter Numerical characteristic of a distribution that generally determine its probability density function, mean, variance, and other characteristics.

Probability density function (p.d.f.) Value f(x) assigned to every X in the domain of a distribution. The integral of f(x) must be unity (continuous distribution) or the f(x) values must sum to unity (discrete distribution).

Probability plot Comparison of each sample observation with the expected value of this observation assuming that the hypothesized distribution is correct (the sample is first sorted). If the hypothesized distribution is correct, the probability plot should be roughly linear. This provides a simple visual test for conformity between the sample and the hypothesis. The normal probability plot is most common.

Skewness Measure of relative symmetry. Zero indicates symmetry, positive values show a long right tail, and negative values show a long left tail.

Standardized Z value Obtained from an observation when we subtract the mean and divide by the sample standard deviation. These transformed data are called Z values because they may be used to see how closely the sample resembles a standard normal distribution, to spot outliers, and to check for asymmetry about the mean.

Sturges' Rule Rule of thumb suggesting that the number of histogram bins should be $1 + \log_2(n)$ where n is the sample size (e.g., 4 bins for 8 observations, 5 bins for 16 observations, 6 bins for 32 observations). It is a guideline to avoid too many or too few classes. If the data are skewed, Sturges' Rule may not provide enough classes to reveal adequate detail.

Theoretical distribution Hypothesized model of the population from which a sample is drawn, generally with specified parameter values.

Uniform distribution Continuous or discrete distribution describing a random variable whose p.d.f. is constant for all values in its domain. Its parameters are its upper and lower limits.

Solutions to Self-Evaluation Quiz

1. b Read the Overview of Concepts. Do Team Project 3.
2. b Do Exercise 5. Consult the Glossary. Read the Overview of Concepts.
3. e Do Exercises 6–12. Consult the Glossary. Read the Overview of Concepts.
4. e Do Exercises 5–12. Do Individual Project 1 or Team Projects 1 or 2.
5. b Do Exercises 12–14. Consult the Glossary.
6. e Do Exercises 2, 12, and 15. Read the Overview of Concepts.
7. b Do Exercises 13–15. Consult the Glossary. Read the Overview of Concepts.
8. a Do Exercise 16. Consult the Glossary. Read the Overview of Concepts.
9. b Do Exercises 17–20. Consult the Glossary.
10. d Do Team Project 2. Do Team Project 2.
11. c Do Individual Project 3. Consult the Glossary.
12. e Do Exercise 24. Consult the Glossary.

CHAPTER 14

Visualizing Bivariate Data Analysis

CONCEPTS
- Scatter Plot, Box Plot, Column Box Plot, Correlation Coefficient, Regression Line, Coefficient of Determination, t Statistic, F Statistic, Cross-Tabulation, Chi-Square Test for Independence, P-Value

OBJECTIVES
- Become familiar with alternative ways to display bivariate data and assess their strengths and weaknesses

- Understand alternative measures of association in bivariate data and recognize their underlying assumptions

- Be able to interpret bivariate regression statistics and assess their significance

- Know how to use and interpret a chi-square test for independence using cross-tabulated frequencies

Overview of Concepts

Bivariate data analysis refers to any technique that helps us analyze relationships between two variables X and Y with n observed data pairs (X_1, X_2), (X_2, X_2), ..., (X_n, X_n). Simply displaying the data pairs on a **scatter plot** may reveal much of what we want to know. Descriptive statistics and **box plots** allow us to analyze X and Y separately (to appraise central tendency, dispersion, and skewness). **Column box plots** for subgroups of Y based on values of X may provide further insight. These initial analytical steps require few assumptions.

A further step is to examine the **correlation coefficient**, a statistical measure of association between X and Y. The correlation coefficient can range from –1 (perfect inverse relationship) to +1 (perfect direct relationship). Uncorrelated data will appear as a random collection of points with a correlation coefficient near zero. Correlation analysis does not require us to specify a "dependent" variable and an "independent" variable. Rather, the variables are considered to covary, without indication of causality. For example, students who tend to score well on history exams may also tend to score well on literature exams. However, high history scores do not "cause" high literature scores (both variables may instead reflect the students' general abilities and study habits).

Often (but not always) one variable is regarded as a cause and the other as an effect. For example, we might suppose that quarterly software revenue is affected by advertising expenditures (but not vice versa). From pairs of sample data, we may estimate the coefficients of a simple **regression line** $Y_i = \beta_0 + \beta_1 X_i$. Its slope (change in Y for a unit change in X) and intercept (value of Y when X = 0) can help us answer policy questions (e.g., how much extra revenue is generated by an extra dollar's advertising expenditure?). Although the regression line reveals average change in Y for a unit change in X, it does not prove causation.

Since the fit of a linear model to observed data is usually imperfect, there is a *residual* for each observation (difference between observed Y_i and estimated Y_i). The Ordinary Least Squares (OLS) method chooses the slope and intercept so the fitted regression yields the smallest possible sum of squared residuals. Residuals are the vertical distances from the fitted regression line to each point on the scatter plot. The significance of each estimated coefficient is assessed using its **t statistic** (ratio of the estimated slope or intercept to its standard error) and corresponding **p-value**.

To assess overall fit we examine R^2 (the **coefficient of determination**), the standard error of the regression, and the **F statistic** (and its p-value). R^2 ranges from 0 (poor fit) to 1 (perfect fit). A small standard error signifies a good fit. The larger the F statistic, the more likely it is that the observed association between Y and X is not due to chance.

Regression analysis assumes that X is nonstochastic and that the errors are independent, normally distributed stochastic disturbances with zero mean and constant variance. If we feel that these assumptions are unwarranted, we might merely construct a grid on the scatter plot and count the number of points within each grid cell (**cross-tabulation** of frequencies). This table of frequencies (also called a contingency table) permits a nonparametric **chi-square test for independence** to be used as a measure of association. The chi-square test compares the expected cell frequency in row j and column k with the corresponding observed cell frequency. The expected frequencies are calculated based on the assumption that X and Y are independent of one another. A chi-square statistic near zero indicates that X and Y are independent, while a large chi-square test statistic indicates that X and Y are not independent.

Illustration of Concepts

Renée is a statistics student who works part-time in a supermarket seafood department. As a project in her university statistics class, she decides to record the weight and cost of customers' fish purchases. For a sequential sample (every third customer) she records the type of fish, its weight, and the cost that is printed on the bar-code stick-on label when the fish is weighed. She records 51 purchases and makes a **scatter plot**. The **box plots** for X and Y (Figure 1) reveal that both variables are right-skewed, and a **column box plot** (Figure 2) reveals that higher weight groups have higher median cost and greater interquartile range.

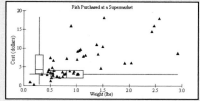

Figure 1: Individual Box Plots

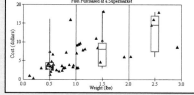

Figure 2: Column Box Plots

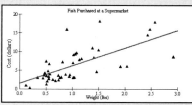

Figure 3: Regression Line

The scatter plot shows a positive association, as expected. Actually, the relationship between weight and cost would be linear (except for measurement error) for a given *type* of fish. But the sample contains 28 different kinds of fish, so the relationship isn't exact. The **correlation coefficient** (R = 0.679) indicates a strong association. Renée proposes a regression model: Cost = β_0 + β_1 Weight. Her hypotheses are based on her prior beliefs about the slope:

H_0: $\beta_1 \leq 0$ (cost does not increase as weight of fish increases)
H_1 $\beta_1 > 0$ (cost increases as weight of fish increases)

The estimated **regression line** (Figure 3) is Cost = 1.415 + 4.744 Weight. On average, cost rises \$4.74 for each extra pound of weight. For d.f. = 49 and α = 0.05, the one-tail critical value of Student's t is 1.677. The **t statistic** for the slope (t = 6.48) leads to a strong rejection of the null hypothesis. This decision is supported by its **p-value** (p < 0.01), which says that the slope estimate probably is not due to chance. In contrast, the intercept's t statistic (t = 1.67) suggests that the intercept does not differ significantly from zero. The **coefficient of determination** (R^2 = 0.461) says that fish weight "explains" about 46% of the variation in cost. The **F statistic** (F = 41.97) has a p-value below 0.01, so the overall regression is significant.

But is regression appropriate? As an alternative, Renée places a 2 × 2 grid on her scatter plot (Figure 4) and examines the **cross-tabulation** of frequencies in each grid cell (Figure 5). Expected and observed frequencies differ markedly, and the chi-square statistic (19.062) is significant (p < 0.001). But the small expected frequency in one cell (E_{12} = 1.1) violates Cochran's Rule (which requires $E_{ij} \geq 5$), so the **chi-square test for independence** is suspect in this case. A different grid might help.

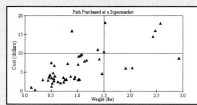

Figure 4: Grid on Scatter Plot

Cost (dollars)	Weight (lbs)		
	Low	High	Total
High	2 / 5.9	5 / 1.1	7
Low	41 / 37.1	3 / 6.9	44
Total	43	8	51

Chi-square test statistic = 19.062 (p < .001)

Figure 5: Cross-Tabulation

Orientation to Basic Features

This module helps you learn to recognize and display bivariate data, and to interpret common measures of association between two variables. It permits regression analysis and a chi-square test for independence of two variables. You can enter your own data, choose a scenario, use a Do-It-Yourself simulation control panel, use built-in real databases, or choose a real example.

1. **Select an Example**
   Start the module by clicking on the module's icon, title, or chapter number in the *Visual Statistics* menu and pressing the Run Module button. When the module is loaded, you will be on the introduction page of the Notebook. Read the questions and then click the Concepts tab to see the concepts that you will learn. Click the Examples tab. Click Consumer. Select an example, read it, and press OK. Read the Hint that appears. Press OK.

2. **Scatter Plot Display**
   The initial display contains a Scatter Plot, the Control Panel, an Example window, and a Descriptive Statistics window. The Grid Options panel is initially disabled. Click on any point to reveal its (X,Y) coordinates and its label (if any). Any data point can be dragged to a new location (this is not recommended at this time) to see what effect it has on the analysis.

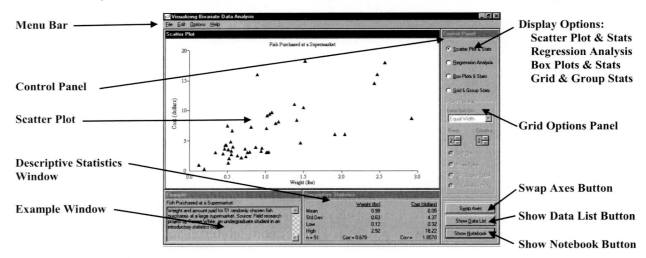

3. **Control Panel: Display Options**
   Click the Swap Axes button to interchange the X and Y variables. Both the data and the axis labels are switched. Click Swap Axes again to restore the initial display. Click the Show Data List button to see a list of the data pairs and their labels. At the top of the Control Panel, select Box Plots & Stats to display box plots (in red) for both variables along the axes of the scatter plot. Their descriptive statistics appear in the Descriptive Statistics window.

4. **Regression**
   Click Regression Analysis to display a fitted regression line (in red) on the scatter plot and to show the Regression Statistics window. Click Options on the menu bar and choose Regression. The Always Show Y Intercept option changes the scale of the scatter plot so that X = 0 is displayed. Otherwise, the scale is chosen to display the maximum graph detail. It has no effect if the scale already includes X = 0. If you choose Suppress Intercept, the regression is forced through the origin (a major change in model specification).

5.   Control Panel: Grid Options

Select Grid & Group Stats to superimpose a grid on the scatter plot. Use the Rows and Columns spin buttons to change the number of rows or columns. Experiment with the Base Grid On list box (Equal Width, Equal Frequency). Click Grid Only to display a simple grid. Click Cross Tabs to replace the two lower display windows with a single window showing a tabulation of frequencies. Click Chi-Square Table to see expected and actual frequencies along with a chi-square test statistic and its p-value. Click Column Box Plots to show column box plots.

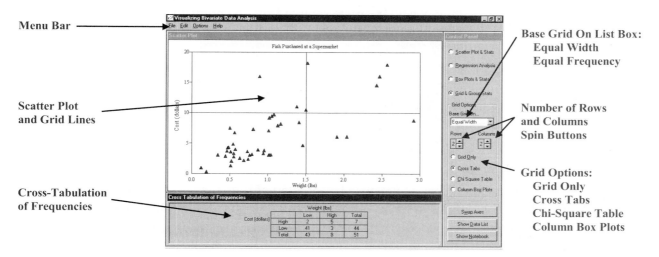

6.   Scenarios

Press the Show Notebook button, choose the Scenarios tab, pick a category and click OK. The scenarios are hypothetical, but this type of data would be likely to exhibit the proposed correlation and population shape. Variable descriptions appear in the Data Sets window. Press Take Samples to see a sample. You can't change the correlation or population type, but you can modify the sample size (though this may distort the scenario's logic).

7.   Databases

Click Show Notebook and choose the Databases tab. Click on U.S. States or World Nations to see a list of variables. Categories labeled + can be clicked to display an expanded list of variables within the category (or click – to collapse the category). You must choose two variables. Click OK. Descriptions of each variable appear in the Data Sets window.

8.   Copying a Display

Click the display you wish to copy. Its window title will be highlighted. Select Copy from the Edit menu (on the menu bar at the top of the screen) or Ctrl-C to copy the display.

9.   Help

Click Help on the menu bar at the top of the screen. Search for Help lets you search a topic index, Contents shows a table of contents, Using Help gives instructions on how to use Help, and About gives licensing and copyright information about *Visual Statistics*.

10.   Exit

Close the module by selecting Exit in the File menu (or click ☒ in the upper right-hand corner of the window). You will be returned to the *Visual Statistics* main menu.

Orientation to Additional Features

1. **Do-It-Yourself Data**
    To create a simulated data set of your own, click the Scatter Plot & Stats option. Press the Show Notebook button. Choose the Do-It-Yourself tab, and click OK. On the DIY Data control panel, use the horizontal scroll bars to change μ and σ and the vertical scroll bar to set ρ (the desired correlation coefficient, where $-1 \leq \rho \leq +1$). Use n to set the sample size (up to 150). Click Take Sample to display a new bivariate sample from the populations you have specified.

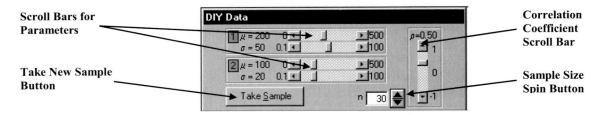

2. **Options: Population Being Sampled**
    Select Options on the menu bar and choose Distribution of Variables. You may specify the distribution of the populations to be sampled as Normal, Uniform, Skewed, or Very Skewed. The default is Normal. Both population distributions will be the same. Click Take Sample to see the effects of varying the distribution's shape.

3. **Data Editor**
    To enter your own data, click Show Notebook, choose the Data Editor tab, and click OK. Each row is an observation (a person, a team, etc.). The first column is an optional label for the observation (a person's name, a team's name, etc.). Use the menu bar File commands (New, Open, Save, Save As) to read existing files or save files in *Visual Statistics* format. Use the menu bar Edit commands (Cut, Copy, Paste, Insert Row, Delete Row) to edit your data or copy/paste data from another spreadsheet using the clipboard. Use the menu bar Options commands (Format, Sort, Typing Replaces Cell) to adjust the decimal places displayed or sort the data. When you are finished editing your data, click Close Editor and Use Data (or click the "smiling face" icon). If you don't want to use the data , click Close Editor and Discard Data (or click the "sad face" icon).

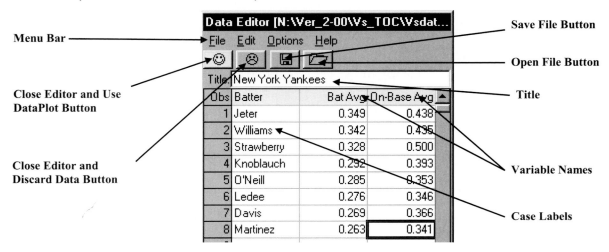

Basic Learning Exercises   **Name** _____

Press the Show Notebook button and select the Databases tab. Choose U.S. States. For your first variable (upper window) select Demographics (click + to expand its categories) and highlight Pop 65 and Up (%). For your second variable (lower window) select Health (click + to expand its categories) and highlight Heart Deaths per 100,000. Then press OK.

Scatter Plots and Correlation

1. Define each variable. Are the variables corrected for the effects of population size? Why would this correction be important (i.e., why not use totals)?

2. Describe the general appearance of the scatter plot. If you see any unusual data points, identify them by clicking on them (but be careful *not* to drag them).

3. Click Show Data List. Scroll down the list. Identify the state with the highest and lowest values for each variable. Can you suggest reasons? **Hint:** You can also find out by clicking on individual data points.

4. What is the value of the correlation coefficient? What is its p-value? What do these statistics tell you about the association between X and Y?

5. Click a point in the middle of the scatter plot and drag and drop it near the extreme lower right corner. What happens to the correlation coefficient? The p-value? How influential was this single data point?

Box Plots

6. The data have been altered by dragging a data point. Restore the correct data by clicking Show Notebook and clicking OK (to select the same two database files). Make sure the scatter plot has its original appearance. Record the means for both variables, then click Box Plots & Stats. Record the medians. Explain what the means, box plots, and quartile statistics tell you about each variable.

    X = Percent of population age 65 and over   Y = Death rate from heart disease
    Mean _____   Median _____   Mean _____   Median _____

7. Click Grid & Group Stats to display a 2 x 2 grid. Click Column Box Plots. Note the sample sizes (column statistics). In the Base Grid On list box, choose Equal Frequency instead of Equal Width and again note the sample sizes. Why is there a difference? Under what circumstances would Equal Width and Equal Frequency yield the same statistics?

8. Using Equal Width, increase the number of columns to 3, and then to 4. What happens to the column box plots, and why?

9. Repeat exercise 8 using the Equal Frequencies option. Discuss the advantages and disadvantages of these two options.

10. Using Equal Frequencies and 2 columns, compare the column box plots and their medians. What does this comparison suggest about the relationship between X and Y? Increase the number of columns to 3, and then to 4. Does the same conclusion hold?

Intermediate Learning Exercises   Name _____

Press the Show Notebook button, select the Databases tab, and choose U.S. States. For your first variable select Demographics and highlight Pop 65 and Up (%). For your second variable select Health and highlight Heart Deaths per 100,000. Then press OK.

Regression Analysis

11. Select Regression Analysis. Examine the regression line. Does it represent the data well?

12. Examine the regression statistics. a) Write the equation for the estimated regression line and interpret it. b) Is the sign of the slope believable? c) In this particular example, is the intercept meaningful? d) Would you have any reservations if a state were to use this estimated regression equation to make a health care policy decision? Explain.

13. What does the R^2 tell you? How much variation in the dependent variable is unexplained?

14. Click any point in the middle of the scatter plot and drag and drop it near the extreme lower right corner. a) What happens to the R^2? b) What happens to the estimated slope? c) How great was the effect of this single data point on the fitted regression line?

Cross Tabulations

15. The data have been altered by dragging a data point. Restore the correct data by clicking Show Notebook and clicking OK (to select the same two database files). Click Grid & Group Stats. Verify that the Equal Frequency option is selected. Choose 2 rows and 2 columns. Choose the Cross Tabs option. Examine the cross-tabulation and compare its frequencies to the grid (i.e., pick any grid cell and try to count its data points to see if your count agrees with the cross-tabulation). If you encounter any difficulties checking the frequencies, explain why.

16. a) Are the row totals equal? Are the column totals equal? b) Would this be the case in any
    2 × 2 table? Explain. c) How do you imagine the categories (Low, High) were formed? d)
    Are the cell frequencies similar in all four cells of the contingency table?

Chi-Square Table

17. Click Chi-Square Table. a) How different are the observed and expected cell frequencies? b)
    Does the chi-square test indicate that the two variables are independent? c) Is Cochran's Rule
    violated? **Hint:** If you're unfamiliar with chi-square tests, click Help or consult the Glossary.

18. In this particular bivariate data analysis, why might the chi-square test offer advantages
    (compared with regression) in assessing the possibility of association between X and Y?

19. Use the Rows and Columns spin buttons to increase the table size to 3 x 3. a) What happens
    to the chi-square test statistic? b) Does the test indicate independence? c) Is Cochran's Rule
    violated? **Hint:** You may have to scroll down the chi-square window to see everything.

20. Should the size of the table be increased further (say to 4 x 4)? Explain.

Advanced Learning Exercises   Name _____

Press the Show Notebook button, select the Do-It-Yourself tab, and click OK. Use the default means and standard deviations ($\mu_1 = 200$, $\sigma_1 = 50$, $\mu_2 = 100$, $\sigma_2 = 20$) and keep the default sample size ($n = 30$). Set the desired correlation at $\rho = 0.25$.

Correlation and Regression: Effects of Sample Size

21. Click Scatter Plot & Stats. Press Take Sample 10 times and record each estimated correlation coefficient and its p-value. Find the average correlation coefficient and average p-value. How close did the average correlation coefficient come to the desired correlation? How many of the estimated correlations were negative? How much variation was there? How many p-values were below 0.10? How much *visual* evidence of a positive correlation did you see in a typical scatter plot (take a few more samples if you wish).

Sample	1	2	3	4	5	6	7	8	9	10	Average
r	____	____	____	____	____	____	____	____	____	____	0___
p-value	____	____	____	____	____	____	____	____	____	____	0

22. Increase the sample size to $n = 100$ and repeat exercise 20. What difference does sample size have on the estimates and their p-values?

Sample	1	2	3	4	5	6	7	8	9	10	Average
r	____	____	____	____	____	____	____	____	____	____	0___
p-value	____	____	____	____	____	____	____	____	____	____	0

23. Click Regression Analysis. Press Take Sample 10 times. How often was the estimated slope positive (just by looking at the red regression line on the scatter plot)? Does having the regression line help you see evidence of a positive correlation?

Correlation and Regression: Varying the Correlation

24. Choose n = 30 and set the desired correlation to $\rho = 0.50$. a) Click Take Sample until you obtain an estimated correlation coefficient within the range 0.48 to 0.52. How hard was it? b) Now click the point farthest from the regression line and drag and drop it on the line. What happened to the correlation coefficient? c) Continue this exercise, watching the estimated correlation coefficient, until you have increased the estimated correlation to 0.99. How nearly linear is the data when you are finished? d) What is the t statistic for the slope? The F statistic? e) Do you expect such samples to occur very often?

Correlation and Regression: Intercept Options

25. Click Take Sample a few times and watch the left end of the X-axis scale. Note that the Y-intercept is not revealed in most of these samples, because X = 0 is not visible. Choose Options and then Regression and select Always Show Y Intercept. Click Take Sample a few times. Discuss advantages and disadvantages of showing the intercept.

26. Choose Options and then Regression and select Suppress Intercept. Examine the scatter plot and regression statistics as you press Take Sample a few times. How is suppressing the intercept different from merely turning off the Always Show Y Intercept option?

27. Choose Options and Regression. Deselect both Suppress Intercept and Always Show Y Intercept (so that neither option is checked). Click Scatter Plot & Stats to eliminate the regression line. Click Take Sample. Click Options again and choose Distribution of Variables. Instead of Normal select Uniform. Press Take Sample a few times. Repeat for Right Skewed and Left-Skewed. Discuss the appearance of the scatter plots. What effects would you expect the non-normal distributions to have on a fitted regression line?

Individual Learning Projects

Write a report on one of the three topics listed below. Use the cut-and-paste facilities of the module to place the appropriate graphs in your report.

1. Use the Data Editor to create a bivariate data set of your own. Choose X, Y data from your own experience (e.g., phone call cost versus length of call from your phone bill) or from a secondary source (e.g., an almanac or the *Statistical Abstract of the United States*) or, if nothing else is available, from a textbook. Explore the data set thoroughly using the tools of bivariate data analysis. Which tools are most helpful, and why? Include in your report a copy of graphs and/or tables you feel are relevant for each different experimental setup.

2. Use column box plots and chi-square analysis to analyze a pair of variables from the U.S. States database, or from the World Nations database that you believe *a priori* will be related. Vary the number of columns in the box plots, and vary the number of rows and columns in the chi-square analysis, to see whether a consistent impression is given of the possible association between the two variables (i.e., does varying the size of the contingency table affect the outcome of the significance test). Tell whether a regression or correlation analysis would be appropriate, and why (or why not). Repeat using a pair of variables from the World Nations database. Include in your report a copy of graphs and/or tables you feel are relevant for each different experimental setup.

3. Select the Scenarios tab in the Notebook. Choose a scenario representing each degree of correlation (ranging from Large Positive to Large Negative) and examine a scenario from each. Set each sample size to 30 so the scatter plots will be comparable. Compare the appearance of the scatter plots and comment on the differences that are due to population shape and note the effects of the data's characteristics on the appropriate methods of analysis. What conclusions can you draw from this experiment? Include in your report a copy of graphs and/or tables you feel are relevant for each different experimental setup.

Team Learning Projects

Select one of the three projects listed below. In each case, produce a team project that is suitable for an oral presentation. Use presentation software or large poster boards to display your results. Graphs should be large enough for your audience to see. Each team member should be responsible for producing some of the graphs. Ask your instructor if a written report is also expected.

1. This is a project for a team of two. One team member should investigate the U.S. States database and the other should investigate the World Nations database. Using logic and trial-and-error, try to find examples of variables that exhibit strong negative correlation, near-zero correlation, and positive correlation. For each example that you finally decide to present, discuss the characteristics of each variable (central tendency, dispersion, skewness) as revealed by box plots, and comment on the possible policy implications and degree of believability of a regression fitted to the data. Discuss which tools are best for each data set, and explain why. Include in your report a copy of all graphs and statistics that you evaluated.

2. This is a project for a team of two. Investigate the effects of population non-normality and sample size on the accuracy of estimates for the regression slope. Use the Do-It-Yourself controls with a true correlation of 0.60. Use the Options to select each of the four population types. Using five samples, find the average and the range of estimates for the slope. One team member should use a sample of size 10 and the other should use a sample of size 50. Explain your conclusions clearly. Include in your report a copy of all graphs and statistics that you evaluated.

3. This is a project for a team of three or more. Investigate the effects of sample size on accuracy of estimation of the correlation coefficient. Use the Do-It-Yourself controls, and set the true correlation to $\rho = 0.00$. Each team member should select a different sample size between 10 and 120 so that the range is covered. Take several samples and average the estimated correlation coefficients. How often would you mistakenly conclude there is a non-zero correlation? Repeat for a true correlation of $\rho = 0.80$. Repeat the experiment using a skewed population and then a uniform population. Display the team's findings in a simple visual summary (table or chart). Include in your report a copy of all graphs and statistics that you evaluated.

Self-Evaluation Quiz

1. A scatter plot of X and Y
    a. gives little information about the actual correlation.
    b. requires that a linear regression be calculated and displayed.
    c. indicates causal direction since X is the independent variable.
    d. makes too many restrictive assumptions to be used in Exploratory Data Analysis.
    e. has none of the above characteristics.

2. Which is *not* a common characteristic of real bivariate data sets?
    a. The populations are not normally distributed.
    b. The data are skewed to the right.
    c. The data may contain extreme values.
    d. The data are inversely related.
    e. The data are not a random sample.

3. The p-value for the correlation coefficient shows
    a. the probability that the true correlation is non-zero.
    b. the probability of obtaining the sample correlation if the true correlation is zero.
    c. the probability of Type I error if the hypothesis of zero correlation is rejected.
    d. more than one of the above.
    e. none of the above.

4. Which is indicative of an *inverse* relationship between X and Y?
    a. A scatter plot whose points are shaped like a circle.
    b. A scatter plot with points mostly in the lower left and upper right quadrants.
    c. A negative correlation coefficient.
    d. A negative p-value for the correlation coefficient.
    e. None of the above.

5. Column box plots on a scatter plot *cannot* reveal
    a. significance of the correlation coefficient.
    b. skewness of the data within each column group.
    c. dispersion of the data within each column group.
    d. central tendency of the data within each column group.
    e. whether the relationship between X and Y is direct or inverse.

6. A box plot on the X-axis of a scatter plot is *least* likely to reveal which of these?
    a. Number of modes in X.
    b. Skewness in X.
    c. Non-normality in X.
    d. The range of X.
    e. Central tendency of X.

7.   The regression line that is superimposed on the scatter plot
     a.   is computed using the Ordinary Least Squares method.
     b.   guarantees the largest possible sample variance.
     c.   guarantees that the slope and intercept are minimized.
     d.   guarantees all of the above.
     e.   guarantees none of the above.

8.   Which is *not* correct regarding the estimated slope of the regression line?
     a.   It is divided by its standard error to obtain its t statistic.
     b.   It shows the change in Y for a unit change in X.
     c.   It is chosen so as to minimize the sum of squared errors.
     d.   It may effectively be regarded as zero if its p-value is below 0.01.
     e.   Its magnitude is an unreliable indicator of significance.

9.   An important attractive feature of the chi-square test for independence is
     a.   its one-to-one correspondence to the magnitude of the slope.
     b.   its lack of reliance on sophisticated assumptions.
     c.   its insensitivity to small expected frequencies.
     d.   its ability to reveal directionality of the relationship (direct or inverse).
     e.   its high power relative to regression or correlation analysis.

10. Which is *least* likely to be adversely affected by outliers?
     a.   the chi-square test statistic.
     b.   the regression slope.
     c.   the sample correlation coefficient.
     d.   the R^2 statistic.
     e.   the p-value for the slope.

11. Which is a characteristic of the chi-square test for independence?
     a.   It requires a large observed frequency in each cell.
     b.   It is a parametric test.
     c.   It requires at least 30 observations for a 4×4 table.
     d.   Its results do not depend on the X–Y grid boundaries.
     e.   None of the above is a correct characteristic.

12. In a simple regression, which would suggest a relationship between X and Y?
     a.   Large p-value for the estimated slope.
     b.   Large t statistic for the slope.
     c.   Large p-value for the F statistic.
     d.   All of the above suggest a relationship.
     e.   None of the above suggests a relationship.

Glossary of Terms

ANOVA table Summary of decomposition of variance. For a bivariate regression, the ANOVA table is shown below. See also **Sums of squares**, **Mean square**, and **Degrees of freedom**.

Source	Sum of Squares	d.f.	Mean Square
Regression	SSR	1	MSR = SSR/1
Error (residual)	SSE	$n - 2$	MSE = SSE/$(n - 2)$
Total	SST	$n - 1$	

Bivariate data Sample of n observations on two random variables X and Y. Each data pair is denoted (X_i, Y_i) where i = 1, 2, . . . , n.

Box plot Graphic representation of X_{Min}, Q_1, Q_2, Q_3, and X_{Max} . A simple box plot is sometimes called a "five-number summary" or a "box and whisker plot". The box encloses the quartiles and the span of the "whiskers" indicates the range.

Chi-square test for independence Test for association between two cross-tabulated variables X and Y in a contingency table with R rows and C columns. If X and Y are truly independent, the chi-square test statistic should be near zero. The test statistic is

$$\sum_{j=1}^{R} \sum_{k=1}^{C} \frac{\left(O_{jk} - E_{jk}\right)^2}{E_{jk}}$$

where O_{jk} and E_{jk} are the respective observed and expected cell frequencies in row j and column k. For a valid test, E_{jk} should not be too small. See **Cochran's rule** and **Degrees of freedom**.

Cochran's rule A rule of thumb that suggests that the minimum expected frequency (E_{jk}) in each cell of a contingency table should be at least 5 for a valid chi-square test.

Coefficient of determination In a bivariate regression, the coefficient of determination is a measure of overall fit. R^2 near 0 signifies a lack of fit while R^2 near 1 signifies a near-linear fit. It is calculated from sums of squares using the equation $R^2 = $ SSR / SST. See **ANOVA table**.

Column box plot For a bivariate data set, a box plot for Y values corresponding to X values within a certain range.

Conditional mean In a regression, the expected value of the dependent variable *given* the observed value(s) of the dependent variable(s). In contrast, the unconditional mean is just the expected value of the dependent variable (i.e., the mean).

Contingency table A cross-tabulation of sample observations (X_i, Y_i) on two random variables into categories (the number of categories need not be the same for X and Y). A contingency table with R rows and C columns is called an R × C contingency table. See **Bivariate data**, **Observed frequency**, **Expected frequency**, and **Chi-square test for independence**.

Correlation coefficient Measure of fit in a bivariate regression, equal to the sample covariance divided by the product of the sample standard deviations of X and Y. A correlation of -1 indicates a perfect inverse relationship, 0 indicates no relationship, and $+1$ indicates a perfect direct relationship. The formula for the correlation coefficient is:

$$r = \frac{\sum_{i=1}^{n}(X_i - \overline{X})(Y_i - \overline{Y})}{\sqrt{\sum_{i=1}^{n}(X_i - \overline{X})^2 \sum_{i=1}^{n}(Y_i - \overline{Y})^2}} \qquad \text{or} \qquad r = \frac{Cov(X,Y)}{S_X S_Y}$$

Cross-tabulation See **Contingency table**.

Degrees of freedom Number of independent pieces of information in a sample. In a chi-square test, degrees of freedom will be $(R - 1)(C - 1)$, where R is the number of rows and C is the number of columns in the contingency table. In a regression ANOVA table, total degrees of freedom will be $n - 1$, error degrees of freedom will be $n - k - 1$, and the regression degrees of freedom will be k, where n is the sample size and k is the number of independent predictors in the model ($k = 1$ for a bivariate model).

Dependent variable In a regression, the variable (denoted Y) that is placed on the left-hand side of the equation and may be assumed to be affected by the independent variable (denoted X). On the scatter plot, the dependent variable is customarily shown on the vertical axis.

Expected frequency In a contingency table, the number of observations in a cell that would be expected if X and Y were independent. For row j and column k, the observed frequency may be denoted E_{jk} and is $n_j n_k / n$, where n_j and n_k are the respective row and column totals for the contingency table. See **Observed frequency** and **Chi-square test for independence**.

F statistic In a regression ANOVA table, the ratio of the regression mean square to the error mean square ($F = MSR / MSE$). The larger the F statistic, the less likely it is that the association between Y and X is due to chance. An F statistic close to zero would suggest the regression line does not give a good fit to the sample data.

Frequency See **Expected frequency** and **Observed frequency**.

Grid Grouping of X and Y into categories on a scatter plot.

Independence See **Chi-square test for independence**.

Independent variable In a regression, the variable (denoted X) that appears on the right-hand side of the equation and is thought to cause variation in the dependent variable (denoted Y). On a scatter plot, the independent variable is usually shown on the horizontal axis.

Intercept Value of the dependent variable when $X = 0$ in the regression model $Y = \beta_0 + \beta_1 X$. On a graph, the intercept β_0 is the point where the regression line intersects the Y-axis. See **Ordinary Least Squares**.

Mean square In a regression ANOVA table, the sums of squares due to regression or error, divided by their respective degrees of freedom. In a bivariate regression the regression mean square is $MSR = SSR/1$ and the error mean square is $MSE = SSE/(n - 2)$. See **ANOVA table**.

Model Proposed regression equation whose coefficients (i.e., slope and intercept) are to be estimated from sample data. The model is generally based on a theory.

Observed frequency In a contingency table, the number of observations in each cell. For row i and column j, the observed frequency is often denoted O_{ij}. See **Expected frequency**.

Ordinary Least Squares Abbreviated OLS, this is a calculus-based method of choosing the regression coefficients so that the fitted regression model yields the smallest possible sum of squared errors (SSE). OLS estimates are widely used in spreadsheets and statistical packages.

Sum of Squared Errors:

$$SSE = \sum_{i=1}^{n}\left(Y_i - \hat{Y}_i\right)^2$$

Estimated Slope:

$$\hat{\beta}_1 = \frac{\sum_{i=1}^{n}\left(X_i - \overline{X}\right)\left(Y_i - \overline{Y}\right)}{\sum_{i=1}^{n}\left(X_i - \overline{X}\right)^2}$$

Estimated Intercept:

$$\hat{\beta}_0 = \overline{Y} - \hat{\beta}_1\overline{X}$$

P-value In a regression, the probability of Type I error if we reject a particular hypothesis about a parameter (such as an estimated slope). For example, if we hypothesize that the true slope of a regression line is zero, a small p-value (say, $p = 0.01$) would suggest rejection of the hypothesis because in so doing we are unlikely to commit Type I error.

Regression line Numerical estimates of the slope and intercept of a bivariate regression model.

Residual Difference between the actual and estimated value of the dependent variable.

R-squared See **Coefficient of determination**.

Scatter plot Visual display in which each of n observed (X_i, Y_i) pairs is plotted as a symbol (usually a dot) at the correct coordinate on the graph.

Slope The change in Y for a unit change in X in the bivariate model $Y = \beta_0 + \beta_1 X$. On a graph, the slope β_1 is the rise divided by the run. See **Ordinary Least Squares**.

Standard error Estimated standard deviation of an unknown parameter. Formulas for some of the standard errors used in this chapter are:

Regression:

$$S_{Y|X} = \sqrt{\frac{SSE}{n-2}}$$

Intercept:

$$S_{\hat{\beta}_0} = S_{Y|X}\sqrt{\frac{1}{n} + \frac{\overline{X}^2}{\sum_{i=1}^{n}\left(X_i - x\right)^2}}$$

Slope:

$$S_{\hat{\beta}_1} = \frac{S_{Y|X}}{\sqrt{\sum_{i=1}^{n}\left(X_i - x\right)^2}}$$

Sum of squares In regression, total variation in the dependent variable around its mean (SST) is partitioned into variation explained by the regression (SSR) and variation that is unexplained by the regression (SSE). They are used in ANOVA to find the mean squares and F statistic. Their formulas are shown below.

Total Variation:

$$SST = \sum_{i=1}^{n}\left(Y_i - \overline{Y}\right)^2$$

Explained (Regression):

$$SSR = \sum_{i=1}^{n}\left(\hat{Y}_i - \overline{Y}\right)^2$$

Unexplained (Error):

$$SSE = \sum_{i=1}^{n}\left(Y_i - \hat{Y}_i\right)^2$$

t statistic Generally, the ratio of an estimated coefficient in a regression model to its standard error, which can be used to test whether the estimated coefficient is equal to zero. If the errors in a regression are normal, this ratio is distributed as Student's t and its magnitude may be used to judge the null hypothesis. For example, a large t statistic for the slope would suggest that the true slope is not zero.

Test for Independence See **Chi-square test for independence**.

Y-intercept The value of Y when X is zero. See **Intercept**.

Solutions to Self-Evaluation Quiz

1.   e   Do Exercises 2–5. Read the Overview of Concepts. Consult the Glossary.
2.   d   Do Exercises 1–3. Read the Overview of Concepts. Consult the Glossary.
3.   d   Do Exercises 4–5. Read the Overview of Concepts.
4.   c   Do Exercises 1–5. Do Individual Learning Project 3.
5.   a   Do Exercises 6–10. Read the Illustration of Concepts. Consult the Glossary.
6.   a   Do Exercise 6. Consult the Glossary.
7.   a   Read the Overview of Concepts. Consult the Glossary.
8.   d   Do Exercises 11–14. Read the Illustration of Concepts. Consult the Glossary.
9.   b   Read the Overview of Concepts. Consult the Glossary.
10. a   Do Exercises 5, 14, 18. Read the Overview of Concepts. Consult the Glossary.
11. e   Do Exercises 15–20. Consult the Glossary. Read Overview of Concepts.
12. b   Do Exercises 21–24. Read the Overview of Concepts and Illustration of Concepts.

CHAPTER 15

Visualizing Simple Regression

CONCEPTS
- Estimated Model, True Model, Conditional Mean, Dependent Variable, Independent Variable, Ordinary Least Squares (OLS), Disturbance, Residual, Estimator, Parameter, Confidence Interval, Prediction Interval, Distribution of $\hat{\beta}_0$, Distribution of $\hat{\beta}_1$

OBJECTIVES
- Understand OLS terminology

- Understand how sample size, standard error, true parameters, and the range of the independent variable affect estimation accuracy

- Understand the sampling and population distribution of OLS estimators

- Understand the difference between confidence intervals for $E(y|x)$ and prediction interval for $y|x$ and the reason for their parabolic shape

Overview of Concepts

A simple regression model relates a **dependent variable** Y to an **independent variable** X. This model is used when the mean of each observation or value of y_i is conditional upon the value of x_i. This **conditional mean** is written as $E(y_i|x_i) = \beta_0 + \beta_1 x_i$, where β_0 is the intercept and β_1 is the slope. β_0 and β_1 are unknown **parameters**. The conditional mean is not observable. However, the actual values of y_i are observed and do not generally lie at this conditional mean. The deviations of the values of y_i from this conditional mean are called **disturbances**, or errors, and are denoted u_i. Combining the conditional mean with these disturbances results in the **true model** $y_i = E(y_i|x_i) + u_i = \beta_0 + \beta_1 x_i + u_i$. Since the conditional mean $E(y_i|x_i)$ is not known, the disturbances are not known or observed.

An example of this model occurs in macroeconomics. John Maynard Keynes theorized that the amount spent by all consumers (consumption) depends upon their total income. In statistical terms this is written as $E(\text{Consumption}|\text{Income}) = \beta_0 + \beta_1 \text{Income}$. This is the conditional mean. The true model is Consumption $= \beta_0 + \beta_1 \text{Income} + u$.

If data were collected on consumption and income, β_0 and β_1 could be estimated using the method of **Ordinary Least Squares (OLS)**. OLS is an estimation technique that is used to derive an **estimator** (an equation) for β_0 and β_1. It does this by minimizing the sum of the squared deviations between y_i and the estimated regression line. The OLS estimates obtained for β_0 and β_1 are generally denoted $\hat{\beta}_0$ and $\hat{\beta}_1$. Using this notation results in the **estimated model** $\hat{y}_i = \hat{\beta}_0 + \hat{\beta}_1 x_i$. This is the equation of the estimated conditional mean or estimated regression line. The difference between each estimated value $\hat{y}_i$ and the corresponding observed value of y_i is called the **residual**. The residual $\hat{u}_i$ equals $y_i - \hat{y}_i$. The residuals sum to zero. The OLS technique guarantees unbiased estimates of $\hat{\beta}_0$ and $\hat{\beta}_1$ that minimize $\Sigma \hat{u}_i^2$.

Just as the sample mean $\overline{Y}$ is a point estimate of the population mean μ_y, $\hat{y}_i$ is a point estimate for the conditional mean $E(y_i|x_i)$. Similarly, just as an interval estimate for μ_y is based on a confidence interval using $\overline{Y}$, an interval estimate for $E(y_i|x_i)$ is based on a **confidence interval** using $\hat{y}_i$. However, using regression analysis we can also create a **prediction interval** for $y_i|x_i$. The confidence interval describes the location of the *conditional mean*, while the prediction interval describes the location of the *individual observation* y_i for a given value x_i.

Recall that the Central Limit Theorem states that the estimator $\overline{Y}$ has a normal distribution (if n is large enough) with a mean μ_y and a standard error $\sigma/\sqrt{n}$. Similar results have been derived for the estimators $\hat{\beta}_0$ and $\hat{\beta}_1$. Statisticians have derived the **distribution of $\hat{\beta}_0$** and the **distribution of $\hat{\beta}_1$** when the disturbances, or errors, u_i are independently and identically distributed with a normal distribution having a mean of zero and a variance of σ^2. In that case, $\hat{\beta}_0$ will be normally distributed with a mean β_0 and a standard error $\sigma\{\Sigma x_i^2 / [n \Sigma(x_i - \overline{X})^2]\}^{0.5}$, and $\hat{\beta}_1$ will be normally distributed with a mean β_1 and a standard error of $\sigma/[\Sigma(x_i - \overline{X})^2]^{0.5}$, where n is sample size and σ is the standard error of the true model.

Illustration of Concepts

Suppose we have a sample of income tax returns for 20 married couples (no dependents). We hypothesize the model Taxes = β_0 + β_1 Income + u, where Taxes are the **dependent variable**, Income is the **independent variable**, u is the **disturbance** (or error) term, and β_0 and β_1 are the unknown **parameters**. In this model, β_1 is the marginal tax rate on each dollar of additional income and β_0 is the average tax for a married couple without dependents with zero income.

Suppose this model is estimated using **ordinary least squares (OLS)** with 20 pairs of observations on taxes and income to obtain the **estimated model** Predicted Taxes = 580.4 + 0.035 Income. The estimated intercept (580.4) and slope (0.035) are the OLS estimates of β_0 and β_1. The OLS **estimators** of these parameters are the equations that are used to obtain the estimates, not the estimates themselves. The **residual** is the difference between the predicted tax and actual tax each family paid to the state. On a graph, a residual is the vertical distance between a data point and the estimated model. Figure 1 shows a scatter plot with the estimated model and two residuals labeled.

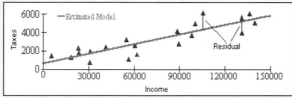

Figure 1: Estimated Model and Residuals

For the estimated intercept, the t-value for the estimated intercept is 1.52, suggesting that the true intercept is possibly close to zero. For the estimated slope, the t-value is 7.71, suggesting that the true slope is positive.

Although the **true model** is not known, based on the structure of the tax law, a financial economist in the state treasurer's office believes that the **conditional mean** is E(Taxes|Income) = −135 + 0.045 Income. If this conditional mean is correct, the true model becomes Taxes = −135 + 0.045 Income + u. The u in this model is the disturbance, or error, term. If the economist is correct, and if the disturbances are normally distributed with a mean of zero and a constant variance, then the **distribution of $\hat{\beta}_0$** is normal with a mean of 135 and the **distribution of $\hat{\beta}_1$** is normal with a mean of 0.045.

Using the estimated model, a **confidence interval** for the conditional mean and a **prediction interval** for y can be constructed (assuming that the disturbances are normally distributed). A 99% confidence interval is shown in Figure 2 along with the line of conditional means. Note that the confidence interval contains this conditional mean. Figure 3 shows a 90% prediction interval. Note that, as expected, one point and maybe two points are outside the interval's boundary.

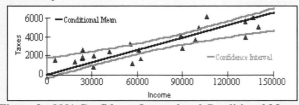

Figure 2: 90% Confidence Interval and Conditional Mean

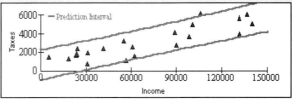

Figure 3: 90% Prediction Interval

Orientation to Basic Features

This module generates data from a true regression model that you create and then estimates the model. You can examine similarities and differences between the true and estimated models and between the residuals and disturbances. You can display a confidence interval for $E(y|x)$ and a prediction interval for $y|x$. You can replicate the experiment and display the estimated models and histograms of the estimated slopes, intercepts, standard errors, R^2, and correlation coefficients.

1. **Opening Screen**

   Start the module by clicking on the module's icon, title, or chapter number in the *Visual Statistics* menu and pressing the Run Module button. When the module is loaded, you will be on the introduction page of the Notebook. Read the questions and then click the Concepts tab to see the concepts that you will learn. Click on the Scenarios tab. Click on Firms, select a scenario, read it, and press OK. A scatter plot appears with a Control Panel at the bottom. Click on the scatter plot. A toolbar appears at the top of the screen.

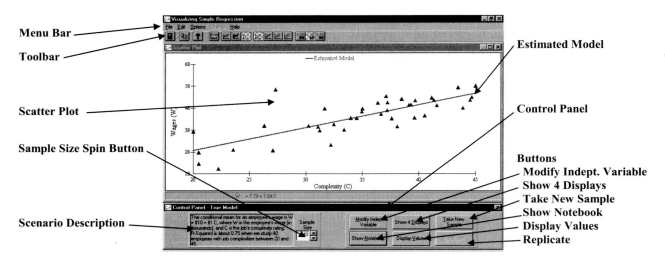

2. **Control Panel**

   The Control Panel contains a short description of the scenario, a Sample Size spin button, and six buttons. Press the Modify Indept. Variable button to bring up a new window that controls the independent variable's minimum value, maximum value, type of variable (integer or decimal), and whether the sample contains the x end points. Press the Take New Sample button to draw a new sample. The Show Notebook button reveals the Notebook allowing you to change scenarios or use the Do-It-Yourself controls. Press the Display Values button to see a table of the x values, y values, predicted y values, residuals, and standardized residuals.

3. **Scatter Plot**

   Click on the scatter plot graph. Its header changes color indicating that the display is active. The red line is the estimated model. The estimated model equation is shown below the graph. New toolbar buttons appear on the toolbar to the right of the ? button. Move the cursor over a button and its description appears in a tooltip. The ? button and the ones to its left are always visible. The buttons to its right vary depending on the display that is active. The Exit Module button ends the program, the Copy button copies the active display, and the ? button activates Help. The remaining toolbar buttons control the scatter plot display. The Zoom button changes the scale of the X and Y axes. This lets you show the X origin or the minimum value of X. The Show Residuals button displays the residuals. The Show Disturbances button displays the disturbances. The Scatter Plot button displays the scatter plot. Only one of these three buttons is active at a time. When the Scatter Plot button is active, all of the toolbar buttons to its right are active. The Estimated Model button displays or removes the estimated model line from the scatter plot. The True Model button displays or removes the true model from the scatter plot (its equation is at the bottom of the display). The Confidence Interval button displays the confidence interval for E(y|x), and the Prediction Interval button displays the prediction interval for y|x. The Interval Level buttons control $1 - \alpha$ (99%, 95% is the default, 90%).

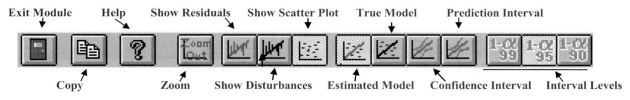

4. **Additional Displays**
    Press the Show 4 Displays button to display four quadrants. The scatter plot is in the upper left quadrant, an ANOVA table is in the lower left quadrant, a histogram of the standardized residuals is in the lower right quadrant, and a Control Panel is in the upper right quadrant. Two buttons on the panel have changed. The Show 4 Displays button has been renamed Main Display (returns you to the scatter plot and Control Panel display), and the Replication button has become active.

5. **Standardized Residuals Display**
    Activate the standardized residuals histogram by clicking on the display. Four new toolbar buttons appear to the right of the ? button. The first two determine whether a bar graph or a histogram of the standardized residuals is shown. The third button (active only if the histogram is chosen) superimposes a standard normal distribution ($\mu = 0$, $\sigma = 1$) for comparison. The last button superimposes the disturbances on the display.

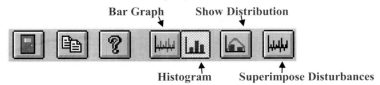

6. **Copying a Display**
    Click on any graph or the ANOVA Table. Press the Copy button on the toolbar or select Copy from the Edit menu on the menu bar. The copied display can be pasted into another application.

7. **Help**
    Press the ? button on the toolbar or click Help on the menu bar at the top of the screen. Search for Help lets you search an index, Contents shows a table of contents for this module, Using Help gives instructions on Help, and About gives licensing and copyright information.

8. **Exit**
    Close the module by selecting Exit in the File menu (or click ☒ in the upper right-hand corner of the window). You will be returned to the *Visual Statistics* main menu.

Orientation to Additional Features

1. **Enlarging a Graph**
   The scatter plot or standardized residuals display can be maximized (or minimized) with the windows buttons in the upper right corner. When the scatter plot is maximized, a Take New Sample button appears.

2. **Replication**
   a. Press the Replicate button. Read the Hint that appears. A Control Panel enables you to start an experiment, set the number of replications (50, 100, 200, 500, or 1000), or exit replication mode. Press the Start Experiment button. Press the Pause Experiment button to halt the experiment and Continue Experiment button to resume sampling. Press the Finish Experiment button and the experiment is completed without building the displays one replication at a time. The other quadrants contain a graph of all estimated models, a histogram of the estimated slopes, and a histogram of the estimated intercepts.
   b. Click on the Estimates of Model display (upper left quadrant). Five new icons appear on the toolbar. The first will draw the True Model on the graph and the second will draw an Interval about the True Mean (the percentage is indicated by the last three icons) to illustrate why regression confidence intervals have a parabolic shape.
   c. Click on the histogram of estimated slopes or intercepts to add two new toolbar buttons. The first superimposes a normal curve on the histogram and the second brings up a table that compares the observed and expected frequencies in each interval.
   d. Right-click on any quadrant. A menu of other displays appears. Select one to replace the display you clicked on. You can superimpose a chi-square distribution on the histogram of estimated variances, but there is no distribution for the correlation coefficients or R^2.
   e. Press the Exit Replication Mode button to return to nonreplication mode.

3. **Do-It-Yourself Controls**
   Click on the Show Notebook button and select the Do-It-Yourself tab. Click OK. A scroll bar for the intercept, slope, and standard error replace the scenario description on the Control Panel. If you

   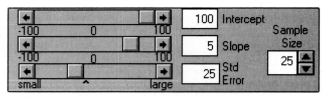

   prefer to control the error by setting the desired R^2 rather than the standard error, click on Options on the menu bar and select Set Error Using and then Desired R-Squared.

Basic Learning Exercises   Name _____

The Estimated Model

1. If you are displaying the four quadrants, press the Main Display button. Only the estimated model should be displayed on the scatter plot (use the toolbar buttons to control this feature). Press the Show Notebook button, select the Scenarios tab, click on Firms, and select the Wage vs. Job Complexity scenario. Read the scenario and click OK. What is the estimated model? **Hint:** The estimated model is displayed below the scatter plot.

2. Interpret this estimated model. **Hint:** Press the Zoom Out toolbar button.

3. What are the advantages and disadvantages of seeing the entire horizontal axis?

4. Use the toolbar button to either show or hide the origin. Press the Show Residuals toolbar button. a) What are residuals? b) How are they calculated. c) How many are there? d) Why do the residuals sum to zero? **Hint:** See Ordinary Least Squares in Help or the Glossary.

5. Press the Show 4 Displays button. A histogram of the standardized residuals is being displayed. a) Why have the residuals been standardized? b) How are the residuals standardized? c) Click on the Standardized Residuals window (lower right quadrant) to activate the display. Use the toolbar to change the display to a bar graph of the standardized residuals. What is the difference between the bar graph display and the histogram? **Hint:** Use the Glossary.

6.   What is the relationship between this display and the scatter plot of the residuals?

7.   What is the R^2 and standard error of your estimated model? What is the standard error and t-value of your estimated intercept and slope? Is the estimated intercept statistically different from zero? Is the slope statistically different from zero?

$R^2 = $ _____   Standard Error of Model _____

β_0: Standard Error _____   t-value _____   Decision _____

β_1: Standard Error _____   t-value _____   Decision _____

8. Interpret the estimated standard error of the model and the R^2?

The True Model
9.   The true model in this scenario is Wage $= \beta_0 + \beta_1$ Complexity $+ u$. a) Identify the parameters of this model. b) What does β_1 represent? c) Why are the parameters of the true model rarely known? d) What does the u represent?

10. In this module we know the conditional mean of the true model. This enables us to see the relationship between the true model and the estimated model. Press the Show Notebook button and reread the scenario. In this hypothetical situation what are the values of β_0 and β_1? What is the true model? Press the Cancel button to return to your previous screen.

11. Press the Show Scatter Plot toolbar button to bring back the scatter plot with the estimated model displayed. Press the Show True Model toolbar button. Why isn't the estimated model exactly equal to the true model?

12. Press the Show Disturbances toolbar button. What are disturbances? Can they be calculated?

13. Click on the Standardized Residuals window to activate it. The bar graph of the residuals should be displayed. Press the Superimpose Disturbances toolbar button. The disturbances are shown in black. What is the relationship between the black bars and the scatter plot displaying the disturbances? Compare the residuals (shown in red) and the disturbances.

14. Press the Histogram of Residuals toolbar button. A histogram of the disturbances is superimposed in green on top of the histogram of residuals. Compare the two histograms. In this model the disturbances are normally distributed with a mean of 0 and a standard deviation of 5. Press the Show Distribution toolbar button to superimpose this distribution on the histogram. Press the Take New Sample button 10 times. In general, are the disturbances and residuals approximately distributed as expected?

15. Activate the Standardized Residuals window. Press the Bar Graph of Residuals toolbar button. The true and estimated models should be displayed on the scatter plot. Press the Take New Sample button 10 times. Each time, record each R^2 value and compare the true and estimated models, and the disturbances and residuals. In this case, is the estimated model a good predictor of the true model? Are its residuals good predictors of the disturbances?

    R^2: _____ _____ _____ _____ _____ _____ _____ _____ _____ _____

16. Press the Show Notebook button and select the Test Scores vs. Job Performance scenario. Read the scenario. Click OK. Repeat exercise 15 using this scenario. Did having a low R^2 change your answers appreciably?

    R^2: _____ _____ _____ _____ _____ _____ _____ _____ _____ _____

Confidence Intervals and Prediction Intervals

17. Activate the scatter plot, click on the Confidence Interval for $E(y|x)$ toolbar button, and push the 90% Confidence Level toolbar button. Click the maximize button in the upper right corner of the scatter plot display. Only the estimated model and confidence interval should be displayed. Why is the estimated model in the middle of the confidence interval?

18. Remove the estimated model and display the true model on the scatter plot by using the toolbar buttons. Press the Take New Sample button in the lower right corner of the computer screen. Note the relationship between the confidence interval and the true model. Repeat this 20 times. What did you observe about the confidence interval and the true model?

19. Press the 95% Confidence Level toolbar button. Repeat exercise 18.

20. Interpret a 95% confidence interval.

21. Press the Prediction Interval for $y|x$ toolbar button. Remove the true model from the display. What is the relationship between the confidence interval and prediction interval?

22. Record the number of data points that lie outside the prediction interval. Repeat this process for nine more samples. Of the 500 observations, what percentage were outside the interval?

Number outside interval											%
Trial Number	1	2	3	4	5	6	7	8	9	10	

23. Describe what a 95% prediction interval shows.

Intermediate Learning Exercises   Name _____

Replication Experiment

24. Press the Show Notebook button, select the Scenarios tab, click on Firms, and select the Wage vs. Job Complexity scenario. Read the scenario and click OK. What is the true model in this scenario?

25. Press the Replicate button. Read the hint if it appears. Set Number of Replications to 500 (use 1,000 if you have a fast computer or 100 if you have a slow computer). Press the Start Experiment button. After the experiment has finished, activate the Estimates of the Model window (upper left quadrant). This display shows every model you estimated during the experiment. Describe the shape of the shaded area. Press the Conditional Mean toolbar button. Where is the conditional mean located in relation to the shaded area? Press the Interval about the Conditional Mean toolbar button. Describe the interval's shape. Compare the interval's shape with the shape of the shaded area.

26. Why do the various OLS estimates of the model form an hourglass shape? **Hint:** Use 50 replications and pay special attention to estimated models that are very flat or steep.

27. Reset replications and start the experiment. Describe the shape of the histogram of estimated slopes. What is its mean and standard error? How does this show that the estimated slope is an unbiased estimator β_1 (read exercise 24)? **Hint:** Read the bottom labels on the histogram.

28. Assume that you are testing H_0: $\beta_1 = 0$ versus H_a: $\beta_1 \neq 0$. Using two standard deviations (approximate α-level is 0.05) as the critical values, what percentage of the estimated slopes would reject H_o? Why is this the power of the test? Activate the histogram window and use the toolbar buttons to show the true distribution and the table of frequencies. Why are the expected and observed results similar? **Hint:** Consider the regression assumptions.

29. Describe the shape of the histogram of estimated intercepts. What is its mean and standard error? Is it an unbiased estimator? Why, or why not?

30. Assume that you are testing H_0: $\beta_0 = 0$ versus H_a: $\beta_0 \neq 0$. Using two standard deviations (approximate α-level is .05) as a critical value, what percentage of the estimated slopes would reject H_o? Why is the power so low? What lesson can you learn from this result?

31. Right-click on the Histogram of Intercepts and select Histogram – R-Squared. Describe the shape of the histogram. Decrease the sample size to 5. Press Start Experiment. Describe the shape of the histogram. Increase the sample size to 100. Press Start Experiment. Describe the shape of the histogram. Why don't we use R^2 as a test statistic?

Advanced Learning Exercises   Name _____

Effect of Sample Size

32. Press the Show Notebook button and select the Number of Bar Scanning Errors scenario. Read it and press OK. Set sample size to n = 15. Run an experiment with 1000 replications and use the histograms to visually estimate the mean and range of the estimated intercept, slope, variance, R^2, and correlation coefficient (r). Double the sample size (to 30) and rerun the replication experiment. Double the sample size again (to 60) and rerun the experiment.

n	Statistic	Intercept	Slope	Variance	R^2	r
15	Mean					
	Range					
30	Mean					
	Range					
60	Mean					
	Range					

33. What is the effect of increasing the sample size on the mean value of the estimated intercept, estimated slope, estimated variance, R^2, and r? What is the effect on the range of the estimated intercept, estimated slope, standard error of the model, R^2, and r? Explain these results.

Effect of Range of X

34. Press the Show Notebook button and select a scenario. Read it and press OK. Conduct an experiment with 1000 replications and use the histograms to estimate the mean and range of the estimated intercept, slope, variance of the model, R^2, and r. Press the Modify Indept. Var. button. Increase the maximum value and decrease the minimum value so that the range is doubled, and repeat the experiment. Again, double the range and repeat the experiment.

X Range	Statistic	Intercept	Slope	Variance	R^2	r
Small	Mean					
	Range					
Medium	Mean					
	Range					
Large	Mean					
	Range					

35. What is the effect of increasing the range of the independent variable on the mean value of the estimated intercept, slope, variance of the model, R^2, and r? What is its effect on the range of the estimated intercept, slope, standard error of the model, R^2, and r?

36. Explain the results in exercise 35.

Distribution of Estimated Variance

37. Run a replication experiment. What is the distribution of the estimated variance of the model? Why does it have this distribution? Why isn't the histogram of the standard error used instead of the variance?

Distribution of the Correlation Coefficient

38. Run a replication experiment. Examine the shape of the histogram of correlation coefficients. Use several different sample sizes and rerun the replication experiment. Each time, reexamine the shape of the histogram of correlation coefficients. Is the histogram normally distributed?

Individual Learning Projects

Write a report on one of the three topics listed below. Use the cut-and-paste facilities of the module to place the appropriate graphs in your report.

1. Explain and illustrate the difference between the confidence interval for $E(y|x)$ and the prediction interval for $y|x$. What does each mean? What is the importance of the confidence level $1 - \alpha$? Why are both intervals parabolic in shape? **Hint:** The replication feature may help you answer this question.

2. Explain and illustrate how the slope, intercept, standard error of the model, sample size, and range of the independent variable (take care not to change its midrange) affect the distribution of an estimator. Investigate *either* the estimated slope, estimated intercept, or estimated variance of the model. Use the Do-It-Yourself controls to create a true model. Run a replication experiment using this model. The histogram of each estimator (either slope or intercept) is your benchmark. Change one of the factors you are to investigate (larger changes are generally better). Run another replication experiment. Examine the estimator's histogram. Return the factor to its original setting and change another factor. Continue the process for all five factors you are investigating. What effect did each factor have on the distribution of the estimator? Which factor affected the distribution the most? The least?

3. Explain and illustrate how the slope, intercept, standard error, sample size, and range of the independent variable affect the R^2 statistic. Use the Do-It-Yourself controls to create a true model. Run a replication experiment using this model. The histogram of R^2 is your benchmark. Change one of the factors you are to investigate (larger changes are generally better). Run another replication experiment. Examine the histogram of R^2. Return the factor to its original setting and change another factor. Continue the process for all five factors you are investigating. What effect did each factor have on the distribution of R^2? Did it change its mean, its standard error, or its shape? Which factor affected the distribution the most? The least?

Team Learning Projects

Select one of the three projects listed below. In each case, produce a team project that is suitable for an oral presentation. Use presentation software or large poster boards to display your results. Graphs should be large enough for your audience to see. Each team member should be responsible for producing some of the graphs. Ask your instructor if a written report is also expected.

1. This project is for a team of three. Investigate the effect sample size has on the distribution of five statistics: the estimated slope, intercept, variance of the model, R^2, and correlation coefficient. The team should decide on a true model (its slope, intercept, standard error of the model, minimum value of X, and maximum value of X). Each team member will run a replication experiment using two different sample sizes. For each experiment the distribution of the five statistics will be examined. The team should cover the range of sample sizes from 2 to 100. What effect did increasing the sample size have on each statistic? Did it affect its mean, its standard error, or its shape? What statistic was affected the most? The least? If your team was hired to estimate a model, what do these results suggest about the sample size you should use?

2. This project is for a team of three to four. Investigate the effect the independent variable has on the distribution of five statistics: the estimated slope, intercept, variance of the model, R^2, and correlation coefficient. The team should decide on a true model (its slope, intercept, standard error of the model), sample size, and the midrange of the independent variable (between 50 and 100). Each team member will use a different range for the independent variable (the team should cover the range 10 to 100). The team member will modify the independent variable so that it has the correct range and midrange and will then run a replication experiment. The team member will then run a second replication experiment after modifying the independent variable so that its midrange is *five* times the first midrange but has the same range. For each experiment, the distribution of the five statistics will be examined. What effect did increasing the midrange of the independent variable have on each statistic? What effect did increasing the range of the independent variable have on each statistic? Did it affect its mean, its standard error, or its shape? What statistic was affected the most? The least? If your team was hired to estimate a model, do these results suggest that you should use an independent variable with a large variance or a small variance?

3. This project is for a team of two. Investigate the distribution of the correlation coefficient r. The team should decide on the initial true model (intercept, slope, and standard error), minimum value of X, maximum value of X and sample size. Use the Do-It-Yourself controls to set up this model. Run a replication experiment. The histogram of r from this experiment is your benchmark. Each team member should select another value of the six factors (large changes generally work better). A replication experiment should be run using each one of these new factor values (always return to the initial true model). How did each factor affect the distribution of r? Did it affect its mean, its standard error, or its shape? Did it affect the probability that r would be judged to be different from zero? **Hint:** Remember the rule of thumb that an estimate that is within 2 standard errors of zero is statistically equal to zero.

Self-Evaluation Quiz

1. In the simple regression model, the disturbance is *not* assumed to
    a. be observable.
    b. be normally distributed.
    c. have zero mean.
    d. have constant variance.
    e. be uncorrelated with X.

2. The conditional mean of y is written as
    a. $E(y|x)$.
    b. $y|x$.
    c. μ.
    d. $x|y$.
    e. $E(x|y)$.

3. Residuals have which characteristic?
    a. They give clues about unobservable disturbances.
    b. If their sum is non-zero, a mistake has been made in the OLS calculations.
    c. They are used to calculate R^2.
    d. All of the above.
    e. Only b and c.

4. The residuals can be thought of as predictors of
    a. the slope.
    b. the the true model.
    c. the disturbances.
    d. the intercept.
    e. none of the above.

5. In a simple regression, which does *not* suggest a relationship between X and Y?
    a. Small Error Sum of Squares and large Regression Sum of Squares in the ANOVA table.
    b. Large F statistic in the ANOVA table.
    c. Small p-value for the F statistic.
    d. Large p-value for the estimated slope.
    e. All of the above suggest a relationship.

6. Which is indicative of an *inverse* relationship between X and Y?
    a. A negative coefficient of determination.
    b. A negative estimated intercept.
    c. A negative p-value for the slope.
    d. A negative F statistic for ANOVA table.
    e. A negative correlation coefficient.

7. When x = 100 the confidence interval for E(y|x)
   a. is narrower than the prediction interval for y|x.
   b. is wider than the prediction interval for y|x.
   c. is equal to 50 for the lower interval and 150 for the upper interval.
   d. is an equal distance above and below the true model.
   e. None of the above.

8. A 95% prediction interval for y|x
   a. is inside a 90% confidence interval for E(y|x).
   b. will always contain 95% of your observations.
   c. is outside a 90% prediction interval for y|x.
   d. will on average contain the true model 95% or less of the time.
   e. has none of the above characteristics.

9. Which is *not* correct of the estimated slope of the regression line?
   a. It is divided by its standard error to get its t-value.
   b. It shows the change in y for a unit change in x.
   c. It is measured in the units of y per unit change in x (e.g., miles per gallon).
   d. It may effectively be regarded as 0 if its t-value is 8.
   e. It is an unbiased estimator of the true slope.

10. A 95% confidence interval for the E(y|x) means, on average, that
    a. 95% of the observations will be contained within the confidence interval.
    b. the confidence interval will contain the true mean 95% of the time.
    c. the true mean will lie within that interval 95% of the time.
    d. out of 100 confidence intervals the true mean will be contained in 95 of them.
    e. none of the above is correct.

11. If the assumptions about the disturbance term are correct then the Ordinary Least Squares method guarantees
    a. unbiased estimators.
    b. a large R^2.
    c. that the slope and intercept are minimized.
    d. all of the above.
    e. two of a, b, or c.

12. Which is *not* normally distributed for regression with normally distributed disturbances?
    a. R^2.
    b. Estimated slope.
    c. Estimated intercept.
    d. Residuals.
    e. All of the above are normally distributed.

Glossary of Terms

ANOVA table Summary of decomposition of variance in a regression, showing total sum of squares and its sources (regression, error) along with degrees of freedom and mean squares.

Coefficient Estimated value of a regression parameter (slope or intercept) based on sample data.

Coefficient of determination See **R-squared**.

Conditional mean In a regression, the expected value of the dependent variable *given* the observed value(s) of the independent variable(s).

Confidence interval In a regression, the range of Y values that is expected to enclose the true *conditional mean* of Y. For a 95% confidence interval, on average, 95 out of 100 such intervals will contain the conditional mean. See **Confidence level**.

Confidence level The desired probability of enclosing an unknown parameter, equal to $1 - \alpha$. Typical confidence levels are 90%, 95%, and 99%.

Correlation Measure of fit in a bivariate regression (−1 indicates a perfect inverse relationship, 0 indicates no relationship, and +1 indicates a perfect direct relationship). It is the square root of R^2 in the simple regression model. More generally, it is the sample covariance divided by the product of the sample standard deviations of X and Y.

Degrees of freedom In a regression ANOVA table, *total* degrees of freedom are $n - 1$, *error* degrees of freedom are $n - k - 1$, and the *regression* degrees of freedom are k, where n is the sample size and k is the number of predictors in the model (k = 1 for a bivariate model).

Dependent variable In a regression, the variable (denoted Y) that is placed on the left-hand side of the equation and is assumed to be affected by the independent variable (denoted X). On the scatter plot, the dependent variable is customarily shown on the vertical axis.

Disturbance An unobservable random error. It is the difference between the conditional mean and the observed value of y (the dependent variable). Disturbances are assumed to be independent and normally distributed with zero mean and constant variance.

Error See **Disturbance**.

Estimated model Bivariate regression equation whose slope and intercept are the coefficients that are estimated using the ordinary least squares method from sample data.

Estimator In a simple regression model, the equations for $\hat{\beta}_0$ and $\hat{\beta}_1$ that are used with sample data to estimate the unknown parameters β_0 and β_1.

F statistic In a regression ANOVA table, the ratio of the *regression* mean square to the *error* mean square.

Independent variable In a regression, the variable (denoted X) that appears on the right-hand side of the equation and is thought to cause variation in the dependent variable (denoted Y). On a scatter plot, the independent variable is usually shown on the horizontal axis.

Intercept Value of the dependent variable when $x_i = 0$ in the regression model $y_i = \beta_0 + \beta_1 x_i$. On a graph, the intercept β_0 is the point where the regression line intersects the Y-axis.

Ordinary Least Squares (OLS) Method of estimating a regression that guarantees that the smallest possible sum of squared residuals. Using the OLS method the residuals sum to 0.

Parameters Values that define a particular distribution. For example, in a simple regression model, β_0 and β_1 are parameters that describe the conditional mean of the distribution of y.

Prediction interval In a regression, range of y_i values that would enclose the true *individual* y_i values a given percentage of the time (typically 90%, 95%, or 99%).

P-value Probability of Type I error if we reject the null hypothesis (e.g., that the true slope is zero). For example, a small p-value (such as 0.01) for the estimated slope would incline us to reject the hypothesis that the true slope is zero.

Residual Difference between an actual and estimated value of the dependent variable.

R-squared Ratio of the *regression* sum of squares to the *total* sum of squares. R^2 near 0 indicates the fit is poor while R^2 near 1 indicates the fit is good.

Scatter plot Visual display in which each observed pair of data values (x_i, y_i) is plotted as a symbol (e.g., a dot) at the correct coordinate on the graph. It allows visual assessment of "fit" of an estimated regression line to the observed data.

Slope The change in Y for a unit change in X in the bivariate model $Y = \beta_0 + \beta_1 X$. On a graph, the slope β_1 is the rise divided by the run.

Standard error Estimate of the standard deviation of the disturbances, calculated as the square root of the sum of the squared residuals divided by $n - k - 1$. See **Degrees of freedom**.

Standardized residual For each observation, the residual divided by the estimated standard error.

Sum of squares In a regression ANOVA table, the total sum of squares is decomposed into two parts: *regression* sum of squares and *error* sum of squares.

True model An unobservable equation assumed to underlie the observed bivariate data.

T-value Ratio of an estimated coefficient in a regression model to its standard error (distributed as Student's t if the parameter is zero). A large t-value suggests that the parameter is not zero.

Solutions to Self-Evaluation Quiz

1. a   Do Exercises 9–12. Read the Overview of Concepts.
2. a   Read the Overview of Concepts and Illustration of Concepts.
3. d   Do Exercises 4, 5, and 12–15.
4. c   Do Exercises 12-15. Read the Overview of Concepts.
5. d   Do Exercises 1–7.
6. e   Do Exercises 1, 2, and 9.
7. a   Do Exercises 17–23. Read the Illustration of Concepts.
8. c   Do Exercises 21–23. Read both the Overview and the Illustration of Concepts.
9. d   Do Exercises 1–9 and 24–27.
10. d   Do Exercises 17–26. Read both the Overview and the Illustration of Concepts.
11. a   Do Exercises 15, 16, and 24–27.
12. a   Do Exercises 14 and 27–31. Read the Overview of Concepts.

CHAPTER 16

Visualizing Regression Assumptions

CONCEPTS
- Regression Assumptions, Homoskedasticity, Mutually Independent Disturbances, Normally Distributed Disturbances, Zero Mean, Independence of Fixed X and Disturbance, Autocorrelation, Heteroskedasticity, Unbiased, Efficient, Consistent, Normally Distributed

OBJECTIVES
- Know the five assumptions that are required to ensure desirable properties of least-squares regression estimates

- Learn the various ways in which each assumption may be violated

- Be able to identify effects of each violation on the residuals and the estimated parameters

- Understand the types of violations that are likely to arise in time series and cross-sectional data

- Recognize how the properties of estimators may be affected by each type of violation

Overview of Concepts

The regression model $Y_i = \beta_0 + \beta_1 X_i + u_i$ is based on five **regression assumptions**: (1) The disturbances u_i have constant variance, i.e. $E(u_i^2) = \sigma^2$ (**homoskedasticity,** also spelled homoscedasticity); (2) The disturbances are independent of one another, i.e., $E(u_i u_j) = 0$ for $i \neq j$ (**mutual independence**); (3) The disturbances u_i are **normally distributed**; (4) The disturbances u_i have **zero mean**, i.e., $E(u_i) = 0$; and (5) The values of the independent variable X_i are **fixed and independent of the disturbance**. Under these assumptions, the ordinary least squares (OLS) estimators for β_0 and β_1 are **unbiased** (the expected value is the true parameter), **consistent** (the variance of the estimator approaches zero as sample size increases, so the estimator collapses on the true parameter), **efficient** (the smallest variance among all unbiased estimators), **normally distributed**, and BLUE (Best Linear Unbiased Estimators).

Heteroskedasticity (non-constant error variance) is a major violation. The OLS estimators are unbiased, consistent, and normally distributed, but are neither efficient nor BLUE. In a given sample, the validity of a confidence interval for $E(Y|X)$ is in doubt over some regions of the X range. If the underlying constant variance is denoted σ^2, some commonly assumed patterns are $k X_i^c \sigma^2$ (variance proportional to a power of X_i), $k E(Y)_i^c \sigma^2$ (variance proportional to expected value of Y), $k Z_i^c \sigma^2$ (variance proportional to a power of another variable), or $k i^c \sigma^2$ (variance proportional to a power of the observation order). Homoskedastic errors should exhibit no discernible pattern in the residuals on the Y-X scatter plot. Heteroskedasticity may be seen as a "fan-out" pattern of residuals (increasing variance as we move to the right) or a "funnel-in pattern" of residuals (decreasing variance as we move to the right).

Autocorrelation (non-independent disturbances) is common in time series data, and is a major violation. The OLS estimators are unbiased, consistent, and normally distributed, but are neither efficient nor BLUE. The first-order autocorrelation model is $u_t = \rho u_{t-1} + v_t$ where ρ is a constant such that $-1 \leq \rho \leq +1$ and v_t is a "well-behaved" disturbance that fulfills all assumptions. If $\rho < 0$ (negative autocorrelation) then u_{t-1} tends to be followed by u_t of the opposite sign. If ρ is near 0 (non-autocorrelation) then u_t is unrelated to u_{t+1}. If $\rho > 0$ (positive autocorrelation) then u_{t-1} tends to be followed by u_t of the same sign. Runs of residuals of the same sign (e.g., $+ + + - - - + + +$) suggest *positive* autocorrelation (common) while runs of residuals of alternating sign (e.g., $+ - + - + - + - + -$) suggest *negative* autocorrelation (rare).

With *non-normal disturbances*, the OLS estimators are unbiased, consistent, and BLUE, but are neither efficient nor normally distributed. However, they are asymptotically efficient, so in large samples confidence intervals for $E(Y|X)$ may be acceptable. Non-normal disturbances are not a major violation, because the OLS method is fairly robust to non-normality. Evidence may be sought in the probability plot of residuals, which is nearly linear under normality.

Non-zero mean exists when the disturbances are not centered on the true regression line. It may be an annoyance or a major violation. A *constant* non-zero mean is a trivial problem, since it will merely be reflected in the intercept estimate and will not even be observable. A *non-constant* non-zero mean is a severe problem due to *incorrect functional form* or an *omitted variable Z*, making the OLS slope estimates biased and inconsistent (although if Z and X are uncorrelated, desirable asymptotic properties of the slope may still exist).

Stochastic X (X is not fixed) is a minor violation causing no loss of desirable properties *unless* X is correlated with the disturbance u_t (non-independence of X and disturbances). In the latter case, the estimator for the slope loses all desirable properties.

Illustration of Concepts

Figure 1 illustrates a positive relationship between years of employment (X) and home value (Y) for a sample of 100 public school teachers. Lack of **homoskedasticity** is evident in the "fan-out" pattern of points on the scatter plot. The residual plot in Figure 2 clearly shows the **heteroskedastic** pattern of increasing variance. Despite this violation of the **regression assumptions**, the slope and intercept estimates are **unbiased** and **consistent**. However, they are not **efficient** and their t-values may be unreliable. Specifically, regression estimates of home value will be more precise (smaller variance) for teachers with less experience and less precise (larger variance) for those with more experience. This makes sense, because new teachers generally cannot afford expensive homes, so the Y value varies within a smaller range. Conversely, experienced teachers generally (but not always) own more expensive homes (greater range) so their home values are harder to predict.

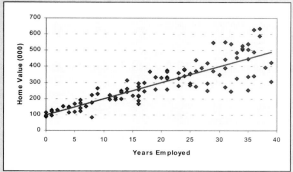

Figure 1: Home Value and Years Employed

Figure 2: Heteroskedastic Residuals

Another serious problem is **autocorrelation**. Figure 3 shows a scatter plot and fitted regression line relating aggregate personal taxes (PT) to aggregate personal income (PI) for the U.S., 1960-1997 (data are in billions of dollars). The fitted equation is PT = -8.620 + .1337 PI with $R^2 = 0.99$. The excellent fit disguises the fact that the errors lack **mutual independence**. A bar chart of the residuals against time (Figure 4) reveals a pattern with "runs" of positive and negative residuals. Figure 4 also suggests heteroskedasticity (increasing variance). This reminds us that more than one assumption can be violated. In this case, the OLS. estimates are unbiased and consistent, but not efficient. Other violations of assumptions may exist, but are not illustrated here.

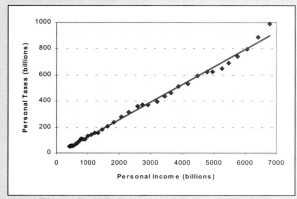

Figure 3: U.S. Income and Taxes, 1960-1997

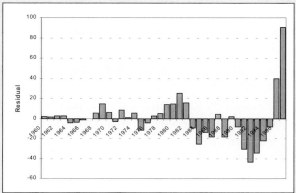

Figure 4: Autocorrelated Residuals

Orientation to Basic Features

This module generates data from a true regression model that meets all five regression assumptions, but then lets you violate any *one* assumption. You can examine similarities and differences between the true and estimated models and between the residuals and disturbances. You can display a confidence interval for E(y|x) and a prediction interval for y|x. You can replicate the experiment and display the estimated models and histograms of the estimated slopes, intercepts, standard errors, R^2, t-statistics, F ratios, and correlation coefficients.

1. **Opening Screen**
   Start the module by clicking its Run Module button in the *Visual Statistics* menu. When the module is loaded, you will be on the introduction page of the Notebook. Click the Introduction and the Concepts tabs to see topics that are covered in this module. Click on the Scenarios tab. Click on No Violations, select the Wage vs Job Complexity scenario, read it, and press OK.

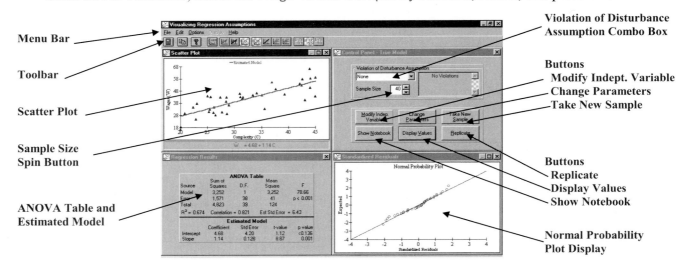

2. **Control Panel**
   The control panel is in the upper right quadrant. The Sample Size spin button sets the sample size. Press the Modify Indept. Variable button to bring up a new window to change the independent variable's minimum value, maximum value, type of variable (integer or decimal), and whether the X end points are included. Press the Change Parameters button to see a control panel that allows you to change the model. Press the Take New Sample button to draw a new sample. The Show Notebook button reveals the Notebook allowing you to change scenarios or use the Do-It-Yourself controls. Press the Display Values button to see a table of the x values, y values, predicted y values, residuals, and standardized residuals. Click on the Violation of Disturbance Assumption combo box to change the assumption being violated (this is specified by the scenario). The text window states the violation that has been chosen. You may only choose one violation at a time (otherwise, the violations are too muddled to be distinguished).

3. **Scatter Plot and Regression Results**
   The other three quadrant displays are identical to Chapter 15, Visualizing Simple Regression. When you click on the scatter plot, the menu bar buttons become active, to display residuals, disturbances, true model, estimated model, confidence intervals, or prediction intervals.

4. **Normal Probability Plot Display**
   Activate the normal probability plot display by clicking on it. Five toolbar buttons appear to the right of the ? button. They are identical to Chapter 15 except for the third button, which shows the probability plot. The fourth button is inactive unless the histogram of residuals is displayed. Any graph (scatter plot, probability plot, residual histogram) can be maximized (or minimized) with the windows buttons in its upper right corner.

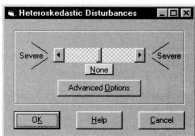

5. **Assumption of Homoskedasticity**
   Click on the Violation of Disturbance Assumption combo box and select Homoskedastic to produce the control panel for this assumption. Use the scroll bar to select the desired degree of "fan-out" (right side of the scale) of "funnel-in" (left end of the scale). Do *not* click Advanced Options at this time.

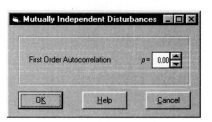

6. **Assumption of Mutual Independence**
   Click on the Violation of Disturbance Assumption combo box and select Mutual Independence to produce the control panel for this assumption. Use the spin button (or type in any ρ value from -1 to +1) to select the desired degree of autocorrelation. The default is ρ = 0 (none).

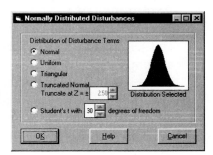

7. **Assumption of Normally Distributed Disturbances**
   Click on the Violation of Disturbance Assumption combo box and select Normal Distribution to produce the control panel for this assumption. Instead of Normal (the default) you can choose Uniform, Triangular, Truncated Normal (you specify the truncation point), or Student's t (you specify the degrees of freedom). All are symmetric. Click on each and watch how the diagram varies, then click Cancel to return to the main control panel.

8. **Copying a Display**
   Click on any graph or the ANOVA Table. Press the Copy button on the toolbar or select Copy from the Edit menu on the menu bar. The copied display can be pasted into another application.

9. **Help**
   Press the ? button on the toolbar or click Help on the menu bar at the top of the screen. Search for Help lets you search an index, Contents shows a table of contents for this module, Using Help gives instructions on Help, and About gives licensing and copyright information.

10. **Exit**
    Close the module by selecting Exit in the File menu (or click ☒ in the upper right-hand corner of the window). You will be returned to the *Visual Statistics* main menu.

Orientation to Additional Features

1. **Assumption of Independent Fixed X**

   Click on the Violation of Disturbance Assumption combo box and select Independent of Fixed X to produce the control panel for this assumption. The default is Fixed Independent Variable X (no violation). You can select Stochastic Independent Variable X and (to achieve the worst violation) you can have X be correlated with the disturbance (the default is no correlation). *Note: The latter violation can cause such severe bias as to make the graphs difficult to read.*

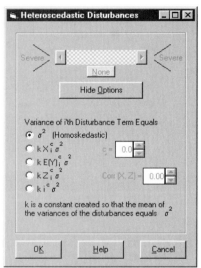

3. **Assumption of Homoskedasticity**

   Click on the Violation of Disturbance Assumption combo box, select Homoskedastic, and press Advanced Options to produce the control panel to the right. Select a form of the heteroskedasticity and a value for the exponent c. If the form is $kZ_i^c\sigma^2$, select the correlation between Z and X. Press the Cancel button to return to the main screen.

4. **Assumption of Zero Mean of the Disturbances**

   Click on the Violation of Disturbance Assumption combo box and select Zero Mean to see the control panel for this assumption (bottom figure to the right). If you select Non-Zero Mean you must specify if the violation is caused by omitting a variable Z or if the wrong functional form was estimated. If the Omitted Variable Z option is selected, you must specify its coefficient, correlation with X, mean and variance. If the Incorrect Functional Form option is selected you must select the true and estimated functional form from the four options provided. Press the Cancel button to return to the main screen.

4. **Replication and Do-It-Yourself Controls**

   The Replicate button works the same as in Chapter 15, except that three additional replication histograms are available (F statistics and t-statistics for slope and intercept). The Do-It-Yourself tab is identical to Chapter 15, allowing you to set the intercept, slope, and standard error (or, if you prefer, you can set the desired R^2 rather than the standard error, by clicking on Options on the menu bar and select Set Error Using and then Desired R-Squared).

Basic Learning Exercises

Name _____

Visualizing Heteroskedasticity

1. Press the Show Notebook button and select the Scenarios tab. Select No Violation and select the Wage vs. Job Complexity scenario. Read it and press the OK button. Click on the Violation of Disturbance Assumption combo box and select Homoskedastic. Move the slider bar to the right to generate severe "fan-out" heteroskedasticity. Press OK. Click on the Normal Probability Plot to select it and use the toolbar below the menu bar to select a bar graph (4th icon from the left). The bar graph displays the residuals *against the ordered X values*. Press the Take New Sample button a couple of times and describe the bar graph and the scatter plot. Why does this "fan-out" pattern indicate that the disturbances are heteroskedastic?

2. Click again on the Assumption combo box and again select Homoskedastic. Move the scroll bar to the left to generate "funnel-in" heteroskedasticity. Press the OK button. Press the Take New Sample button a couple of times and describe the bar graph and the scatter plot. Why does this "funnel-in" pattern indicate that the disturbances are heteroskedastic?

3. Press the Show Notebook button and click on Next page twice to see scenarios with heteroskedasticity. Select the Heteroskedasticity Related to X scenario read it and press OK. a) Press the Take New Sample button a couple of times and describe the bar graph and scatter plot. b) Why would the variance of the error term increase with Money Growth? c) In many regression programs, the bar graph is replaced with a scatter plot of the residuals *against X*. What is a possible advantage and disadvantage of such a scatter plot? d) Press the Show Notebook button, select the Heteroskedasticity Related to E(Y) scenario, read it and press OK. Press the Take New Sample button a couple of times and describe the bar graph and the scatter plot. e) Rather than this bar graph, a scatter plot of the residuals *against predicted Y* (since E(Y) is not observed) is usually used to reveal this type of heteroskedasticity. Why?

4. Press the Show Notebook button, select the Heteroskedasticity Related to 3rd Variable scenario, read it and press OK. Press the Take New Sample button a couple of times and describe the bar graph and the scatter plot. Why does neither graph reveal the heteroskedasticity?

Visualizing Autocorrelation

5. Press Show Notebook and click on Previous page for scenarios with autocorrelation. Select Severe Positive Autocorrelation. Read it, and press OK. a) Press the Take New Sample button a couple of times and describe the bar graph and the scatter plot. b) Take 10 samples, in what percent is the autocorrelation evident? c) Why is this called first-order autocorrelation? d) Why does this violation occur most often in time series data? e) In many regression programs, the bar graph is replaced with a scatter plot of the residuals *against the observation number*. Why would a graph versus the *observation number* generally be more reliable at revealing first-order autocorrelation than a graph versus the *ordered X values*.

6. Press the Show Notebook button, select the Moderate Positive Autocorrelation scenario, read it, and press OK. a) Press the Take New Sample button a couple of times and describe the bar graph and the scatter plot. b) Take 10 samples, in what percent is the autocorrelation evident? What is the value of rho (read the description in the panel above the buttons)? c) Click on the Assumptions combo box, select Mutual Independence, reduce ρ (rho) to 0.2, and press the OK button. Press Take New Sample. Take 10 samples. In what percent is the autocorrelation evident? d) What can you conclude about the value of rho and the ability to detect first-order autocorrelation on a graph?

7. Press the Show Notebook button, select the Negative Autocorrelation scenario, read it, and press OK. a) Press the Take New Sample button a couple of times and describe the bar graph and the scatter plot. b) Increase rho using the Mutual Independence dialog box (as in question 6). Is it still harder to detect visually when rho is closer to zero? c) Why do you think negative autocorrelation would be more unusual in real world data?

Visualizing Non-normally Distributed Disturbances

8. Press Show Notebook and click on Previous page for scenarios with no violations. Select the State Income Tax vs. Income scenario. Read it, and press OK. Replace the bar graph of residuals with a histogram of the standardized residuals (use the toolbar after clicking on the bar graph). a) Press the Take New Sample button a couple of times and describe the histogram. b) Replace the histogram with the normal probability plot. Press the Take New Sample button a couple of times and describe the probability plot. **Hint:** If you don't know how to use a normal probability plot, click Help in the menu bar, select Contents, and select Displays: Normal Probability Plot of Residuals under the heading Using the Program.

9. Press Show Notebook and click on the Scenarios tab. Select Non-normality and select the Uniformly Distributed Error Term scenario. Read it, and press OK. a) Press the Take New Sample button a couple of times and describe the normal probability plot. b) Replace the normal probability plot with the histogram. Press the Take New Sample button a couple of times and describe the histogram. c) Do you think either graph could be effectively used to detect residuals that are uniformly distributed?

10. Press Show Notebook and select the Peaked Error Term scenario. Read it, and press OK. a) Press the Take New Sample button a couple of times and describe the histogram. b) Replace the histogram with the normal probability plot. Press the Take New Sample button a couple of times and describe the probability plot. c) Do you think either graph could be effectively used to detect residuals that are more peaked than a normal distribution?

11. Click on the Assumptions combo box and select Normal Distribution. The sketch shows that the disturbances currently are distributed with a Student's t distribution with 3 degrees of freedom. Increase the degrees of freedom to get an idea of how peaked this distribution really is. Select Triangular distribution and press the OK button. a) Press the Take New Sample button a couple of times and describe the normal probability plot. b) Replace the normal probability plot with the histogram. Press the Take New Sample button a couple of times and describe the histogram. c) Superimpose a normal distribution on the histogram. What do you now observe? d) Do you think either graph could be effectively used to detect residuals that are triangularly distributed? **Hint:** Use the Assumption combo box to bring up normally distributed disturbances and see what you observe.

Intermediate Learning Exercises   Name _____

Visualizing Unbiasedness, Consistency, Normality and Efficiency

12. Press Show Notebook and click on the Scenarios tab. Select No Violation and select the Job Performance vs. Test Scores scenario. Read it, and press OK. a) Write down the true model. Press the Replicate button. Read the Hint that appears and press OK. Set the number of replications to 1000 by using its combo box. Reduce the sample size to 10 using its spin button. Press the Start Experiment button. Press the Pause Experiment button after a few replications. The current estimate of the slope and intercept are entered into their respective histograms in red. The corresponding estimated regression line is shown in red in the upper left quadrant. Press the Continue Experiment button to restart the experiment. Press the Finish Experiment button to fast forward to the end of the experiment. b) The true standard error of this model is 40 (variance is 1600). Since all of the assumptions are true, what is the theoretical distribution of the estimated slope histogram? Be sure and specify its parameters. c) Click on the histogram for the estimated slope and superimpose the true distribution (toolbar below the Menu bar). How does this show that the estimated slope is unbiased? d) normally distributed? e) Is the estimated intercept normally distributed? f) unbiased? **Hint:** Click on Search for Help on in Help and type "slope" to find the true distribution,

13. To be consistent, an estimator *must* be unbiased (or the bias must go to zero as the sample size n increases to infinity) and its variance must decrease as n increases. Write down the minimum and maximum value for the estimated slope and intercept. Increase the sample size to 100. Press the Start Experiment button and then the Finish Experiment button. How does this experiment show that both estimators are consistent? (The sophisticated user will recognize this as *mean square error consistency*.)

Slope: Minimum _____ Maximum _____   Intercept: Minimum _____ Maximum _____

14. To be efficient an estimator *must* to be unbiased and either have the minimum variance of *all* unbiased estimators or achieve the Cramer-Rao lower bound. In this case, this lower bound can be verified visually by comparing the histogram of the estimated variances for the model, to its theoretical distribution. The theoretical distribution is a scaled χ^2, where the scale factor is $\sigma^2 / (n-2)$. Right click on the Estimates of Model window (upper left) and select Histogram – Estimates of Variance. Superimpose its theoretical distribution. Does the theoretical distribution outline the histogram? If it does, then it achieves the lower bound and the slope and intercept estimators are efficient.

15. Because the estimators for the slope and intercept are unbiased, the test statistics for the estimated parameters have a Student's t distribution with n – 2 degrees of freedom. Press the Exit Replication Mode button. Press the Change Parameters button. Change the intercept's value from –50 to 0. Press the Change Assumptions button to bring back the assumption panel. Press the Replicate button. Press the Start Experiment button and then the Finish Experiment button. Replace both estimated parameter histograms with their t-statistic histograms. Superimpose the true distribution on both t statistic histograms. Since the true value of the *intercept* is 0, the null hypothesis is true (H_0: $\beta_0 = 0$). The histogram of t-statistics has the traditional t distribution with 98 (n – 2) degrees of freedom. The critical values for $\alpha = 0.05$ are approximately ±2 (shown in magenta). a) Approximately, how many rejections out of 1000 are in each tail? b) Now look at the t-statistic for the slope. In this case the true value of the slope coefficient is 2 (check your answer to question 12a). Therefore, the null hypothesis that $\beta_1 = 0$ is false. The magenta lines are the critical values. What are their approximate values? c) Approximately, what percentage of the 1000 estimates is outside these critical values? Because the null hypothesis is false, the distribution being displayed is the true distribution when $\beta_1 = 2$. It is called a non-central t distribution with n – 2 degrees of freedom. *Notice that the histogram corresponds to what the theory suggests when the assumptions about the disturbances are true.*

Properties of Estimators when Disturbances are Heteroskedastic

16. Click on the Assumptions combo box and click on Homoskedastic. If the advanced options are showing, press the Hide Options button. Move the slider all the way to the right. Press OK. You now have severe heteroskedasticity (fan-out). Make sure n = 100. Use the process outlined in question 12 to determine if the estimated parameters are unbiased and normally distributed (recall that $\beta_0 = 0$ and $\beta_1 = 2$).

17. Use question 13 as a guide to determine if the estimated parameters are efficient. **Hint:** In this module, the average variance of all observations equals σ^2. If this was not done, the form of the heteroskedasticity may shift the histogram. However, the difference in shape between the histogram and the theoretical distribution is what causes inefficiency, not just the shift.

18. Will the t-statistics agree with their theoretical distribution? If yes why, if no why not? Why is this important? Display the t-statistics to see if you were correct. **Hint:** To see a table comparing the expected and actual frequency by interval, select the table icon on the toolbar.

19. Use question 14 as a guide, determine if the estimated parameters are consistent.

20. Select Homoskedastic in the Assumption combo box. Move the slider all the way to the left. Press OK. You now have severe funnel-in heteroskedasticity. Make sure n = 100. Press the Start Experiment button and then the Finish Experiment button. Do you get different conclusions when funnel-in heteroskedasticity is present?

Properties of Estimators when Disturbances are Autocorrelated

21. Click on the Assumptions combo box and click on Mutual Independence. Set ρ to 0.4. Press OK. You now have moderate autocorrelation. Make sure n = 100. Use the process outlined in question 12 to determine if the estimated parameters are unbiased and normally distributed (recall that $\beta_0 = 0$ and $\beta_1 = 2$).

22. Use question 13 as a guide to determine if the estimated parameters are efficient.

23. Will the t-statistics agree with their theoretical distribution? If yes why, if no why not? Why is this important? Display the t-statistics to see if you were correct.

24. Using question 14 as a guide, determine if the estimated parameters are consistent.

25. Click on the Assumptions combo box and click on Mutual Independence. Set ρ to -0.4. Press OK. You now have moderate *negative* autocorrelation. Make sure n = 100. Although the estimators for the slope and intercept are still unbiased, consistent, normally distributed, and inefficient, which histograms are substantially different?   What would these differences imply about hypothesis testing?

Properties of Estimators when Disturbances are Not Normally Distributed

26. Click on the Assumptions combo box, click on Normal Distribution, select Student's t, and set degrees of freedom to 3. Press OK. Set n = 10. a) Are the estimated parameters unbiased? b) Are they normally distributed? c) Are the estimators efficient?

27. a) Display the t-statistics. Are the test statistics distributed as Student's t? If yes why, if no why not? b) Why is this important? c) Are the estimated parameters consistent?

28. With sample size set to 100, do both estimators appear to be normally distributed? Are the test statistics distributed as Student's t?

29. Change the distribution to uniform using the Assumptions combo box. Set n = 10. a) Are the estimated parameters normally distributed? b) Are the test statistics distributed as Student's t? c) How can you explain this result given your answer to questions 26 and 27?

Advanced Learning Exercises   Name _____

Omitted Variable

30. Press Show Notebook and click on the Scenarios tab. Select Other Violations, select the Omitted Variable scenario, and read it. a) Write down the true model. b) What model will be estimated? Press OK. c) Write down the estimated model. d) Superimpose the true model on the scatter plot (use the toolbar). What do you see?

31. Press the Replicate button. Set Replications to 1000 and run the experiment. a) Are the estimated parameters unbiased? b) Are the estimated parameters efficient and/or consistent? c) What does this mean about the estimated model? **Hint:** Superimpose the true model on the Estimates of Model graph.

32. Click on the Assumptions combo box and Select Zero Mean. Change the correlation between Z and X to 0. a) What s the mean of Z? b) What is its coefficient? Press OK. Press the Start Experiment button and then the Finish Experiment button. c) Is the estimator of the slope unbiased, normally distributed, efficient, and consistent? d) The mean for the intercept is 6.6 rather than 5. Why is the bias 1.6? **Hint:** The omitted variable Z is years until maturity (Y).

33. Click on the Assumptions combo box and Select Zero Mean. Change the correlation between Z and X to 1. Press OK. Press the Start Experiment button and then the Finish Experiment button. Why is the bias for the estimated slope 0.2? Why is the intercept still biased?

34. What does this tell us about the effect of omitting a variable from the model? **Hint:** 3 cases.

Stochastic Independent Variable

35. Press Exit Replication button, press Show Notebook, select the Omitted Variable scenario, and read it. a) Write down the true model. b) Which assumption is violated? c) Press OK. Change the sample size to 5 and press the Take New Sample button. Look at the scatter plot and press the Take New Sample button again. Do the X values change? d) Click on the Assumption combo box and select Independent of Fixed X. Select Fixed Independent Variable X and press OK. Press Yes when the message box appears. Press the Take New Sample button. Look at the scatter plot and press the Take New Sample button again. Do the X values change? e) What does stochastic X mean?

36. Press the Show Notebook button and OK to reload the scenario. Conduct a replication experiment to determine if the estimators are unbiased, normally distributed, consistent, and efficient?

37. Exit replication and return to the notebook. Select the Error Term and X Variable Correlated scenario and read it. a) Write down the true model. b) Which assumption is violated? c) Look at the scatter plot, probability plot, histogram, and bar graph. Repeatedly take new samples. Do you see any problems? d) Display the true model on the scatter plot. What do you see? e) Do you think the estimated parameters are unbiased?

38. Conduct a replication experiment to determine if the estimators are unbiased, normally distributed, consistent, and efficient.

Incorrect Functional Form

39. End replication and return to the notebook. Select the Incorrect Functional Form scenario and read it. a) What is the true model? b) What model will be estimated? c) Press OK. Look at the scatter plot, probability plot, histogram, and bar graph. Repeatedly take new samples. Do you see any problems? d) Display the true model on the scatter plot. What do you see? e) Do you think the estimated parameters are biased?

40. Press the Zoom Out icon on the toolbar for the scatter plot. a) What do you see? b) What does this suggest about using the wrong model for forecasting? c) Interpret the true model's slope. d) Interpret the estimated model's slope.

41. Press the Replicate button and conduct a replication experiment with 1000 replications. a) Are the parameters unbiased? b) What is the amount of the bias in the slope parameter and the intercept parameter? c) Given these results, are the estimators consistent or efficient?

42. Superimpose the true model and confidence interval on the Estimated Model graph by using their icons on the toolbar. What does this tell you about the effect of using the wrong functional form?

    When the wrong functional form is used, the confidence intervals are no longer valid. In addition, it is clear that on average your estimated model can give misleading information about the underlying model.

43. Examine the t-statistic histograms and the histogram of the variances. Superimpose the distribution of each statistic if the model had been estimated with the correct functional form. a) What do you see? b) Why do you think the histogram of the t-statistic of the slope is similar to its distribution if the model had been estimated with the correct functional form? c) Why is the distribution of the variance similar to its histogram?

44. Examine the F-statistic, R^2, and correlation coefficient. Since the wrong functional form is being used, why is the histogram for the F-statistic and the true distribution similar?

45. Using the histogram, write down approximate mean, minimum value, and maximum value of R^2.

46. Click on the Assumptions combo box and select Zero Mean. Change the estimated model to linear-log using the combo box. The model will now be correctly estimated. Press the OK button. Conduct an experiment to determine if the parameters are unbiased and normally distributed? How do you know?

47. Are the estimated parameters efficient? Explain.

48. Are the estimated parameters consistent? Explain.

49. What do your answers to questions 46 – 48 tell you about estimating nonlinear models?

50. Is the R^2 similar to the experiment you did earlier (see your answer to question 45)? Why?

Individual Learning Projects

Write a report on one of the two topics listed below. Use the cut-and-paste facilities of the module to place the appropriate graphs and tables in your report.

1. From the notebook, select one of the scenarios that have no violation of the assumptions. Using only this scenario, illustrate positive and negative autocorrelation, funnel-in and fan-out heteroskedasticity, and non-normality using a uniform and a Student's t distribution with 3 degrees of freedom. For each of the six cases, provide a scatter plot and indicate if the violation is apparent on the graph. Also, provide a residual display that would be useful in detecting the violation and indicate if the display reveals the violation or not. In studying autocorrelation, indicate the value of ρ you used. In studying heteroskedasticity, indicate the number of clicks on the scroll bar you used or, if you used the advanced options, the form of the heteroskedasticity and its parameters. The final paper should *explain and illustrate* the different forms of each of the 3 violations and how each may be detected visually.

2. Study either heteroskedasticity or autocorrelation. Select a scenario from the notebook with no violation of the assumptions. Using only this scenario, study one of the violations by creating different amounts and types of the violation. For autocorrelation, 6 different values of ρ should be used (both positive and negative). For heteroskedasticity, 6 different degrees of heteroskedasticity should be used (both funnel-in and fan-out). For each of the 6 cases, illustrate the problem with a scatter plot or one of the residual graphs. Also for each case, since the estimated parameters are inefficient, select a replication graph that illustrates the degree of inefficiency for that case. The final paper should *explain and illustrate* the different forms and degrees of the violation and the effect the violation has on efficiency.

3. Study the effect of estimating a linear model when it is *not* the correct model. Select a scenario from the notebook with no violation of the assumptions. Use this scenario to create a true model that is log-linear. Conduct a replication experiment. Illustrate and explain why the estimators are biased, inefficient, and inconsistent. Which t-statistic (slope or intercept) is approximately what it should have been and why? Since this is the wrong functional form, explain why R^2 is so large. What is the interpretation of the slope and intercept term in the linear model and in the log-linear model? Use the scatter plot and/or estimated model graph to explain the effect of incorrectly estimating a linear model. Repeat the process using a linear-log model and a log-log model.

Team Learning Projects

Select one of the three projects listed below. In each case, produce a team project that is suitable for an oral presentation using presentation software or large poster boards. Graphs should be large enough for your audience to see. Each team member should be responsible for producing some of the graphs. Ask your instructor if a written report is also expected.

1. This is a project for a team of 2 or 3. The purpose of the project is to study the ability to detect non-normality visually and the effect it has on the test statistics. The team should select a scenario to study throughout this project. Create a model that has a disturbance term that is uniformly distributed. This is a very platykurtic distribution. What effect did this distribution have on the t-statistics (copy the t-statistic histograms)? Is this violation evident on the probability plot (copy this diagram)? Repeat this process for a triangular distribution (less platykurtic), a normal distribution (a mesokurtic distribution), and a Student's t distribution with 24, 12, 6, and 3 degrees of freedom (increasingly leptokurtic). The presentation should focus on the ability to detect violations and the effect on the t-statistics.

2. This project is for a team of 2 or 3. The purpose is to study the effect of an omitted variable on the estimated included parameters. The team should select a scenario to study throughout this project and agree on the coefficient of the omitted variable, its mean, and its variance. Create a model that has an omitted variable that is not correlated with the included variable. Conduct a replication experiment to determine the bias in both the slope and intercept. Illustrate these biases. Repeat the process for correlations of 0.25, 0.50, 0.75, 1.00, −0.25, −0.50, −0.75, and −1.00. Derive the bias arithmetically in any situation where it is possible. The presentation should focus on the relationship between the correlation and the amount of bias in both estimators.

3. This project is for a team of 4. The purpose is to study the effect of estimating models with transformed variables. The team should select a scenario to study throughout this project. One team member should create a linear true model and estimate it with a linear-log model. Using a replication experiment show that both estimators are biased. Why are they also inefficient, and inconsistent? Why is R^2 so large, considering that the estimated model has the wrong functional form? Why is the distribution of the t-statistic for the slope about the same as it would have been if the model were estimated with a linear model? Use either the scatter plot or the Estimated Models graph to explain the cost of using the wrong functional form. Repeat the estimation process using a log-linear, a log-log, and a linear model. When the model is correctly estimated show that the estimators are unbiased, efficient, consistent, and normally distributed. The second team member should repeat the process with a log-linear model that is estimated with a linear, log-linear, linear-log, and log-log model. The third team member should repeat the process with a linear-log model that is estimated with a linear, log-linear, linear-log, and log-log model. The last team member should repeat the process with a log-log model that is estimated with a linear, log-linear, linear-log, and log-log model. The presentation should show: (a) that the parameters of any model correctly estimated will have all desirable properties, (b) that the parameters of any model estimated with the wrong functional form will have no desirable properties, (c) that models incorrectly estimated will still have large R^2s, and appropriate t-statistics, and (d) that regardless of the redeeming features, there are substantial costs of using the wrong functional form.

Self-Evaluation Quiz

1. Which is *not* one of the five assumptions of regression?
    a. The disturbances are observable.
    b. The disturbances are independent of each other.
    c. The disturbances are normally distributed.
    d. The disturbances have a constant variance.
    e. The disturbances have zero mean.

2. If the disturbances u_1, u_2, ..., u_n in a time series model exhibit autocorrelation, then
    a. u_t is independent of u_{t-1}.
    b. u_t is the same as u_{t-1}.
    c. u_t is related to u_{t-1}.
    d. u_t is related to X_t.
    e. u_t has non-zero mean.

3. Autocorrelation would most likely show up in
    a. the intercept estimate.
    b. the slope estimate.
    c. the R^2 statistic.
    d. the time plot of residuals.
    e. the histogram of residuals.

4. Which pattern of residual signs is most likely to indicate *positive* autocorrelation?
    a. + + + + + + – – – – – – – + + + + + + + + + + + – – – – – – – – – – + + + + +.
    b. + – + – + – + – + – + – + – + – + – + – + – + – + – + – + – + + – + – +.
    c. – + + – + – + – + – + – + – – – + + – – + – – + + – + + – – + + – + – –.
    d. Any of the above indicates positive autocorrelation.
    e. Either a. or b. indicate positive autocorrelation.

5. If there is heteroskedasticity, it would be most evident in
    a. a plot of the residuals against X or $\hat{Y}$.
    b. a histogram of the residuals.
    c. the fitted regression equation.
    d. the probability plot of standardized residuals.
    e. the ANOVA table and R^2.

6. In a time-series regression model, which violation of an assumption is *most* likely?
    a. Heteroskedasticity.
    b. Non-zero mean.
    c. Non-stochastic X.
    d. Autocorrelation.
    e. Incorrect functional form.

7. Non-normality of errors
   a. can be detected from the residual probability plot.
   b. is often considered a relatively minor violation.
   c. will not bias the estimates of the slope and intercept.
   d. is likely to affect the t-tests for the slope and intercept.
   e. All of the above are correct.

8. If the disturbances are autocorrelated, then it is *incorrect* to say that
   a. the OLS estimators for the slope will be unbiased.
   b. the OLS estimators for the slope will be consistent.
   c. the OLS estimators for the slope will be efficient.
   d. the OLS estimator of the intercept is unbiased.
   e. the OLS formulas can still be used for the slope and intercept.

9. If the disturbances are heteroskedastic, the OLS estimators of β_0 and β_1 would no longer be
   a. unbiased.
   b. consistent.
   c. normally distributed.
   d. efficient.
   e. BLUE.

10. If a variable Z is inadvertently omitted from the regression model, then
    a. the slope estimate is biased if Z_i is correlated with X_i.
    b. the intercept estimate is biased.
    c. the slope estimate is not consistent if Z_i and X_i are correlated.
    d. the intercept estimate is not consistent.
    e. all of the above are correct.

11. If the functional form of the regression is misspecified, then
    a. the OLS estimators for the slope and intercept will be unbiased.
    b. the OLS estimators for the slope and intercept will be consistent.
    c. the OLS estimators for the slope and intercept will be efficient.
    d. the regression results will be completely invalid.
    e. the consequences may be considered relatively minor.

12. If the independent variable X is stochastic instead of being fixed then
    a. the consequences are minor unless X_i is correlated with u_i.
    b. the probability plot will reveal non-normality of the residuals.
    c. the distribution of the slope estimate is distinctly non-normal.
    d. the t-statistic for the slope is reliable if X and the error term are correlated.
    e. Two of the above are correct.

Glossary of Terms

ANOVA table Summary of decomposition of variance in a regression, showing total sum of squares and its sources (regression, error) along with degrees of freedom and mean squares. See **Error sum of squares** and **Regression sum of squares**.

Autocorrelation Non-independent errors in a regression model. Evidence of autocorrelation may be sought by examining the residuals in a regression. Runs of residuals with the same sign (e.g., $+ + + - - -$) would suggest *positive* autocorrelation, while runs of residuals with alternating sign (e.g., $+ - + - + -$) would suggest *negative* autocorrelation. Autocorrelation (particularly positive) is common in time series data, and is considered a major violation. See **Mutually independent disturbances**.

Coefficient of determination See **R-squared**.

Confidence interval Upper and lower limits that are expected to enclose the true model. For a 95% confidence interval, on average, 95 out of 100 such intervals will contain the true model in repeated sampling. See **Confidence level** and **Prediction interval**.

Confidence level Desired probability of enclosing an unknown parameter, equal to $1 - \alpha$. Typical confidence levels are 90%, 95%, and 99%.

Correlation coefficient Measure of association between two variables, equal to the sample covariance divided by the product of the sample standard deviations of X and Y. A correlation of -1 indicates a perfect inverse relationship, 0 indicates no relationship, and $+1$ indicates a perfect direct relationship. The formula for the correlation coefficient is:

$$r = \frac{\sum_{i=1}^{n}(X_i - \overline{X})(Y_i - \overline{Y})}{\sqrt{\sum_{i=1}^{n}(X_i - \overline{X})^2 \sum_{i=1}^{n}(Y_i - \overline{Y})^2}}$$

Degrees of freedom In a regression ANOVA table, *total* degrees of freedom is $n - 1$, *error* degrees of freedom is $n - k - 1$, and the *regression* degrees of freedom is k, where n is the sample size and k is the number of independent predictors in the model.

Dependent variable In a regression, the variable (denoted Y) that is placed on the left-hand side of the equation and is assumed to be affected by the independent variable X.

Error sum of squares In a regression ANOVA table, the error sum of squares is the portion of the total sum of squares that is not explained by the model.

Estimated coefficient Sample statistic used to estimate a parameter of the regression model. The estimated regression coefficients are denoted $\hat{\beta}_0$, $\hat{\beta}_1$. See **Ordinary least squares**.

Fixed X In a regression, it is assumed that the independent variable X is non-stochastic. That is, X does not have a distribution, but is assumed to have predetermined values.

F statistic In a regression ANOVA table, the ratio of the *regression* mean square to the *error* mean square.

Heteroskedasticity Non-constant variance of errors in a regression. If the underlying constant variance is denoted σ^2, some commonly assumed patterns are $k\,X_i^c\,\sigma^2$ (variance proportional to a power of X_i), $k\,E(Y)_i^c\,\sigma^2$ (variance proportional to expected value of Y), $k\,Z_i^c\,\sigma^2$ (variance proportional to a power of another variable), or $k\,i^c\,\sigma^2$ (variance proportional to a power of the observation order). If the disturbances are heteroskedastic, the OLS estimators are still unbiased, consistent, and normally distributed, but are not efficient. Also, in a given sample, the predictive validity of a confidence interval for the expected value of Y is in doubt over some regions of the X range. Heteroskedasticity is considered a major violation.

Homoskedasticity Constant variance of errors in a regression model. If the errors are homoskedastic, there should be no discernible pattern in the residuals on a scatter plot that displays the fitted regression. Heteroskedasticity would be suggested by a "fan-out" pattern of residuals (increasing variance as we move to the right) or a "funnel-in" pattern of residuals (decreasing variance as we move to the right).

Independent of fixed X Assumption about the disturbances of a regression, which states that the errors are unrelated to the values of the independent variable X, where X is assumed to be a non-stochastic variable. See **Fixed X**.

Independent variable In a regression, the variable (denoted X) that appears on the right-hand side of the equation and is thought to cause variation in the dependent variable.

Intercept Value of the dependent variable when the independent variable in the regression model is zero. However, zero values may have little or no meaning for some predictors. Although it is often included by default, an intercept is not required in a regression model.

Misspecified model Omission of a relevant predictor or the incorrect functional form (e.g., assuming linearity when the relationship is non-linear). See **Zero mean**.

Mutually independent disturbances Absence of a relationship between errors in a regression. A violation of this assumption is called *autocorrelation*. First-order autocorrelation is the most common form: $u_t = \rho\, u_{t-1} + v_t$ where ρ is a constant such that $-1 \le \rho \le +1$ and v_t is a well-behaved disturbance (normally distributed, mutually independent, homoskedastic, zero mean). If $\rho = -1$ then a disturbance in period $t - 1$ yields an identical disturbance in period t but opposite in sign (negative autocorrelation) plus a random disturbance. If $\rho = 0$ then there is no carryover from period $t - 1$ to period t (non-autocorrelated). If $\rho = +1$ then a disturbance in period $t - 1$ yields the same disturbance in period t (positive autocorrelation) plus a random disturbance. If this violation exists, the OLS estimates are still unbiased, consistent, and normally distributed, but no longer efficient. Moreover, because of the increased variance, a high degree of positive autocorrelation may make it impossible to obtain reasonable estimates of your parameters except in very large samples. See **Autocorrelation**.

Non-normal errors Violation of a basic regression assumption that may affect confidence intervals and hypothesis tests. Evidence may be found in the residuals from a fitted regression. If the disturbances are not normally distributed, the OLS estimators are unbiased and consistent, but are not efficient. However, they are asymptotically efficient, and in large samples the confidence intervals for $E(Y|X)$ may be reasonable. Non-normal disturbances are not usually considered a major violation, since the OLS method is robust to considerable non-normality. Evidence of non-normality may be sought by examining the histogram of residuals or the normal probability plot.

Ordinary Least Squares (OLS) Method of estimating a regression that guarantees the smallest possible sum of squared residuals. The residuals sum to 0 using the OLS method.

Parameter Numerical constant needed to define a particular model or distribution. In a regression model, the parameters are the intercept and the coefficient of the independent variable. They are denoted β_0, β_1. See **Estimated coefficient**.

Prediction interval Upper and lower limits that are expected to enclose the observed data points. For a 95% prediction interval, on average, 95 out of 100 of the observations will lie within the interval. See **Confidence level** and **Confidence interval**.

Predictor An independent variable in a regression model. See **Binary variable**.

Probability plot Comparison of each observed residual with the value that would be expected assuming that it came from a normal distribution. To construct a probability plot, calculate the inverse of the hypothesized normal distribution function for the ith residual, and plot it against the observed i^{th} residual. This is done for all n residuals to produce a scatter plot. If the hypothesized normal distribution is correct, the scatter plot should be roughly linear along the diagonal. This is a simple, powerful visual test for normality of the sample residuals.

P-value Probability (usually two-tailed) of type II error if we reject the null hypothesis of a zero parameter. Thus, a small p-value (such as 0.01) would incline us to reject the hypothesis that the true parameter is zero.

Regression sum of squares In a regression ANOVA table, the regression sum of squares is the portion of the total sum of squares that is explained by the model.

Residual Difference between an actual and estimated value of the dependent variable.

Residual plot Scatter plot of the residuals against a predictor, used to check the residuals for evidence of a violation known as *heteroskedasticity* (non-constant residual variance). For k predictors we get k residual plots. To simplify matters, statisticians sometimes just look at a plot of the residuals against the fitted Y, though this method reveals less than the k plots. If the residuals are *homoskedastic*, there should be no discernible pattern. See **Heteroskedasticity**.

R-squared Also called the coefficient of determination, it is the ratio of the *regression* sum of squares to the *total* sum of squares. R^2 near 0 indicates the fit is poor while R^2 near 1 indicates the fit is good.

Standard error Estimate of the standard deviation of the stochastic disturbances, using the square root of the sum of the squared residuals, divided by $n - k - 1$. It is often called the *standard error of the estimate* to distinguish it from the standard error of each regression coefficient. See **Degrees of freedom**.

Standardized residual For each observation, the residual divided by the estimated standard error of the estimate.

Sum of squares In a regression ANOVA table, the total sum of squares is decomposed into two parts: *regression* sum of squares and *error* sum of squares.

Truncated normal Normal distribution whose tails are cut off. For example, a standard normal that is truncated at ± 2.5 would never have any outliers and would have reduced variation.

t-value Ratio of an estimated coefficient in a regression model to its standard error, used to test the null hypothesis that the parameter is zero. This ratio is distributed as Student's t if the parameter is zero. A large t-value would suggest that the true parameter is not zero.

Zero mean The mean of the disturbances may be thought of as the "center" of the errors around the true regression line. If this mean is non-zero, or if it is non-constant, the OLS estimates will lose some of their desirable properties. Non-zero mean may be an annoyance or a major violation, depending on its form. A constant non-zero mean is a trivial problem, since it will merely be reflected in the intercept estimate and may not be noticeable. An omitted variable Z is a much worse manifestation that can make the OLS slope estimate biased and inconsistent (although if Z and X are uncorrelated it is unbiased and may have other desirable asymptotic properties). Incorrect functional form for the equation can also lead to serious consequences, since the wrong model will be estimated. Bias due to incorrect functional form can be severe.

Solutions to Self-Evaluation Quiz

1. a   Read the Overview of Concepts.
2. c   Do Exercise 5. Read the Overview and Illustration of Concepts.
3. d   Do Exercises 5–7. Read the Overview and Illustration of Concepts.
4. a   Do Exercises 5–7. Read the Overview and Illustration of Concepts.
5. a   Do Exercises 1–4. Read the Illustration of Concepts.
6. d   Do Exercise 5. Read the Illustration of Concepts.
7. e   Do Exercises 8–11, and 26–29.
8. c   Do Exercises 21–25.
9. d   Do Exercises 16–20.
10. e   Do Exercises 30–34.
11. d   Do Exercise 39–44.
12. a   Do Exercises 35–38.

CHAPTER 17

Visualizing Multiple Regression Analysis

CONCEPTS

- Regression Model, Predictor, Parameter, Estimated Coefficient, Standard Error, t-value, p-value, Confidence Interval, Data Conditioning, Multicollinearity, Variance Inflation Factor, Residual Plots, Probability Plot, R-Squared, Adjusted R-Squared

OBJECTIVES

- Recognize and use the terminology of multiple regression

- Be able to perform significance tests and interpret confidence intervals for unknown model parameters

- Understand the importance of data conditioning and the potential effects of ill-conditioned data on a regression

- Detect multicollinearity and recognize its common symptoms

- Learn when a model may be overfitted and why that can be a problem

- Use visual displays to check the residuals for possible non-normality, autocorrelation, and heteroskedasticity

333

Overview of Concepts

A **regression model** proposes a relationship between a dependent variable Y and several independent variables $X_1, X_2, ..., X_k$. We call the independent variables **predictors** for short, since they are intended to help us predict Y. The form of the proposed regression model is $Y = \beta_0 + \beta_1 X_1 + \beta_2 X_2 + ... + \beta_k X_k + \varepsilon$ where ε is a random disturbance. Given a data set of n observations on each variable, the k+1 **parameters** $\beta_0, \beta_1, ..., \beta_k$ can be estimated using the ordinary least squares (OLS) method. These OLS estimates (called **estimated coefficients**) are chosen so as to minimize the sum of squared differences between Y_{actual} and Y_{fitted}.

Dividing a coefficient by its estimated **standard error** gives its **t-value**. A small **p-value** would indicate that the estimated coefficient differs significantly from zero (i.e., that zero is not included in the **confidence interval** for that parameter). The overall fit of a regression model is measured by **R-squared** (or R^2) which lies between 0 and 1. When R^2 is multiplied by 100 it is called the "percent of variation explained" (where 100% would be a "perfect fit"). Since adding more predictors cannot decrease R^2, there may be a temptation to clutter the model with superfluous variables. The **adjusted R-squared** (or R^2_{adj}) includes a penalty for the number of predictors. An added predictor that improves the fit enough to offset the penalty will raise R^2_{adj}, while adding a superfluous predictor will reduce R^2_{adj}. Conversely, removing a weak predictor may raise R^2_{adj} even though R^2 stays the same or declines.

The independent variables may be related to one another (i.e., the predictors may contain redundant information). For example, a person's age, income, years of education, and gender may be related. If we use these four variables to predict the weekly number of hours the person spends watching live professional sports, we face a potential problem called **multicollinearity**. The resulting variance inflation can affect the **standard error** of each estimated coefficient and render its t-tests and p-values misleading. If the **variance inflation factor (VIF)** for a predictor is large (one rule of thumb says above 10) then one might consider discarding that predictor, but *only* if that can be done without damaging the logic of the model.

Other tests of a model's adequacy concern violations of certain assumptions about the disturbances (the ε's) that are supposed to be normally distributed, have constant variance, and be independent of one another. One visual test is to plot the residuals (n differences between Y_{actual} and Y_{fitted}) against each predictor to get a **residual plot**. Ideally, there is no apparent visual pattern. A "fan-shaped" or "funnel-shaped" pattern suggests *heteroskedasticity* (non-constant variance of residuals). Plotting the residuals against entry order (only in time series data) can suggest another problem known as *autocorrelation* (runs of $+ + +$ or $- - -$ in the residuals). We can check for *non-normality* by examining the histogram of residuals, which should be bell-shaped. A more sensitive test is the **probability plot** of residuals, which should resemble a 45° line if the residuals are normal. We look at the list of residuals (or a residual plot) to see if there are outliers (or near-outliers) which may be data errors or may suggest a left-out predictor.

Data conditioning refers to the magnitude of the data. *Ill-conditioned* variables have values that are unnecessarily small or large. For example, sales measured in dollars (e.g., $123,456,789) could be rewritten in millions and rounded to fewer significant digits (e.g., 123.457) without harm and perhaps with increased clarity. *Well-conditioned* data help avoid tiny or huge regression coefficients, and may prevent computational errors.

Illustration of Concepts

Here are some results from a **regression model** of aircraft cockpit noise against seven **predictors**: flight phase (climb, cruise, descent), airspeed, airspeed^2, altitude, and altitude^2.

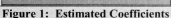

Variable	Est Coeff	Std Error	t	P	VIF	95% Lower	95% Upper
Intercept	83.08	8.075	10.29	0.000	---	66.89	99.27
Climb	-0.8140	0.5649	-1.44	0.155	3.4	-1.9465	0.3185
Descent	-1.661	0.5557	-2.99	0.004	3.3	-2.775	-0.547
AirSpeed	-0.04918	0.05253	-0.94	0.353		-0.15450	0.05613
Altitude	0.3134	0.1328	2.36	0.022		0.0472	0.5796
SpeedSqr	0.1867	0.07992	2.34	0.023		0.0265	0.3470
AltSqr	-.007390	0.003148	-2.35	0.023		-.013700	-.001079

p < .01   p < .05   VIF > 10

Figure 1: Estimated Coefficients

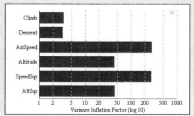

Figure 2: Variance Inflation Factors

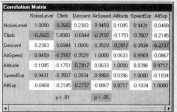

Correlation Matrix	NoiseLevel	Climb	Descent	AirSpeed	Altitude	SpeedSqr	AltSqr
NoiseLevel	1.0000	-0.2682	0.2383	0.9459	0.1095	0.9431	-0.0468
Climb	-0.2682	1.0000	-0.6944	-0.3187	-0.1751	-0.3507	-0.2145
Descent	0.2383	-0.6944	1.0000	0.3529	-0.2817	0.3934	-0.2737
AirSpeed	0.9459	-0.3187	0.3529	1.0000	0.0633	0.9969	-0.0867
Altitude	0.1095	-0.1751	-0.2817	0.0633	1.0000	0.0396	0.9717
SpeedSqr	0.9431	-0.3507	0.3934	0.9969	0.0396	1.0000	-0.1034
AltSqr	-0.0468	-0.2145	-0.2737	-0.0867	0.9717	-0.1034	1.0000

p < .01   p < .05

Figure 3: Correlation Matrix

Figure 1 shows the **estimated coefficient** and **standard error** for each predictor. From the **t-values** and **p-values** and **confidence intervals** we infer that three coefficients differ significantly from zero at $\alpha = 0.05$ (shown in green) and two at $\alpha = .01$ (shown in cyan). The **variance inflation factors** shown in Figure 2 reveal **multicollinearity** among several predictors. However, we may prefer to ignore these indications of variance inflation since they arise from squaring predictors, which was done by design. Figure 3 shows several significant correlations among the predictors (shaded green for $\alpha = 0.05$ or cyan for $\alpha = 0.01$).

ANOVA Table					
Source	Sum of Squares	D.F.	Mean Square	F	P
Regression	860.47	6	143.4	103.2	0.000
Error	75.05	54	1.390		
Total	935.52	60			
R-squared	0.9198		Adj R-sqr	0.9109	
R (mult corr)	0.9591		Durbin Watson	1.21	
Std Error	1.1789		Sample size	61	

Figure 4: ANOVA Table

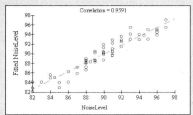

Figure 5: Actual and Fitted Y

Descriptive Statistics for All Variables						
Variable	Mean	S.D.	Min	Max	Range	Type
NoiseLevel	89.68	3.949	82.0	97.0	Medium	Decimal
Climb	0.4098	0.4959	0	1	Small	Binary
Descent	0.4098	0.4959	0	1	Small	Binary
AirSpeed	332.5	48.80	230	420	Medium	Integer
Altitude	19.33	7.533	4.5	39.0	Medium	Decimal
SpeedSqr	112.9	31.91	52.900	176.400	Medium	Decimal
AltSqr	429.5	322.4	20.25	1,521.00	Medium	Decimal

Figure 6: Descriptive Statistics

The ANOVA table in Figure 4 shows that the R^2 and R^2_{adj} for this model are similar (0.92 and 0.91 respectively). The scatter plot in Figure 5 shows that Y_{actual} and Y_{fitted} are reasonably alike, a visual indication of the high R^2. The descriptive statistics in Figure 6 suggest that there are no major **data conditioning** problems.

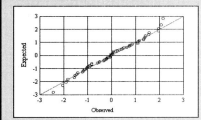

Figure 7: Residual Probability Plot

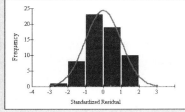

Figure 8: Residual Histogram

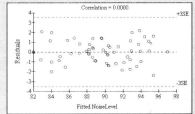

Figure 9 Residuals and Fitted Y

Since the **probability plot** in Figure 7 is linear except for one data point on each end, it supports the view that the residuals are normal. Since the standardized residual histogram in Figure 8 is somewhat bell-shaped and has no outliers, it supports the assumption that the disturbances are normally distributed. Since the **residual plot** against the fitted Y in Figure 9 shows no pattern, it supports the assumption that the variance is constant (homoskedastic).

Orientation to Basic Features

This module does multiple regression. You can analyze a variety of different data sets by selecting them from the Notebook or create your own using the data editor.

1. **Opening Screen**
   Start the module by clicking on the module's icon, title, or chapter number in the *Visual Statistics* menu and pressing the Run Module button. When the module is loaded, you will be on the introduction page of the Notebook. Read the questions and then click the Concepts tab to see the concepts that you will learn. Click on the Examples tab, click on Education, select College Graduates, and press OK to see the Variable Selection screen shown below. After examining this screen, click OK.

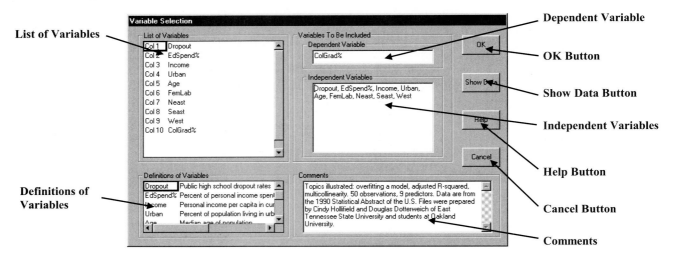

2. **Main Display**
   A Hint appears in the middle of the display. Read it and press OK. The upper left of the screen shows a table of estimated coefficients and related statistics. The Control Panel appears on the right. On the bottom left is an ANOVA table. On the bottom right is a histogram of the residuals. Other displays may be chosen from the menu bar at the top of the screen or by right-clicking a display and using the menu that will appear.

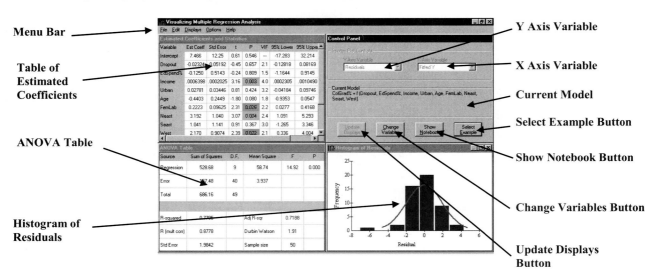

3. **Control Panel**
   a. The control panel is only active when you are displaying one or more scatter plots. The opening screen contains no scatter plots. You can have up to three scatter plots at once. Right-click the quadrant where you want the scatter plot and then select a scatter plot from the menu that will appear. Initially, Scatter Plot 1 plots the residuals against fitted Y, Scatter Plot 2 plots Y_{fitted} against Y_{actual}, and Scatter Plot 3 plots Y_{actual} against the first predictor in your model, but you can change them. Click the scatter plot you want to change. Its title bar will be highlighted and the control panel's Y axis variable and X axis variable will display the variables displayed on the selected scatter plot. Use the variable selection combo boxes on the control panel to change the variables. The Update Displays button will flash if you have changed the Y axis variable or the X axis variable on the selected scatter plot. *The control panel only manipulates one scatter plot at a time.*

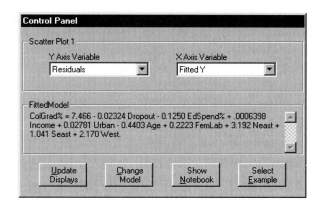

   b. Click the Change Model button to bring up the Variable Selection window again. This permits you to revise the variables in your model. Click the Select Example button to pick a new data set from the list of examples. This button's caption changes to Select Databases or Edit Data depending upon the origin of the data you are analyzing. It is a shortcut to the Notebook tab previously selected.

4. **Copying Graphs**
   Select Copy from the Edit menu (on the menu bar at the top of the screen), or the Copy option when you right click on a display, to copy the display. It can then be pasted into other applications, such as a document or spreadsheet, so it can be printed. Graphs are copied as bitmaps, and tables as tab-delimited text.

5. **Help**
   Click on Help on the menu bar at the top of the screen. Search for Help lets you search an index for this module, Contents shows a table of contents for this module, Using Help gives instructions on how to use Help, and About gives licensing and copyright information about *Visual Statistics*.

6. **Exit**
   Close the module by selecting Exit in the File menu (or click ☒ in the upper right-hand corner of the window). You will be returned to the *Visual Statistics* main menu.

Orientation to Additional Features

1. **Other Displays**

    This module offers four different types of graphs, six types of tables, and a verbal interpretation. The Hint that was displayed as the module began said, "Click the right mouse button on a quadrant to select a different display." This can also be done by selecting a quadrant and clicking on Displays in the menu bar. Only the Control Panel cannot be replaced. Under Graphs you can select a Residual Histogram, Standardized Residual Histogram, Normality Plot of Residuals, or VIF Plot. Under Tables you can select Estimated Coefficients, ANOVA Table, Residual List, Data List, Correlation Matrix, or Descriptive Statistics. Under Scatter Plots you can select up to three scatter plots. Here is a screen showing three of these displays.

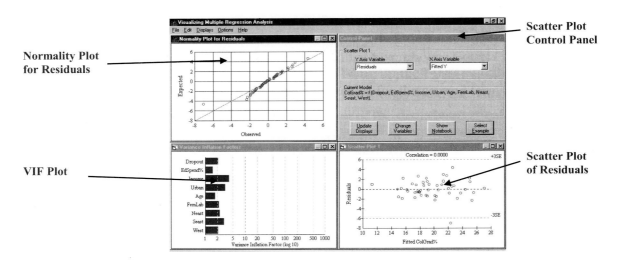

2. **Databases**

    Click the Show Notebook button to bring up the Notebook.. Select the Databases tab. There are seven databases that you can access with this module: Aircraft, Alcoholism, Body Fat, MBA Profile, Statistics Grades, States, and Time Series. Click on the database you want to examine, and you will see its description in the text window. If you use a database, you must specify your own model by selecting a dependent variable and one or more independent variables (in contrast, the Examples tab has already selected them for you). Click the Cancel button to return to the Notebook.

3. **Data Editor**

    Click on the Show Notebook button to bring up the Notebook. To use your own data, select the Data Editor tab, and press OK. A simple multicolumn spreadsheet appears. You can enter variable names, case labels, and data directly into this editor. To title each variable, click the top cell in each column and enter the desired name. You can copy data from another spreadsheet (such as Excel or 123) and paste it into the data editor. To save the data in *Visual Statistics* format, use the File option on the menu bar. When you are finished, choose File and Exit Editor and Use Data. If you want to leave without using the data click on File and select Exit Editor and Discard Data.

Basic Learning Exercises

Name _____

Estimated Regression Model

In the Notebook, click on the Examples tab, click on Education, select College Graduates, and press OK to see the Variable Selection screen.

1.   Examine the variable definitions, the dependent variable, and the independent variables. Does the proposed model seem reasonable? What *a priori* sign would you anticipate for each model coefficient (i.e., would you expect a positive or negative estimated coefficient)? Explain your reasoning about causation. **Hint**: The observations are states, not persons.

Predictor	Reasoning About Expected Sign of Estimated Coefficient
Dropout (public high school dropout rates)	
EdSpend% (percent of personal income spent on K-12 educ)	
Income (personal income per capita in current dollars)	
Urban (percent of population living in urban areas)	
Age (median age of population)	
FemLab (labor force participation rate among females)	
Neast (1 if state is in the northeastern U.S., 0 otherwise)	
Seast (1 is state is in the southeastern U.S., 0 otherwise)	
West (1 if state is in the western U.S., 0 otherwise)	

2.   Click on OK. A Hint appears in the middle of the display. Read it and press OK. Use the table of estimated coefficients and statistics to compare your expected signs (– or + or –/+) with the regression results. Use the p-values to determine significance (for example, p-values below 0.10 are significant at α = 0.10). Describe the results in two or three sentences. **Hint**: Unless a coefficient differs significantly from zero, the actual sign is NA (that is, neither – nor +).

Predictor	Expected Sign of Coefficient	Actual Sign of Coefficient	p-Value	Differs from Zero at		
				α = 0.10?	α = 0.05?	α = 0.01?
Dropout						
EdSpend%						
Income						
Urban						
Age						
FemLab						
Neast						
Seast						
West						

3.   a) Write the equation for the estimated model. b) Is the magnitude of a coefficient a reliable guide to its significance (from Exercise 2)? c) How might this equation be misleading to a novice who did not look at the p-values?

Statistics of Fit
4.   Record the main measures of fit from the ANOVA table and interpret them.

R^2 _____ R^2_{adj} _____   F statistic _____   p-value _____

Intermediate Learning Exercises   Name _____

Residuals

5.   In the Notebook, click on the Examples tab, click on Education, select College Graduates, and press OK to see the Variable Selection screen. Click OK.Describe the histogram of residuals and the fitted normal curve. Based on this histogram, are the residuals normal?

6.   Right-click on the lower left quadrant, choose Graphs, and select Residual Standardized Histogram. a) Based on this histogram, are the residuals normal? Is the visual impression the same as for the residual histogram? b) What percent of the standardized residuals are within ± 2? How does this compare with a normal? c) Are there any outliers?

7.   Right-click on the lower right quadrant, choose Tables, and select Residual List. Identify any outliers (residuals that exceed 3 standard errors) or unusual residuals (residuals that exceed 2 standard errors) and explain what they mean.

8.   Right-click on the lower right quadrant, choose Graphs, and select Residual Normality Plot. Explain what it tells you.

Scatter Plot

9.   a) On the menu bar, click Option and verify that Display Correlation on Scatterplots is selected. Then right-click on the lower right quadrant, choose Scatter Plots, and select Scatter Plot 2. What are the variables? Describe the scatter plot. b) Right-click on the lower left quadrant, choose Tables, select ANOVA Table. What relationship exists between the multiple correlation coefficient, the correlation shown on the scatter plot, and the R^2?

Correlation Matrix

10. Right-click on the lower left quadrant, choose Tables, and select Correlation Matrix. Look at the top row. Describe the p-values. Do the significance levels of the correlations between the dependent variable *ColGrads%* and the nine independent variables correspond to the predictor p-values in the table of estimated coefficients? Should they be the same?

Multicollinearity

11. In the correlation matrix, look only at the correlations among the independent variables. That is, ignore the top row and do not consider duplicates (below the diagonal). a) Among these predictors, how many correlations are significant at $\alpha = 0.05$? At $\alpha = 0.01$? What does this tell you about the data? b) How many of the correlations exceed 0.5000? c) Overall, do you see evidence of multicollinearity?

12. a) Describe the VIFs in the table of estimated coefficients. Are any VIFs large enough to cause alarm? b) What is the sum of the VIFs? Is it large enough to cause alarm? c) If there are different indications (individual VIFs versus the sum of VIFS) what does it suggest? Would removing a predictor help?

13. Right-click on the lower right quadrant, choose Graphs, and select VIF Plot. a) What is the smallest possible VIF, and what would it mean? b) Describe the VIF plot. What is the meaning of the dashed red line? c) Why is the VIF scale shown in log form? d) What is the connection between the VIF plot and the matrix of correlation coefficients?

Advanced Learning Exercises

Name _____

Data Conditioning

14. In the Notebook, click on the Examples tab, click on Education, select College Graduates, and press OK to see the Variable Selection screen. Click OK. Right-click on the lower left quadrant, choose Tables, and select Descriptive Statistics. Examine the magnitude of each variable by examining its minimum, maximum, and mean. Do you see evidence of ill-conditioned data?

15. Right-click on the lower right quadrant, choose Tables, and select Data List. Do you see any evidence of unusual data values in any of the variables? If so, identify them and compare them with their respective means (see Exercise 13).

16. Right-click on the lower right quadrant and select Interpretation. Did it agree with your own analysis? Would this be helpful to a novice?

Heteroskedasticity

17. Right-click on the upper left quadrant, choose Scatter Plots, and select Scatter Plot 1. This scatter plot is called a residual plot because it plots the residuals against other variables. The default should show the residuals against fitted *ColGrad%*. As your eye moves to the right, do you see any pattern that could be called "fan-out" or "funnel-in" (heteroskedastic) or do the residuals appear to have a constant vertical dispersion (homoskedastic)?

18. Click on the Scatter Plot 1 graph to select it, then click on the control panel. The Y axis variable should be *Residuals*. Use the combo box to change the X axis variable to *Dropout* and click Update Displays. Repeat the check for heteroskedasticity (see Exercise 17). Do this systematically for all nine predictors. What do you conclude? What is unique about the binary predictors?

Model Specification

19. On the control panel, click the Change Model button. Deselect the Include Intercept option and click OK. What effect does this have on the statistics of fit in the ANOVA table? Does forcing the intercept through the origin make sense in this model?

20. On the control panel, click the Change Model button. Select the Include Intercept option. Delete the predictor with the highest p-value and click OK. Record the statistics of fit below. Repeat, deleting at each step the predictor with the highest p-value, until you have only one predictor left. Discuss the pattern of change in each statistic and try to interpret its meaning.

Model	Predictor Deleted	R^2	R^2_{adj}	F statistic
1	None	0.7705	0.7188	14.92
2				
3				
4				
5				
6				
7				
8				
9				

Time Series Data

21. Click the Show Notebook button, select Examples and Money Supply, then click OK. On the variable selection screen, also click OK. What is the main problem with this model? Plot the residuals against entry order. What does this graph tell you?

Individual Learning Projects

Write a report on one of the two topics listed below. Use the cut-and-paste facilities of the module to place the appropriate graphs and tables in your report.

1. From the Notebook, select Time Series from the Examples tab and choose either Longley Data or Money Supply. Fit a regression model using all of the independent variables. Examine the correlation matrix and explain what it says. Click Change Model, delete the predictor with the highest VIF, and re-estimate the model. Repeat until only one predictor remains. In a table like the one below, record the variable names, estimated coefficients, t-values, and fit statistics (R^2, R^2_{adj}, standard error, and F statistic). Are the estimated coefficients stable? Discuss what this series of estimates tells you about how variance inflation, fit, and predictor significance change as correlated predictors are eliminated.

	Model 1			Model 2			...	Model k-1		
Var	Est β	t	VIF	Est β	t	VIF	...	Est β	t	VIF
Intcpt	xxx	xxx	xxx	xxx	xxx	xxx	...	xxx	xxx	xxx
X_1	xxx	xxx	xxx	xxx	xxx	xxx	...	xxx	xxx	xxx
X_2	xxx	xxx	xxx	xxx	xxx	xxx	...	xxx	xxx	xxx
:	:	:	:	:	:	...	:	:		
X_k	xxx	xxx	xxx	xxx	xxx	xxx		xxx	xxx	xxx
R^2		xxx			xxx		...		xxx	
R^2_{adj}		xxx			xxx		...		xxx	
Std err		xxx			xxx		...		xxx	
F		xxx			xxx		...		xxx	

2. From the Notebook, select Technology and choose either LCD Monitors or Turbofan Engines. Fit a regression model using all of the independent variables. Identify the weakest predictor (highest p-value), click Change Model, delete the weakest predictor, and re-estimate the model. Repeat until only one predictor remains. In a table like the one below, record the variable names, estimated coefficients, t-values, and fit statistics (R^2, R^2_{adj}, standard error, and F statistic). Discuss what this series of estimates tells you about how overall fit and predictor significance change as predictors are eliminated. Which model seems most appropriate, and why?

	Model 1		Model 2		...	Model k-1	
Var	Est β	t	Est β	t	...	Est β	t
Intcpt	xxx	xxx	xxx	xxx	...	xxx	xxx
X_1	xxx	xxx	xxx	xxx	...	xxx	xxx
X_2	xxx	xxx	xxx	xxx	...	xxx	xxx
:	:	:	:	:	...	:	:
X_k	xxx	xxx	xxx	xxx		xxx	xxx
R^2		xxx		xxx	...		xxx
R^2_{adj}		xxx		xxx	...		xxx
Std err		xxx		xxx	...		xxx
F		xxx		xxx	...		xxx

Team Learning Projects

Select one of the three projects listed below. In each case produce a team project that is suitable for an oral presentation. Use presentation software or large poster board(s) to display your results. Graphs and tables should be large enough for your audience to see. Each team member should be responsible for producing some of the exhibits. Ask your instructor if a written report is also expected.

1. This is a project for a team of two to four. Within one of the databases provided in this module or using another database of the team's choice, the team should agree on a dependent variable. Each team member should independently propose a regression model by choosing explanatory variables that may help explain the dependent variable (explaining the causal logic of including each predictor). Each team member should prepare exhibits that summarize his/her results (predictors used, fitted equation, fit statistics, predictor significance, variance inflation, residual normality tests, check for outliers, and data conditioning). Were the models and results similar or different? Whose model seems "best" overall? The objective of the project is to compare and contrast the choices and results made by independent researchers faced with the same task.

2. A team of three should use the time-series database, choose a dependent variable, propose a regression model (with arguments about causation for all predictors), estimate it, and do an *in-depth* analysis of the results. The first team member should analyze the estimated equation and degree of significance of predictors (estimated coefficients, t-values, p-values, confidence intervals for parameters) and fit statistics (R^2, R^2_{adj}, standard error, and F statistic). The second team member should analyze variance inflation, correlation among predictors, and data conditioning. The third team member should analyze the residual histograms, residual plots, and probability plot for evidence of non-normality, heteroskedasticity, and autocorrelation. The objective of this project is to understand the role of each aspect of model estimation, and to illustrate the special problems that confront researchers who study time series data.

3. This project is for a team of four. Two team members should use the state database, and two should use the economic time series database. Each team member should select a dependent variable, propose a multiple regression model (explaining the causal logic), and estimate it. Each team member should prepare exhibits that summarize his/her estimation results (predictors used, fitted equation, fit statistics, predictor significance, variance inflation, residual normality tests, check for outliers, and data conditioning). Compare and contrast the issues (e.g., fit, variance inflation, and residual behavior) that arise in using cross-sectional data (states) and time series data (economic time series). The objective is to understand that each data type raises its own archetypal set of issues.

Self-Evaluation Quiz

1. A multiple regression model does *not* require
    a. an intercept.
    b. a dependent variable.
    c. independent variables (predictors).
    d. assumptions about the errors.
    e. observed data for all variables.

2. When a multiple regression model is estimated, the overall fit is *not* measured by the
    a. values of the estimated coefficients.
    b. adjusted R-squared statistic.
    c. R-squared statistic.
    d. F-statistic in the ANOVA table.
    e. estimated standard error.

3. The p-value for the estimated regression coefficient for predictor j shows
    a. the probability of rejecting the null hypothesis that $\beta_j = 0$.
    b. the probability of type I error if you reject the null hypothesis that $\beta_j = 0$.
    c. the probability that the null hypothesis $\beta_j = 0$ is true.
    d. the ratio of the estimated coefficient to its standard error.
    e. all of the above.

4. The significance of an individual predictor can be assessed using
    a. the t-statistic for the predictor.
    b. the p-value for the predictor.
    c. the confidence interval for the true parameter of interest.
    d. the ratio of the estimated coefficient to its standard error.
    e. all of the above.

5. Multicollinearity
    a. is a relationship among the predictors.
    b. makes the estimated coefficients more stable.
    c. leads to small VIFs for some of the predictors.
    d. is best revealed in the p-values for the predictors.
    e. has all of these characteristics.

6. The probability plot for the residuals is *primarily* intended to offer a test for
    a. normality.
    b. heteroskedasticity.
    c. autocorrelation.
    d. ill-conditioned data.
    e. multicollinearity.

7. Which is *not* an advantage of a standardized residual histogram?
    a. Greater number of histogram bars.
    b. Easier comparison with a normal distribution.
    c. Better visual detection of outliers.
    d. Common axis scale for all regression models.
    e. Better visual check for asymmetry.

8. Evidence of possible multicollinearity would be found in
    a. several VIF that exceed 10.
    b. a sum of VIFs that is above 10.
    c. insignificant p-values for predictors that are correlated with Y.
    d. significant correlations between several predictors in the correlation matrix.
    e. all of the above.

9. Which is a characteristic of well-conditioned data?
    a. Decimal data are never rounded off to avoid spurious accuracy.
    b. Units (e.g., thousands) are set to avoid unnecessarily large or small values.
    c. Variables should have widely varying magnitudes whenever possible.
    d. Observations must be obtained from a census rather than from a sample.
    e. At least one variable must be a binary variable.

10. Data conditioning can be checked using which table display(s)?
    a. ANOVA table.
    b. Correlation matrix.
    c. Data list.
    d. Descriptive statistics.
    e. None of the above.

11. A residual plot that shows a fan-shaped pattern (more vertical dispersion moving right)
    a. suggests homoskedasticity.
    b. suggests heteroskedasticity.
    c. suggests non-normality.
    d. suggests multicollinearity.
    e. suggests of the above.

12. Overfitting a regression model refers to
    a. including too few predictors.
    b. having an excessive sample size.
    c. using ill-conditioned data.
    d. using too many independent variables.
    e. none of the above.

Glossary of Terms

Adjusted R-squared Alternate measure of the fit of a regression, based on the R^2 but with a penalty for the number of predictors. The intent is to prevent gratuitous inclusion of predictors to improve the fit. If weak predictors are added, the R^2_{adj} may decline. Conversely, R^2_{adj} may increase if weak predictors are deleted. If there are k predictors, the definition is:

$$R^2_{adj} = 1 - (1 - R^2)\left[\frac{n-1}{n-(k+1)}\right]$$

ANOVA table Summary of decomposition of variance in a regression, showing total sum of squares and its sources (regression, error) along with degrees of freedom and mean squares. See **Error sum of squares** and **Regression sum of squares**.

Autocorrelation Non-independent errors in a regression model (violation of a regression assumption). Evidence of autocorrelation may be sought by examining the residuals in a regression. Runs of residuals with the same sign (e.g., $+++---$) would suggest *positive* autocorrelation, while runs of residuals with alternating sign (e.g., $+-+-+-$) would suggest *negative* autocorrelation. Autocorrelation (particularly positive) is common in time series data. See **Durbin-Watson test**.

Binary variable Variable that has only two values, used for qualitative data (e.g., male, female). Generally the values 0 and 1 are assigned, where 1 denotes the presence of the attribute of interest and 0 denotes its absence. However, other values may be used (e.g., 1 and 2). If the attribute has c categories, we need c − 1 binary variables. See **Predictor**.

Coefficient of determination See **R-squared**.

Confidence interval Upper and lower limits that are expected to enclose the true parameter (e.g., regression coefficient). For a 95% confidence interval, on average, 95 out of 100 such intervals will contain the true parameter in repeated sampling. See **Confidence level**.

Confidence level Desired probability of enclosing an unknown parameter, equal to 1 − α. Typical confidence levels are 90%, 95%, and 99%.

Correlation coefficient Measure of association between two variables, equal to the sample covariance divided by the product of the sample standard deviations of X and Y. A correlation of −1 indicates a perfect inverse relationship, 0 indicates no relationship, and +1 indicates a perfect direct relationship. The formula for the correlation coefficient is:

$$r = \frac{\sum_{i=1}^{n}(X_i - \overline{X})(Y_i - \overline{Y})}{\sqrt{\sum_{i=1}^{n}(X_i - \overline{X})^2 \sum_{i=1}^{n}(Y_i - \overline{Y})^2}}$$

Data conditioning Good statistical practice requires that each variable's units be chosen to avoid extremely dissimilar magnitudes of the variables in the data set, that decimals be chosen to avoid extremely large or small values, and that data be rounded to a reasonable number of significant digits to avoid spurious accuracy. Thus, defect rates might be rounded to 4-digit accuracy and defined as defects per 1,000,000 parts (i.e., 75.42 instead of .00007542117).

Degrees of freedom In a regression ANOVA table, *total* degrees of freedom is $n - 1$, *error* degrees of freedom is $n - k - 1$, and the *regression* degrees of freedom is k, where n is the sample size and k is the number of independent predictors in the model.

Dependent variable In a regression, the variable (denoted Y) that is placed on the left-hand side of the equation and is assumed to be affected by the independent variables $X_1, X_2, ..., X_k$.

Durbin-Watson test Test statistic derived from the residuals of a regression to test for first-order autocorrelation. The D-W statistic can range from 0 to 4, with a value near 2 suggesting the absence of autocorrelation.

Error sum of squares In a regression ANOVA table, the error sum of squares is the portion of the total sum of squares that is not explained by the model.

Estimated coefficient Sample statistic used to estimate a parameter of the regression model. The estimated regression coefficients are denoted $\hat{\beta}_0, \hat{\beta}_1, \hat{\beta}_2, ..., \hat{\beta}_k$. See **Ordinary least squares**.

F statistic In a regression ANOVA table, the ratio of the *regression* mean square to the *error* mean square.

Fitted model Regression equation estimated from sample data. For example, the equation ColGrad% = 7.960 + .0008861 Income + 0.02169 Urban - 0.5276 Age + 0.2023 FemLab is an example of a fitted model using data for the 50 states in the U.S.

Heteroskedasticity Non-constant variance of errors in a regression (violation of a regression assumption). Evidence of heteroskedasticity may be sought by plotting the residuals from a fitted regression against each predictor. A "fan-shaped pattern" (increasing variance as we move to the right) or a "funnel-in pattern" (decreasing variance as we move to the right) on a residual plot would suggest heteroskedasticity. See **Residual plot**.

Homoskedasticity Constant variance of errors in a regression model. If the errors are homoskedastic, there should be no discernible pattern in the regression residuals when plotted against any predictor. See **Heteroskedasticity**.

Ill-conditioned data Data set whose variables are of greatly dissimilar magnitudes, or whose values are extremely large or small. See **Data conditioning**.

Independent variable In a regression, the variables (denoted $X_1, X_2, ..., X_k$) that appear on the right-hand side of the equation and are thought to cause variation in the dependent variable.

Intercept Value of the dependent variable when all the independent variables in the regression model are zero. However, zero values may have little or no meaning for some predictors. Although it is often included by default, an intercept is not required in a regression model

Multicollinearity Intercorrelation among the predictors in a regression (i.e., lack of independence among the independent variables). In effect, the predictors contain redundant information, causing potential loss of accuracy in model estimation. Usually one or more predictors can be eliminated from the model without significant loss of fit. See **Variance inflation**.

Multiple correlation coefficient Measure of overall fit in a regression. It is the square root of R^2. It may be interpreted as the correlation between Y_{actual} and Y_{fitted} over all n observations.

Non-normal errors Violation of a basic regression assumption that may affect confidence intervals and hypothesis tests. Evidence may be found in the residuals from a fitted regression. See **Probability plot**.

Ordinary Least Squares (OLS) Method of estimating a regression that guarantees the smallest possible sum of squared residuals. The residuals sum to 0 using the OLS method.

Parameter Numerical constant needed to define a particular model or distribution. A regression model's the parameters are the intercept and the coefficients of the k independent variables, whose true values are denoted $\beta_0, \beta_1, \beta_2, ..., \beta_k$. See **Estimated coefficient**.

Predictor An independent variable in a regression model. See **Binary variable**.

Probability plot Comparison of each observed residual with the value that would be expected assuming that it came from a normal distribution. To construct a probability plot, calculate the inverse of the hypothesized normal distribution function for the ith residual, and plot it against the observed i^{th} residual. This is done for all n residuals to produce a scatter plot. If the hypothesized normal distribution is correct, the scatter plot should be roughly linear along the diagonal. This is a simple, powerful visual test for normality of the sample residuals.

P-value Probability (usually two-tailed) of type II error if we reject the null hypothesis of a zero parameter. Thus, a small p-value (such as 0.01) would incline us to reject the hypothesis that the true parameter is zero.

Regression model Equation representing a relationship between a dependent variable and one or more independent variables. See **Predictor**.

Regression sum of squares In a regression ANOVA table, the regression sum of squares is the portion of the total sum of squares that is explained by the model.

Residual Difference between an actual and estimated value of the dependent variable.

Residual plot Scatter plot of the residuals against a predictor, used to check the residuals for evidence of a violation known as *heteroscedasticity* (non-constant residual variance). For k predictors we get k residual plots. To simplify matters, statisticians sometimes just look at a plot of the residuals against the fitted Y, though this method reveals less than the k plots. If the residuals are *homoskedastic*, there should be no discernible pattern. See **Heteroskedasticity**.

R-squared Also called the coefficient of determination, it is the ratio of the *regression* sum of squares to the *total* sum of squares. R^2 near 0 indicates the fit is poor while R^2 near 1 indicates the fit is good.

Standard error Estimate of the standard deviation of the stochastic disturbances, using the square root of the sum of the squared residuals, divided by $n - k - 1$. It is often called the *standard error of the estimate* to distinguish it from the standard error of each regression coefficient. See **Degrees of freedom**.

Standardized residual For each observation, the residual divided by the estimated standard error of the estimate.

Sum of squares In a regression ANOVA table, the total sum of squares is decomposed into two parts: *regression* sum of squares and *error* sum of squares.

t-value Ratio of an estimated coefficient in a regression model to its standard error, used to test the null hypothesis that the parameter is zero. This ratio is distributed as Student's t if the parameter is zero. A large t-value would suggest that the true parameter is not zero.

Variance inflation Effects arising from interrelationships among the predictors in a model. May lead to unstable coefficient estimates that vary when predictors are added or deleted from the model, inflated standard errors, and unreliable t-values. See **Multicollinearity**.

Variance inflation factor Abbreviated VIF, it is a measure of multicollinearity for each predictor in a regression model. The VIF for predictor k is $VIF_k = [1 - R_k^2]^{-1}$ where R_k^2 is the coefficient of determination that arises when predictor k is regressed against all the other predictors. If R_k^2 is small (indicating that predictor k is not associated with the other predictors) then VIF_k will be near the ideal value of 1. A single VIF that exceeds 10 (or a sum of all VIFs that exceeds 10) is sometimes taken as an indication that multicollinearity is severe. However, data sets (especially time series data) may have VIFS of 100 or more. This can make it difficult to isolate the role of the affected predictors.

Well-conditioned data Variables whose units are chosen so that the magnitudes of the variables in the analysis are not too dissimilar, with decimals adjusted to avoid extremely large or small values, and rounded to a reasonable number of significant digits to avoid spurious accuracy. See **Data conditioning**.

Solutions to Self-Evaluation Quiz

1.   a   Consult the Glossary. Read the Overview of Concepts.
2.   a   Do Exercises 2–4. Consult the Glossary. Read the Overview of Concepts.
3.   b   Do Exercise 2. Consult the Glossary. Read the Overview of Concepts.
4.   e   Do Exercise 2. Consult the Glossary. Read the Overview of Concepts.
5.   e   Do Exercises 10–13 and Individual Learning Project 1. Consult the Glossary.
6.   a   Do Exercises 5–8. Consult the Glossary. Read the Overview of Concepts.
7.   c   Do Exercises 5–7. Consult the Glossary.
8.   e   Do Exercises 10–13 and Individual Learning Project 1. Consult the Glossary.
9.   b   Do Exercises 14–16. Consult the Glossary. Read the Overview of Concepts.
10. d   Do Exercises 14–16. Consult the Glossary.
11. b   Do Exercises 17–18. Consult the Glossary.
12. d   Do Exercises 19–20. Do Individual Learning Project 2.

CHAPTER 18

Visualizing
Regression Models

CONCEPTS
- Transformations, Linear Model, Elasticity Model, Exponential Growth Model, Declining Returns Model, Power Model, Beta Weight, Polynomial Model, Interaction Variable

OBJECTIVES
- Know the types of commonly-used variable transformations and their purposes

- Learn the effects of variable transformations on the fitted regression and its statistics of fit

- Recognize and interpret models that utilize log, reciprocal, standardized, or power transformations of X and/or Y

- Understand how to use polynomial models

- Be able to use and interpret an interaction variable

Overview of Concepts

The familiar **linear model** has the form $Y_i = \beta_0 + \beta_1 X_i + u_i$. β_0 and β_1 can be estimated using the method of Ordinary Least Squares (OLS) even if we perform **transformations** of the data. Common transformations of the variables are the logarithmic transformation [$\ln(X_i)$ or $\ln(Y_i)$], raising to a power [X_i^c or Y_i^c], inversion [$1/X_i$ or $1/Y_i$], or standardization by subtracting the mean and dividing by the standard deviation.

OLS can also be used for some alternative model forms. One example is the family of **polynomial models**. Although they can capture nonlinear patterns and improve the R^2, polynomial models are usually difficult to interpret. In this module, we limit the choices to the quadratic model $Y_i = \beta_0 + \beta_1 X_i + \beta_2 X^2_i$ and cubic model $Y_i = \beta_0 + \beta_1 X_i + \beta_2 X^2_i + \beta_3 X^3_i$ because they are familiar and easily graphed. In both cases, the sign of the slope coefficients affect the specific shape of the polynomial. Of course, the linear model is a special case of the polynomial model family.

In the **elasticity model**, $\ln(Y_i) = \beta_0 + \beta_1 \ln(X_i)$, a 1% change in X_i leads to a β_1% change in Y. For instance, if the fitted model is $\ln(Y_i) = 2.055 - 0.643 \ln(X_i)$ then a 1% change in X_i leads to a -0.643% change in Y. When $\beta_1 > 1$, the function increases at an increasing rate; when $0 < \beta_1 < 1$, it increases at a decreasing rate; and when $\beta_1 < 0$, it is asymptotic to $Y = 0$ from above. In the **exponential growth model**, $\ln(Y_i) = \beta_0 + \beta_1 X_i$, a 1-unit change in X_i causes Y_i to change by $100\beta_1$% . For example, if $\ln(Y_i) = 200 + .075 X_i$, then a 1-unit increase in X would cause Y to increase by 7.5%. When $\beta_1 > 0$, the function increases at an increasing rate; and when $\beta_1 < 0$, it decreases at an decreasing rate. In the **declining returns model**, $Y_i = \beta_0 + \beta_1 \ln(X_i)$, a 1% change in X_i causes Y_i to change by $\beta_1/100$. For example, if $Y_i = 200 + 57.5 \ln(X_i)$ then a 1% increase in X would increase Y by 0.575 units. This function either increases at a decreasing rate ($\beta_1 > 0$) or decreases at a decreasing rate ($\beta_1 < 0$). These models are useful when there is a theoretical reason to expect a nonlinear relationship (such as diminishing returns to scale in the theory of production) or when the data demands a nonlinear form.

Standardized variables are denoted $\text{Std}(Y) = (y_i - \bar{y}) / s_y$ and $\text{Std}(X) = (x_i - \bar{x}) / s_x$. The model $\text{Std}(Y_i) = \beta_0 + \beta_1 \text{Std}(X_i)$ yields the same R^2 as the linear model, since standardizing is a linear transformation of X and Y. Each transformed variable is expressed in standard deviations, and the coefficient β_1 is called a **beta weight**. This model is of interest in fields such as finance, human resources, and psychology. It eliminates units of measurement, and avoids issues of scaling in variables with dissimilar magnitudes. In the model, a 1-standard deviation change in X results in a β_1 standard deviation change in Y. The estimated intercept β_0 is always zero and hence, can be omitted from the model.

A **power model** has the form $Y_i = \beta_0 + \beta_1 X_i^c + u_i$ where c is a constant specified *a priori*. Special cases are $c = 2$ (quadratic model without the X term), $c = 1$ (the linear model), $c = -1$ (the *reciprocal model*), and $c = 0.5$ (a type of diminishing growth model). Alternatively, if Y_i is raised to the power c, the power model has the form $Y_i^c = \beta_0 + \beta_1 X_i + u_i$. In both cases if c is not known beforehand, a search procedure can be used.

An **interaction variable** has the form $X_i Z_i$ (i.e., X_i is multiplied by Z_i), where Z_i is a variable believed to interact with X_i. The model becomes $Y_i = \beta_0 + \beta_1 X_i + \beta_2 X_i Z_i$. One case of interest is when Z_i is a variable that has only two values, but this is not a necessary restriction. Z_i can be multi-valued (e.g., 1, 2, 3) or even continuous. The effect of Z_i is to alter the slope of the regression line (in effect, a different fitted function for each value of Z_i).

Illustration of Concepts

For a sample of 52 architectural firms that specialize in health care, an industry analysis shows the number of architects employed by each firm (X) and the firm's total fees for the year (Y) in millions of dollars. The **linear model** (Figure 1) yields $R^2 = 0.78$. The quadratic model (Figure 2) improves the fit slightly to $R^2 = 0.80$. The cubic model (Figure 3) yields $R^2 = 0.81$ (but note that the coefficient of the X^3 term is nearly zero). Adding an additional variable to the model always improves R^2, even if it adds nothing to the model's explanatory power. The **declining returns model** (Figure 4) requires a Ln **transformation** of the independent variable. It yields $R^2 = 0.67$. In this model, a 1% increase in the number of architects yields an extra 0.083711 (= 8.3711/100) in fees or \$83,711 since the units are in thousands. In contrast, in the linear model each additional architect yielded an extra 0.1755 in fees (i.e., \$175,500). There is no straightforward interpretation of either **polynomial model**. However, all three nonlinear models suggest that total fees increase at a declining rate relative to the number of architects. This is theoretically appealing since it is unlikely that the 200th architect will have the same impact on total fees as the 5th architect.

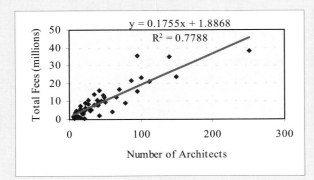

Figure 1: Linear Model

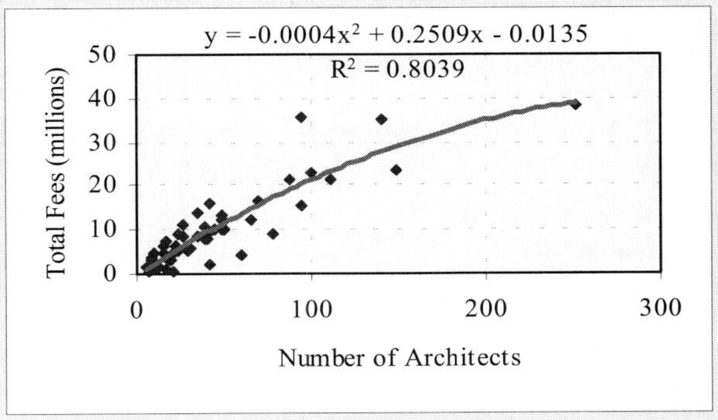

$y = 0.1755x + 1.8868$
$R^2 = 0.7788$

Figure 2: Quadratic Model

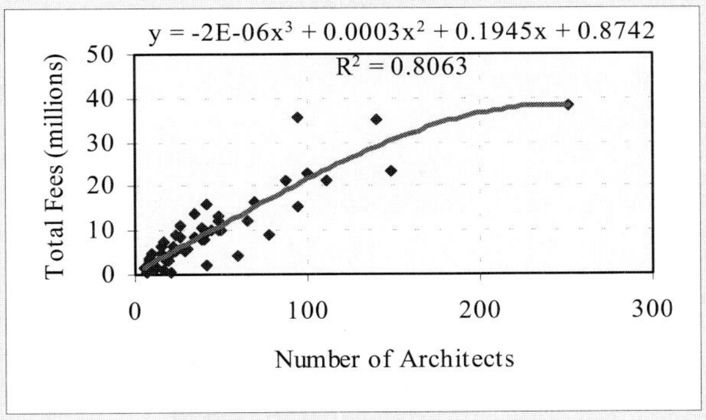

$y = -0.0004x^2 + 0.2509x - 0.0135$
$R^2 = 0.8039$

Figure 3: Cubic Model

$y = -2E\text{-}06x^3 + 0.0003x^2 + 0.1945x + 0.8742$
$R^2 = 0.8063$

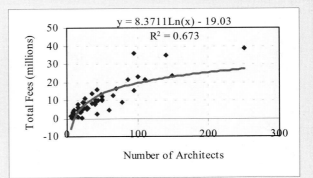

Figure 4: Declining Growth Model

$y = 8.3711Ln(x) - 19.03$
$R^2 = 0.673$

Other models are possible. An **elasticity model** tells us the percentage change in total fees due to a 1% change in the number of architects. A *standardized model* gives the same fit as a linear model, but its **beta weight** tells us the standard deviation change in total fees due to a 1-standard deviation change in the number of architects. An **exponential growth model** does not make sense, given the shape of the data. The **power model** requires *a priori* specification of an exponent, for which we lack any real basis. An **interaction variable** might be appropriate, perhaps by using the number of engineers employed by the firm (Z) since engineers and architects are likely to be complementary in the design of health care facilities.

Orientation to Basic Features

This module estimates a model based on the functional form and variable transformations that you specify. You can examine the shape of the fitted function that is displayed on a scatter plot, or study its estimated coefficients, ANOVA statistics, and examine confidence intervals for E(y|x) and prediction intervals for y|x. Data is brought into the module from the notebook.

1. **Opening Screen**
   Start the module by clicking on the module's icon, title, or chapter number in the *Visual Statistics* menu and pressing the Run Module button. When the module is loaded, you will be on the introduction page of the Notebook. Read the questions and then click the Concepts tab to see the concepts that you will learn. Click on the Scenarios tab. Click on Growth Models, select the Elasticity Models scenario, and read it. Enter a number in the version window at the bottom of the notebook page. The version number allows you to duplicate this same scenario later. The default (0) gives a randomly chosen scenario between 1 and 99. Version 3 is shown below. When you have selected a version, press OK. A scatter plot appears with X and Y control panels on the right. Click the Estimate Model button and you will see a screen similar to the one shown here with the fitted model displayed in red on the scatter plot. After the model has been fitted, the Estimate Model button becomes a Clear Estimates button.

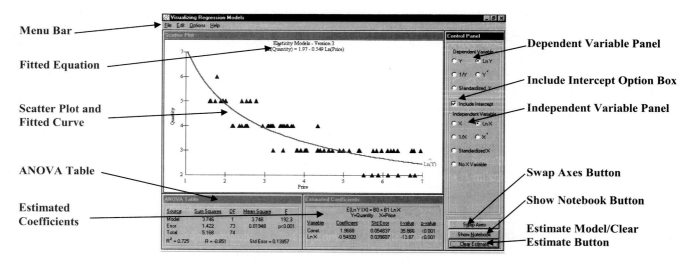

2. **ANOVA Table and Estimated Coefficients**
   Examine the ANOVA table and estimated coefficients at the bottom of the screen. Except for rounding, the coefficients are the same as the fitted equation shown at the top of the scatter plot. Each scenario will generate a different fitted equation. Click the Swap Axes button to interchange the independent and dependent variables.

3. **Control Panel for X and Y**
   The Ln X and Ln Y options are selected in the Control Panel. Select X and Y, then press the Estimate Model button. Note the effects on the fitted equation and displayed curve. Repeat, selecting the 1/X and 1/Y options. Restore the original display by selecting the options Ln X and Ln Y. *To prevent illegal transformations, when the axes are swapped, or data is obtained from the notebook (except scenarios), the model is always returned to options X and Y.*

4. **Options**

   a. On the menu bar, click Options. Select Show Data. You will see a list of the X and Y data values that are displayed on the scatter plot.

   b. On the menu bar, click Options. Select Show Confidence and Prediction Intervals and then Show 90% Confidence and Prediction Intervals. The confidence bands follow the shape of the estimated regression function with additional bend. Note that the prediction intervals (for individual Y values) are wider than the confidence intervals (for the *conditional mean* of Y). Select Show 90%, 95%, and 99% Confidence Intervals to see a visual comparison of three confidence levels. Note that the 95% intervals are wider than the 90% intervals. Finally, select No Confidence or Prediction Intervals to restore the display to its default appearance.

✔ No Confidence or Prediction Intervals
Show 90% Confidence and Prediction Intervals
Show 95% Confidence and Prediction Intervals
Show 99% Confidence and Prediction Intervals
Show 90%, 95%, and 99% Confidence Intervals
Show 90%, 95%, and 99% Predicition Intervals

   c. On the menu bar, click Options. Select Axis Scale and choose Transformed X and Y Units. The fitted regression function immediately changes its appearance. In this example, it becomes a straight line, because *the elasticity function is linear in terms of Ln X and Ln Y*. Observe that the axis scales now are quite different, and are labeled Ln X and Ln Y instead of X and Y. Return to Original X and Y Units.

Original X and Y Units
✔ Transformed X and Y Units

   d. On the menu bar, click Options. Select Show Calculations (note that this option is unavailable unless you have already clicked the Estimate Model button). You will see a dialog box that shows the transformations and formulas used in the OLS calculations for the slope and intercept. This can be useful for understanding how the fitted equation is derived. This option is *not* available if the model has more than one independent variable since the estimation equations are much more complex and not overly instructive.

   Calculations

   $Y = Q$

   $X = P$

   $\bar{x} = \Sigma X/n = 378.55 / 75 = 5.0473$

   $\bar{y} = \Sigma Y/n = 231 / 75 = 3.0800$

   $$\hat{\beta}_1 = \frac{\Sigma (X-\bar{x})(Y-\bar{y})}{\Sigma (X-\bar{x})(X-\bar{x})} = \frac{-132.2961}{262.5230}$$

   $= -0.50394$

   $\hat{\beta}_0 = \bar{y} - \hat{\beta}_1 \bar{x}$

   $= 3.0800 - (-0.50394)(5.0473)$

   $= 5.6235$

5. **Copying a Display**
   Click on any graph or the ANOVA Table. Press the Copy button on the toolbar or select Copy from the Edit menu on the menu bar. The copied display can be pasted into another application.

6. **Help**
   Click Help on the menu bar at the top of the screen. Search for Help lets you search an index, Contents shows a table of contents for this module, Using Help gives instructions on Help, and About gives licensing and copyright information.

7. **Exit**
   Close the module by selecting Exit in the File menu (or click ☒ in the upper right-hand corner of the window). You will be returned to the *Visual Statistics* main menu.

Orientation to Additional Features

1. **Interaction Variable**

    Press the Show Notebook button. Click on the Scenarios tab. Click on Interaction Models, select the Interaction Variable with Three Values scenario, read it, enter 43 in the Version label box, and press the OK button. The new option Interaction Model appears in the Independent Variable panel and has been selected. This option can also be obtained from the menu bar: click Options, select Interaction Model and Allow. Press the Estimate Model button. Three separate regression lines are fitted, each color-coded (red, green, and blue in this example) as are the data points that match the coding of the interaction variable. In this scenario, the interaction variable is number of car cylinders (1 = 4 cylinders, 2 = 6 cylinders, 3 = 8 cylinders).

2. **Other Options**

    a. On the menu bar, click Options. Select Allow Polynomial Models. Two new options appear on the bottom of the Independent Variable panel. Select Quadratic Model and select Y in the Dependent Variable panel. Press the Estimate Model button. Note the shape of the new fitted function. Select Cubic Model and then press the Estimate Model button. Observe that the new function has an inflection point, where the line's slope changes from becoming flatter to becoming steeper, at about 3.2 on the Weight axis. Also note that the R^2 increased slightly. This always occurs when additional variables are added to the model.

    b. On the menu bar, click Options. Select Show Y Intercept. The display shows X = 0. The Y intercept (104.18) can now be seen. If X = 0 is showing, the option has no effect.

    c. Press the Show Notebook button. Select the Interaction Variable with Four Values scenario, read it, and press the OK button. Press the Estimate Model button. On the menu bar, click Options and select Graph Display. The menu offers four choices. The Color Printer option is selected. Select the Black and White Printer. The colored lines and symbols change to lines and symbols that they are easier to differentiate on a non-color printer. If you click Symbols you will see another submenu showing three choices. The default is to display solid symbols unless the sample size exceeds 150, and then to use outline symbols (to reveal more detail as the scatter plot becomes more crowded). However, you can override this choice and choose Solid or Outline Only symbols all the time. If you click Type of Plot, choose Time Plot to connect the points on the scatter plot in their temporal order. *For cross-sectional data, which doesn't have a temporal order, this can result in a graph with a very odd appearance.*

3. **Databases**

    Press the Show Notebook button. Select the Databases tab, select a type of database, and click on a particular database. Read about the database and press OK to create a model. Scroll down the list of variables and select a dependent variable. Press the dependent variable ⇨ button. To remove the variable, press the ⇦ button. Select an independent variable and press the independent variable ⇨ button. The Sample Size button or Time Period button (depending on the database) enables you to change the sample size. You can select an interaction variable now or later if needed. Press OK to create your scatter plot.

Basic Learning Exercises

Name _____

Exponential Growth Model

1. Press the Show Notebook button. Click on the Scenarios tab, select Growth Models and select Exponential Growth Model. Read the scenario. a) What are the variables? Enter 90 in the Version label box, and press OK. b) Describe the scatter plot. b) Press the Estimate Model button. Describe the fitted line. c) Write the estimated equation. d) What does Ln stand for? e) Why is there a ^ above the dependent variable? f) What are the axis labels? **Hint:** This model is sometimes called a Log-Linear model.

2. Even though the estimated model is nonlinear the model was estimated with Ordinary Least Squares (OLS). Select Options on the Menu bar and select Show Calculations. Notice that Y is the Ln of GDP. Also, notice that the estimated slope is the same equation you learned in simple regression. The transformation is what caused the fitted line to be curved. Press the Close button. Select Options on the Menu bar and select Axis Scale and then Transformed X and Y Units. Describe the estimated line and axes labels.

3. Select Options on the Menu bar and select Show Confidence and Prediction Intervals and then Show 95% Confidence and Prediction Intervals. a) What does the confidence interval show? b) What does the prediction interval show? c) Why are they both closest to the estimated line at Period 12.5? d) Select Options on the Menu bar and select Axis Scale and then Original X and Y Units. Describe the confidence and prediction intervals. When are they closest to the estimated nonlinear fitted line?

4. Remove the confidence and prediction intervals using Options on the Menu bar. The table shows the fitted Y value that corresponds to each X value. The ratio Y_2/Y_1 tells us that Y grew 20.7% from period 5 to 10. Raising the ratio to the 1/5 power (5 is the number of periods) gives the growth per period (3.83% from period 5 to 10). Which parameter estimates this growth rate?

X	Y	Y_2/Y_1	$(Y_2/Y_1)^{1/5}$	Growth
5	5.27	NA	NA	NA
10	6.36	1.207	1.0383	3.83%
15	7.68	1.208	1.0384	3.84%
20	9.26	1.206	1.0381	3.81%

5.   Press the Show Notebook button. Click on the Examples tab, select Macroeconomic
      Examples, and select Consumer Price Index. Read the example. a) What years will be
      displayed on the graph? b) Press the OK button. Select Ln Y option button in the Dependent
      Variable panel to estimate an exponential growth model. Press the Estimate Model button.
      What has inflation (growth in prices) averaged over the time period? c) In the late 1990's was
      inflation above or below this historic average?

Declining Returns Model

6.   Press the Show Notebook button. Click on the Scenarios tab, select Growth Models and select
      Declining Returns Model. Read the scenario. a) What are the dependent and independent
      variables? b) Enter 40 in the Version label box, and press the OK button. Describe the scatter
      plot. c) Press the Estimate Model button. Describe the fitted line. d) Write the estimated
      equation. e) Why is this model also called a Linear-Log model?

7.   Select Options on the Menu bar and select Axis Scale and then Transformed X and Y Units.
      Describe the estimated line and axes labels?

8.   The table shows the fitted Y value (in thousands) that corresponds to each X value. The
      difference in Y's, ΔY, is about 64,000 when X is doubled.
      This constant change due to a constant *percentage* increase
      in X (100% in this case) is characteristic of the declining
      returns model. *The estimated model tells how much Y*
      increases if X is increased by 1%. In this case, a 1%
      increase in Employment (X) causes Output (Y) to increase

X	Y(000's)	ΔY(000's)
400	614	NA
800	677	63
1600	741	64
3200	805	64

      by 917.24 units. How was 917.24 obtained? Why didn't doubling X increase Y by 91,724
      units?

9.   Press the Show Notebook button. Click on the Examples tab, select Financials Examples, and Baseball Salaries. Read the example. a) What are the variables and in what units are they measured? b) Press the OK button. Select Ln X option button in the Independent Variable panel to estimate a declining returns model. Press the Estimate Model button. What does this model suggest about baseball salaries and years in professional baseball?

Elasticity Model

10.   Press the Show Notebook button. Click on the Scenarios tab, select Growth Models and select Elasticity Model. Read the scenario. a) What are the dependent and independent variables and their units of measurement? b) Enter 20 in the Version label box, and press the OK button. Describe the scatter plot. c) Press the Estimate Model button. Describe the fitted line. d) Write the estimated equation. **Hint:** *This model is also called a Log-Log or multiplicative model.*

11.   Select Options on the Menu bar and select Axis Scale and then Transformed X and Y Units. Describe the estimated line and axis labels.

12.   The table shows the fitted Y value that corresponds to each X value. The ratio Y_2/Y_1 tells us that Y grew by -35.8% ($= 1 - 0.642$ changed to percent) when price increased from \$1 to \$2 or increased by 100%. This constant *percentage* change due to a constant *percentage* increase in X (100% in this case) is characteristic of the elasticity model. The estimated model tells the percentage Y increases if X is increased by *1%*. In this case, a 1% increase in Price (X) results in Quantity (Y) *decreasing* by 0.635%. -0.635 is called an elasticity. Which

X	Y	Y_2/Y_1	Growth
1	8.1	NA	NA
2	5.2	0.642	−31.4%
4	3.4	0.654	−33.3%
8	2.2	0.647	−31.2%

parameter estimates this elasticity? Why didn't doubling X *decrease* Y by 63.5%?

13. Press the Show Notebook button. Click on the Examples tab, select Health Examples, and Birth Weights. Read the example. a) What are the independent and dependent variables and in what units are they measured? b) Press the OK button. Select Ln X option button in the Independent Variable panel and Ln Y in the Dependent Variable panel to estimate an elasticity model. Press the Estimate Model button. What does this model suggest about gestation period and birth weight? c) What would be the shape of the fitted line if the slope coefficient were –2.57?

14. Press the Show Notebook button. Click on Next Page in the lower right corner and select Utility Costs. Read the example. a) What are the independent and dependent variables and in what units are they measured? b) Press the OK button. Select Ln X and Ln Y to estimate an elasticity model. Press the Estimate Model button. What does this model suggest about gas used and energy cost? c) What would be the shape of the fitted line if the slope coefficient were –0.272?

Intermediate Learning Exercises   Name _____

The Polynomial Model

15. Press the Show Notebook button. Click on the Scenarios tab, select Models Using Exponents, and select Quadratic Model. Read the scenario. a) What are the dependent and independent variables and their units of measurement? b) Enter 5 in the Version label box, and press OK. Describe the scatter plot. c) Notice that two new options have been added to the Independent Variable panel box. These options can be selected by selecting Options on the Menu bar and selecting Allow Polynomial Models. Which model is selected? d) Press the Estimate Model button. Describe the fitted line. e) Write the estimated equation.

16. In a quadratic model selecting Options on the Menu bar and selecting Axis Scale and then Transformed X and Y Units will have no effect since there are two independent variables. The table shows the fitted Y value that corresponds to each X value. The ΔX and ΔY columns show the change in X and Y. The $\Delta Y/\Delta X$ column shows the slope of the fitted curve. Although this table shows how to calculate the slope using the graph, unlike the Ln transformation, there is no straight-

X	ΔX	Y	ΔY	$\Delta Y/\Delta X$
2	NA	4.88	NA	NA
3	1	5.07	0.19	0.19
4	1	5.15	0.08	0.08
5	1	5.14	–0.01	–0.01

forward interpretation of the quadratic model. An alternative approach to calculating the slope is to take the function's derivative: $0.438 + 2\,(-0.505)\,(\text{Revenue})$. a) Calculate the slope using this formula (use the average value of X for Revenue). b) Why aren't the slopes the same as above? c) Why does this parabola have a maximum?

17. Press the Show Notebook button. Click on the Examples tab, select Time Series Examples, and Gasoline Prices. Read the example. a) What are the variables and in what units are they measured? b) Press the OK button. Select Quadratic Model in the Independent Variable panel. Press the Estimate Model button. What does this model suggest about gas prices during this the late 1990's? c) Why does this parabola have a minimum?

18. Select the Cubic Model. Press the Estimate Model button. Describe the fitted line.

The Standardized Model

19. Press the Show Notebook button. Click on the Scenarios tab, select Linear Models, and select Standardized Variables. Read the scenario. a) Define the dependent and independent variables and their units of measurement. b) Enter 20 in the Version label box, and press OK. Describe the scatter plot. c) Press the Estimate Model button. Describe the fitted line. d) Write the estimated equation.

20. In a standardized model selecting Options on the Menu bar and selecting Axis Scale and then Transformed X and Y Units will have no effect since the model is already linear. a) What is the standardization transformation? b) Why is this considered a linear transformation? c) Why is the estimated intercept equal to 0? **Hint:** Unlike the Ln transformation, it is rare to use this transformation on just the independent or dependent variable.

21. a) What is the coefficient of the independent variable called in this model? b) What is the interpretation of the estimated slope? c) Select Y and X in the panels. Press the Estimate Model button. Did the fitted line change? **Hint:** Because this transformation removes all scaling, the size of the beta weight measures the variable's impact on the dependent variable. This is useful in a multiple regression model where you have many independent variables.

22. Press the Show Notebook button. Click on the Examples tab, select Examples with People, and Statistics Course Grades. Read the example. a) What are the independent and dependent variables and in what units are they measured? b) Press the OK button. Select Standardized X in the Independent Variable panel and Standardized Y in the Dependent Variable panel to estimate a standardized model. Press the Estimate Model button. What does this model suggest about the final grade and grade on exam 1?

Advanced Learning Exercises

Name _____

Power and Reciprocal Models

23. Press the Show Notebook button. Click on the Scenarios tab, select Models Using Exponents, and select Power of X Transformation. Read the scenario. a) Define the dependent and independent variables and their units of measurement. b) To what power is X raised? c) Enter 25 in the Version label box, and press OK. Describe the scatter plot. d) Press the Estimate Model button. Notice that the independent variable option selected is $X^{0.2}$. Describe the fitted line. e) Write the estimated equation.

24. The downside of this type of model is that you must know the exponent *before* you estimate the model. One way around this problem is to re-estimate the model with different values of the exponent and select the one that minimizes the Error Sum of Squares (ESS). The key to doing this search efficiently is to set up a systematic approach. Fill in the ESS in the table below (the first one is entered). After each entry, write down *why* the next exponent was selected. To change the power to which X is raised, select the X option and then re-select the X^c option. This will bring up a dialog box where you can enter your exponent. Press OK and the Estimate Model button. Write down the estimate of your final model. *This same process could be used if Y is raised to a power.*

Exponent	ESS	Why Select the Next Exponent to Estimate
0.2	1.558	
0.3		
0.1		
0.01		
0.05		
0.03		
0.02		
Final Model –		

25. Press the Show Notebook button. Select the Reciprocal of X Model. Read the scenario. a) Define the dependent and independent variables and their units of measurement. b) Press OK. Describe the scatter plot. c) Press the Estimate Model button. Describe the fitted line. d) Write the estimated equation. e) What is the elasticity of this demand function? **Hint:** This is a special case of the power model where the exponent is –1.

Interaction Variables

26. Press the Show Notebook button. Click on the Scenarios tab, select Interaction Models, and select Interaction Variable with Two Values. Read the scenario. a) Define the dependent and independent variables and their units of measurement. b) Define the interaction variable and its unit of measurement. c) Enter 35 in the Version label box, and press OK. Describe the scatter plot. d) Press the Estimate Model button. Write the estimated equation. e) Why are there two lines? Describe the fitted lines.

27. a) What is the p-value of the interaction term (i.e., SqFt People)? b) If we tested the coefficient at $\alpha = 0.05$, what does it tell us about the value of the condominium and the number of people living in it? c) Is the size of the condominium important in part (b)?

28. Press the Show Notebook button. Select Interaction Variable with Four Values. Read the scenario. a) What are the dependent and independent variables and their units of measurement? b) What is the interaction variable and its unit of measurement? c) Press OK. Press the Estimate Model button. Write the estimated equation. d) Why are there four lines? Describe the fitted lines.

29. a) What is the p-value of the interaction term (i.e., Exp Ed)? b) If we tested the coefficient at $\alpha = 0.01$, what does it tell us about Income and Education? c) Is Experience important in part (b)?

Individual Learning Projects

Write a report on one of the three topics listed below. Use the cut-and-paste facilities of the module to place the appropriate graphs in your report.

1. Use one of the Databases in this module to select variables that can be estimated with a simple linear model ($Y = \beta_0 + \beta_1 X + u$). Copy the graph with the estimated model for your paper. Define your variables, explain the model, and interpret the estimated coefficients. Repeat each step using a standardized model, an exponential growth model, a declining returns model, and an elasticity model. Your data should be appropriate for the model used.

2. Use data from an Example or a Database in this module, to create a nonlinear model (not a polynomial). Estimate the model and display a 95% confidence and prediction interval on the graph. Copy the graph for your paper. Transform the axes to display the transformed variable(s) on the axes. Copy the graph for your paper. Define your variables, explain the model and interpret the estimated coefficients. Explain in *detail* why graph 2 shows a linear line while graph 1 shows a nonlinear line. Review how a 95% confidence and prediction interval are created. Explain how the intervals were created for graph 2 and then for graph 1. Explain why the two graphs display the intervals differently.

3. Use data from an Example or a Database in this module to create a power model in X. Make sure that neither X nor Y is less than or equal to zero. Define your variables. Estimate the model using the search procedure outlined in Exercise 24. Create a table with your exponents and Error Sum of Squares. Copy at least 2 graphs for your paper. Use the table and graphs to explain how you searched for the best model. Explain your final estimated model. Repeat the process using the same data and a power model in Y. Compare and contrast the two models.

Team Learning Projects

Select one of the three projects listed below. In each case, produce a team project that is suitable for an oral presentation. Use presentation software or large poster boards to display your results. Graphs should be large enough for your audience to see. Each team member should be responsible for producing some of the graphs. Ask your instructor if a written report is also expected.

1. This project is for a team of two or three. Using Examples and Databases from this module, you are to illustrate and interpret 11 different models: simple linear model, standardized model, elasticity model ($\beta_1 > 1$, $0 < \beta_1 < 1$, and $\beta_1 < 0$), exponential growth model ($\beta_1 > 0$, $\beta_1 < 0$), decreasing returns model ($\beta_1 > 0$, $\beta_1 < 0$), and quadratic model ($\beta_2 > 0$, $\beta_2 < 0$). Although you may be able to use the same variables more than once, most models will use different data. For each model define your variables, explain the model, and interpret the coefficients (if they have an interpretation). Each model should have a graphical display. Models that have similar explanations should be presented together. The purpose of this project is to demonstrate the variety of different models that can be estimated with OLS, to understand the similarities and differences in these models, and to understand the importance of the slope coefficient in differentiating these models.

2. This project is for a team of three. The purpose of this project is to investigate and explain different types of interaction variables. Data will come from any cross sectional database in this module. The team will select the dependent and independent variable, and sample size. Each variable should be defined. One team member will use an interaction variable with two or three values, another member will use an interaction variable with 5 to 10 values, and the last member will use a continuous interaction variable (more than 12 different values). Each team member will estimate their model and create a graph of this estimation. The model will be explained and the interaction term interpreted and tested for significance. The team should compare and contrast the three models. The project should be repeated using a time series database from this module. Compare and contrast the process using cross-sectional data and time series data.

3. This project is for a team of three or four. Use data from an Example or a Database in this module, to create a power model in X. Make sure that neither X nor Y is less than or equal to zero. Define your variables. Estimate the model using the search procedure outlined in Exercise 24. Create a table with your exponents and Error Sum of Squares. Show at least 2 graphs for your presentation. Use the table and graphs to explain how you searched for the best model. Explain your final estimated model. Repeat the process using the same data and a power model in Y. Use the final exponents for X and Y to *begin* a search for the best model using *both* an exponent for X and Y. In searching for the best exponents in this new model you must search simultaneously over both exponents. Your table of ESS should have exponents for Y across the top and exponents for X down the side. The table should be filled in completely (i.e., for any value of the exponent of Y that is used you need to estimate the model with every value of the exponent of X that you used). You should use at least 8 different exponents for both X and Y. At least 3 graphs from this search should be included in your presentation. The focus of this project is how to estimate a model using a search procedure when both X and Y are raised to a power.

Self-Evaluation Quiz

1. In the model $Ln(Y) = 4 + 5Ln(X) + u$, the interpretation of the slope coefficient is that
    a. a 1% change in X results in a 5 unit change in Y.
    b. a 1% change in X results in a 5% change in Y.
    c. a 1% change in X results in a 0.05 unit change in Y.
    d. a 1-unit change in X results in a 5 unit change in Y.
    e. a 1-unit change in X results in a 500% change in Y.

2. Which model could show a 3% growth rate?
    a. $Std(Y) = \beta_0 + \beta_1 Std(X)$.
    b. $Y = \beta_0 + \beta_1 X^2$.
    c. $\ln Y = \beta_0 + \beta_1 X$.
    d. $Y = \beta_0 + \beta_1 \ln X$.
    e. $\ln Y = \beta_0 + \beta_1 \ln X$.

3. Which of the following is a declining returns model?
    a. $Std(Y) = \beta_0 + \beta_1 Std(X)$.
    b. $\ln Y = \beta_0 + \beta_1 \ln X$.
    c. $Y = \beta_0 + \beta_1 X^2$.
    d. $\ln Y = \beta_0 + \beta_1 X$.
    e. $Y = \beta_0 + \beta_1 \ln X$.

4. For any transformed bivariate model, a 95% prediction interval for y | x
    a. will be narrower than a 95% confidence interval for Y.
    b. will be widest near the mean of the transformed variable X.
    c. will contain the individual Y values about 95% of the time.
    d. will contain the true conditional mean of Y about 95% of the time.
    e. will be linear if the transformed equation is linear.

5. Which equation represents a nonlinear variable transformation?
    a. $\ln Y = \beta_0 + \beta_1 X$.
    b. $Y = \beta_0 + \beta_1 (1/X)$.
    c. $\ln Y = \beta_0 + \beta_1 \ln X$.
    d. $Y = \beta_0 + \beta_1 X^{1/2}$.
    e. All of the above.

6. Which do you expect from the polynomial model $Y = \beta_0 + \beta_1 X + \beta_2 X^2 + \beta_3 X^3$?
    a. It is generally easier to interpret than a linear or quadratic model.
    b. It is incapable of fitting data with an inflection point.
    c. It is likely to yield a better fit than the simple linear model.
    d. It is impossible to estimate using the OLS method.
    e. It cannot be graphed on a simple X-Y scatter plot.

7. The standardized variable model $Std(Y) = \beta_0 + \beta_1\,Std(X)$
   a. is a simple linear transformation of X and Y.
   b. is sometimes called a beta-weight model.
   c. improves the scaling of variables of dissimilar magnitudes.
   d. no longer uses the original units of X and Y (e.g., kilograms).
   e. All of the above.

8. Which model can be displayed as a curve that increases at a decreasing rate as X increases?
   a. $Y = 200 - 0.5\,(1/X)$.
   b. $Y = 200 + 5\ln X$.
   c. $Y = 200 + 15\,X - 0.5\,X^2$.
   d. $Y = 200 + 5\,X^{1/2}$.
   e. All of the above.

9. Which is *not* a feature of the reciprocal model relating quantity (Q) and price (P)?
   a. It cannot be estimated using the OLS method because it is nonlinear.
   b. It has the form $Q = \beta_1\,(1/P) + u_i$.
   c. It represents constant elasticity.
   d. Its form is a hyperbola except for the disturbance.
   e. Other things being equal, a 1% increase in P will result in a 1% rise in P.

10. Which is a power of Y transformation that represents *declining* growth in Y?
    a. $Y^{0.5} = 12 + 10\,X$.
    b. $Y^2 = 12 + 10\,X$.
    c. $Y^{-0.5} = 12 + 10\,X$.
    d. $Y^{-2} = 12 + 10\,X$.
    e. None of the above.

11. Which model uses an interaction variable?
    a. $Y = \beta_0 + \beta_1\,X + \beta_2\,X^2$.
    b. $\ln Y = \beta_0 + \beta_1\,X + \beta_2\,Z$.
    c. $Y = \beta_0 + \beta_1\,X^{1/2}$.
    d. $\ln Y = \beta_0 + \beta_1\,X + \beta_2\,XZ$.
    e. Two of the above.

12. An interaction variable
    a. can have only two values (generally 0 or 1).
    b. may have several discrete values (such as 1, 2, 3).
    c. may be a continuous variable.
    d. can result in a changing slope of the fitted equation.
    e. could have any of these characteristics.

Glossary of Terms

ANOVA table Decomposition of variance in a regression, showing total sum of squares and its sources (regression, error) along with degrees of freedom and mean squares. *Total* degrees of freedom equals $n - 1$, *error* degrees of freedom equals $n - k - 1$, and the *regression* degrees of freedom equals k, where n is the sample size and k is the number of independent variables.

Beta weight Coefficient of the independent variable in a regression model of the form $Std(Y_i) = \beta_0 + \beta_1 Std(X_i)$ where $Std(Y) = (y_i - \bar{y}) / s_y$ and $Std(X) = (x_i - \bar{x}) / s_x$. β_0 is always zero. It is unusual not to transform both the independent and dependent variables.

Confidence interval for mean of Y With probability $1 - \alpha$ the upper and lower values of the range of estimates for the *conditional mean* of Y. When plotted over the entire range of X they comprise a *confidence band*. Individual Y values often lie outside this confidence band.

Cubic model Regression model of the form $Y_i = \beta_0 + \beta_1 X_i + \beta_2 X_i^2 + \beta_3 X_i^3 + u_i$. It will have two extrema (over the displayed range of X, it may not be possible to see them) and an inflection point. See **Polynomial model**.

Declining returns model Regression model of the from $Y_i = \beta_0 + \beta_1 Ln(X_i) + u_i$. In this model, a 1% change in X results in a $\beta_1/100$ unit change in Y. It is also called a Linear-Log model.

Elasticity model Regression model of the form $Ln\, Y_i = \beta_0 + \beta_1 Ln(X_i) + u_i$. Economists use it to describe a relationship between price and quantity demanded or supplied. In this model, a 1% change in X_i leads to a β_1% change in Y_i. It is also called a Log-Log or multiplicative model.

Exponential growth model Regression model of the form $Ln\, Y_i = \beta_0 + \beta_1 X_i + u_i$. In this model, a 1-unit change in X results in a $100 \times \beta_1$% change in Y. It is also called a Log-Linear model. It is commonly used for financial or economic data.

F statistic In a regression ANOVA table, the ratio of the *regression* mean square to the *error* mean square. It is used to test the overall significance of the regression. See **p-value**.

Interaction variable An interaction variable is a transformation where a third variable Z_i enters the analysis through an interaction with X_i. It has the form $Z_i X_i$, i.e., Z_i is multiplied by X_i. If entered into a simple linear model it has the form $Y_i = \beta_0 + \beta_1 X_i + \beta_2 Z_i X_i + u_i$. Although it requires multivariate estimation techniques, it can be viewed on a scatter plot as line segments or as a series of different lines (one for each unique value of Z_i).

Multiple correlation coefficient Measure of overall fit in a regression. It is the square root of R^2. It may be interpreted as the correlation between Y_{actual} and Y_{fitted} over all n observations.

Ordinary Least Squares (OLS) Method of estimating a regression that guarantees the smallest possible sum of squared residuals. The residuals sum to 0 using the OLS method.

Parameter Numerical constant needed to define a particular model or distribution. A regression model's the parameters are the intercept and the coefficients of the k independent variables, whose true values are denoted $\beta_0, \beta_1, \beta_2, ..., \beta_k$. See **Estimated coefficient**.

Prediction interval for individual Y Upper and lower values of the range of estimates for an *individual value* of Y conditional upon the value of the independent variable(s). The prediction interval for Y is wider than the confidence interval for the mean of Y. Individual Y values generally will lie within the prediction interval unless the assumptions are violated.

P-value Probability (usually two-tailed) of committing Type I error if we reject the null hypothesis that a parameter is zero (for example, a regression coefficient). A small p-value (such as 0.01) would incline us to reject the hypothesis that the true parameter is zero.

Polynomial model Since a polynomial model only involves X and Y, it can be graphed in two dimensions. However, it requires multivariate methods of estimation because it has more than one independent variable. Adding polynomial terms will improve the R^2, but the resulting model may have no meaningful interpretation. Nonetheless, a the model does offer a useful test for non-linearity. If the quadratic and cubic coefficients are near zero (i.e., insignificant t-value) it essentially collapses to a linear model. See **Quadratic model** and **Cubic model**.

Power model Regression model of the form $Y_i = \beta_0 + \beta_1 X_i^c + u_i$ where c is specified *a priori*. Special cases are c = 2 (quadratic model without the X term), c = 1 (the linear model), c = −1 (the reciprocal model), and c = 0.5 (a declining growth model). Alternatively, it can be of the form $Y_i^c = \beta_0 + \beta_1 X_i + u_i$.

Quadratic model Regression model of the $Y_i = \beta_0 + \beta_1 X_i + \beta_2 X_i^2 + u_i$. The quadratic model has a single peak or trough, However, over the displayed range of X, it may not be possible to see them. See **Polynomial model**.

Reciprocal model Regression model of the form $Y_i = \beta_0 + \beta_1(1/X_i) + u_i$ or of the form $1/Y_i = \beta_0 + \beta_1 X_i + u_i$. **See Power model**.

R-squared Ratio of the *regression* sum of squares to the *total* sum of squares. R^2 near 0 indicates the fit is poor while R^2 near 1 indicates the fit is good. Also called coefficient of determination.

Standard error Estimate of the standard deviation of the stochastic disturbances, using the square root of the sum of the squared residuals, divided by n − k − 1, where n is the sample size and k is the number of independent variables.

Transformed variable Common transformations include taking logarithms [$\ln(X_i)$ or $\ln(Y_i)$], raising to a power [X_i^c or Y_i^c], inversion [$1/X_i$ or $1/Y_i$], or standardizing by subtracting the mean and dividing by the standard deviation. As long it contains only two variables, the transformed model is still a simple regression model and may be estimated using the OLS method. However, on a graph the fitted regression equation may be nonlinear. Some variable transformations may be impossible if there are zero or negative values (e.g., 1/X).

Solutions to Self-Evaluation Quiz

1. b   Do Exercises 10–14. Read the Overview of Concepts.
2. c   Do Exercises 1–5. Read the Overview of Concepts.
3. e   Do Exercises 6–9. Read the Overview of Concepts.
4. c   Do Exercise 3.
5. e   Do Exercises 1, 10, 23–25. Read both the Overview and the Illustration of Concepts.
6. c   Do Exercises 15–18.
7. e   Do Exercises 19–22. Read the Overview of Concepts.
8. e   Do Exercises 6–9, 15–17, 23–25.
9. a   Do Exercise 25.
10. b   Do Exercises 6–9, 23, 24. Individual Learning Project 3.
11. d   Do Exercises 26–29. Read the Overview of Concepts.
12. e   Do Exercises 26–29. Read the Overview of Concepts.

CHAPTER 19

Visualizing Binary Predictors in Regression

CONCEPTS
- Binary Variable, Qualitative Variable, Quantitative Variable, Intercept Binary, Slope Binary, Interaction, Seasonal Binary, Median Split

OBJECTIVES
- Recognize the difference between quantitative and qualitative predictors in a regression model

- Be able to interpret the results of a fitted regression model that has either an intercept binary or a slope binary or both

- Learn how to interpret seasonal binaries for time series data

- Recognize if the data is time series or cross-sectional

- Understand how to create binary predictors from a third variable

Overview of Concepts

It is natural to think of regression modeling as a method of studying relationships among **quantitative variables** (data whose values are integers or decimal numbers). Examples would be home size (square feet), educational attainment (years), or credit card debt (dollars). However, researchers also study **qualitative variables** (attribute data whose values are non-numerical). Such data are usually encoded as **binary variables** using either 0 or 1. For example, we could create a binary variable Q_i to represent gender by defining $Q_i = 1$ if the ith individual is female, or $Q_i = 0$ if the ith individual is male. Similarly, a binary could denote a college graduate (yes = 1, no = 0). For time-series data, a binary could designate a recession year (recession = 1, none = 0). The choice of which is 0 and which is 1 is arbitrary, although 1 often is the condition of interest to the researcher. A special case is the **seasonal binary** that is used to represent a season (e.g., 1 if it is January, 0 otherwise). Binary predictors may be freely used in OLS regression, and cause no special problems.

A regression model *cannot* include a multi-valued attribute that is encoded numerically (for example, 1 = liberal, 2 = moderate, 3 = conservative) since the numbers themselves have no intrinsic meaning. Rather, we would define a binary for each category (e.g., Liberal = 1 if the individual is liberal, 0 otherwise; Moderate = 1 if the individual is moderate, 0 otherwise; Conservative = 1 if the individual is conservative, 0 otherwise). To avoid multicollinearity, the number of binaries allowed in the regression is always one *less* than the number of categories. Thus, gender (two categories) requires *one* binary, and political orientation (three categories) requires *two* binaries. If a qualitative predictor has c categories, we omit one so that only c–1 binaries enter the model. Although the decision of which to omit is arbitrary, the estimated coefficients and the interpretation of the results will be affected by the decision.

Binary predictors may enter the model in several ways. For an **intercept binary** the model is $Y_i = \beta_0 + \beta_1 X_i + \beta_2 Q_i$. If $Q_i = 0$ then the intercept is β_0, while if $Q_i = 1$ the intercept is $\beta_0 + \beta_2$. In other words, Q_i shifts the *intercept* of the regression line. For a **slope binary** the model is $Y_i = \beta_0 + \beta_1 X_i + \beta_2 X_i Q_i$. If $Q_i = 0$, the slope of X is β_1, while if $Q_i = 1$, the slope is $\beta_1 + \beta_2$. In other words, Q_i changes the *slope* of the regression line. The term $X_i Q_i$ is called an **interaction** because the quantitative predictor X_i interacts with the qualitative predictor Q_i. We can also have both an intercept binary *and* a slope binary, using a model of the form $Y_i = \beta_0 + \beta_1 X_i + \beta_2 Q_i + \beta_3 X_i Q_i$. This amounts to a separate regression for each binary value, albeit with a common error term (not shown), i.e., when $Q_i = 0$, the model is $Y_i = \beta_0 + \beta_1 X_i$ whereas when $Q_i = 1$ the model is $Y_i = (\beta_0 + \beta_2) + (\beta_1 + \beta_3) X_i$.

A binary (qualitative predictor) can be created from a quantitative variable Z_i. One common way to do this is a **median split**, in which we assign $Q_i = 1$ for all Z_i values above the median, and assign $Q_i = 0$ to all values of Z_i below the median. This method would be appropriate when we feel that Z_i may influence Y_i, but are unwilling to assume a continuous effect. It is also useful when Z_i has outliers. We could also create multiple quantitative variables from Z_i by choosing appropriate cutpoints (e.g., divide Z_i at its quartiles to create four qualitative predictors, then omit one of them from the model). There are four common methods for creating binary variables based on a third predictor Z_i: create binaries based on intervals of equal width (e.g., 10-20, 20-30, 30-40, etc), based on intervals of equal frequency (e.g., median split or quartiles), assigning one binary to each category (e.g., conservative, liberal, etc.), or selecting convenient cutpoints on Z_i (e.g., 10-25, 25-50, 50-100, etc.).

Illustration of Concepts

Using 1990 data for the 50 states in the U.S., we want to estimate the simple regression model $Y_i = \beta_0 + \beta_1 X_i$, where Y is a state's average score on the verbal portion of the SAT (Scholastic Aptitude Test) and X is the state's per capita income (dollars). Both X and Y are **quantitative variables**. Is the fitted regression different in the 15 Midwestern states than in the other 35 states? To investigate this question, we create a **qualitative variable** coded $Q_i = 1$ if the ith state is in the Midwest and $Q_i = 0$ otherwise. Because Q_i has only two values, it is a **binary variable**. For an **intercept binary** the model is $Y_i = \beta_0 + \beta_1 X_i + \beta_2 Q_i$. If $Q_i = 0$, the intercept is β_0, while if $Q_i = 1$, the intercept is $\beta_0 + \beta_2$. In other words, Q_i shifts the *intercept* of the regression line (see Figure 1). Both fitted lines have a negative slope, indicating that higher income is associated with lower SAT scores. This somewhat unexpected result may reflect a phenomenon known as *selection bias* (most universities and colleges require the ACT rather than the SAT test, while the most selective universities and colleges, generally located in more-affluent states, require the SAT test). The two regression lines are parallel. That is, they have the same *slope* but different *intercepts*. After accounting for effects of income, the Midwestern states ($Q_i = 1$) appear to have higher SAT scores than the other states ($Q_i = 0$).

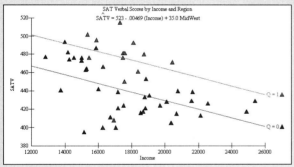

Figure 1: Model Using Intercept Binary

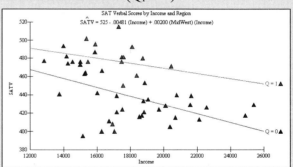

Figure 2: Model Using Slope Binary

Alternatively, for a **slope binary**, the model is $Y_i = \beta_0 + \beta_1 X_i + \beta_2 X_i Q_i$. If $Q_i = 0$, the slope of X is β_1, while if $Q_i = 1$, the slope is $\beta_1 + \beta_2$. In other words, Q_i changes the *slope* of the regression line. The term $X_i Q_i$ is called an **interaction** because the quantitative predictor X_i interacts with the qualitative predictor Q_i. Figure 2 shows the results of this model. Both slopes are negative, but the slope is flatter for the Midwestern states ($Q_i = 1$) than for the non-Midwestern states ($Q_i = 0$). In all cases, the p-values (not shown) indicate that these regression coefficients differ significantly from zero. This means that both X_i and $X_i Q_i$ are significant predictors of Y_i.

We could create a binary predictor from a third variable Z (e.g., per capita spending on grades K-12). For example, a **median split** would assign $Q_i = 1$ if Z_i is above its median and $Q_i = 0$ if Z_i is below its median. This approach is appropriate when we believe that Z_i may influence Y_i, but does *not* have a *continuous* effect. For example, if the coefficient for Q is 10, we conclude that students living in states that spend above the median on K-12 education score on average 10 points higher on the SAT test. The amount above the median is not considered.

If we have time-series data (e.g., quarterly or monthly data) we can include a **seasonal binary** to test for systematic effects. For c seasons, we use c – 1 binaries. For example, with quarterly data, we could include the three binaries Qtr2, Qtr3, Qtr4, arbitrarily omitting Qtr1. The omitted season is the reference point to which the other seasons are compared.

Orientation to Basic Features

This module estimates models with binary variables. You can analyze a scenario that uses artificial data created to illustrate a concept, an example that uses real data, create your own models using one of the nine databases, or create your own model using the data editor. The choice is made in the Notebook.

1. **Opening Screen**

   Start the module by clicking on the module's icon, title, or chapter number in the *Visual Statistics* menu and pressing the Run Module button. When the module is loaded, you will be on the introduction page of the Notebook. Read the questions and then click the Concepts tab to see the concepts that you will learn. Select the Scenarios tab, click on One Binary Variable, and select Binary Intercept 1. Read the scenario, type 40 in the Version box to see version 40 of the 99 versions of this scenario and press OK. A Hint will appear; read it and press OK. Press the flashing Estimate Model button to estimate the binary model; your computer screen should appear as below.

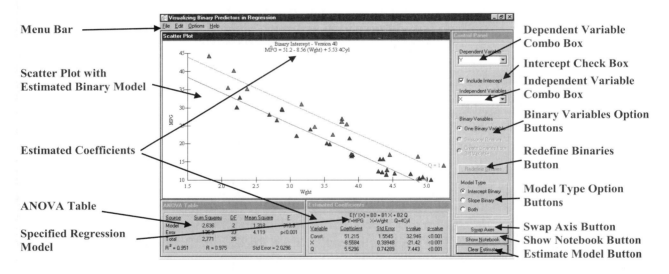

2. **Control Panel**

   Use the Dependent or Independent Variable combo boxes to select a transformation of the variable (studied in Visualizing Regression Models, Chapter 18). Deselect the Intercept check box to specify a regression model without an intercept. Use the Model Type option buttons to select the type of binary variable to include in the model: intercept binary, slope binary, or both. The Swap Axis button switches the variables on the axes and the Show Notebook button returns you to the Notebook. The model to be estimated is displayed at the top of the Estimated Coefficients window (if it is too long for the display, click on the message to display the model). Press the Estimate Model button to estimate this model, display its statistics in the ANOVA and Estimated Coefficients windows, display the fitted binary model (red and blue lines) and its fitted equation on the scatter plot, and rename the button the Clear Model button. Pressing this button clears the statistics and regression lines. Use the Binary Variables option buttons (active only when the data are consistent with their operation) to select the type of binary variable. The Redefine Binaries button allows you to redefine the binary variables if you select either the Seasonal Binaries or Create Binaries from 3rd Variable options.

Seasonal Binaries

Press the Show Notebook button, select the Examples tab, click
on Examples Using Time Series Data, and select Traffic Deaths.
Read the example, and press OK. Since this is time series data the
Seasonal Binaries option button is active (some Scenarios, and
Databases also use time series data). Select the Seasonal
Binaries option button and the dialog box to the right is displayed.
The first spin button displays the number of seasonal periods. The
second spin button shows the period number assigned to
observation 1. Both spin buttons are only active if you are using your own data (from the Data
Editor) since this information is known for data contained in this module. The last spin button
specifies which binary to eliminate from the model. Press the OK button. Notice that the scatter
plot is now color-coded. The legend shows the color assigned to each period. The legend for S0
shows the color of the period whose binary was omitted from the model.

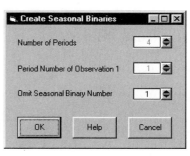

4. **Options**
    a. Select Options from the menu bar and Show Y Intercept to show $X = 0$ on the horizontal
        axis (the Y intercept can now be seen). If $X = 0$ is already showing, it has no effect.
    b. The legend for each regression line is normally next to the line. If it is difficult to read
        because it overlaps another legend, select Options, Legend and Place Right of Graph.
    c. Selecting Graph Display under Options allows you to control the display. Color Printer uses
        different colors to differentiate the regression lines and symbols, while Black and White
        Printer uses different types of lines and symbols that are easier to see on a non-color printer.
        The default symbols are solid if the sample size is less than 150 or an outline of the symbol
        otherwise. Select Symbol and Solid or Outline Only to override the default. For time series
        data, data points can be connected by selecting Type of Plot and Time plot (select Scatter
        plot to remove the connecting line).
    d. Selecting Equation Display and Hide hides the equation on the scatter plot. If the estimated
        equation is too long, it is displayed as a label box that can be moved and resized (select
        Resize). To copy the label box, right click, choose Select All, right click and choose Copy.
        Select Use Moveable Display to display the equation as a label box.
    e. Select Show Data to display the data. It can also be copied and pasted into a spreadsheet.

5. **Copying Graphs**
    Click on the window you want to copy and select Copy from the Edit menu on the menu bar at
    the top of the screen. It can then be pasted into a word processor or spreadsheet program.

6. **Help**
    Click on Help on the menu bar at the top of the screen. Search for Help lets you search an index
    for this module, Contents shows a table of contents for this module, Using Help gives
    instructions on how to use Help, and About gives licensing and copyright information about this
    module.

7. **Exit**
    Close the module by selecting Exit in the File menu (or click ☒ in the upper right-hand corner of
    the window). You will be returned to the *Visual Statistics* main menu.

Orientation to Additional Features

1. Using Databases

Press the Show Notebook button, select the Databases tab, click on Individual Consumer Cross Sectional Data and select Interview Data (read description). Press OK. The Variable Selection window (left below) appears. The bottom right frame describes the database. The upper left frame lists the database's variables (binary variables end in ?) grouped in categories (blue headings). The bottom left frame defines the variable selected. The upper right frame defines the model. Press the ⇨ button to write the selected variable in the adjacent box (⇨ changes to ⇦). Pressing a ⇦ button removes the variable from the box (⇦ changes to ⇨). Create the model: Food$ (Dependent Variable), Earnings$ (X Variable), Child? (Binary Variable), and NumChild (Z Variable). Press the Sample Size button, to select a portion of the database (middle below). Select the Use a portion of the database option button. The bottom frame becomes active. Select the top option. Enter 100 into the box (option reads Use first 100 observations). The second option selects a random sample. Press OK. Press the Show Database button to display the *entire* database. Highlight a portion of the table and it can be copied by pressing Ctrl-c. Close the table. Press the OK button.

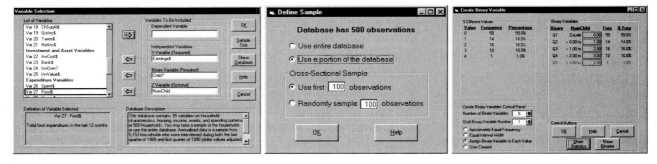

2. Creating Binaries from a 3rd Variable

Select the Create Binaries from 3rd Variable option button (window above right appears). Since there are fewer than 13 values (5 in this case), a frequency table is shown. Press the Show Statistics button to display summary statistics. Four options for creating binary variables are listed; select Assign Binary Variable to Each Value. Read the message that appears and press OK. The fifth binary variable is in red (only 1 observation equals 4). Click the User Created option button. Reduce the Number of Binary Variables to 4. The last 2 groups are combined. Pressing the Show Binaries button displays a table of the created binary variables. The second spin button specifies which binary to eliminate from the model. Press the OK button. The scatter plot is now color-coded using the 4 new binaries. The legend shows the color assigned each binary. The legend for S0 shows the color of the binary omitted from the model.

3. Data Editor

To use your own data, click on the Show Notebook button, select the Data Editor tab, and press OK. A five-column spreadsheet appears. You can enter variable names (top row), labels (col 1), and data into this editor. The third variable (col 4) *must* be a binary variable. The fourth variable (Var3 – col 5) is optional. Data from another spreadsheet can be pasted into the data editor. To save data in *Visual Statistics* format, select File and Save or press the 🖫 button. When finished, select File and Exit Editor and Use Data or press the ☺ button. To leave the editor and not use the data, select File and Exit Editor and Discard Data or press the ☹ button.

Basic Learning Exercises   Name _____

Binary Intercept

1. In the Notebook, click on the Scenarios tab, click on One Binary Variable, and select Binary Intercept 2 scenario. Read the scenario, enter 39 in the Version box, and press OK. a) Write the model that will be estimated. b) When you estimate this model how many lines will appear? c) What relation do you expect between the lines?

2. Click on Estimate Model. a) Write down the estimated model. b) Why are there two lines? c) Why are the two lines parallel? c) What is the vertical distance between the two lines?

3. a) If your model is Scps $= \beta_0 + \beta_1$ Tmp $+ \beta_2$ Ovr40, $\alpha = 0.05$, and your null and alternative hypotheses are H_0: $\beta_2 = 0$, H_a: $\beta_2 = 0$, would you reject or not reject H_0 and why? b) How would you interpret this result about people over 40? c) If your null and alternative hypotheses are H_0: $\beta_2 \geq 0$, H_a: $\beta_2 < 0$, would you reject or not reject H_0? d) How would you interpret this result about people over 40? e) What would be an underlying reason for using the hypotheses in a) versus c)?

Binary Slope

4. Press the Show Notebook button and select the Binary Slope scenario. Read the scenario, enter 59 in the Version box, and press OK. a) Write the model that will be estimated. b) When you estimate this model how many lines will appear? c) What relation do you expect between the lines?

5. Click on Estimate Model. Click Options and select Show Y Intercept. a) Write down the estimated model. b) Why are there two lines with the same intercept but different slopes?

6. If your model is StUn $= \beta_0 + \beta_1$ CtyUn $+ \beta_2$ (Urbn)(CtyUn) $+ \varepsilon$, $\alpha = 0.01$, and your null and alternative hypotheses are H_0: $\beta_2 \leq 0$, H_a: $\beta_2 > 0$, would you reject or not reject H_0 and why? How would you interpret this result about urban areas? Why would this be true?

Binary Intercept and Slope
7. Press the Show Notebook button and select the Binary Intercept and Slope scenario. Read the scenario, enter 39 in the Version box, and press OK. a) Write the model that will be estimated. b) When you estimate this model how many lines will appear? c) What relation do you expect between the lines?

8. Click on Estimate Model. a) Write down the estimated model. b) Why are there two lines with different intercepts and slopes? c) What does a different intercept mean? d) What does a different slope mean?

9. a) Suppose your model is Inc $= \beta_0 + \beta_1$ (Exp) $+ \beta_2$ Male $+ \beta_3$ (Male) (Exp) $+ \varepsilon$, $\alpha = 0.05$, and your null and alternative hypotheses are H_0: $\beta_2 = 0$, H_a: $\beta_2 \neq 0$. Would you reject or not reject H_0 and why? b) How would you interpret this result regarding starting salaries? c) Would this result support the contention of gender discrimination? Why?

10. a) Suppose your null and alternative hypotheses are H_0: $\beta_3 = 0$, H_a: $\beta_3 \neq 0$. Would you reject or not reject H_0 and why? b) How would you interpret this result regarding starting salaries? c) Would this result support the contention of gender discrimination? Why? d) What other factors would need to be examined to confirm this result?

Intermediate Learning Exercises   Name _____

Seasonal Period Binaries

11. In the Notebook, click on the Scenarios tab, click on Seasonal Binary Variables, and select the Quarterly Seasonal Binaries scenario. Read the scenario, enter 40 in the Version box, and press OK. a) Write the model that will be estimated. b) When you estimate this model how many lines will appear? c) What relation do you expect between the lines?

12. Click on Estimate Model. Click Options on the menu bar and select Show Y Intercept. a) Write down the estimated model. b) Why are there four lines with different intercepts and slopes? c) What does a different intercept mean? d) What does a different slope mean?

13. Suppose your model is Clos $= \beta_0 + \beta_1$ (Pop) $+ \beta_2$ S2 $+ \beta_3$ (S2) (Pop) $+ \beta_4$ S3 $+ \beta_5$ (S3) (Pop) $+ \beta_6$ S4 $+ \beta_7$ (S4) (Pop) $+ \varepsilon$, $\alpha = 0.05$, and your null and alternative hypotheses are H_0: $\beta_6 = 0$, H_a: $\beta_6 \neq 0$. Would you reject or not reject H_0 and why? How would you interpret this result?

14. If your null and alternative hypotheses are H_0: $\beta_7 = 0$, H_a: $\beta_7 \neq 0$. a) Would you reject or not reject H_0 and why? b) How would you interpret this result regarding clothes sales? c) Redo a) and b) for parameters β_2, β_3, β_4, and β_5.

15. Press the Redefine Binaries button and change the omitted period binary from 1 to 4. Press OK. Press the Estimate Model button. Write down the estimated model. Compare this result with question 12 above. How do the results differ because you omitted a different period?

Other "Seasonal" Binaries

16. Press the Show Notebook button. Select the Daily Binaries scenario. Read the scenario, enter 41 in the Version box, and press OK. Click Options and deselect Show Y Intercept. In this scenario, the "seasonal" or period binaries have nothing to do with seasons. However, since these period binaries are used in the same way as seasonal binaries, period binaries are usually called seasonal binaries. a) Write the model that will be estimated. b) When you estimate this model how many lines will appear? c) What relation do you expect between the lines?

17. Click on Estimate Model. a) Write down the estimated model. b) Why does each line have a different intercept? c) What does the intercept mean? d) Why do the lines have the same slope?

18. The model is Cars $= \beta_0 + \beta_1$ (Per) $+ \beta_2$ S2 $+ \beta_3$ S3 $+ \beta_4$ S4 $+ \beta_5$ S5 $+ \varepsilon$. Many auto experts believe that sales increase during the month because dealerships are more willing to deal near the end of a month in order to earn incentive awards from the automaker. If true, what would be the null and alternative hypotheses? Test this hypothesis at $\alpha = 0.10$. Interpret this result.

19. a) Why would many experts believe that sales for this dealership should be less on Wed., Thurs., and Fri.? b) To test this, what are the three null and alternative hypotheses? c) Using $\alpha = 0.05$, do these estimates support the belief that dealerships should be open more hours?

20. Press the Show Notebook button, select the Data Editor tab, and press OK. Press the 📂 button to open Ques19.vsq. Select the file and press the Open button. The data is from the dealership scenario with a binary (WThF) for Wed.-Thurs.-Fri.. Press the ☺ button to use the data. The red points are WThF. Press the Estimate Model button. The model is Cars $= \beta_0 + \beta_1$ Period $+ \beta_2$ WThF. a) What is the estimated model? b) Test $H_0: \beta_2 \geq 0$, $H_a: \beta_2 < 0$ ($\alpha = 0.05$)? c) Answer question 18. d) Why is the answer different than before?

Advanced Learning Exercises   Name _____

Median Split

21. In the Notebook, click on the Scenarios tab, click on Creating Binaries from 3rd Variables, and select the Equal Frequencies – Median Split scenario. Read the scenario, enter 40 in the Version box, and press OK. Press the Redefine Binaries button to see how the binary variable was defined. a) How many binaries were created? b) Which criterion was used to create the binaries? c) How many observations are there for each binary variable? d) How was the value 2594.5 selected? e) Why is this called a median split? f) Which binary will be omitted from this model?

22. a) What model will be estimated. b) When estimated, how many lines will appear? c) What relation do you expect between the lines?

23. Press the Estimate Model button. a) What is the estimated model? b) If you believe that the wealthy are more risk averse, what are the null and alternative hypotheses? c) Using $\alpha = 0.05$, would you reject or not reject H$_0$ and why?

24. Press the Redefine Binaries button. Click the down arrow on the Omit Binary Variable Number spin button to change the option to None. Press the OK button. The model to be estimated is now Per = $\beta_o + \beta_1$ (Q1) (Rsk) + β_2 (Q2) (Rsk) + ϵ. Notice that Rsk is not in the model as a variable by itself and that *both* binary variables are now in the model. a) What do β_1 and β_2 mean in this model? b) Given your answer above, what will be the estimate for β_1 and β_2? c) Press the Estimate Model button. Read the message that appears and press OK. What is the estimated model? d) Using the results from above, how is the 1.29 calculated?

25. Press the Redefine Binaries button. Click the up arrow on the Omit Binary Variable Number spin button to change the option back to 1. Press the OK button. Select the Intercept Binary option button. How does this model differ from the model with a slope binary?

26. Press the Estimate Model button. What is the estimated model? Using $\alpha = 0.10$, do wealthy investors earn a *different* rate of return on their investments?

Nonlinear Binary Models

27. Click on the Dependent Variable combo box and select Ln Y. The hypothesized model is now $\text{Ln(Per)} = \beta_0 + \beta_1 \text{(Rsk)} + \beta_2 \text{Q2} + \varepsilon$. Press the Estimate Model button. a) Seeing the estimated model, what does the model say about the relationship between percent return and risk? b) Since there is only a binary intercept (therefore the slopes are the same), why does the gap between the two lines increase as Per increases?

28. Select the Slope Binary option button. The proposed model is $\text{Ln(Per)} = \beta_0 + \beta_1 \text{(Rsk)} + \beta_2 \text{(Q2)(Rsk)} + \varepsilon$. Press the Estimate Model button. a) Using $\alpha = 0.05$, test the hypothesis H_0: $\beta_2 \leq 0$, H_a: $\beta_2 > 0$. b) Based on this test, what would you conclude about how wealthy versus the non-wealthy view the relationship between percent return and risk?

One Value per Category

29. Press the Show Notebook button and select the One Value per Category scenario. Read the scenario. a) What do the 1, 2, and 3 represent? Use version 50 and press OK. b) Press the Redefine Binaries button. How many binaries were created? c) How were they created? d) Which binary is being omitted?

30. Using categorical data is one of the most common methods to create binary variables. Press the OK button. The model being estimated is $\text{Con} = \beta_0 + \beta_1 \, 26 \, \text{(Inc)} + \beta_2 \, \text{Q2} + \beta_3 \, \text{(Q2)(Inc)} + \beta_4 \, \text{Q3} + \beta_5 \, \text{(Q3)(Inc)} + \varepsilon$. How many lines will be drawn when the model is estimated? Press the Estimate Model button. Using $\alpha = 0.05$, is there any difference between the three types of individuals?

Individual Learning Projects

Write a report on one of the three topics listed below. Use the cut-and-paste facilities of the module to place the appropriate graphs and tables in your report.

1. The purpose of this project is to demonstrate the use and interpretation of the three types of models using a single binary variable. Select an example to investigate (not a scenario). Describe the dependent, independent and binary variable. For *each* of the three models (binary intercept, binary slope, both binary intercept and slope) present the regression model, explain how the binary variable is used in the model and the question it enables you to answer. Based on this discussion, develop a null and alternative hypothesis. Estimate the model. Provide a table of the model's statistics, an ANOVA table, and a scatterplot showing the estimated model. Discuss these results, interpreting each of the estimated coefficients. Test your hypothesis regarding the binary variable and explain what it means. Before starting this project, make sure you have completed the Basic Learning Exercises.

2. The purpose of this project is to demonstrate that you know how to use and interpret seasonal binary variables. Select either a time series example (not a scenario) or develop your own model using one of the 3 Not Seasonally Adjusted Time Series Data databases. Define your dependent, independent, and seasonal binary variables. Indicate the number of periods in a time frame and the number of time frames covered, e.g., 5 days per week over 10 weeks equals 50 observations. Develop a regression model using an intercept binary (don't forget to tell which period is omitted). Explain how binary variables are used in the model and the questions they enable you to answer. Based on this discussion, develop null and alternative hypotheses that can be tested. Estimate the model. Provide a table of the model's statistics, an ANOVA table, and a scatterplot showing the estimated model. Discuss these results, interpreting each of the estimated coefficients. Test your hypothesis regarding the binary variable and explain what it means regarding the binary variable. Repeat the exercise using either a slope binary model or a slope and intercept binary model. Before starting this project, make sure you have completed the Intermediate Learning Exercises.

3. The purpose of this project is to demonstrate that you know how to interpret a model with multiple binary variables regardless of which binary variable is omitted. You can do this project by using seasonal binaries (do the Intermediate Learning Exercises first) or create your own binaries using a 3rd variable (do the Advanced Learning Exercises first). You can obtain your data from one of the examples (not a scenario) or develop your own model using one of the databases. Your data must have at least four binary variables. Define your dependent, independent, and binary variables. Select a binary model type (intercept, slope, or both). Explain how the binary variables are used in the model and the questions they enable you to answer. Which binary was omitted and why was it selected? Based on this discussion, develop null and alternative hypotheses that can be tested. Estimate the model. Provide a table of the model's statistics, an ANOVA table, and a scatterplot showing the estimated model. Discuss these results, interpreting each of the estimated coefficients. Test your hypothesis regarding the binary variable and explain what it means regarding the binary variable. Re-estimate the model omitting a different binary variable and a third time omitting no binary variable. Show that although the overall results are the same, your estimated coefficients are different (show the relationships between them).

Team Learning Projects

Select one of the projects listed below. In each case, produce a team project that is suitable for an oral presentation using either presentation software or large poster board(s). Graphs and tables must be large enough for your audience to see. Each team member is responsible for producing some of the exhibits. Ask your instructor if a written report is also expected.

1. In this project, a team of four will use the single binary variable model (this is covered in the Basic Learning Exercises). The team should select a dependent variable, two independent variables, and two binary variables from a database. Each independent and binary variable should be expected to affect the dependent variable. Define each variable. Each team member will use the dependent variable, one independent, and one binary variable (there are four combinations) to estimate three binary models (binary intercept, binary slope, both binary intercept and slope). The focus of the presentation should be on the similarities and differences obtained when different variables are used to estimate a dependent variable. The presentation should consider interpretation issues (what questions does the model answer and how is this affected by the type of binary model), as well as statistical results (coefficients, t-statistics, summary statistics). If the scatterplot reveals a nonlinear relationship, variable transformations should be used (see exercises 27 and 28).

2. In this project, a team of three to five will use a seasonal binary model (this is covered in the Intermediate Learning Exercises). The team will model either the number of people employed or unemployment rates. The data is in one of the three databases containing Not Seasonally Adjusted data. The team should select a period of between 96 and 120 months to analyze (press the Time Period button in the Variable Selection window to set the time period). One team member will use the U.S. data, and the rest will use *different* state data. Alternatively, one team member will use the U.S. data, two will use different state data and two will use city data (selecting one city from each state). The independent variable will be the period number (Period). Select any binary variable (e.g., 4thQ?). Analyze three seasonal binary models (intercept binaries, slope binaries, and both intercept and slope binaries). If your scatterplot reveals a nonlinear relationship, variable transformations should be used (see exercises 27 and 28). You may also find that using a single binary variable (i.e., 4thQ? or Jan?) works better than the 12 monthly seasonal binaries (if so, this must be explained *and* illustrated). The focus of the presentation should be on the similarities and differences between the U.S. model and the state models (and city models for teams of five).

3. In this project, a team of four will create binary variables from a 3rd variable (this is covered in the Advanced Learning Exercises). The data must come from one of the databases. The team agrees on the number of observations to use (between 100 and 150, *don't* select the data randomly) and on a dependent and independent variable. Each team member will select a 3rd variable from which to create *at least* 3 binary variables. Each team member will create binary variables in a different way: equal frequencies, equal widths, user created, and one binary per value (use categorical data). Each team member will estimate three models (intercept binaries, slope binaries, and both intercept and slope binaries). If the scatterplot reveals a nonlinear relationship, variable transformations should be used (see exercises 27 and 28). The focus of the presentation will be on how to create binary variables and the similarities and differences in interpreting models using these types of binary variables.

Self-Evaluation Quiz

1. A binary variable
    a. has more than two values.
    b. is a quantitative variable.
    c. is a qualitative variable.
    d. cannot be used in a regression.
    e. is not important to researchers.

2. Depending on how it is used, a binary predictor in a regression could affect
    a. the intercept.
    b. the slope.
    c. the fit.
    d. the t-values.
    e. all of the above.

3. Which statement is *not* correct for an intercept binary Q_i?
    a. The form of the equation is $Y_i = \beta_0 + \beta_1 X_i + \beta_2 Q_i + u_i$.
    b. The coefficient of Q_i is added to the intercept if $Q_i = 1$.
    c. The coefficient of Q_i is subtracted from the intercept if $Q_i = 0$.
    d. The fitted regression line's intercept is shifted up or down by β_2.
    e. We may use a standard t-test for significance for the binary Q_i.

4. Which statement is *incorrect* for a slope binary $X_i Q_i$?
    a. The form of the equation is $Y_i = \beta_0 + \beta_1 X_i + \beta_2 X_i Q_i + u_i$.
    b. The coefficient of X_i is added to the intercept if $Q_i = 1$.
    c. The coefficient of $X_i Q_i$ is added to the slope if $Q_i = 1$.
    d. The fitted regression slope is shifted by β_2 if $Q_i = 1$.
    e. The equation is $Y_i = \beta_0 + \beta_1 X_i + u_i$ if $Q_i = 0$.

5. In a regression of the form $Y_i = \beta_0 + \beta_1 X_i + \beta_2 X_i Q_i + u_i$
    a. the $X_i Q_i$ term is called an interaction.
    b. the intercept may be shifted but not the slope.
    c. both the slope and intercept can shift.
    d. neither the slope nor the intercept will be shifted.
    e. we will see parallel lines on the graph of fitted regression lines.

6. If we see two fitted regression lines with different slopes,
    a. the researcher included only an intercept binary.
    b. the researcher used both a slope and an intercept binary.
    c. the researcher used only a slope binary.
    d. the researcher included an interaction term.
    e. the researcher's slope binary is significantly different from 0.

7. In assigning values to a binary variable, which statement is *incorrect*?
    a. The values assigned usually are 1 and 0.
    b. It is arbitrary which condition is assigned 1 and which is assigned 0.
    c. The value 1 often represents a condition of interest, but this is up to the researcher.
    d. For multiple conditions, we can use a multi-valued variable (e.g., $Q_i = 1, 2, 3, 4$).
    e. 1 represents the presence of an attribute and 0 its absence.

8. A valid set of seasonal binary predictors (each 0 or 1) to use in a regression would be
    a. Jan, Feb, Mar, Apr, May, Jun, Jul, Aug, Sep, Oct, Nov.
    b. Qtr1, Qtr2, Qtr3, Qtr4.
    c. Jan, Feb, Mar, Apr, May, Jun, Jul, Aug, Sep, Oct, Nov, Dec.
    d. Feb, Mar, Apr, May, Jun, Jul, Aug, Sep, Oct, Nov, Dec.
    e. Two choices are correct.

9. If you used quarterly seasonal binaries (Q1, Q2, Q3, Q4) and omitted Q3 from your model
    a. then the regression estimates would be invalid.
    b. then the coefficient of Q1 shows how quarter 1 differs from the average quarter.
    c. then the coefficient of Q2 shows how quarter 2 differs from quarter 3.
    d. then the coefficient of Q2 shows how quarter 2 differs from quarter 1.
    e. then we cannot use a slope binary.

10. To use an attribute variable with 5 categories in a regression we would
    a. create 5 binary predictors but omit one from the model.
    b. create 5 binary predictors and include them all in the model.
    c. include 5 binary predictors in the model and see which were significant.
    d. utilize a single predictor with values 1, 2, 3, 4, 5.
    e. do none of the above.

11. Use of a median split on a third variable Z_i would *not*
    a. free the researcher from having to specify a linear relationship with Z_i.
    b. require that Z_i be normally distributed with no outliers
    c. create two groups of observations of roughly equal size.
    d. permit a simplified t-test test for significance of Z_i.
    e. shift the intercept or slope, depending on how the created binary enters the model.

12. A third variable Z_i can be used
    a. to divide the observations into two groups using a median split.
    b. to divide the observations into four groups using the quartiles.
    c. to divide the observations into k groups using equal Z_i intervals.
    d. to divide the observations into k groups using equal Z_i frequencies.
    e. to divide the observations in any of the above ways.

Glossary of Terms

ANOVA table Decomposition of variance in a regression, showing total sum of squares and its sources (regression, error) along with degrees of freedom and mean squares. *Total* degrees of freedom equals $n - 1$, *error* degrees of freedom equals $n - k - 1$, and the *regression* degrees of freedom equals k, where n is the sample size and k is the number of independent variables.

Binary predictor Independent variable that has only two values, used for qualitative data (e.g., male, female). Generally, 1 denotes the presence of the attribute of interest and 0 denotes its absence, but other values may be used (e.g., 1 and 2). If the attribute has c categories, we need c – 1 binary variables. See **Intercept binary, Slope binary,** and **Seasonal binary**.

Estimated coefficient Sample statistic used to estimate a parameter of the regression model. The estimated regression coefficients are denoted $\hat{\beta}_0$, $\hat{\beta}_1, \hat{\beta}_2, ..., \hat{\beta}_k$. See **Ordinary least squares**.

F statistic In a regression ANOVA table, the ratio of the *regression* mean square to the *error* mean square. It is used to test the overall significance of the regression. See **p-value**.

Interaction See **Slope binary**.

Intercept Value of the dependent variable when all the independent variables in the regression model are zero. Zero values of X_i may have little or no meaning for some models.

Intercept binary A simple regression model can be modified to fit *two* regression lines with different intercepts by including a binary predictor ($Q = 0$, $Q = 1$). The form of the equation is $Y_i = \beta_0 + \beta_1 X_i + \beta_2 Q_i + u_i$. When $Q_i = 0$ the equation's intercept is β_0. When $Q_i = 1$ the equation's intercept is $\beta_0 + \beta_2$. Since β_2 could be negative, the line might be shifted either up or down. See **Slope binary**.

Median split Binary predictor created from another variable Z_i by defining $Q_i = 0$ if Z_i is below its median and $Q_i = 1$ if Z_i is above its median. In this way, a researcher can investigate whether "low" and "high" values of Z_i have different effects.

Multiple binary predictors More than one qualitative predictor can be included in a model. If an attribute has c categories, we use c– 1 binaries. For example, an individual's marital status (single, married, divorced, widowed) can be coded using *three* binaries. See **Seasonal binary**.

Multiple correlation coefficient Measure of overall fit in a regression. It is the square root of R^2. It may be interpreted as the correlation between Y_{actual} and Y_{fitted} over all n observations.

Parameter Numerical constant needed to define a particular model or distribution. A regression model's parameters are the intercept and the coefficients of the k independent variables, whose true values are denoted β_0, $\beta_1, \beta_2, ..., \beta_k$. See **Estimated coefficient**.

P-value Probability (usually two-tailed) of committing type I error if we reject the null hypothesis that a parameter is zero (for example, a regression coefficient). A small p-value (such as 0.01) would incline us to reject the hypothesis that the true parameter is zero.

Qualitative predictor One whose value is not a number (e.g., eye color). In contrast, a *quantitative* variable is one whose value is numerical (e.g., income). See **Binary predictor**.

R-squared Ratio of the *regression* sum of squares to the *total* sum of squares. R^2 near 0 indicates the fit is poor while R^2 near 1 indicates the fit is good. Also called coefficient of determination.

Seasonal binary The number of seasonal binaries is always one less than the number of seasons. One seasonal period must be omitted. Thus, quarterly data (four periods) will require three binaries, and monthly data (12 periods) will require 11 binaries. The choice of which seasonal period to omit is arbitrary. For example, in quarterly data we could omit the first quarter:

Qtr2 = 1 if it is the 2nd quarter, 0 otherwise

Qtr3 = 1 if it is the 3rd quarter, 0 otherwise

Qtr4 = 1 if it is the 4th quarter, 0 otherwise

The omitted period (Qtr1) may be viewed as the baseline, reflected in the intercept when the other binaries are all zero. Failure to omit one seasonal binary creates perfect multicollinearity (in this example, Qtr1 = 1− Qtr2 − Qtr3 − Qtr4) which poses a dire estimation problem.

Slope Coefficient of an independent variable. If $Y_i = \beta_0 + \beta_1 X_i$ then β_1 is the change in the Y for a *one unit* change in X. If $Y_i = \beta_0 + \beta_1 \ln X_i$ then $\beta_1/100$ is the change in Y for a *one percent* change in X. If $\ln Y_i = \beta_0 + \beta_1 X_i$ then $100\beta_1$ is the *percent* change in Y for a *one unit* change in X. If $\ln Y_i = \beta_0 + \beta_1 \ln X_i$ then β_1 is the *elasticity*, or *percent* change in Y for a *one percent* change in X.

Slope binary A simple regression can be modified to fit *two* regression lines with different slopes by including an *interaction* term equal to the independent variable X_i multiplied by a qualitative predictor Q_i. The form of the equation is $Y_i = \beta_0 + \beta_1 X_i + \beta_2 X_i Q_i + u_i$. When $Q_i = 0$ the slope is β_1. When $Q_i = 1$ the slope is $\beta_1 + \beta_2$. Since β_2 can be negative, the slope for $Q_i = 1$ may be either greater or smaller than β_1. See **Intercept binary**.

Standard error Estimate of the standard deviation of the stochastic disturbances, using the square root of the sum of the squared residuals, divided by $n - k - 1$, where n is the sample size and k is the number of independent variables.

Transformed variable Common transformations of the variables are the logarithmic transformation $[\ln(X_i)$ or $\ln(Y_i)]$, raising to a power $[X_i^c$ or $Y_i^c]$, inversion $[1/X_i$ or $1/Y_i]$, or standardization by subtracting the mean and dividing by the standard deviation.

t-value Ratio of an estimated coefficient in a regression model to its standard error, used to test the null hypothesis that the parameter is zero. This ratio is distributed as Student's t if the parameter is zero. A large t-value would suggest that the true parameter is not zero.

Solutions to Self-Evaluation Quiz

1. c Read the Overview of Concepts, Illustration of Concepts. Consult the Glossary.
2. e Do Exercises 1–6. Read the Overview of Concepts, Illustration of Concepts.
3. c Do Exercises 1–3. Read the Overview of Concepts, Illustration of Concepts.
4. b Do Exercises 4–6. Read the Overview of Concepts, Illustration of Concepts.
5. a Do Exercises 4–6. Read the Overview of Concepts, Illustration of Concepts.
6. d Do Exercises 1–10. Read the Overview of Concepts, Illustration of Concepts.
7. d Do Exercises 1–10. Read the Overview of Concepts, Illustration of Concepts.
8. e Do Exercises 11–15. Read the Overview of Concepts, Illustration of Concepts.
9. c Do Exercises 11, 12, 15. Read the Overview of Concepts, Illustration of Concepts.
10. a Do Exercises 29, 30. Read the Overview of Concepts, Illustration of Concepts.
11. b Do Exercises 21–26. Read the Overview of Concepts, Illustration of Concepts.
12. e Do Exercises 21–26. Read the Overview of Concepts, Illustration of Concepts.

CHAPTER 20

Visualizing Trends and Seasonality

CONCEPTS
- Time series, Periodicity, Trend, Cycle, Seasonal, Error, Decomposition, Fitted Trend, Additive Model, Multiplicative Model

OBJECTIVES
- Understand periodicity

- Recognize the difficulty in separating trend, seasonality and error, and why sample size is important

- Understand the difference between additive and multiplicative seasonality

- Recognize the difference between the true and fitted trend and the importance of selecting the correct functional form for the fitted trend

- Understand common fit statistics (MAPE, R^2, standard error) and what they tell us about the model

Overview of Concepts

Time series data consists of observations on a variable over several periods of time. For example, a firm uses time series data to monitor its financial situation (e.g., unit sales, market share, return on assets, stock prices), the quality of its product (e.g., warranty claims, defect rates, customer satisfaction), or general economic conditions (e.g., inflation, prime rate, S&P 500 stock index). Time series **periodicity** is most commonly annual (1 observation per year), quarterly (4 observations per year), or monthly (12 observations per year). Time series **decomposition** seeks to separate a time series into four components: trend, cycle, seasonality, and error. These components are assumed to follow an additive or a multiplicative model:

Additive Model	Time Series = Trend + Cycle + Seasonality + Error
Multiplicative Model	Time Series = Trend × Cycle × Seasonality × Error

Trend is the general pattern over many periods (change over a few periods is not a trend). The statistician estimates the trend by using a **fitted trend** model. We may imagine three general trends: growth, stability, or decline. Yet a trend may not be that simple, as illustrated in Figures 1, 2, and 3, which depict graphs whose Y-axes show the variable of interest and whose X-axes show time. Specific trend models (linear, quadratic, cubic, exponential) may be used to try to estimate such trends. Forecasters prefer the simplest trend model that adequately matches the trend (the principle of Occam's Razor) because simple models are easier to interpret and explain to others.

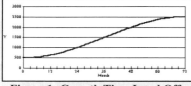
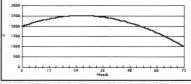
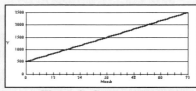
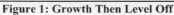

| Figure 1: Growth Then Level Off | Figure 2: Peak Then Decline | Figure 3: Constant Increase |

Cycle is a repetitive up-and-down movement about a trend over several years. For example, analysts have studied cycles for sales of new automobiles, new home construction, inventories, and investment. But this module omits cycles because their timing is erratic, their causes are complex, and over a small number of years they are undetectable or may resemble a trend.

Seasonal pattern is a repetitive cyclical movement within a year (months, quarters). For example, many retail businesses experience strong sales during the fourth quarter because of Christmas. Automobile sales rise when new models are released. Peak demand for airline flights to Europe occurs during summer vacation travel. Although often imagined as sine waves, seasonal patterns may not be smooth. Peaks and valleys can occur in any month or quarter, and each industry may face its own unique seasonal pattern.

Error is a random disturbance that follows no pattern. This "random noise" reflects all factors other than trend, cycle, and seasonality. Large error components are common. For example, daily prices of volatile stocks are important to financial analysts. When the error is large, it may be difficult to isolate other individual model components.

Illustration of Concepts

Motor vehicle deaths are an example of **time series** data. Many states have enjoyed a downward trend in motor vehicle deaths over the past few decades. The graph below shows this **trend** using data with monthly **periodicity**. In this example, a linear **fitted trend** model is shown by the heavy red line. The slope of this line says that monthly traffic deaths have declined at an average rate of 0.2198 deaths per month from a starting point of 171.6 (forecasts could be rounded to integers). Other trend models (quadratic, cubic, or exponential) might give a better fit (note the low R^2) but all would support the idea of a slow decline in deaths. The linear model has the advantage of simplicity.

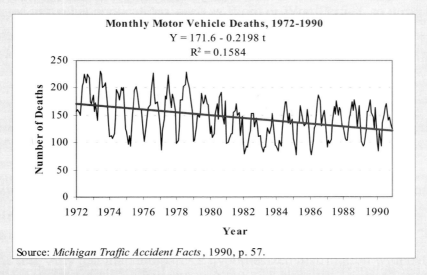

Source: *Michigan Traffic Accident Facts*, 1990, p. 57.

In addition to trend, you can see a distinct **seasonal** pattern in this time series: Deaths are higher in the warm months and lower in the cool months. This is probably due to increased travel during the summer months. No **cycles** can be inferred from this graph (at least using "eyeball" methods). But you can see that trend and seasonality still do not account for all the variation in the data. Any remaining variation is nonsystematic **error** due to unpredictable events (such as mild or severe weather). For example, the summer "high" is not as pronounced in 1982 and 1983, and the winter "low" is less apparent in 1988 and 1989. Overall, the error component appears relatively small, and we might conclude that variation in monthly traffic deaths is mostly due to trend and seasonal patterns.

Time series **decomposition** separates these overlaid components and assesses their relative magnitude. Two general types of time series models are **additive models** and **multiplicative models**. The first step in estimating either of these models is to estimate the fitted trend models. The *linear* trend is the simplest (constant growth or decline with no turning points). Non-linear trends include the *quadratic* trend (growth or decline with one turning point), *cubic* trend (growth or decline with two turning points), or *exponential* trend (constant percent growth or decline with no turning points). Once we have a fitted trend, seasonal factors may be estimated in relation to the fitted trend. Estimates will be better if the researcher has more data to work with. Finally, the cyclical component could be estimated. The rest is error.

Orientation to Basic Features

This module generates monthly, quarterly or yearly data that conforms to a model that you specify, consisting of trend, seasonality, and error. You can fit a linear, quadratic, cubic, or exponential model to the sample and estimate the seasonality. You can compare the estimated trend and seasonality to the true trend and seasonality.

1. **Opening Screen**

    Start the module by clicking on the module's icon, title, or chapter number in the *Visual Statistics* menu and pressing the Run Module button. When the module is loaded, you will be on the introduction page of the Notebook. Read the questions and then click the Concepts tab to see the concepts that you will learn. Click on the Scenarios tab. Select Monthly Data, choose a scenario, and press OK. The top of the screen shows a graph of the sample data. The module's Control Panel appears on the bottom. A flashing New Sample button will indicate when you have changed one or more control settings.

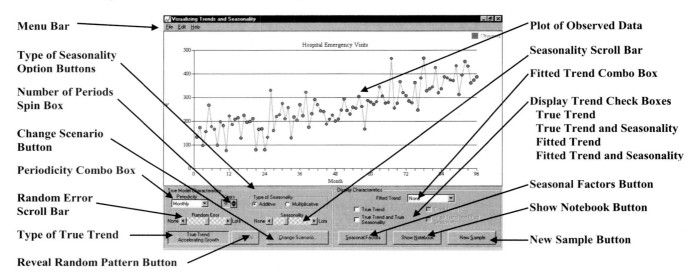

2. **Selecting a Trend**

    The true trend can be selected in two simple ways:

    a. You can use a scenario that you selected from the Notebook. To change this scenario click the Change Scenario button (lower left corner of display). Four situations (monthly, quarterly, and yearly data) are available.

    b. You can select from a menu of 15 different trends by clicking on the Show Notebook button, selecting the Templates tab, and pressing OK. A screen like the one to the right will appear. Any of these trends (or a random trend, indicated by the question mark button) can be selected. Click the Describe button to see an explanation of the selected trend. Click OK to use the trend selected, or Cancel to return to the Notebook. Once a template has been selected the Change Scenario

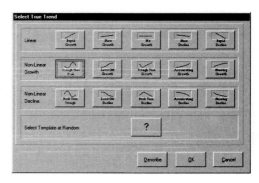

    button becomes a Change Template button, providing easy access to this template.

3. **Seasonality and Random Error**

   When you return to the main screen, use the Seasonality and Random Error scroll bars to change the amount of seasonality and random error. Click New Sample. The graph shows a sample of data, based upon the true model, seasonality, and error you specified.

4. **Fitted Trend**

   Click on the Fitted Trend combo box to select the type of trend you wish to fit (None, Linear, Quadratic, Cubic, Exponential). The equation of the fitted model is shown at the top of the graph, along with its fit statistics (R^2, MSE, and MAPE) and the Fitted Trend check box becomes active. Click it to display the fitted trend as a red line on the graph.

5. **Fitted Trend and Seasonality**

   If you have chosen a trend from the Fitted Trend combo box, the Fitted Trend and Seasonality check box becomes active. Click it to see the fitted trend with seasonality as a magenta line on the graph. If seasonality is present, the magenta line should provide a better visual fit to your sample. There can be fitted seasonality even if you set the Seasonality scroll bar to None, because random error alone can erroneously suggest a seasonal pattern.

6. **True Trend and True Seasonality**

   Deselect the Fitted Trend and Seasonality check box. Select the True Trend check box to see the true trend displayed as a blue line on the graph. Select the True Trend and Seasonality check box, to see the true trend with its seasonality as a cyan line. The effect of seasonality is easily seen. In real data, these two lines are unknown. Being able to visualize these lines is one of the advantages of a simulation. Deselect True Trend. Select Fitted Trend and Seasonality to see how well your fitted model reflects the components of the true model. This is illustrated to the right.

   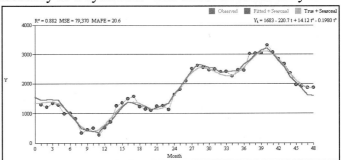

7. **Copying a Display**

   Click on the display you wish to copy. Its window title will be highlighted. Select Copy from the Edit menu (on the menu bar at the top of the screen) or Ctrl-C to copy the display. It can then be pasted into other applications, such as Word or WordPerfect, so it can be printed.

8. **Help**

   Click on Help on the menu bar at the top of the screen. Search for Help lets you search an index for this module, Contents shows a table of contents for this module, Using Help gives instructions on how to use Help, and About gives licensing and copyright information.

9. **Exit**

   Close the module by selecting Exit in the File menu (or click ☒ in the upper right-hand corner of the window). You will be returned to the *Visual Statistics* main menu.

Orientation to Additional Features

1. **Additive or Multiplicative Model**
   Two types of seasonality can be modeled (Additive, Multiplicative). Select the desired check box and click the New Sample button to update the display.

2. **Periodicity and Number of Periods**
   Click on the Periodicity combo box to choose between yearly, quarterly, and monthly data. The Number of Periods spin button specifies the number of periods to sample.

3. **Do-It-Yourself Trend**
   There are two ways you can create your own trend:

   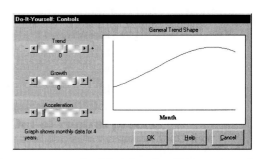

   a. You can create your own trend by opening the Notebook, selecting the Do-It-Yourself tab, clicking on Scroll Bar Controls, and pressing OK. A screen like the one to the right will appear. The scroll bars control the trend, growth, and acceleration parameters. Your trend is shown on the accompanying graph. Click Help to get more information, OK to use the trend created, or Cancel to return to the Notebook. Once a trend has been created, the Change Scenario button becomes a Change Trend button, providing easy access to the scroll bar controls.

   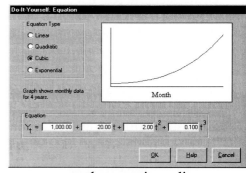

   b. You can create your own equation by opening the Notebook, selecting the Do-It-Yourself tab, clicking Enter Equation Parameters, and pressing OK. A screen like the one to the right will appear. Select an equation type and enter its parameter values. Your trend is shown on the small graph. Click Help to get more information, OK to use the trend created, or Cancel to return to the Notebook. Once you have created a trend, the Change Scenario button becomes a Change Trend button, providing easy access to the equation editor.

4. **Seasonal Factors**
   Click on Seasonal Factors to reveal a bar graph of the true seasonal factors and fitted seasonal factors. An example is to the right. Click on Show 95% CI to display a confidence interval about the fitted seasonal factors. Press Ctrl-C to copy the seasonal factors graph to the clipboard.

   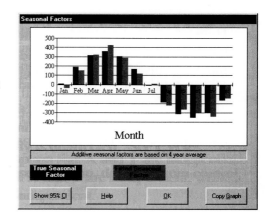

Basic Learning Exercises

Name _____

Trend Component

Press the Show Notebook button, select the Scenarios tab, click on Monthly Data, and select General Aviation Shipments. Read the scenario and click OK.

1. Click on Options on the menu bar (top of screen) and select Display True Trend. Why would general aviation shipments have this type of trend (Peak then Trough)?

2. Under Fitted Trend, select Cubic. Use the check boxes to deselect True Trend and select Fitted Trend. Look at the fit statistics. Record the smallest and largest value of R^2, MSE, and MAPE from 10 different samples. If you extrapolated the fitted cubic trend for a few periods, would it give reasonable forecasts?

    R^2 _____   MSE _____   MAPE _____

3. Use the scroll bar to increase Random Error to Lots (all the way to the right). Take 10 samples and again record the smallest and largest value of R^2, MSE, and MAPE. Note any irregularities in the behavior of these statistics.

    R^2 _____   MSE _____   MAPE _____

4. When you increased the random error, what happened to the fit? Does a larger or smaller value for R^2, MSE, and MAPE signify a "better fit"?

5. Change Fitted Trend to Quadratic. Take 10 samples and record the smallest and largest value of R^2, MSE, and MAPE. What happened to the fit statistics, compared with the cubic trend you estimated in exercise 3? If you extrapolated the fitted quadratic trend for a few periods, would it give reasonable forecasts? Explain.

    R^2 _____   MSE _____   MAPE _____

6. Click Show Notebook, select the Templates tab and click OK. Select the Peak then Decline Template (third row, middle button). Click the Describe button. Read the description, click OK, and click OK again. Set Fitted Trend to Linear. Take 10 samples and record the smallest and largest values of R^2, MSE, and MAPE. Would forecasts based on the linear model be too low, too high, or about right? Explain. Give an example of when this trend could occur.

    R^2 _____   MSE _____   MAPE _____

7. Choose a quadratic fitted model. Take 10 samples and record the smallest and largest values of R^2, MSE, and MAPE. Then choose a cubic fitted model and do the same. Compared to the linear, do the quadratic and cubic models offer improved fit? All things considered, which of the three fitted trend models is preferable? Explain.

    Quadratic: R^2 _____   MSE _____   MAPE _____
    Cubic: R^2 _____   MSE _____   MAPE _____

8. Explain why the cubic model cannot give a worse fit than a linear or quadratic model. Since this is so, why wouldn't a cubic trend always be preferable? Explain.

9. Change Fitted Trend to Quadratic. Increase the number of years to 8. Take 10 samples and record the smallest and largest value of R^2, MSE, and MAPE. Then reduce the number of years to 3 and do the same. How does a smaller sample size affect the fit statistics?

    8 years: R^2 _____   MSE _____   MAPE _____
    3 years: R^2 _____   MSE _____   MAPE _____

10. In general, are larger samples preferred? If you had data over 8 years, but during the first four years the country was at war, would using all 8 years of data be a good idea? Explain.

Intermediate Learning Exercises   Name _____

Seasonal Component

Press the Change Scenario button, select Hospital Emergency Visits, read the scenario, and click OK. Set Seasonality to Lots and Random Error to None. Select Display True Trend.

11. What is the shape of the true trend? Use the combo box to select a fitted trend. Then use the check boxes to select both Fitted Trend and True Trend so that both are displayed (true trend in blue, fitted trend in red). Which fitted trend works the best? The worst? Explain.

12. Choose an exponential fitted trend. Uncheck both Fitted Trend and True Trend (to reduce screen clutter). Then check both True Trend and True Seasonality and Fitted Trend and Fitted Seasonality. Notice that the estimated model (magenta line) and true model (cyan line) are almost identical. Click the Seasonal Factors button. Click Show 95% CI. Why is seasonality so accurately estimated? Is this situation realistic?

13. Increase the error on the Random Error scroll bar by eight clicks (the middle of the scroll bar). Take a new sample and compare the true model (cyan line) and estimated model (magenta line). Click Seasonal Factors. Click Show 95% CI. Is this what you expected? How many of the twelve confidence intervals contain 0? What does this mean?

14. Increase the error to its maximum on the Random Error scroll bar. Take a new sample and visually compare the true model (cyan line) and estimated model (magenta line). Click Seasonal Factors. Click Show 95% CI. a) What do you notice about the length of the confidence intervals? b) How many of the 12 intervals now contain 0? c) Interpret this result. Why do more of the intervals contain 0?

15. What role does random error play in estimating seasonality?

Periodicity

Click Change Scenario and click on Next page in the lower right corner of the current page to display scenarios using quarterly data. Click on Maternal Hospital Stay. Read the scenario and click OK. Select a cubic fitted trend. Select True Trend and True Seasonality and Fitted Trend and Fitted Seasonality. Change the number of years to 5.

16. Set the Seasonality scroll bar to Lots and click New Sample. Why is the fitted model (magenta line) jagged? Does it resemble the true model (cyan)?

17. Change the amount of random error to Lots. Take a new sample. Compare the fitted model (magenta line) with the true model (cyan). Click on Seasonal Factors. Compare the red bars and the blue bars. Click Show 95% CI. Do this experiment two or three times. Evaluate the quality of your seasonal estimates.

18. Triple the number of years to 15 (you now have 60 quarterly observations) and repeat the process in exercise 17. Evaluate the quality of your seasonal model and the estimated seasonal factors and their confidence intervals relative to those with five years of data.

19. Return the number of years to 5 but change the periodicity to monthly (you now have 60 monthly observations). Repeat the process in exercises 16 and 17. Evaluate the quality of your seasonal estimates and confidence intervals relative to those in exercises 16 and 17.

20. Why do you think that using 60 quarterly estimates gives more accurate estimates of seasonality than does using 60 monthly observations?

Advanced Learning Exercises   **Name** _____

Exploring Multiplicative Time Series Models
Click Show Notebook, select the Scenarios tab, click on Monthly Data, and select Residential
Security Systems. Read the scenario and click OK. Select a Cubic trend. Use the check boxes to
display the True Trend and True Seasonality and Fitted Trend and Fitted Seasonality.

21. Set Random Error to None. Press the New Sample button. How does the fitted model
     (magenta) compare with the true model (cyan)? What do you notice about the magnitude of
     the seasonality of the true time series displayed on the graph? Why?

22. Press the Change Scenario button. Select the General Aviation Shipments scenario. Read
     the scenario and click OK. Set Random Error to None and set Seasonality to the midpoint of
     its scroll bar. Select a Cubic trend. Press the New Sample button. What do you notice about
     the magnitude of the seasonality?

23. Press the Show Notebook button. Click on the Templates tab and click OK. Select the No
     Growth template (3rd button, 1st row) and click OK. Select a Linear trend. What do you
     notice about seasonality?

24. Interpret what multiplicative seasonality means. Give an example of this type of seasonality.
     Do you think this type of seasonality is rare or common?

25. Press the Show Notebook button, select the Scenarios tab, click on Monthly Data, select the
     General Aviation Shipments scenario, and click OK. Set Random Error to Lots, set
     Seasonality to the midpoint of its scroll bar, and set Fitted Trend to Cubic. Press the New
     Sample button. Press the Seasonal Factors button and click Show 95% CI. Is multiplicative
     seasonality more easily estimated than additive seasonality (look at exercise 13 above)? Why
     or why not?

Exploring the Do-It-Yourself Methods of Creating a Time Series

26. Set Periodicity to Annual, choose 15 years of data, press Show Notebook, select the Do-It-Yourself tab, click on Scroll Bar Controls, and click OK. Play with each control one at a time, setting it back to zero before going on to the next control. Explain what each control does.

27. How would you get a U-shaped curve? An upside down U-shaped curve? A curve with a peak, followed by a trough?

28. Press Show Notebook, click on Next page to bring up the Enter Equation Parameters option. Click OK. Select Exponential. Try various values for the second term between 0.7 and 1.3. Describe what happens to the function.

29. Recall that in exercise 26 you set the Periodicity to Annual. What does a coefficient of 1.05 for the second term mean? If this were quarterly or monthly data, what would it mean? Is this a likely growth rate for someone's annual salary? Someone's monthly salary?

30. Select Cubic Equation. How would you get a U-shaped curve? An upside-down U-shaped curve? A curve with a peak followed by a trough?

31. Under what circumstances would you prefer to use the Do-It-Yourself methods to create an equation rather than the buttons on the template pallet?

Individual Learning Projects

Write a report on one of the three topics listed below. Use the cut-and-paste facilities of the module to place the appropriate graphs in your report. For each project, generate data by using the Scenario, Template or Do-It-Yourself tabs. If the data comes from a scenario, discuss the reason for its apparent trend, type of seasonality (multiplicative or additive), amount of seasonality, and amount of random error. Otherwise, give an example of the type of situation that would have the trend, type of seasonality (multiplicative or additive), amount of seasonality, and amount of random error you selected.

1. The amount of seasonality or random error in a data set affects the reliability of estimation. However, the two components have very different meanings. Use monthly data. Estimate the model with different amounts of random error and seasonality. Explain and illustrate the role each factor plays in reliably estimating the data's trend and seasonality.

2. Fit statistics show how well a fitted trend explains the data. Evaluate their effectiveness in leading a statistician to use the best fitted trend. Choose the Templates tab in the Notebook, and click the Random button. Generate 60 observations of data using an additive model with no seasonality and lots of random error. Fit three different trends to the data before you click Reveal Random Trend. How effective were the fit statistics in guiding you to the correct fitted trend? Repeat this process two more times.

3. Larger sample sizes are generally preferred. Suppose you have five years of quarterly sales data and are given ten more. Alternately, imagine that you replace five years of quarterly sales data with monthly sales data covering the same five years. Either would result in a threefold increase in your sample size. Explain and illustrate the different issues you would encounter in estimating trend and seasonality with these two larger data sets.

Team Learning Projects

Select one of the three projects listed below. In each case, produce a team project that is suitable for an oral presentation. Use presentation software or large poster boards to display your results. Graphs should be large enough for your audience to see. Each team member should be responsible for producing some of the graphs. Include in your report a copy of all graphs and statistics that you evaluated. Ask your instructor if a written report is also expected. If the data comes from a scenario, discuss the reason for its apparent trend, type of seasonality (multiplicative or additive), amount of seasonality and amount of random error. Otherwise, give an example of the type of situation that would have the trend, type of seasonality (multiplicative or additive), amount of seasonality, and amount of random error you selected.

1. This is a project for a team of three or more. Investigate the role sample size plays in estimating models with different amounts of error. Generate data by using the Template or Scenario tab. The team should agree on an amount of seasonality, the true trend, the periodicity, three sample sizes (number of years), and three fitted trends (one should be the correct trend). Each team member should select a different amount of error (the team should cover the entire error range). Using that error, each team member should take five samples for each sample size and fitted trend combination. For each sample record the estimated model, its fit statistics, and its fitted seasonal factors. After you have finished estimation, analyze the statistics you recorded. Illustrate and explain how sample size aids in estimating the correct trend and seasonality.

2. This is a project for a team of three or more. Investigate the role sample size plays in estimating trend models with different amounts of seasonality. Generate data by using the Template or Scenario tab. The team should agree on an amount of error, the true trend, the periodicity, three sample sizes (number of years), and three fitted trends (one should be the correct trend). Each team member should select a different amount of seasonality (the team should cover the entire seasonality range). Using that seasonality, each team member should take five samples for each sample size and fitted trend combination. For each sample record the estimated model, its fit statistics, and its fitted seasonal factors. After you have finished estimation, analyze the statistics you recorded. Illustrate and explain how sample size aids in estimating the correct trend and seasonality.

3. This is a project for a team of three. Each team member should use the Do-It-Yourself Equation method to generate a realistic time series exhibiting appropriate amounts of seasonality and random error. The team should interact in planning each member's contribution. The first team member should create a time series representing monthly measurements of ozone concentrations in a city over a 10-year period during which successful government efforts are being made to reduce this pollutant (use 280 parts per billion as the starting point). The second team member should create a time series representing monthly earnings by a free-lance computer systems consultant during the first 60 months of acting as a solo consultant. The third team member should create a time series representing quarterly sales of a new product over a 5-year life cycle, during which sales rapidly increase, and then drop off sharply (use any starting point that works). In each case, explain how the levels of seasonality and randomness were chosen, and determine whether the seasonal factors can be estimated accurately from the generated data.

Self-Evaluation Quiz

1. Which is *not* a component of a time series?
   a. Trend.
   b. Error.
   c. Cycle.
   d. Amplitude.
   e. Seasonality.

2. Cycles often are ignored in time series decomposition because
   a. there is no agreed-upon theory of cycles.
   b. their periodicity is irregular.
   c. their interpretation is not primarily a statistical question.
   d. their underlying causes are varied.
   e. all of the above.

3. Which statements are *not* correct concerning fitted trend?
   a. The quadratic model allows a single peak or trough.
   b. The linear model allows no peak or trough.
   c. The cubic model allows three peaks or troughs.
   d. The exponential model allows no peak or trough.
   e. The cubic model is particularly dangerous if extrapolated.

4. Which model allows a constant percent rate of growth?
   a. Linear.
   b. Quadratic.
   c. Cubic.
   d. Exponential.
   e. None of the above.

5. Which statistic(s) of fit will be unit-free?
   a. MAPE.
   b. MSE.
   c. R-squared.
   d. Only a and c.
   e. Only a and b.

6. If a cubic trend is fitted instead of a quadratic trend
   a. the R-squared cannot fall.
   b. the R-squared cannot rise.
   c. the R-squared can be higher or lower.
   d. the R-squared is irrelevant.
   e. none of the above is correct.

7. If the true trend is cubic and we fit a quadratic model
   a. the MAPE will be too low.
   b. the seasonal factors may be poorly estimated.
   c. the R-squared will be low.
   d. all of the above.
   e. both b and c.

8. If we fit a linear trend to data that are growing exponentially
   a. the fitted trend will be too low at the beginning and end.
   b. the fitted trend will be too high in the middle.
   c. the forecasts (if extrapolated) will be too low.
   d. the fit could probably be improved by fitting a quadratic model.
   e. all of the above.

9. Seasonal factors
   a. always form a smooth, sinusoidal monthly cycle.
   b. are irrelevant for annual data.
   c. are calculated before the trend is estimated.
   d. are ratios between 0 and 1 in the additive model.
   e. are irrelevant for most business data.

10. Which is *not* true of confidence intervals for seasonal factors?
    a. They are wider if there is little seasonality.
    b. They are wider if the number of observed years is small.
    c. They are wider if the random error is high.
    d. They are wider if an inappropriate trend model is fitted.
    e. They are wider if outliers are present.

11. If random error is large but the correct functional form is specified, which is *most likely* to be estimated well in monthly data?
    a. Mean seasonal factors.
    b. Fitted trend.
    c. Estimated cycles.
    d. Confidence intervals for seasonality.
    e. Forecasts for the next period.

12. Which statement is *not* correct in comparing additive with multiplicative models?
    a. The additive model may be too simplistic for financial data that reflect inflation.
    b. The multiplicative model may be harder to explain to the average manager.
    c. Relative growth is best handled by a multiplicative model.
    d. Additive models may fail when long time periods are covered.
    e. Monthly data works best with additive models due to seasonality.

Glossary of Terms

Additive model Model of time series decomposition of the form $Y = T + C + S + E$ where Y is the time series, T is the trend, C is the cycle, S is the seasonal, and E is the error. Generally, the linear model is appropriate for a series with little trend or over short periods of time. Since financial data usually has trend (e.g., due to inflation) the additive model is used less often.

Cubic trend Polynomial trend model of the form $Y = \beta_0 + \beta_1 t + \beta_2 t^2 + \beta_3 t^3$ which is used to fit a time series trend with two turning points. The disadvantage of a cubic trend (or any higher-order polynomial) is that they are harder to interpret or explain, and may give strange forecasts when extrapolated more than a few periods.

Cycle Component of time series data that represents repetitive movement about a trend over several years. Cycles are difficult to analyze unless the theoretical basis for their existence can be described in a formal model (e.g., a capital goods replacement cycle based on life of the good). For this reason, they are not considered in this module.

Decomposition Attempt to divide a time series into four components: trend (long-term tendency), cycle (fluctuation over several years), seasonal (fluctuation within a year), and error (random "noise" that is not systematic). See **Additive model** and **Multiplicative model**.

Error Irregular component of a time series which follows no detectable pattern. The error may be assumed additive or multiplicative.

Exponential Trend Trend model of the form $Y = \beta_0 t^{\beta_1}$ which is used to fit a non-linear time series trend with constant percent growth ($\beta_1 > 1$) or decline ($\beta_1 < 1$) each period. It is an attractive choice for modeling growth in economic data or biological populations. It is considered intrinsically linear because its logarithmic form is a straight line.

Fit statistics Collective name given to certain statistics such as R^2, MAPE, and MSE. These statistics measure the correspondence between observed data and a proposed model.

Fitted trend Mathematical equation based on historical data for a time series that attempts to define the long-term pattern of change (e.g., linear, quadratic, cubic, exponential).

Linear trend Trend model of the form $Y = \beta_0 + \beta_1 t$ which is used to fit a time series trend with no turning points (constant change each period). It is the most common trend model because it is simple and easy to explain.

MAPE Mean absolute percent error of a fitted time series model. Because it is a percent, it is unit-free, allowing us to compare MAPE between time series variables that are measured in different units (e.g., dollars and yen). MAPE is easy to understand, but is sensitive to division by small data values, and cannot be used with negative data. Other things equal, smaller MAPE signifies a better fit.

MSE Mean squared error, obtained by summing the squared residuals from a fitted time series model and dividing by the number of time periods. It is not unit-free, so it cannot be used to compare time series variables that are measured in different units (e.g., dollars and yen). Its meaning is unintuitive, but it works with any kind of data and has useful mathematical properties. Other things equal, smaller MSE signifies a better fit. The MSE is sometimes called MSD (mean squared deviation).

Multiplicative model Model of time series decomposition of the form $Y = T \times C \times S \times E$ where Y is the time series, T is the trend, C is the cycle, S is the seasonal, and E is the error. Generally, this model is preferred for strongly trended data observed over many time periods, because it expressed variation in *relative* terms. It is useful, for example, for financial data whose growth over time reflects inflation (e.g., sales).

Periodicity Number of subperiods over which a regular cycle or seasonal pattern is observed (e.g., months or quarters). If the data are annual, no seasonality can be observed.

Quadratic trend Polynomial trend model of the form $Y = \beta_0 + \beta_1 t + \beta_2 t^2$ which is used to fit a time series trend with one turning point. It is harder to explain and interpret than a linear model. However, it may produce useful forecasts in the very short run.

R-squared Ratio of the fitted model's sum of squares to the total sum of squares. It is unit-free, so it can be used to compare variables that are measured in different units (e.g., dollars and yen). R^2 near 0 indicates the fit is poor, while R^2 near 1 indicates a good fit.

Seasonal Repetitive cyclical movement about a trend within a calendar year (e.g., over 12 months or 4 quarters). Also, a reference to the seasonal component of time series data. The concept can be generalized to include other kinds of sub-period variation, such as weekly, daily, hourly, and so on. However, this module considers only monthly and quarterly seasonality.

Time series Any observed data that is recorded over time.

Trend General pattern over many periods. Generally considered the most important component of time series data. Removal of trend is the customary starting point for the statistical task of time series decomposition.

Solutions to Self-Evaluation Quiz

1. d   Read the Overview of Concepts. Consult the Glossary.
2. e   Consult the Glossary. Read the Overview of Concepts.
3. c   Do Exercises 1–10. Read the Overview of Concepts.
4. d   Read the Overview of Concepts. Consult the Glossary.
5. d   Consult the Glossary.
6. a   Do Exercises 7–8. Consult the Glossary. Read the Overview of Concepts.
7. e   Do Exercises 1–5. Read the Overview of Concepts.
8. e   Do Exercise 11.
9. b   Do Exercises 11–15. Read the Overview of Concepts. Consult the Glossary.
10. a   Do Exercises 11–20. Consult the Glossary.
11. b   Do Exercises 1–3 and 11–15. Read the Overview of Concepts.
12. e   Do Exercises 21–25. Read the Overview of Concepts. Consult the Glossary.

CHAPTER 21

Visualizing Statistical Process Control

CONCEPTS
- Statistical Process Control, Control Chart, Control Limits, Control Chart Factors, Mean, Range, X-Bar Chart, R-Chart, Centerline, In-Control Process, Out-of-Control Process, Rules of Thumb

OBJECTIVES
- Understand how control limits are constructed

- Be able to interpret simple control charts

- Recognize out-of-control processes (level shift, trend, cycle, oscillation, instability, mixtures) and their typical causes

- Understand pattern recognition rules

Overview of Concepts

Products or services can be defined by measurable characteristics (such as diameter, weight, or waiting time) or by customer perceptions (such as color, courtesy, or defects). **Statistical process control** (SPC) allows monitoring of process parameters to ensure that quality standards are met. The broader goal of continuous quality improvement (CQI) is to increase customer satisfaction and reduce cost through better conformance to customer requirements. To this end, organizations must analyze customer needs, design their products and services to meet these needs, monitor their processes of production and distribution, and implement appropriate management systems. Variation is a natural phenomenon that cannot be eliminated, but it can be reduced toward the *asymptotic* goal of zero variation. The attainable degree of variation depends on equipment, technology, processes, management, and worker training.

An **in-control process** performs as expected, exhibiting only *common cause* variation (normal or random variation). An **out-of-control process** exhibits *special cause* anomalies (not due to random variation) such as instability, trend, level shift, cycle, mixture, or oscillation. Samples are used to monitor a process when measurements are costly, time-consuming, or destructive (100 percent inspection is not discussed here). Sample size and frequency of sampling will depend on the situation, but small samples (under 10) are typical. This module focuses on two well-known statistics: the **mean** (a measure of centrality) and the **range** (a measure of variation). These sample statistics are plotted over time on **control charts**, which guide decisions to continue, adjust, or halt the process.

The control chart for a mean is an **X-bar chart** (or $\bar{\text{X}}$-chart) while the control chart for the range is an **R-chart**. The **centerline** of a control chart is the expected value of the statistic. Statistical theory is used to establish an upper control limit (UCL) and lower control limit (LCL) around the desired centerline. **Control limits** in this module are based on **control chart factors** (found in tables) so that, when a process is in control, the sample statistic will lie within the control limits about 99 percent of the time. The X-bar chart's control limits are symmetric (based on a normal distribution), while the R-chart's control limits are asymmetric.

The position of sample statistics in relation to these control limits will tell us whether or not the process is in control. We are willing to accept a certain amount of variation, which is normal and expected. Excessive variation would indicate that a process may be out of control. Statisticians use **rules of thumb** to detect abnormal patterns so that management can take corrective action. The initial hypothesis is that the process is in control. Rejecting this hypothesis when it is true is *Type I error*, while accepting this hypothesis when it is false is *Type II error*. Failure to make timely corrections (Type II error) may lead to poor quality, excess scrap, re-work, and customer dissatisfaction. But unnecessary adjustments (Type I error) may cause loss of production and unnecessary expense.

Upper and lower control limits are established empirically by taking repeated samples from a new process once it is stable (even if engineering specifications are available). The overall mean becomes the assumed centerline of the X-bar chart, while the average range becomes the centerline for the R-chart. Walter A. Shewhart pioneered techniques for control charts, but SPC was further developed by other twentieth century experts, including W. Edwards Deming, Joseph M. Juran, Armand V. Feigenbaum, and Genichi Taguchi.

Illustration of Concepts

Rear axle shafts for a certain truck are supposed to have a diameter of 8.679 centimeters. Experience has shown the process standard deviation to be 0.005 centimeters. **Statistical process control** recognizes that variation exists in actual diameters because the hard-turn machining cell that produces the axle shafts is subject to vibration, wear, and other random perturbations. Samples of five axles are taken every hour and are measured to determine the actual diameter to the nearest 0.001 centimeters.

   Control charts are constructed for the **mean** and **range**, using **control chart factors** for n = 5 to set the **control limits**. The 99 percent upper and lower control limits (UCL and LCL) are shown as dashed blue lines. On the X-bar chart, dashed green lines are also used to display ± 1 sigma limits and ± 2 sigma limits on either side of the **centerline** ("sigma" refers to the standard deviation of the sample mean). To check for patterns that might indicate an **out-of-control process**, the quality monitoring staff applies these **rules of thumb** to the **X-bar chart**:

Rule 1:	*Single mean outside the 3 sigma limits (UCL and LCL)*
Rule 2:	*2 of 3 means outside the 2 sigma limits (same side of centerline)*
Rule 3:	*4 of 5 means outside the 1 sigma limits (same side of centerline)*
Rule 4:	*8 means on same side of centerline*

   One Thursday, the X-bar chart below showed four of five consecutive observations on the same side of its centerline (a violation of Rule 3). While this could be due to chance, it might also signal increased variation or a developing trend. Should the process be stopped?

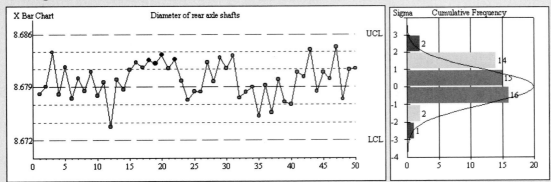

   As a further test, the histogram of the sample means was compared with the normal bell-shaped curve. This histogram is based on 50 sample means, so inferences about the distribution are guarded. Its general appearance resembles the normal curve that is superimposed, yet upon closer inspection it has too many means above zero and too few means below zero. The **R-chart** (not shown) indicated no violations.

   A decision was made to halt production and to inspect the machine tools. It was discovered that a small adjustment screw had loosened, allowing axle diameter to increase slightly. Only 10 minutes of equipment downtime were lost. If an adjustment had not been made (i.e., if an **in-control process** had been assumed) the axle shafts would have been slightly oversized, on average, leading to excessive friction, overheating, and shorter axle life.

Orientation to Basic Features

This module helps you learn how to create and read control charts. It illustrates both in-control and out-of-control processes using a variety of scenarios that represent manufacturing and service sector applications. You can use samples from processes to establish control limits and display samples on the resulting control charts.

1. **Select a Scenario**

   Start the module by clicking on the module's icon, title, or chapter number in the *Visual Statistics* menu and pressing the Run Module button. When the module is loaded, you will be on the introduction page of the Notebook. Read the questions and then click the Concepts tab to see the concepts that you will learn. Click the Scenarios tab. Select the Quantity of fill in a soft drink bottle scenario, read it, and press OK.

2. **Establish Control Limits**

   The Establish Control Limits Empirically screen contains a blank data matrix. Use the Sample Size scroll bar to alter the sample size (from 2 to 10). Changing the sample size changes the number of observations used to calculate each $\overline{X}$. Click the flashing Take More Samples button. At the bottom of each column you will see each sample's mean, range, and standard deviation. At the right are the control limits based on the samples taken so far. Below them are shown the cumulative mean, average range, and average standard deviation. Click the Take More Samples button to increase the number of samples used to calculate the control limits (the limit is 1,000). Click Accept Control Limits when you feel you have taken enough samples (or click Accept Default Limits to get control limits based on the true process parameters). Click the Help button to get more information.

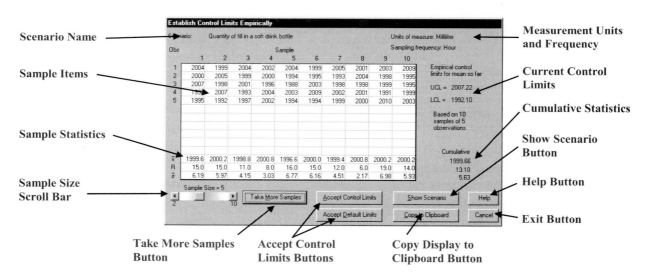

3. **Main Screen**
   The main screen shows the $\overline{X}$ chart (upper left), R-chart (lower left), and cumulative histogram of sample means (upper right) with a superimposed normal curve. On the $\overline{X}$ chart and R-chart, the centerline is a blue dashed line, and the upper control limit (UCL) and lower control limit (LCL) are shown as dashed red lines. The dotted green lines on the X-bar chart represent the 1 sigma and 2 sigma limits (here, "sigma" refers to the standard error of the mean $\sigma/\sqrt{n}$ where σ is estimated when you establish the control limits empirically or is given by the scenario if you choose Accept Default Limits). Sampling experiments are controlled by the buttons in the Control Panel (lower right), as well as by the menu bar at the top of the screen.

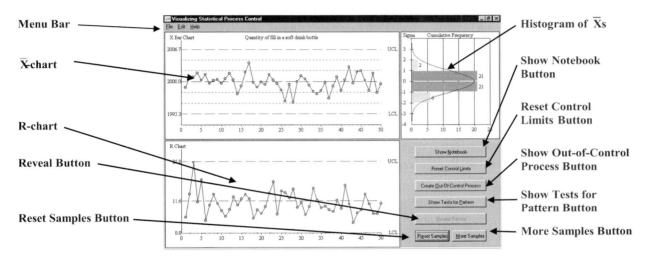

4. **Taking Samples**
   Click the More Samples button to generate 50 more samples of means (you are limited to 1,000 samples). Examine the $\overline{X}$-chart and R-chart to determine if the process is in control. The color-coded histogram shows the number of sample means in each zone: green (within ±1 sigma), yellow (within ±2 sigmas), magenta (within 3 sigmas), and red (outside 3 sigmas). These results can be compared with what is predicted by the normal distribution. Click the Reset Samples button to start over using the same control limits.

5. **Copying a Display**
   Click on the display you wish to copy. Its window title will be highlighted. Select Copy from the Edit menu (on the menu bar at the top of the screen) or Ctrl-C to copy the display. It can then be pasted into other applications, such as Word or WordPerfect, so it can be printed.

6. **Help**
   Click on Help on the menu bar at the top of the screen. Search for Help lets you search an index for this module, Contents shows a table of contents for this module, Using Help gives instructions on how to use Help, and About gives licensing and copyright information about *Visual Statistics*.

7. **Exit**
   Close the module by selecting Exit in the File menu (or click ⊠ in the upper right-hand corner of the window). You will be returned to the *Visual Statistics* main menu.

Orientation to Additional Features

1. **Create an Out-of-Control Process**
   Click the Create Out-of-Control Process button to obtain the choices for out-of-control processes shown on the next page. The default is None. Click the Describe Problem button to get more information about the problem you have selected. Drag or click the scroll bar(s) for the problem selected to set its level of severity (often, a severe problem is easiest to see). Click on Help if you want more information about the causes and consequences of out-of-control processes. Choose OK or Cancel to return to the main screen. Select Random Problem to have a random problem chosen with the severity you indicated. On the main screen, click on the Reveal Problem button to see if you correctly identified the problem.

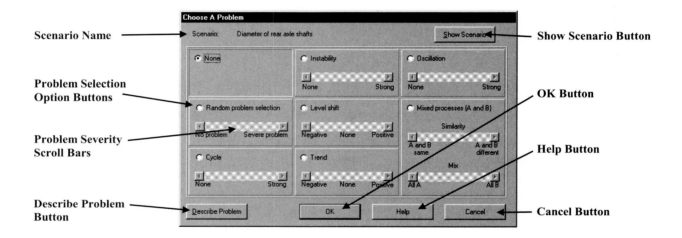

2. **Show Tests for Pattern**
   Click the Show Test for Pattern button to illustrate various tests for special cause. Choose a test and click OK. The Random selection tells the computer to choose a pattern (so you can test your ability to recognize them). Click the Reveal Pattern or Reveal Random Pattern button to highlight the points that demonstrate the pattern (there may be other patterns, but the points that were created to demonstrate the pattern are the ones highlighted).

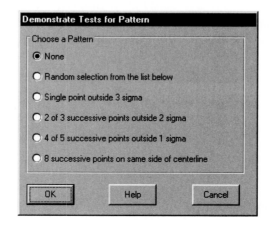

Basic Learning Exercises

Name _____

Press the Show Notebook button, select the Scenarios tab, click on Manufacturing I, and select Quantity of Fill in a Soft Drink Bottle. Read the scenario and click OK.

In-Control Processes

1. What is the desired mean? What are the units of measurement? What is the frequency of sampling? What is the sample size?

   Desired mean _____   Units of measurement _____
   Sampling frequency _____   Sample size _____

2. From the Establish Control Limits Empirically screen click Accept Default Limits. This will cause the control limits to be set using the true process parameters (usually unknown to the statistician but used initially in this exercise to be sure the control limits are exact). The main screen will appear. Record the centerline (dashed blue line) and control limits (dashed red lines) from the $\overline{X}$-chart and R-charts. How often should the sample statistics lie between the upper control limit (UCL) and lower control limit (LCL)?

$\overline{X}$-chart		R-chart	
Upper Control Limit (UCL)	_____	Upper Control Limit (UCL)	_____
Centerline (Actual Mean)	_____	Centerline (Actual Mean)	_____
Lower Control Limit (UCL)	_____	Lower Control Limit (UCL)	_____

3. Click Help on the menu bar at the top of the screen. Choose Search for Help and enter the key word "sigma limits." The titles of relevant screens appear in the window below. In the lower window, double-click on the title of a screen that sounds relevant (Histogram of Sample Means, Histogram Bar Colors). Explain why the UCL and LCL on the $\overline{X}$-chart are sometimes called "3 sigma limits," and explain how they are related to the normal distribution. What percent of the means are within ± 1 sigma, ± 2 sigma, and ± 3 sigma? Close Help by selecting Exit from the File menu on the Help screen.

4. Press the More Samples button once to take 50 samples. From the $\overline{X}$-chart, count the number of sample means that lie above the centerline of the chart. From the R-chart, count the number of sample ranges that lie above the centerline of the chart. Are any sample statistics outside the control limits (dashed red lines)? Do these sample frequencies differ significantly from what you would expect? Should we generalize from 50 samples?

<table>
<tr><td></td><td>$\overline{X}$-chart</td><td></td><td></td><td>R-chart</td></tr>
<tr><td>Frequency above centerline</td><td>_____</td><td></td><td>Frequency above centerline</td><td>_____</td></tr>
<tr><td>Frequency below centerline</td><td>_____</td><td></td><td>Frequency below centerline</td><td>_____</td></tr>
<tr><td>Frequency outside limits</td><td>_____</td><td></td><td>Frequency outside limits</td><td>_____</td></tr>
</table>

5. Press the More Samples button again, to accumulate 100 samples. Look at the cumulative histogram of sample means. How closely does it resemble the bell-shaped curve?

6. Based on the cumulative histogram, record the number of sample means that lie above and below the centerline of the $\overline{X}$-chart. Referring to the "sigma limits" (dotted green lines), record the number of sample means within ± 1 sigma (sum of the green bars), ± 2 sigma (sum of the green and yellow bars) and ± 3 sigma (sum of the green, yellow, and magenta bars). Are any sample means outside the control limits (dashed red lines)? Do these sample frequencies differ significantly from a normal distribution? Should we generalize from 100 samples? **Hint:** Use Help on the menu bar to find out more about the normal distribution.

	Frequency	Percent	Percent if Normal
Above centerline	_____	_____	50.00
Below centerline	_____	_____	50.00
Within ± 1 sigma	_____	_____	68.26
Within ± 2 sigma	_____	_____	95.44
Within ± 3 sigma	_____	_____	99.73
Outside ± 3 sigma	_____	_____	0.27

Intermediate Learning Exercises   Name _____

Press the Show Notebook button, select the Scenarios tab, click on Manufacturing I, and select Quantity of Fill in a Soft Drink Bottle. Read the scenario and click OK.

Out-Of-Control Processes

7.   Press the Reset Samples button. Click Create Out-of-Control Process and then click Instability. Click Describe Problem. a) What is instability? b) Why is it a problem? c) What might cause it (in the service sector as well as in manufacturing)? d) How might we detect it?

8.   Make sure the Instability scroll bar is in the exact middle between None and Strong (the scroll bar should initially appear in this position, but make sure). This will generate a problem of moderate instability. Click OK. How many of the 50 samples violate the R-chart control limits? Using only the R-chart, do you see clear indications of instability? Explain.

9.   Press More Samples again (now you have 100 samples). How does the cumulative histogram of sample means compare with the normal curve? From the histogram, record the number of sample means that lie above and below the centerline of the $\overline{X}$-chart, within $\pm$ 1 sigma (sum of the green bars), $\pm$ 2 sigma (sum of the green and yellow bars), within $\pm$ 3 sigma (sum of the green, yellow, and magenta bars), and outside UCL and LCL. Do these sample frequencies differ greatly from a normal distribution? What does this reveal about instability's effects?

	Frequency	Percent	Percent if Normal
Above centerline	_____	_____	50.00
Below centerline	_____	_____	50.00
Within $\pm$ 1 sigma	_____	_____	68.26
Within $\pm$ 2 sigma	_____	_____	95.44
Within $\pm$ 3 sigma	_____	_____	99.73
Outside $\pm$ 3 sigma	_____	_____	0.27

10. Click Create Out-of-Control Process. Click on Trend, then press Describe Problem. a) What is trend? b) Why is it a problem? c) What might cause it (in the service sector as well as in manufacturing)? d) How might you detect it?

11. Set the Trend scroll bar all the way to the end labeled Positive (the scroll bar should initially be set just to the right of None). This will generate strong upward trend. Click OK. Examine the R-chart and then the $\overline{X}$-chart. a) For these 50 samples, do you see any indication of trend on either chart? Explain. b) Click More Samples again until the trend is obvious. How many samples did you have to take to see the trend? c) Which chart reveals the problem?

Show Tests for Pattern

12. Click Show Tests for Pattern (this will automatically reset the process to being in control). Each rule offers a method for detecting problems on the $\overline{X}$-chart (which is supposed to be free of any patterns). Click Single Point Outside 3 Sigma and look at the $\overline{X}$-chart to see if you can spot the violation. Click Reveal Pattern to verify that you have found the problem. Repeat this exercise for each of the other rules of thumb. Evaluate the degree of difficulty in detecting each pattern. Why might an observer overlook some of the patterns? Do you see more than one violation (that is, a violation other than the one the computer revealed)?

Advanced Learning Exercises   Name _____

Setting Control Limits

Press the Show Notebook Button, select the Scenarios tab, click on Manufacturing II, and select Diameter of Rear Axle Shafts. Read the scenario and click OK.

13. a) Why might a firm need to set its control limits empirically (that is, by taking a number of preliminary samples to estimate the overall process mean and its average range)? b) Haven't engineers or systems analysts already designed the process and its parameters? c) Even after extensive sampling, might the resulting control limits be imperfect?

14. On the Establish Control Limits Empirically screen, use the Sample Size scroll bar to set the sample size to n = 8. Press the Take More Samples button once. This will display 10 samples. Examine the statistics (mean, range, standard deviation) at the bottom of each column and the cumulative statistics over all 10 samples (at the right side of the screen) and record the information requested below. Choose any sample and verify its column statistics to be sure you understand how they were calculated.

Smallest column mean	_____	Largest column mean	_____
Smallest column range	_____	Largest column range	_____
Smallest column std. dev.	_____	Largest column std. dev.	_____

Cumulative average mean   _____
Cumulative average range   _____
Cumulative average std. dev.   _____

15. Continue to press the Take More Samples button until you are satisfied that you have obtained a good estimate of the true mean, range, and standard deviation. (**Hint:** Watch the cumulative statistics.) Record the cumulative statistics here.

Cumulative average mean   _____
Cumulative average range   _____
Cumulative average std. dev.   _____
Number of samples taken   _____

16. Use the formulas shown below to calculate the estimated control limits, plugging in your cumulative mean ($\overline{\overline{X}}$) and range ($\overline{R}$) from exercise 15. Show each step of your calculations clearly in the space provided. **Hint:** Find control chart factors for d_2, D_3, and D_4 in the Glossary (or click Help).

   a. Your estimated upper control limit for sample mean:

   $$UCLX = \overline{\overline{X}} + 3 \frac{\overline{R}}{d_2 \sqrt{n}} =$$

   b. Your estimated lower control limit for sample mean:

   $$LCLX = \overline{\overline{X}} - 3 \frac{\overline{R}}{d_2 \sqrt{n}} =$$

   c. Your estimated upper control limit for sample range:

   $$UCLR = D_4 \overline{R} =$$

   d. Your estimated lower control limit for sample range:

   $$LCLR = D_3 \overline{R} =$$

17. To assess the accuracy of your estimates (exercise 16), from the Establish Control Limits Empirically screen click Accept Default Limits to find the control limits using the true process parameters (rather than using your sample estimates). These true control limits will appear on the main screen. How close were your calculated control limits to the true UCL and LCL that are displayed on the screen? If there are differences, explain why they might exist.

   $\overline{X}$-chart true control limits:

   True UCL   _____
   True LCL   _____

   R-chart true control limits:

   True UCL   _____
   True LCL   _____

18. Press the Show Notebook button, select the Scenarios tab, click on Manufacturing II, **and** select Diameter of Rear Axle Shafts. Read the scenario and record the true process parameters. How do they compare with your cumulative mean and standard deviation from exercise 15? If there is a difference, how might the difference have arisen? What difference would it make? Why wasn't this question asked earlier?

> True process mean   _____   Your cumulative mean   _____
> True process std. dev. _____   Your cumulative std. dev. _____

19. Press the Show Notebook button, select the Do-It-Yourself tab, and click OK. Enter 500 for the mean and 50 for the standard deviation, and then click OK. On the Establish Control Limits Empirically screen, choose a sample size of 5 and press Take More Samples once (to generate 10 samples). Record the cumulative mean and standard deviation (shown on the right-hand side of the screen) in the spaces below. Repeat this process until you have accumulated 100 samples. After each round of sampling, do the cumulative estimates always move closer to the true process parameters? Is the 100th estimate better than the 10th? Are 100 samples enough that you feel comfortable accepting the control limits? Why might a firm be unable to take as many samples as it would like?

> True process parameters   Mean _____   Standard Deviation _____
>
> 10 samples accumulated   Mean _____   Standard Deviation _____
> 20 samples accumulated   Mean _____   Standard Deviation _____
> 30 samples accumulated   Mean _____   Standard Deviation _____
> 40 samples accumulated   Mean _____   Standard Deviation _____
> 50 samples accumulated   Mean _____   Standard Deviation _____
> 60 samples accumulated   Mean _____   Standard Deviation _____
> 70 samples accumulated   Mean _____   Standard Deviation _____
> 80 samples accumulated   Mean _____   Standard Deviation _____
> 90 samples accumulated   Mean _____   Standard Deviation _____
> 100 samples accumulated   Mean _____   Standard Deviation _____

Out-Of-Control Processes

20. Click Create Out-of-Control Process and then click Level shift. Click Describe Problem.
     a) What is level shift? b) What might cause it (in the service sector as well as in
     manufacturing)? c) Which chart would show it? d) Which rule might detect it?

21. Set the Level shift severity scroll bar about halfway between None and Positive to create a
     moderate level shift. Click OK. From these 50 samples, does the R-chart reveal this level
     shift? Does the $\overline{X}$-chart reveal it? Click More Samples again to accumulate 100 samples.
     Does the histogram of means reveal this level shift? Discuss.

22. Click Create Out-of-Control Process and then click Cycle. Click Describe Problem. a) What
     is a cycle? b) How is it detected? c) What might cause it?

23. Set the Cycle severity scroll bar to Strong (all the way to the right) to create a strong cycle.
     Click OK. a) In these 50 samples, does the R-chart reveal the cycle? b) Does the $\overline{X}$-chart
     reveal it? If not, click More Samples again. c) Which rule is most likely to reveal a cycle?

Individual Learning Projects

Write a report on one of the three topics listed below. Use the cut-and-paste facilities of the module to place the appropriate graphs in your report. Include in your report a copy of at least one X-bar chart, R-chart, and histogram for each different experimental setup.

1. Investigate out-of-control processes by choosing any scenario that interests you, accepting the default control limits, and then using the Create Out-of-Control Process button to select one of the following problems: oscillation, level shift, or cycle. Include three different scroll bar settings for problem severity (low, moderate, strong) and take 50 samples for each severity level. Can you see the problem? If not, take more samples until you are sure. Explain how you detected the problem (or if it was undetectable, why not). Which control chart shows the problem most clearly? Are both charts needed? Repeat using a different problem from this list. Based on your experience, which problem was hardest to detect?

2. Investigate out-of-control processes by choosing any scenario that interests you, accepting default control limits, and then using the Create Out-of-Control Process button and selecting Random Problem Selection. Start with the problem severity scroll bar in the Strong position (to create a severe problem) and take 50 samples. Can you see the problem? If not, take more samples until you are sure. Explain how you detected the problem (or if it was undetectable, why). Which control chart shows the problem most clearly? Are both charts needed? Do this again, until you have seen at least three *different* random problems. Click the Create Out-of-Control Process button, change the problem severity to moderate (scroll bar halfway between None and Strong) and repeat these questions. Compare the ease of evaluating the two sets of three experiments.

3. Investigate rules of thumb. Select a scenario that interests you and accept the default control limits. Press Show Tests for Pattern and Random Selection. Each time you press More Samples you will get a new illustration of the same pattern, which you must try to identify. Look at all three charts. Tell which ones reveal the pattern, how clearly it is revealed, and whether more than one rule of thumb is violated. In the context of the scenario, what could cause this type of pattern? When you have identified the pattern, press the Reset Samples button to get a new random pattern. Do this until you have seen each rule of thumb illustrated twice. Which pattern violations are easiest to detect, and why? Why do you suppose this project asked you to use default control limits instead of setting the control limits empirically?

Team Learning Projects

Select one of the three projects listed below. In each case, produce a team project that is suitable for an oral presentation. Use presentation software or large poster boards to display your results. Graphs should be large enough for your audience to see. Each team member should be responsible for producing some of the graphs. Include in your report a copy of *relevant* X-bar charts, R-charts, and histograms you evaluated. Ask your instructor if a written report is also expected.

1. This is a project for a team of three or more. Investigate mixtures by choosing any scenario that interests you, accepting default control limits, and clicking Create Out-of-Control Process. Select Mixture. Each team member should choose a different setting on the Similarity scroll bar (ranging from A and B Same to A and B Different) and should investigate five settings for the Mix scroll bar (including All A, 50-50, and All B). What are the symptoms of a mixture? When is it difficult to detect? Which charts are needed?

2. This is a project for a team of two. Investigate two new rules of thumb that may help you detect cycles and oscillation:

    Rule 5: Six points in a row steadily increasing or decreasing
    Rule 6: Fourteen points in a row alternating up and down

    Choose a scenario, accept default control limits, and click Create Out-of-Control Process. One team member should select Cycle and the other should select Oscillation. Try five settings for the problem severity scroll bar (starting just above None and ending at Strong). Take 50 samples for each severity level. Can you see the problem? If not, take 50 more samples. Continue until you are sure. Explain how you detected the problem (or if it was undetectable, why). Did Rule 5 and Rule 6 help you detect the out-of-control processes, or were Rules 1 through 4 sufficient?

3. This is a project for a team of two. Press the Show Notebook button, select the Do-It-Yourself tab, and click OK. Enter any mean and standard deviation, make up a scenario that fits these parameters, and click OK. On the Establish Control Limits Empirically screen, choose any sample size and press Take More Samples once (to generate 10 samples). Record the cumulative mean and standard deviation (shown on the right-hand side of the screen). Repeat this process until you have accumulated at least 500 samples. Plot your cumulative sample statistics results in a graph and discuss the pattern. Do the cumulative estimates move closer to the true process parameters? How many samples are enough that you would feel comfortable accepting the control limits?

Self-Evaluation Quiz

1. Process control charts are primarily associated with which statistical expert?
    a. Joseph M. Juran.
    b. W. Edwards Deming.
    c. Armand V. Feigenbaum.
    d. Genichi Taguchi.
    e. Walter A. Shewhart.

2. Control limits are *least likely* to be based on
    a. detailed knowledge of engineering technology.
    b. repeated sample measurements of the mean.
    c. knowledge of the normal distribution.
    d. tables of control chart factors.
    e. repeated sample measurements of the range.

3. Quality improvement would probably *not* entail
    a. reducing variance.
    b. identifying sources of variance.
    c. blaming employees who do poor work.
    d. improving technology.
    e. monitoring processes continually.

4. Quality in a product is best assessed by
    a. trained statisticians.
    b. skilled mechanical engineers.
    c. attorneys who handle product liability.
    d. government quality inspectors.
    e. customers.

5. The R-chart is most likely to reveal which problem?
    a. Instability.
    b. Cycle.
    c. Oscillation.
    d. Trend.
    e. Level shift.

6. Which is *not* a characteristic of instability?
    a. A larger than normal amount of variation.
    b. Higher-than-expected frequencies in tails of the histogram of means.
    c. Could be caused by untrained operators.
    d. Could indicate that equipment tolerances are too tight.
    e. Could indicate that two processes are mixed.

7.   A slow drift of measurements either up or down from the process centerline suggests
     a.   mixed processes.
     b.   instability.
     c.   oscillation.
     d.   cycle.
     e.   trend.

8.   Which is *not* a characteristic of a trend?
     a.   Variance is essentially unchanged in each sample.
     b.   The cumulative histogram grows skewed in one tail.
     c.   It is easily detected visually if enough measurements are taken.
     d.   Rules of thumb can be established to detect it.
     e.   It is often due to mixing two batches of materials.

9.   Which is *not* a rule of thumb to indicate an out-of-control process on the X-bar chart?
     a.   three out of four points beyond ±2 sigma.
     b.   two out of three points beyond ±2 sigma.
     c.   four out of five points beyond ±1 sigma.
     d.   one point outside ±3 sigma.
     e.   eight consecutive points on same side of the centerline.

10. Likely reasons for inaccurate control limits would include which of the following?
     a.   The engineering parameter for variance is unknown.
     b.   The engineers were underpaid for their work.
     c.   There was insufficient preliminary sampling.
     d.   Process variation was not zero, as expected.
     e.   None of the above.

11. A cycle
     a.   is a series of high measurements followed by a series of low measurements.
     b.   is usually detectable visually.
     c.   is somewhat sinusoidal in shape.
     d.   is all of the above.
     e.   is none of the above.

12. If we see measurements near the upper or lower edges of the chart with fewer than expected
     near the centerline, we would be *least likely* to suspect which problem?
     a.   Cycle.
     b.   Oscillation.
     c.   Instability.
     d.   Stratification.
     e.   Mixed processes.

Glossary of Terms

Centerline Expected value of a process parameter (for example, mean or range). On a control chart, it is shown as a horizontal line.

Common cause Random variation in sample measurements that is inherent in the underlying process. It does not require action, because it is normal and expected. It cannot be reduced unless the process itself changes.

Control chart Plot of sample statistics (such as the mean or range) over time on a graph that shows the process centerline and its control limits.

Control limits For each process parameter, an upper control limit (UCL) and lower control limit (LCL) are established above and below the centerline. If the sample statistics lie within these control limits, we conclude that the process is in control. See **Control chart factors**.

Control chart factors D_3 and D_4 are based on percentiles of the distribution of the range, while d_2 relates the average range to the process standard deviation ($\sigma = \overline{R} / d_2$). They are derived from the normal and chi-square distributions.

n	d_2	D_3	D_4
2	1.128	0	3.267
3	1.693	0	2.575
4	2.059	0	2.282
5	2.326	0	2.215
6	2.534	0	2.004
7	2.704	0.076	1.924
8	2.847	0.136	1.864
9	2.970	0.184	1.816
10	3.078	0.223	1.777

Control limits for X-bar chart

$$\text{UCLX} = \overline{\overline{X}} + 3 \, \frac{\overline{R}}{d_2 \, \sqrt{n}} = \text{upper control limit of sample mean}$$

$$\text{LCLX} = \overline{\overline{X}} - 3 \, \frac{\overline{R}}{d_2 \, \sqrt{n}} = \text{lower control limit of sample mean}$$

where

$\overline{\overline{X}}$ is the empirical sample mean (centerline of $\overline{X}$ chart)

$\overline{R}$ is the empirical average range (centerline of R chart)

n is the size of each sample taken

d_2 is the control chart factor for samples of size n (from a table)

Control limits for R chart

UCLR $=$ $D_4\,\overline{R}$ $=$ upper control limit of sample range

UCLR $=$ $D_3\,\overline{R}$ $=$ lower control limit of sample range

where

$\overline{R}$ is the empirical average range based on repeated sampling

D_3 is the control chart factor for samples of size n (from a table)

D_4 is the control chart factor for samples of size n (from a table)

Cycle An out-of-control process in which means tend to follow a cyclic pattern (runs of high and then low values in relation to the centerline). It may be difficult to identify on the X-bar chart unless it is extreme. The R-chart typically is unaffected. See **Oscillation**.

Histogram of sample means If the process is in control, the histogram of sample means should form a normal (bell-shaped) distribution centered on the centerline of the control chart.

In-control process A certain amount of variation is normal and acceptable. As long as variation is within the control limits, the process is in control. See **Out-of-control process**.

Instability An out-of-control process in which sample means vary more than expected (in effect, the control limits are too narrow relative to the actual process). It may be detected directly from inspection of the R-chart, or by applying various rules of thumb to the X-bar chart.

Level shift An out-of-control process in which the sample means shift abruptly to a new level either above or below centerline, and stay there. It differs from a trend, which is a slow, gradual movement. The R-chart typically is unaffected. See **Trend**.

Lower control limit See **Control limits**.

Mean Average of n sample observations ($\overline{X} = \dfrac{1}{n}\sum_{i=1}^{n} x_i$), often referred to as X-bar. It is a measure of central tendency. Its theoretical distribution is normal if the population is normal or if n is large enough. Its expected value is the process mean μ.

Mixture An out-of-control process in which sample items come from two different populations that may differ. Very difficult to detect, and may be confused with instability. The R-chart may be affected, depending on how the samples are drawn.

Normal distribution If the sampling distribution is normal, the histogram of sample means should be symmetric about the centerline, with 68.26% within $\mu \pm 1\,\sigma/\sqrt{n}$, 95.44% within $\mu \pm 2\,\sigma/\sqrt{n}$, and 99.73% within $\mu \pm 3\,\sigma/\sqrt{n}$ where σ is the process standard deviation. The quantity $\sigma/\sqrt{n}$ is called the standard error of the mean. See **Sigma limits**.

Oscillation An out-of-control process in which the sample means tend to alternate (high-low-high-low) in "sawtooth" fashion. It may be difficult to identify on the X-bar chart unless it is extreme. It is an uncommon problem. The R-chart typically is unaffected. See **Cycle**.

Out-of-control process Process characterized by special-cause variation, detected from control charts (often by applying rules of thumb).

Parameter In the context of quality control, a numerical descriptor of a process, such as the its mean (μ, a measure of central tendency) or its standard deviation (σ, a measure of variation).

Process Method of producing a good or service, characterized by one or more measurable parameters. See **Parameter**.

Quality Quality of products or services can be defined by measurable characteristics (such as diameter, weight, or waiting time) or by customer perceptions (such as color variation, employee courtesy, or defects). Slight variation may not affect customer satisfaction, but variation that affects real or perceived performance of the product or service requires remedy.

Range Difference between the largest and smallest sample data values ($R = X_{max} - X_{min}$). It is a measure of dispersion.

R-chart Control chart for the sample range. The centerline is the average range (from past experience). The upper and lower control limits (UCLR and LCLR) are not symmetric, and are calculated using a table. See **Control chart factors**.

Rules of thumb Rules of pattern recognition to decide when a process is out of control:
Rule 1: Single mean outside 3 sigma limits
Rule 2: Two of three means outside 2 sigma limits (on the same side of the centerline)
Rule 3: Four of five means outside 1 sigma limits (on the same side of the centerline)
Rule 4: Eight consecutive means on same side of centerline.

Sample size In some situations (e.g., destructive testing) the sample size for a measurable characteristic is usually small (typically about five items). Sample size can be increased if more accuracy is needed or decreased in order to reduce sampling cost. In many modern factories every item may be inspected automatically ($n = 1$).

Sigma limits Informal way of referring to control limits. For example, the "3 sigma" control limits are $\mu \pm 3\ \sigma/\sqrt{n}$, where σ is the process standard deviation (often estimated from a sample) and n is the sample size. Similarly, $\mu \pm 2\ \sigma/\sqrt{n}$ would be called the "2-sigma" limits.

Special cause Variation in sample measurements attributed to nonrandom factors that are *not* inherent in the underlying process. It requires that action be taken, because it signifies that there is something wrong with the system.

Statistical process control The entire collection of statistical techniques that are applicable to quality management. More narrowly, it often refers to control charts.

Trend An out-of-control process whose means drift slowly either upward or downward, forming a trend. Trends may usually be detected visually on a control chart.

Type I error Making unnecessary adjustments to a process that is in control. It causes downtime, loss of production, added expense, diminished profit, and stockholder disappointment.

Type II error Failing to correct a process that is out of control. It leads to poor quality, excess scrap, unnecessary re-work, customer dissatisfaction, or litigation due to defective products.

Upper control limit See **Control limits**.

Variation Normal, expected deviation from an intended process parameter, due to a multiplicity of random causes, such as differences in raw material, equipment, and/or worker skill. The role of statistics is to measure variation, define attainable quality standards, and identify problems.

Variance reduction Multi-step process to improve quality: (1) analyze the process until it is well-understood and its parameters are known; (2) ensure that the process is stable and in control; (3) decide whether the process is capable of meeting the desired specifications; (4) over time, work to reduce variation so that measured variation approaches the unattainable ideal of zero.

X-bar chart A control chart for a sample mean. The centerline is the mean (from product specifications or past experience). The upper and lower control limits (UCLX and LCLX) are symmetric and are calculated using the normal distribution. When a process is in control, the sample mean will lie within the control limits almost all the time, and will be free of patterns. See **Sigma limits**.

Solutions to Self-Evaluation Quiz

1. e   Read the Overview of Concepts.
2. a   Do Exercises 2 and 13. Read the Overview of Concepts.
3. c   Consult the Glossary (see Variance reduction).
4. e   Read the Overview of Concepts.
5. a   Do Exercises 7 and 8. Consult the Glossary.
6. d   Do Exercises 7–9. Consult the Glossary.
7. e   Do Exercises 10 and 11. Consult the Glossary.
8. e   Do Exercises 10 and 11. Consult the Glossary.
9. a   Do Exercise 12. Consult the Glossary.
10. c   Do Exercises 13–19. Read the Overview of Concepts.
11. d   Do Exercises 22 and 23. Consult the Glossary. Read the Overview of Concepts. Do Team Learning Project 2.
12. d   Consult the Glossary.